THE NEW
IMPERIAL
PRESIDENCY

CONTEMPORARY POLITICAL AND SOCIAL ISSUES

Alan Wolfe, Series Editor

Contemporary Political and Social Issues provides a forum in which social scientists and seasoned observers of the political scene use their expertise to comment on issues of contemporary importance in American politics, including immigration, affirmative action, religious conflict, gay rights, welfare reform, and globalization.

Putting Faith in Partnerships: Welfare-to-Work in Four Cities,
  by Stephen V. Monsma

The New Imperial Presidency: Renewing Presidential Power after Watergate, by Andrew Rudalevige

Self-Financed Candidates in Congressional Elections,
  by Jennifer A. Steen

THE NEW IMPERIAL PRESIDENCY

Renewing
Presidential Power
after Watergate

A N D R E W   R U D A L E V I G E

The University of Michigan Press   *Ann Arbor*

Copyright © by the University of Michigan 2005
All rights reserved
Published in the United States of America by
The University of Michigan Press
Manufactured in the United States of America
♾ Printed on acid-free paper

2008   2007   2006   2005   4   3   2   1

A CIP catalog record for this book is available from the British Library.

Library of Congress Cataloging-in-Publication Data

Rudalevige, Andrew, 1968–
    The new imperial presidency : renewing presidential power after
Watergate / Andrew Rudalevige.
        p.   cm. — (Contemporary political and social issues)
Includes index.
    ISBN-13: 978-0-472-11430-6 (cloth : alk. paper)
    ISBN-10: 0-472-11430-1 (cloth : alk. paper)
    1. Presidents—United States—History—20th century.   2. Presidents—United
States— History—21st century.   3. Executive power—United States—
History—20th century.   4. Executive power—United States—History—
21st century.   5. United States—Politics and government—1945–1989.
6. United States—Politics and government—1989–   I. Title.   II. Series.

JK511.R83   2005
973.92—dc22   2005007415

To Christine, Eliza, & Owen;
& to Suzanne
& Donald Rudalevige
with love and thanks

Ad id quod ne timeatur fortuna facit minime tuti sunt homines.
(Men are least safe from what success induces them not to fear.)
—Livy

PREFACE &
ACKNOWLEDGMENTS

The first version of this book took shape in my mind before September 11, 2001, but it was largely written after the mass murders of that day. The American reaction to September 11 has of course been extensive. Furthermore, both in formulation and execution, it has been driven largely by the presidency. The authority exercised by President George W. Bush, both granted by legislative action and claimed beyond those grants—for instance, to unilaterally designate American citizens as "enemy combatants" out of reach of the judicial system or the Constitution—was astonishing in its scope. Presidential assertiveness, and legislative deference, seemed at unprecedented levels.

Perhaps this was fair enough in the wake of events that had "changed everything." Yet it struck me that these developments also flowed naturally, if at a quicker pace and higher volume, from other aspects of recent American history—specifically the ebbs and flows of presidential power leading up to and away from the Vietnam/Watergate era. Back in 1973 the historian Arthur M. Schlesinger Jr. had affixed an enduring adjective to the Nixon presidency: it was, he said, "imperial." This didn't mean that the president literally had become emperor, as some anti-Federalist authors had feared back in the 1780s. But it did suggest both that the occupant of the office exercised more absolute power over more issues than the constitutional framework suggested and, more broadly, that the office itself had expanded in its power relative to other governmental actors. The presidency had breached old boundaries, bringing more and more authority over more and more aspects of American governance under its control.

Still, no sooner had Schlesinger written his magisterial indictment than Congress began to fight back. Nixon was forced to resign his office as the full scope of the Watergate scandal became known, and a wide range of laws were passed that, collectively, reinserted Congress into the key areas of policy Nixon had claimed for himself. Legislators grabbed back the power of the purse and the sword and committed themselves to policy leadership and aggressive oversight of executive behavior. James Sundquist captured the era in his own reply to Schlesinger, *The Decline and Resurgence of Congress.*

My primary goal in this book is to add an installment or two to this ongoing narrative. As Sundquist rightly concluded, it was up to Congress to make the resurgence stick: I suggest that Congress did not live up to that challenge and that the resurgence therefore receded. The 1970s framework that was meant to guide and constrain presidential behavior, in times of war and peace both, slowly eroded over the decades that followed.

Going back to the framing of the presidency in the Constitution, I describe the evolution of executive power in our separated system of governance; discuss the abuses of power that prompted what I will call the "resurgence regime" against the imperial presidency; and ask how and why, over the three decades that followed Watergate, presidents regained their standing. September 11 and the reaction to it rightly receive special treatment in a separate chapter; still, when considered within this broader sweep, they represent developments different in degree but perhaps not in kind.

This is a book about politics, not of political science. I have taken on the task the historian John Lewis Gaddis once assigned to "lumpers" (as opposed to "splitters"): to systematize, to generalize, to reduce the "chaos, disorder, and sheer untidiness of history to neat patterns."[1] The questions herein are complicated, and those looking to find a counterexample to the trends I delineate will, in fact, find many. But the pattern, I think, prevails. And if the narrative here is in large measure synthesis, that synthesis aggregates into an argument: that the freedoms secured by the checks and balances of government are not automatic but depend on the exertions of public servants and the citizens they serve. Such an argument is hardly new—yet it is gravely relevant to the present day. As Schlesinger noted in the preface to *The Imperial Presidency,* "much of the historical recital in these pages is at least a thrice-told tale. Yet the contemporary argument rushes along with astonishingly little reference to the national experience."[2] One might argue that the present volume brings the count to at least four times told—yet on the arguments rush, similarly ungrounded. At the least, I hope this volume will capture in one place for students and policymakers the fate of the post-Watergate regime built by Congress and the courts. At best, I hope it will serve to remind them that without considering our history we will not act in a way true to the ideals that underlie it. Most of all, I hope, along with Justice Stevens, that we will not "wield the tools of tyrants even to resist an assault by the forces of tyranny."[3]

No book can provide the final word on a set of topics so broad. Anyone dealing with contemporary events must choose an endpoint, and this narrative stops on November 3, 2004, the day Sen. John F. Kerry conceded the vote count in Ohio and thus President Bush's narrow reelection victory. That election's full ramifications will not be known for some time, but the developments traced here did not depend on its outcome. Had Senator Kerry become President Kerry, I suggest, he would have been a very different person in office but perhaps not such a different chief executive. All presidents try to push the limits of their power: it is inherent in the office's position in the constitutional framework. The key question becomes, then, Will other political actors push back? Part of the point of this volume is to argue that they must. Presidential leadership is a necessity, given the challenges that face us as citizens—but it comes with risks of its own. How to resolve that balance deserves careful thought, not the mindless denunciations that have too often substituted for debate in our recent politics.

I owe thanks to a wide array of scholars, without whom this book would not have been possible or would at the least have made less sense. Obviously Arthur Schlesinger heads the list; I have enjoyed rediscovering the eloquence of *The Imperial Presidency,* which is perhaps more cited than read these days—a pity if so. James Sundquist deserves special mention for his comprehensive research on the "resurgence" Congresses, as does Louis Fisher for his thoughtful writings on presidential-congressional interaction and their constitutional ramifications. Many others have written with far more erudition than I on specific aspects of the subjects treated herein, and I hope I have done right by their research. They are too many to name here (and I fear leaving someone out), but my debts are made clear in the references to each chapter.

I also want to thank those who helped more tangibly with the writing of this book. I am grateful to Provost Neil Weissman of Dickinson College and to the college's Research and Development Committee for their financial support of this project. Dickinson has been a warm and supportive setting not just for teaching but for pursuing my research agenda; I thank all my colleagues in the Department of Political Science and across the campus, with a special nod to Vickie Kuhn for her inexhaustible supply of good-natured assistance of all stripes and Harry Pohlman for his vast knowledge of constitutional precedent and principle. Harry read the entire manuscript and provided many valuable suggestions, along with a frightening amount of aged scotch. (Thanks to Pat Pohlman for putting up with the latter.) I also want to thank several semesters' worth of students for tolerating and improving my musings on the "world after Watergate." I am especially grateful to one of those students, Brendan Lilly, who later served as a research assistant for this project.

Princeton University's Center for the Study of Democratic Politics (CSDP) served as my base for the final round of revisions to the manuscript; many thanks to Larry Bartels for bringing me aboard, to Diane Price and Helene Wood for their help and humor, and to all those associated with CSDP for their hospitality and collegiality. At the University of Michigan Press, warm thanks go to the manuscript's reviewers; to Kevin Rennells and his copyediting staff; to Jim Reische, acquisitions editor; and to Alan Wolfe, this series' editor. Jim has been unwaveringly supportive, even of my bliss-induced lack of work ethic during the 2004 baseball playoffs, and made important substantive and stylistic suggestions along the way. Alan prodded this book into being when, visiting our campus, he came to speak about political ethics to my freshman seminar. There was, we realized, no single book available for the course I wanted to teach. So I decided to write it, and have been in good hands ever since.

Two more acknowledgments are warranted. We all owe a debt to those in government, who work hard in the face of general derision, and especially at times like these to those men and women in the armed services, who do what most of us won't. A special appreciation goes to two specific public servants: first, to my brother-in-law, Corporal Jim Burns of the Army's Second Infantry Division, who actually reads books like this and who, as I write, is serving us all in Ramadi, Iraq; and second, to Richard E. Neustadt. Dick, a member of the Truman administration and (less memorably for him and history) of my dissertation committee at Harvard, died in the fall of 2003 before this manuscript took final shape. The author of the touchstone work on the modern presidency, *Presidential Power,* Dick was a valued adviser to a half century's worth of presidents but always took time to share his vast knowledge of politics and polity with the most junior of graduate students. I am forever grateful for that kindness and for his contribution to the field I study.

Finally, I thank my family for their love, inspiration, and immense generosity. My wife, Christine, will never recoup what I owe her; she made it possible to write this book in a compressed period of time, with grace and loving patience. My children, Owen and Eliza, provided many joyous reminders of my real-world priorities. And my parents, Don and Sue Rudalevige, have always impressed upon me the vital necessity of principled activism in the public sphere. It is to all of them, with deep gratitude for the lessons they continue to teach me, that I dedicate this book.

CONTENTS

I. "FREEDOM FRIES" & PRESIDENTIAL POWER   1

II. THE "FOETUS OF MONARCHY" GROWS UP   19

III. THE "OLD" IMPERIAL PRESIDENCY   57

IV. THE WORLD AFTER WATERGATE
The Resurgence Regime Takes Shape   101

V. THE RESURGENCE RECEDES, PART I
Money & Morals   139

VI. THE RESURGENCE RECEDES, PART II
Peace & War   167

VII. TIDAL WAVE   *The World after September 11*   211

VIII. "PRACTICAL ADVANTAGES & GRAVE DANGERS"
Imperial Presidency or Invisible Congress?   261

NOTES   287

INDEX   341

1. "FREEDOM FRIES" & PRESIDENTIAL POWER

As the cherry trees budded around Washington, D.C., in the spring of 2003, war was already in full bloom. The brutal regime of Saddam Hussein, in control of Iraq since 1979, had resisted the efforts of United Nations (UN) weapons inspectors to catalog its violations of that body's past resolutions and the cease-fire that ended the 1991 Gulf War. Every day new headlines blared, telling of (mainly unsuccessful) negotiations seeking support for the war from nations large and small, of American and British troop buildups in Kuwait and Qatar, of covert operations searching for Iraqi arms caches, of demonstrations for and against the war, of preparations for terrorist retaliation against the American homeland.[1]

President George W. Bush appeared in practically every one of those articles, a commander in chief very much in command. General Tommy Franks, Secretary of Defense Donald Rumsfeld, Secretary of State Colin Powell, their aides, and other military and intelligence staffers also played key roles as the drama unfolded. Congress, however, did not. Indeed, a careful reader of the *Congressional Record* would have been hard-pressed to glean from its pages a sense of the frenetic nature of events. The Senate spent most of mid-March debating the emotionally polarizing but substantively limited question of partial-birth abortion procedures. The House of Representatives had its official photograph taken, named a room after former majority leader Richard Armey, and expressed its unanimous sense that fires in nonresidential buildings and executions conducted by stoning were bad things. Of the thirty-five March roll call votes in the House before the war started, just one, a broad statement of support for American military personnel, had any relationship to the impending hostilities. As Sen. Robert C. Byrd (D-WV) lamented, the legislative branch was "ominously, dreadfully silent. You can hear a pin drop. . . . We stand passively mute, paralyzed." What would the Constitution's framers say? Byrd asked plaintively. "What would these signers of the Constitution have to say about this Senate which they created when they note the silence, that is deafening, that emanates from that Chamber on the great issue of war and peace?"[2]

Congressman Paul Ryan (R-WI), speaking for most of his colleagues, replied that silence was golden. After all, "there's nothing for us to do. . . . We don't have any role on Iraq." Majority Whip Roy Blunt (R-MO) added: "the truth is that in time of war . . . there is not a whole lot for Members of Congress to do."[3] In a legal brief, the Bush administration enthusiastically agreed.

> Irrespective of any Congressional assent, the President has broad powers as Commander in Chief of the Armed Forces under the Constitution that would justify the use of force in Iraq. . . . The Constitution vests the President with full "executive Power," and designates him "Commander in Chief" of the Armed Forces. Together, these provisions are a substantive grant of broad war power that authorizes the President to unilaterally use military force in defense of the United States's national security.[4]

In truth, the Constitution *is* uncharacteristically unequivocal on the subject of warfare—but in the other direction. The president is, of course, assigned the role of commander in chief. However, there is meant to be little to command without congressional approbation. In Article I, Section 8, Congress is given the power "to declare war, grant letters of marque or reprisal, and make rules concerning captures on land and water," along with other responsibilities for governing and supporting the armed forces. The framers of the Constitution, most scholars agree, clearly saw the initiation of war as a congressional function. As James Wilson put it at Pennsylvania's ratification convention, "this system will not hurry us into war; it is calculated to guard against it. It will not be in the power of a single man, or a single body of men, to involve us in such distress."[5]

But in 2002 and 2003, members of Congress seemed happy to accept the administration's argument for presidential preeminence. As Rep. Scott McInnis (R–CO) put it, "We elected our President, and President after President we put confidence in our administration and our leadership. They know a lot more than we know." Indeed, after the bombs began falling on Baghdad, deference to President Bush's conduct of the war extended even to tax policy. On March 21, 2003, arguing that one couldn't undercut the president in wartime, House leaders rammed through the president's proposed $726 billion in tax cuts by three votes, suggesting that moderates perturbed by the recurrence of massive budget deficits were unpatriotic.[6]

Upset by the failure of the French government to support the war, however, the chairman of the House Administration Committee announced on March 11 that he had ordered "French toast" and "French fries" stricken from the menu of the House cafeteria. In their place would be "freedom toast" and "freedom fries."[7] Congress had taken a stand.

RETURN TO TONKIN?

It was true that, from most members' perspective, Congress had already taken its only relevant stand: some five months prior, the House and Senate had voted by wide margins to pass a resolution concerning Iraq.[8] Rather than tackling the decision by voting war up or down, however, the legislators voted to delegate that problematic choice to President Bush—leaving him both to know and to do. The president was granted authority to "use the Armed Forces of the United States as he determines to be necessary and appropriate . . . against the continuing threat posed by Iraq." Congress found, in the words of the resolution, that Iraq continued "to possess and develop a significant chemical and biological weapons capability"; that it was "actively seeking a nuclear weapons capability"; and that it was "supporting and harboring terrorist organizations," including "members of al Qaida." This pairing of malicious intent and destructive capacity, the resolution went on, "combine[s] to justify action by the United States to defend itself." Some legislators, especially on the Democratic side of the aisle, expressed their opposition to actually taking such action, at the time of the vote and when it came;

but since many of them voted "yes" nonetheless, it was natural to ask if they had read what they had just voted for. Others had no hesitancy: Democratic House leader Dick Gephardt, for example, joined the president in a showy Rose Garden ceremony trumpeting unity and marginalizing dissenters.[9]

While they slightly amended the president's preferred draft—which would have given him authority to act militarily anywhere in the Middle East to "restore international peace and security" in the region—legislators were eager to strengthen the president's hand as he entered into negotiations with the UN and just as eager to rid themselves of the pesky issue of war and peace before the midterm elections in November. While the National Intelligence Estimate summarizing American knowledge about the threat posed by Iraq was available to all members of Congress, no more than a dozen ever read it. (Had they done so, the preamble of the resolution might have been less certain regarding Iraq's weapons capacity and recent ties to terrorism.) Within three days of debate in each chamber—by contrast, the full Senate debated the 2001 education bill for twenty-one days and an energy bill for twenty-three— the president had been granted the authority to do as he wished in Iraq. Bombs started falling on Baghdad on March 19, 2003.[10]

War with Iraq may have been the right choice. But Congress chose to delegate that choice rather than to make it. Sen. Patrick Leahy (D-VT) was among a number of legislators to make a direct comparison to an earlier debate: "the key words in the resolution we are considering today," Leahy noted, "are remarkably similar to the infamous resolution of thirty-eight years ago which so many Senators and so many millions of Americans came to regret. Let us not make that mistake again. Let us not pass a Tonkin Gulf resolution."[11]

The analogy was carefully chosen. The 1964 resolution that took its name from the Gulf of Tonkin—granting President Lyndon Baines Johnson a similar blank check concerning the conflict in Vietnam—was symbolic of an earlier era of congressional deference to the executive in a time of crisis. Johnson's actions and, even more so, those of his successor, Richard M. Nixon, were famously assailed by the historian Arthur M. Schlesinger Jr. as exemplifying an "imperial Presidency," an institution "created by wars abroad" and "making a bold bid for power at home." Schlesinger charged that Nixon "had produced an unprecedented concentration of power in the White House and an unprecedented attempt to transform the Presidency of the Constitution into a plebiscitary Presidency." Under such a system chief executives could do what they wanted, regardless of checks and balances, so long as the voters approved at quadrennial intervals.[12] The Vietnam War, Schlesinger and others felt, represented "the presidency rampant," with the president acting unilaterally and often in secret, unconstrained by Congress or Constitution, misrepresenting to the public both American interests and their own actions. "When the President does it, that means that it is not illegal," Nixon would later say; and this arrogation of power was evident throughout his presidency, whether in the bombing and invasion of Cambodia, the wiretapping at the Watergate (and elsewhere), the huge slush fund payments during and after the 1972 campaign, or the impoundments that subverted Congress's "power of the purse." Vietnam and Watergate were tightly linked; the latter, at least in its broadest sense, could not have happened without the former.[13]

The Vietnam/Watergate era has shaped our current era in numerous tangible ways, both in reaction and counterreaction. As discussed later, the framework of presidential-congressional relations established in the wake of Watergate is critically important for understanding a wide range of current issues, from war powers to budgeting to government ethics to executive secrecy. World War II, the cold war (including its hot interludes), and the various "wars of Watergate"[14] led presidents to secrecy, to deceit, and to the unilateral and sometimes careless exercise of power. These were justified as they happened, and often in retrospect, by the challenges that these crises posed to the national interest. And obviously the new mandates of the "global war on terror" and its expansion into Iraq gave new resonance to many of these topics. The terrorist mass murders of September 11, 2001, spurred a reassessment of the questions posed in the 1970s and forced a new appreciation for strong presidential leadership. But Leahy's analogy suggested a specter lurking behind that development: Had the imperial presidency returned?

THE NEW IMPERIAL PRESIDENCY?

That is the basic question of this book. It is a question that might have seemed silly just a few years ago. After all, one did not need to go back to the revolutionary period, as Senator Byrd urged, to find evidence of strong legislative initiative in the face of aggressive executive action. One had to return only to the first "imperial" era. On March 31, 1968, Lyndon Johnson, his political capital and credibility fatally wounded on the battlefields of Vietnam, announced that he would not seek reelection as president. Six years later, on August 9, 1974, Richard M. Nixon resigned his office, the first and only American president to do so.

Nixon's decision, especially, was barely voluntary. It came some two weeks after the House of Representatives' Judiciary Committee approved in bipartisan fashion three articles of impeachment, alleging presidential abuse of power and obstruction of justice. The votes followed a unanimous ruling by the Supreme Court forcing Nixon to surrender tapes of conversations relevant to criminal trials arising from the June 1972 burglary of the Democratic National Committee (DNC) headquarters in Washington's Watergate complex. Most critical was the release of Nixon's conversation with Chief of Staff H. R. Haldeman a week after the break-in, when Nixon told his aide to have the CIA short-circuit the FBI's criminal investigation: "[T]hey should call the FBI in and say that 'we wish for the country, don't go any further into this case, period!'" That discussion became known as the "smoking gun," placing the metaphorical murder weapon in the president's hands, and as its details were made public, Nixon's remaining political support melted away. The prospects of impeachment by the full House and removal by the Senate became a near certainty. Instead, Nixon chose to resign.[15]

In the aftermath, new president Gerald R. Ford declared that "our Constitution works." And such was the lesson of Watergate, as presented by the punditocracy: that the system worked, that constitutional malfeasance had been ferreted out and punished by constitutional process. Certainly, the actions of Congress and the Court seemed to fulfill the desire of the framers of the Constitution for interinstitutional policing through the aggressive use of checks and balances. In 1788 James Madison had argued that "the great security against a gradual concentration of the several powers in the same department consists in giving to [each branch] . . . the necessary constitutional means and personal motives to resist encroachments. . . . Ambition must be made to counteract ambition."[16] With Watergate—considered here not just as the burglary itself but as a blanket term covering a wide range of executive abuses—presidential ambition was checked, and checked hard. The political actors who impelled Nixon to resign were self-interested, to be sure; but as Madison and his colleagues hoped, self-interest was channeled into constitutional duty and into the public interest.

As Nixon's hold on the Oval Office weakened, and for several years thereafter, Congress, the courts, and even the bureaucracy reined in unilateral presidential authority on a variety of fronts. The War Powers Resolution (WPR) of 1973 sought to enhance legislators' ability to control presidents' use of force. The Hughes-Ryan Amendment of 1974, the Domestic Intelligence Guidelines of 1976, the Foreign Intelligence Surveillance Act (FISA) of 1978, and the Intelligence Oversight Act of 1980 aimed to likewise limit the autonomy of executive branch law enforcement and intelligence activities at home and abroad. The Federal Election Campaign Act (FECA) of 1974 and the Ethics in Government Act (EGA) of 1978 (creating, among other things, the office of the independent counsel) were to diminish the role of money in the political process and thus to reduce corruption—and to provide a neutral mechanism for investigating high-level corruption that might occur nonetheless. *U.S. v. Nixon* set bounds on the ability of presidents to claim confidentiality over executive branch procedures; the Presidential Materials and Preservation Act (PMPA), the Freedom of Information Act (FOIA) amendments of 1974, and the Presidential Records Act (PRA) of 1978 opened public access to the workings of the executive branch, including the White House; and the Privacy Act of 1974 protected individuals from the misuse of information they had provided the government. The Congressional Budget Act (CBA) and Impoundment Control Act of 1974 reinvented the legislative budget process while prohibiting presidents from unilaterally manipulating how, and whether, budgetary appropriations were actually spent.

One after another, then, the assumptions and processes that had extended the president's power, his ability to shape governmental behavior and outcomes, were reformed or removed. In the wake of congressional resurgence, it seemed the "imperial presidency" was an outdated period piece.[17] Indeed, as the Ford and Carter presidencies wound on, many scholars feared these limiting changes might have crippled the office. President Ford himself claimed that the presidency, far from imperial, had become "imperiled."[18] While the strong leadership of Ronald Reagan banished this fear for a time, especially after his first-year budget triumphs, even the Great Communicator ran ashore on the shoals of the Iran-contra scandal. Further limits on covert operations and intelligence resulted. By 1995, after his massive health-care plan was defeated and the first fully Republican Congress in forty years elected and in active opposition, President Bill Clinton was forced to insist that "the Constitution gives me relevance. . . . The president is relevant here."[19] Three years later, of course, Clinton would be impeached by the House of Representatives, though not removed from office, over charges arising from his efforts to keep secret an extramarital affair. Longtime political reporter R. W. Apple summed up the presidency, and the president, circa 1998: "his ability to function effectively, already eroded, would be further curtailed [if impeached]. Even now, he is neither trusted on Capitol Hill nor feared by Saddam Hussein and other enemies of the United States."[20]

The contrast with the spring of 2003 seems rather stark.

In between, of course, came September 11. Yet the events and claims of the post-9/11 political world are in many ways merely an acceleration of recent history. The current wars came as the strictures of the aftermath of Vietnam and Watergate no longer held much sway and a new set of rules was already being negotiated: had September 11 never happened, this book would be shorter by one chapter but no less pertinent. Over time, the legal institutions that marked what I will call Congress's "resurgence regime" proved to be built on sand—and, like sand, they eroded away, leaving a new landscape. Some parts crumbled more quickly than others; and to be sure, Congress maintains much latent power. But developments to date point the compass of presidential-congressional relations in a direction much more favorable to presidential authority.

This progression will be mapped in some detail over the course of the narrative that follows. But the broad outlines—the reasons why the Tonkin Gulf analogy, broadly conceived, hit home—are worth considering here. Even in the decade following Nixon's resignation, the office of the presidency retained a solid base of authority grounded in its ability to grab the public spotlight and to set the agenda, in the commander-in-chief power, in its potential control over regulations and policy implementation, in its role in appointments, and in its veto leverage. A wide range of recent scholarship, indeed, has stressed—with varying degrees of normative concern—the inherent ability of the president to take unilateral action in the absence of legislative authority.[21] As Clinton himself suggested after the Democrats lost Congress, "I think now we have a better balance of both using the Presidency as a bully pulpit and the President's power of the Presidency to *do* things, actually accomplish things, and . . . not permitting the presidency to be defined only by relations with the Congress." Clinton took unilateral military action around the globe, ordering cruise missile strikes even as the House pondered impeachment. And on Capitol Hill itself, the pre- and postimpeachment Clinton could claim a fair measure of success in pursuing his policy priorities through budget bargaining with the Republican majority.[22]

Presidents since Watergate have resisted probes for information and have asserted "executive privilege" over a wide range of records while protecting even historical material from public release. The Clinton administration went to court several times to protect conversations and documents, with mixed success; the George W. Bush administration has been perhaps even more aggressive in this area, holding fast against congressional requests for documentation in a variety of areas, even where the confidential advice protected by the privilege was not given directly to the president. Vice President Richard Cheney, for instance, refused to provide the General Accounting Office (GAO)[23] with even the barest records of his stewardship of the process that produced the administration's energy proposals in 2001. The GAO's subsequent lawsuit against the vice president was unsuccessful and was not appealed; the Supreme Court declined in a parallel suit to force the administration to release the information. Bush also delayed the release of records from the Ronald Reagan Library scheduled under the PRA and then issued an executive order rewriting the act to limit access to material in presidential libraries more broadly.

The Independent Counsel Act was allowed to expire at the end of June 1999. In 2000 presidential candidates spent more than $800 million in their quest for election—compared to the then shocking $90 million spent by both parties in 1972—and in 2002 FECA was seriously modified by the McCain-Feingold amendments, which hoped to root out the role of "soft money" in the system and whose very passage implied that FECA had failed. Both major presidential candidates opted out of the FECA system in 2004, and as soft money made its way back into campaigns through organizations ostensibly unconnected to the parties or candidates, spending skyrocketed toward $1 billion.

The CBA, likewise, failed to discipline federal spending, which continued in deficit into the early twenty-first century, with a brief blip into surplus in the late 1990s. By 2004 the federal government's annual budget was over $400 billion in the red, with additional spending in Afghanistan and Iraq still on tap and the first-term Bush tax cuts yet to fully kick in. Further, the deliberative process laid out in 1974 was often honored in the breach: in fiscal 2002, for example, not a single budget bill (of the thirteen required) was approved before the start of the new fiscal year beginning October 1. In 2003 just two were approved, in 2004 just three, in 2005 just one. The result each year was one or more massive omnibus spending bills cobbled together as late as February of the next year. Given that the single thing Congress *has* to do each year is to pass a budget, its failure to do so spoke volumes. So did the legalization of impoundment by the Line-Item Veto Act of 1996, a delegation of power too extreme for the Supreme Court, which overturned it in 1998. Looking at these developments, the departing head of the Congressional Budget Office said in late 2002 that the process should be pronounced "dead."

The situation was even more dramatic in the realm of foreign policy. Covert operations remained frequently covert even from their legislative overseers, and members of Congress seeking to make decisions about questions of war and peace often received carefully selected intelligence information. While the WPR remains on the books, its effect is uncertain in the face of presidential use of troops in places ranging from Grenada to Kosovo without express congressional approval.

Many of these trends were cast in sharp relief in the aftermath of September 11. Almost immediately, President George W. Bush and his administration took decisive action at home and abroad. Much of the power unleashed was also unchecked, either by congressional consent or its silent assent. On September 14 Congress passed a resolution arguing that "the president has authority under the Constitution to take action to deter and prevent acts of international terrorism against the United States" and granting the president the ability to use all "necessary and appropriate force" against those he determined had committed, planned, authorized, or aided the attacks or helped those who had.[24] The first target was the repressive Taliban regime in Afghanistan, starting in early October. The next was Iraq: starting in the summer of 2002 the administration argued for deposing Saddam Hussein and claimed the inherent constitutional right to make war, even preventively; it finally settled for the broad congressional delegation of authority discussed at the start of this chapter and promptly utilized it. As of Election Day 2004, over 1,100 American soldiers had been killed either during the invasion or during the subsequent occupation of Iraq, along with thousands of noncombatant Iraqis. Some 140,000 troops remained there, at a cost of over $1 billion per week, itself spent with little legislative oversight.

Meanwhile, hundreds, perhaps thousands, of prisoners captured around the world, all with suspected ties to the al Qaeda terrorist network, were being held in military custody. More than six hundred were imprisoned at the custom-built "Camp X-Ray" at the U.S. naval base in Guantánamo Bay, Cuba. They were designated not as prisoners of war but rather as "unlawful enemy combatants," without the rights that prisoner-of-war status confers and without formal charges being brought against them. Secretary of Defense Donald Rumsfeld noted in February 2004 that the prisoners at Guantánamo, some held for more than two years at that point, would be detained "as long as necessary." Charges that detainees' human rights had been violated in Cuba, Afghanistan, and especially Iraq made headlines in the spring of 2004 and beyond as photographs of prisoner abuse and administration memos seeming to justify the use of torture came to light. According to the president's top lawyers, the executive powers flowing from the September 11 attacks and the September 14 resolution were practically unlimited. "Congress can no more interfere with the President's conduct of the interrogation of enemy combatants than it can dictate strategic or tactical decisions on the battlefield," the Justice Department declared. In this view, laws banning torture were themselves unconstitutional to the extent that they constrained presidential discretion during wartime.[25]

On the domestic front, the USA PATRIOT Act[26] was designed to enhance the executive branch's prosecutorial tools and power to conduct criminal investigations by relaxing limits on surveillance. The Bush administration closed immigration hearings and held most aliens appealing violations of visa charges without bond. The president claimed the authority to create military tribunals outside the normal judicial system for terrorism suspects and issued an executive order doing just that. Most dramatically, the administration claimed that some defendants—even American citizens, arrested within the United States—could be held indefinitely without charge or lawyer if they too were labeled as enemy combatants. The determination of who qualified as an enemy combatant was, according to the president, entirely up to him, not the courts or legislature, and was not even reviewable by those branches of government. "The capture and detention of enemy combatants during wartime falls within the President's core constitutional powers as Commander in Chief," argued the Justice Department. "The Court owes the executive branch great deference."[27]

As 2002 closed, observers suggested that Bush had "created one of the most powerful White Houses in at least a generation"[28] as part of a specific strategy aimed at recovering executive powers ceded to—or seized by—Congress during the Watergate era. In the 2002 elections, Bush's frantic campaigning was credited with providing an unusual midterm boost to the president's party in Congress, strengthening the GOP's House majority and winning back the Senate outright. The iron discipline of legislative Republicans meant that through his entire term President Bush did not find it necessary to use the veto pen. Indeed, a string of successes made it appear that he could get Congress to do most anything he wanted. Lyndon Johnson, it was said late in his presidency, was so unpopular that he would have failed to get a resolution favoring Mother's Day passed by Congress. George W. Bush, one suspects, could have had Mother's Day repealed. And on November 2, 2004, he was reelected to a second term. He soon made clear that there would be no retreat. "I earned capital in the campaign, political capital," he said— "and now I intend to spend it."[29]

Was the imperial presidency back? Many have concluded so. Even Schlesinger returned to the fray with a brief essay entitled "The Imperial Presidency Redux."[30] It should already be clear, however, that the question is not as simple as institutional partisans of all sides might prefer. For one thing, it is hard to affix a label to a work in progress. In fact, the intertwining of presidential power and congressional prerogative goes back to the framing of the Constitution. Congress is the first branch of government and remains the actor with the most potential authority over the workings of the public sphere. Against this backdrop it should come as no surprise that the Bush administration—that *any* administration—would try to expand its power. Though temperament certainly matters for presidential behavior, the question here is not one of personality but one of positionality. Presidents since the beginning of the republic have sought to better their status in the constitutional order. The powers used and abused by Nixon were not plucked from thin air; as Nixon constantly complained, the Watergate charges were "chickenshit. I mean, it's nothing"—"Kennedy did it all the time." Nixon apologist Victor Lasky likewise proclaimed, "It didn't start with Watergate," and he had a point: executive authority had grown dramatically over the course of American history and especially since the energetic response of Franklin D. Roosevelt to the dark days of the Depression and war in the 1930s and 1940s.[31] From the vantage of the Oval Office, Congress is sluggish, cacophonous, and fragmented. As an aide to President Kennedy once put it, "Everybody believes in democracy—until he gets to the White House."[32]

Further, despite the pejorative slant of the very term *imperial,* such unbelief is not always unwarranted. The presidency is a natural focal point for leadership, and its structural unity gives the president both great opportunity and great responsibility for exercising that leadership in perilous times. There is a threat to liberty from an overweening executive; but there is a threat, too, from those who target liberty with bullet and bomb, and that reality must inform our debate.

But the word *debate* remains the right one. Much as he might prefer it, the president is not alone in his responsibilities. Nor, even if he will not admit to mistakes, is the president always right. One of his mandates is therefore to exercise his leadership through coalition, not command, justifying his choices in a way that persuades a range of constituencies and their representatives to follow his lead. The genius of American government flows from the interaction of the branches, from the contending self-interests and ambitions Madison foresaw. Justice Robert Jackson of the Supreme Court, writing as the United States fought in Korea in a war Congress never voted on, put it best: "While the Constitution diffuses power the better to secure liberty, it also contemplates that practice will integrate the dispersed powers into a workable government. It enjoins upon its branches separateness but interdependence, autonomy but reciprocity. Presidential powers are not fixed but fluctuate depending upon their disjunction or conjunction with those of Congress."[33] If power in government is defined as effective influence over governmental outcomes, then the relative power of the legislative, judicial, and executive branches has always ebbed and flowed over time. Across the sweep of American history, each branch continually pushes the boundaries of its power and is met, or not, by resistance from the others. The players change, but the dance goes on, with different steps and divergent grace.

It is critical that Congress not act the wallflower here. If the framers expected ambition in the American executive—and that quality unifies the otherwise very different men who have served as president—they expected counterbalancing ambition elsewhere. "The history of human conduct," warned Alexander Hamilton in *Federalist* No. 75, "does not warrant that exalted opinion of human virtue which would make it wise in a nation to commit interests of so delicate and momentous a kind, as those which concern its intercourse with the rest of the world, to the sole disposal of a magistrate created and circumstanced as would be a President of the United States." The tragedies of September 11 made it clear that strong presidential leadership is essential to the nation. But they made it equally clear that Congress has a critical role to play in determining national policy in times of crisis. As Justice Jackson put it a half century ago:

> The claim of inherent and unrestricted presidential powers has long been a persuasive dialectical weapon in political controversy. . . . By his prestige as head of state and his influence upon public opinion, he exerts a leverage upon those who are supposed to check and balance his power which often cancels their effectiveness. . . .
>
> [But] a crisis that challenges the President equally, or perhaps primarily, challenges Congress. If not good law, there was worldly wisdom in the maxim attributed to Napoleon that "The tools belong to the man who can use them." We may say that power to legislate for emergencies belongs in the hands of Congress, but only Congress itself can prevent power from slipping through its fingers. With all its defects, delays and inconveniences, men have discovered no technique for long preserving free government except that the Executive

be under the law, and that the law be made by parliamentary deliberations.

If so, the idea of *inherent* "imperialism" must be rejected: there is no "imperial presidency" in the structure of American government. Any such creature is conditional, fragile, and revocable. The presidency, in other words, is contingently imperial.

The flip side of the "imperial presidency," then, is the invisible Congress. Congress itself has not been run over so much as it has lain supine; it has allowed or even encouraged presidents to reassert power in the world after Watergate. We should ask why it has been such a willing party to its own victimization.

It may be, of course, too early to draw such a conclusion. Short-term assessment carries with it the distinct risk of being outrun by events (though, on the other hand, Keynes's famous assessment of the long run places its own premium on timely analysis). In 2004 the Supreme Court heard appeals from the inmates at Guantánamo Bay and the American-born "enemy combatants," ruling that executive prerogative could not override a suspect's access to the courts and due process. Though President Bush called for the permanent extension (and expansion) of the Patriot Act in his 2004 State of the Union address, a number of legislative voices rose in resistance. They were emboldened, perhaps, by rising concerns about the occupation in Iraq and the justification for the war in the face of mounting evidence that Saddam Hussein did not, in fact, possess weapons of mass destruction or anything close to them by the time of the U.S. invasion. The approaching 2004 election also served to spur mounting criticism of the administration's stewardship of the post–September 11 world. As noted previously, Congress retained the tools to counteract the assertions of presidential prerogatives—if it could muster the will to do so.

Still, when George W. Bush took the oath of office for the second time in January 2005, he presided over a presidency much stronger in absolute and relative terms than the framers had conceived it. Increased partisan polarization and the structural divide between executive and legislature enhanced the incentives for the president, whoever the incumbent, to claim unilateral authority and to try to make it stick. Thus, however it is resolved in the war on terror, the basic balance of power between the branches will remain at the very heart of our democracy. It is not entirely correct to see their interaction as a zero-sum game: what benefits one branch does not always harm another in equal and opposite measure. But making that relationship a positive one depends both on our political actors and, perhaps most crucially, on we the people. How we choose to balance the advantages and dangers of presidential power has great ramifications for American self-government and its ability to handle the crises that already define the twenty-first century.

THE PLAN OF THE BOOK

The remainder of this book delves into these issues. In so doing it veers across three possible approaches. The first is historical: how has presidential power developed over time? The second is institutional: how have other branches of government reacted to that development? A third, far briefer, is normative: how much presidential power does American governance require?

Chapter 2 will discuss the constitutional framework undergirding American government. In 1787, when the framers met in Philadelphia, they wanted to produce a president strong enough to resist legislative tyranny—the situation, as they saw it, in many of the thirteen states—but himself clearly held in check. There was, after all, little desire to substitute one king for another. The president's enumerated powers in the Constitution are fairly limited; his authority lies in the vague grant of prerogative inherent in "the executive Power" assigned at the start of Article II, in his ability to insert himself in the legislative process through the veto, and in his role as chief executive.

Still, presidents pushed to define the vague terms of their charter in practice. Sometimes Congress pushed back; sometimes it did not. The result was an accretion of precedent, of prerogative—of presidential power—over time. Further, as the government grew enormously in size and scope, presidents' administrative authority grew with it. By the 1940s the "modern presidency" was born.

Chapter 3 will center the discussion on the first "imperial presidency," detailing the events of Vietnam and Watergate as they expressed presidential power. The centralization of authority in the executive branch by Presidents Johnson and especially Nixon will be analyzed. This review is surprisingly necessary: a poll taken on the thirtieth anniversary of the break-in, in 2002, found that only 35 percent of Americans—and just 16 percent of those under thirty-five years of age—claimed to know enough about the events of Watergate to explain their gist to someone else. Yet those events have played out across the political and civic landscapes of three decades. As Suzanne Garment has noted, "The post-Watergate laws, like fossils, present a lasting record of the cast of the Watergate-era mind."[34]

Chapters 4 through 6 examine the responses of other institutions to the "imperial presidency" and how those responses held up over time. The chapters are organized in parallel, covering four broad areas: unilateral executive authority and "executive privilege"; budget politics (given that politics is, after all, about the distribution of resources); war powers and intelligence oversight; and governmental ethics more generally, including the role of money in politics. These chapters trace what happened in the 1970s in these areas and then what happened to the reforms beginning in the 1980s. As traced previously and detailed subsequently, Congress sought to "fix" Vietnam and Watergate by reshaping the institutional balance of power through a series of major statutory changes. They limited presidential initiative in a wide variety of areas. They assumed, in many ways, that the relationship between the branches of government could be legislated rather than negotiated.

But by and large, this assumption failed. The processes created in the 1970s proved unworkable or unsatisfactory in important ways—sometimes because they were evaded by presidents, sometimes because Congress failed to follow through on the burden it assigned itself, and sometimes because they fed an adversarial culture where civility leaked away and the ordinary pursuit of politics was deemed dirty or corrupt. As suggested previously, the events of September 11, 2001, and their own aftermath have only accelerated that process; bringing that story through the presidential election of 2004 is the subject of chapter 7.

The concluding chapter revisits the broader question of the balance of power in American government. In a system as large and fragmented as ours, there is a clear need for clear leadership. Did the erosion of the 1970s resurgence regime simply reflect the need for a strong executive in a government infinitely more complex than the framers could have imagined? If so, the relative aggrandizement of the executive office is simply a natural development and a rather efficient one, helping to solve the enormous governance issues facing the United States—from globalization and terrorism to skyrocketing health-care costs and an aging population and infrastructure. American government favors the status quo; empowering the president allows decisive action.

Or, as suggested earlier, is the issue less an imperial president (even if for good) and more an intentionally invisible Congress eager to shirk hard choices? The latter possibility is less benevolent. The goal of legislative deliberation is not to foster trust in government for its own sake; indeed, a healthy distrust of government is part of American history and a valuable tool of accountability. But both reflexive distrust and reflexive trust carry the seeds of disengagement, of apathy. Our government is built to respond—if we know what we want to ask it to do.

As the Watergate-era reform regime has crumbled, little systematic has arisen to replace it. Crafting a new balance of power within our government—and between polity and public—means making difficult decisions and trade-offs about the powers and goals of American government, about its very scope and direction; thus, doing so is our highest national priority. But it will require the active involvement of *all* our ambitions. "We must recognize," said a young John F. Kennedy, campaigning in his first election in 1946, "that if we do not take an interest in our political life, we can easily lose at home what so many young men so bloodily won abroad."[35]

II. THE "FOETUS OF MONARCHY" GROWS UP

Little at the Constitutional Convention of 1787 provoked more debate than the shape and scope of the executive branch. Delegates had to determine how the president would be selected, how long he should serve, whether he should be able to run for office more than once, how much power he should have—and even whether the president would be a "he" or a "they."[1] Indeed, when James Wilson of Pennsylvania moved that the executive should consist of a single person, the room lapsed into an uncomfortable silence. Some of the framers were unconvinced of the need for an executive branch in the first place. Others thought that executive power, like legislative power, must be strictly divided as a bar to future tyranny. For them, a single executive was, in Virginia governor Edmund Randolph's phrase, "the foetus of monarchy."[2]

Monarchy, of course, was what the framers wanted to avoid. The American colonies' experience under King George III and his colonial governors made that model of executive leadership both normatively and politically a nonstarter. Concentrating power in one individual, as the pseudonymous "Cato" later wrote in opposition to the Constitution, "would lead to oppression and ruin. . . . The world is too full of examples, which prove that to live by one man's will became the cause of all men's misery." The power to make war, to conduct diplomacy, to appoint administrators and judges, to pardon crimes, to convene and dismiss the legislature—all these needed to be checked and controlled.[3]

At the same time, the first U.S. government under the Articles of Confederation had lacked any separate executive branch. State constitutions drafted subsequent to the Declaration of Independence, with a few notable exceptions, had provided for extremely weak governors. Under the Articles of Confederation, the administration of government—thus, of the war for independence—was erratic at best; only the notable exertions of financier Robert Morris, ambassador Ben Franklin, and General George Washington kept the government solvent and its armies in the field. In most states, governors were required to act in concert with advisory bodies selected separately and had few powers to act unilaterally in any area. The Virginia Constitution of 1776, for example, required that the governor work in conjunction with a Council of State and limited executive powers to those specifically granted by the legislature.

Defending the work of the Constitutional Convention in *Federalist* No. 48, Madison argued that the result of such institutional restrictions was merely to substitute the risk of one form of tyranny for another. Indeed, legislative tyranny was in some ways more dangerous than executive tyranny, since the legislature was closer to the passions of the people and could degenerate into mob rule. "The legislative department is everywhere extending the sphere of its activity and drawing all power into its impetuous vortex," Madison warned. This vortex was blocked in the state constitutions only by "parchment barriers" insufficient to withstand it. So Madison sought a framework that would provide "those who administer each department the necessary constitutional means and personal motives to resist encroachments of the others." The goal was to separate institutions rather than to separate powers per se; in fact, powers would necessarily be shared to the extent required to give each branch some ability to prevent unilateral action by the others.[4]

The framers, then, wanted an executive that would be constrained but still competent. Two unsatisfactory executive models stood before them: one too strong and one too weak. Like Goldilocks, they sought a balance that would be just right. Yet striking that balance would require a resort to ambiguity that has only been clarified, when at all, in the political practice and precedent of more than two hundred years of American history. The presidential powers dictated by Article II of the Constitution are barely modified from the framers' work in 1787. But in fits and starts the American presidency has grown to fill the enormous demands placed upon it by American expansion, industrialization, and globalization. The "foetus of monarchy" has grown up.

THE CONSTITUTIONAL CONVENTION

The rough draft of the Constitution outlined a president rather different from the one we know today. That president was to be selected by Congress; he was to serve a single seven-year term, ineligible for reelection; and the powers of treaty making and of appointing ambassadors and judges were to be vested in the Senate.

Getting even this far had been a struggle. A large minority of the delegates, led by Randolph, favored a plural executive of some kind—perhaps a committee of three, or six, or even a number that would vary according to the will of Congress. Others, including Madison, thought presidents should garner legislative advice from and share the veto power with a "council of revision" that brought together the executive with members of the judiciary or a Constitutional Council made up of regional representatives of the states. The key, divisive questions were inseparably intertwined: pondering the nature of presidential powers required establishing how the president was to be elected, how long he might serve, and whether he might be removed (and, if so, by whom). Unable to agree even on what order to take up these questions—form before powers? powers before form?—the delegates settled on what seemed the least bad alternative. Many were unwilling to hand the election of the president over to the public, fearing at best that the larger population in the north would dictate the choice and at worst that voters might be swayed by demagogues plotting a return to monarchy. Given the rudimentary state of mass communication and education, it seemed quite likely to the framers that most in the wider electorate would be uninformed about political issues and events, especially about potential leaders not from their own state.

Still, congressional selection, though it placed the choice of president in the hands of those most knowledgeable about politics and policy, made it hard for the president to be independent of the legislative branch. A long, single term was one answer: it would prevent a reelection-minded president from cozying up to Congress, trading favors for votes. But it seemed prudent as well to minimize the powers the president might exert, in case his strings were pulled by legislative puppet-masters nonetheless.

So matters stood for much of the convention, until the notion of an Electoral College emerged in early September 1787 from the catchall committee dealing with postponed matters. The idea of having some intermediary body of electors, independent of the legislature but made up of informed elites, had been floated earlier in the convention and cast aside. Yet as Georgia delegate Abraham Baldwin put it, the proposal was "not so objectionable when well considered, as at first view."[5] As refined by the committee, the Electoral College provided for a compromise between those who wanted direct election and legislative selection (since state legislatures could pick electors directly if so desired) and between those who wanted proportional representation and equal states' rights. It also provided that electors meet in their own states, minimizing travel, but also that they vote for at least one person not from their own state, minimizing parochialism. Presidents would serve for four years and would be able to run as many times as they wished. While (as later decided) the House of Representatives, voting by state delegation, would make the final selection if no victor emerged with a majority of the electoral votes, nominees would at least have been chosen independent of the legislative "vortex."

With this jury-rigged system in place the framers could revisit the powers assigned to the executive. For example, the appointment and treaty powers were restored to the president, though linked to senatorial consent. After some haggling the congressional threshold for overriding a presidential veto was increased to two-thirds of each chamber. And the House and Senate were respectively given the ability to impeach and remove the president from office, for treason, bribery, or "other high crimes and misdemeanors."

These provisions did not prevent renewed criticism of a unified executive as the Constitution went to the states for ratification. In the Virginia ratifying convention, for example, Patrick Henry suggested that the document had many "deformities," chief among them "an awful squinting: it squints towards monarchy." After all, Henry went on, "Your President may easily become king. . . . If your American chief be a man of ambition, and abilities, how easy is it for him to render himself absolute?" In New York Cato piled on, arguing that an "arbitrary and odious aristocracy or monarchy" awaited the United States, since presidential power under the Constitution "differs but very immaterially" from that of the British king. And not merely a king but an emperor might be in store. "You do not believe that an American can be a tyrant?" Cato scorned. "[Y]our posterity will find that great power connected with ambition, luxury, and flattery, will . . . readily produce a Caesar, Caligula, Nero, and Domitian in America."

Alexander Hamilton soon fired back. "If, in this particular, there be a resemblance to the king of Great Britain," he mocked, "there is not less a resemblance to . . . the Man of the Seven Mountains." Unlike a hereditary monarch, Hamilton went on, the president would be elected for a fixed term; further, the president could be impeached and removed from office; his vetoes could be overridden by Congress; and his taxes, treaties, and appointments could be rejected. He would have no power to dismiss the legislature and, unlike the king (who led the Church of England), had "no particle of spiritual jurisdiction." The president's powers, in short, were checked on all sides. There was thus "no pretense for the parallel which has been attempted."

This argument was not meant to downplay the importance of having a single executive in charge. With the requisite structural defenses in place, a vigorous president was actually a good thing, since his ambition would both check and be channeled by the ambition of others in government. And as Hamilton later wrote, "energy in the executive" sprang largely from the fact that the "unity" of having a sole individual as president made it possible for the executive branch to act decisively, quickly, and, where necessary, in secrecy. The very title of *president,* narrowly construed, simply means "presider"—in this case, an officer who would preside over the execution of the will of Congress. Hamilton, though, in keeping with the Madisonian imperative that each branch be able to withstand the "encroachments" of the other branches of government, argued that the president must be able to resist legislative aggression. The president's powers, not kingly but "competent," provided one bulwark. The structural advantages of unity, as contrasted with the collective (and thus slow) deliberative processes of the bicameral Congress, provided another. Third, unity enhanced executive accountability. That is, come election time, it allowed the public to know who to blame.[6]

The Federalists won the argument, winning narrow ratification in

Virginia and New York to bring eleven states into the new union by July 1788.[7] And on February 4, 1789, the Electoral College made George Washington the first president of the United States.

CONSTITUTIONAL POWERS & CONSTRAINTS

Most of the powers of the president are listed in Article II of the Constitution. Article I, much longer and more detailed, is devoted to Congress, and it is here that the president's veto power is defined. That power, of course, is checked; it must be utilized within ten days of a bill's passage, and a two-thirds majority of each legislative chamber may join to transform a bill into law despite the president's objections.

More than half of Article II describes the presidential selection process. Presidential powers are then delineated in two concise sections, which can be summarized even more concisely. Namely, the president is commander in chief of the armed forces and of the state militias when they are placed in federal service. He can receive ambassadors and other public officials from other countries. He can negotiate treaties—and appoint judges as well as executive officials. He can grant pardons and commute sentences. The president may demand the written opinion of his department heads on any topic within their purview; and he is to give his own opinion to Congress about legislation he judges "necessary and expedient" as well as to provide the legislature with updates, "from time to time," on "the state of the Union." If Congress is out of session, "on extraordinary occasions" he may bring them back in. And he "shall take care that the laws be faithfully executed."

This short list is truncated further since many of these powers, like the veto, come with an asterisk. The president may suggest laws, but Congress must pass them. The president may conduct wars, but the power to declare war in the first place belongs to Congress. The president has control of his department heads, but Congress decides what departments exist in the first place. The president executes the laws—but within the language, and budget, approved and appropriated by Congress. A president's treaties must be ratified by two-thirds of the Senate and his appointments confirmed by a Senate majority. He may call Congress into session but cannot get them out. Pardons cannot be granted when impeachment by Congress is the trial at hand. And the president himself may be impeached by majority vote in the House, then removed from office by two-thirds of the Senate.

The framers' immediate concern was to get the Constitution ratified by the states. As a result, much of the document is built on compromise—the "Great Compromise" between large and small states that shaped representation in the House and Senate no less than the not-so-great compromise between northern and southern states that counted each slave as three-fifths of a human being for the purposes of legislative apportionment. As noted previously, the Electoral College is likewise very much a salesman's straddle, allowing proponents of popular election and legislative selection both to tout its provisions to their respective constituencies.

A parallel strategy was simply to be vague, to leave the definition of terms and powers to be worked out in practice. Examples of imprecision are scattered throughout the Constitution—for example, which legislative powers might be "necessary and proper"? But Article II wins out, as legal scholar Edward Corwin has commented, as "the most loosely drawn chapter of the Constitution. To those who think a constitution ought to settle everything beforehand it should be a nightmare."[8] Where does the power to command troops break off from the power to declare war? Which positions require Senate confirmation—and if the Senate gets to approve appointments, does it get to weigh in if the president wants to remove those appointees? What are the "high crimes and misdemeanors" for which a president can be impeached?

This vagueness begins—and is most crucial, perhaps—in the very first sentence of Article II: "The executive power shall be vested in a President of the United States of America." Note that the parallel grant of power in Article I adds a key qualifier, that "all legislative powers *herein granted* shall be vested in a Congress." That might imply that "the executive power" goes beyond the list of powers delineated in the rest of the article. But what is that power, exactly? Are there inherent executive powers of some sort? What do they allow the president to do? On this point the document is silent, and we must turn to history.

In so doing, though, it is worth emphasizing that the terseness of Article II means the historical narrative is animated not by how presidents used constitutional strength but by how they sought to overcome constitutional weakness. On the face of it, the president is hemmed in. He is given powers adequate to his needs but not sufficient for expending much affirmative authority. Even the amendments to the Constitution, to the extent they have affected presidential power, have enervated rather than enhanced that power.[9] Congress is the first branch of government for a reason: executive power is subordinate to legislative power in many ways, including the ultimate power of removal (since Congress can get rid of the president but not vice versa). In short, the president is necessary for others to do their jobs, but his own job is rather undefined. As H. L. Mencken put it in 1926, "No man would want to be President of the United States in strict accordance with the Constitution." And, indeed, for the eighteenth and much of the nineteenth centuries, presidential leadership of government was the exception, not the rule.[10]

But people do want to be president, for the powers of the modern presidency go beyond anything the framers foresaw. By building up a "presidential branch"[11] separate from—and often opposed to—the wider executive branch; by strategically using the powers the Constitution does grant; and, not least, by continually and creatively interpreting constitutional vagueness in their favor, U.S. presidents have built their office into the most powerful executive platform in the world.

ESTABLISHING PRESIDENTIAL POWER: ARE THERE INHERENT POWERS?

THE FEDERALIST ERA

The *Federalist Papers* partnership of James Madison and Alexander Hamilton did not survive the 1790s. Hamilton became treasury secretary in the new Washington administration, quickly becoming a stalwart of the new Federalist Party, while Madison went to Congress, where he led the faction that would become Thomas Jefferson's Democratic-Republican Party.

As Washington's second term began in 1793, the United States was pressed to take sides in the breaking war between England and France. Washington chose instead to issue a Neutrality Proclamation. But could he do so? The policy of neutrality made sense to most (indeed, the United States had little power to add to either side of the conflict), but could the president choose such a course without congressional input? Could he decide on his own to implement—or fail to implement— treaty provisions in a manner consistent with a neutral course?

Hamilton, writing as "Pacificus," produced a series of essays defending the proclamation and Washington's related policies. He argued that this was a decidedly executive sphere: "the Legislative Department is . . . charged neither with *making* nor *interpreting* Treaties," and to maintain a state of peace was no change in the law. The power to declare war rested with Congress, true, but it was "on the other [hand] the duty of the Executive to preserve Peace until war is declared; . . . it becomes both its province and its duty to enforce the laws incident to that state of the Nation."

Madison, in turn, insisted that the proclamation was a change in policy equivalent to a new statute or peace treaty. Only legislators could make law or ratify treaties; "all [the president's] acts therefore, properly executive, must pre-suppose the existence of the laws to be executed." Presidents could not end a state of war or implement new policies of peace (many of them altering domestic "code" as well as external relations, Madison held) unless Congress gave its consent. To argue otherwise, he claimed, was to borrow executive powers not from the text of the Constitution but from "*royal prerogatives* in the *British government*."[12]

As that last gibe suggests, the argument really turned on the notion of inherent executive authority. John Locke, in his *Second Treatise* of 1690, had discussed "prerogative," defined as the power of the executive "to act according to discretion, for the publick good, without the prescription of the Law, and sometimes even against it." Legislatures were slow, Locke argued, and the law could not foresee all "Accidents and Necessities" that might arise. Indeed, even where statutes were in place, strict adherence to their letter might do more harm than good in certain cases. Thus the executive needed discretion to implement the law or to set a policy course when law was lacking.

However, Locke's version of prerogative had natural limits. It was only legitimate as it reflected the public commonweal and could only be temporary: executive control in the absence of legislative direction stood only until "the Legislature can be conveniently assembled to provide for it."[13]

Hamilton made a broader claim. He argued that the divergent wording that introduced Articles I and II was clear evidence that "the executive power of the Union is completely lodged in the President." The
subsequent discussion of presidential powers in Article II thus merely
specified limits on various aspects of that "more comprehensive grant,
contained in the general clause." Madison countered that "to see the
laws faithfully executed constitutes the essence of the executive authority." From this might be deduced the power to remove subordinate
officers responsible for executing the law (itself a question at issue in the
first Congress in 1789) but for little else—and certainly not the power to
make war, or even peace, unilaterally. "Those who are to conduct a war
cannot in the nature of things, be proper or safe judges, whether a war
ought to be commenced, continued, or concluded," he argued; to give
the president power beyond his specified grants of authority would
threaten "a great principle in free government," namely, the separation
of policy formulation from its implementation.

This dispute has echoed throughout American history. Reduced to its
essence, the question is simple: Is a president limited to the specific powers affirmatively listed in the Constitution, or can he take whatever
actions he deems in the public interest so long as those actions are not
actually prohibited by the Constitution? President Theodore Roosevelt's version of the Hamilton position put it clearly: "My belief was
that it was not only [the president's] right but his duty to do anything
that the needs of the Nation required unless such action was forbidden
by the Constitution or by the laws." Roosevelt's successor, William
Howard Taft, clarified the opposing view. "The President can exercise
no power which cannot be fairly and reasonably traced to some specific
grant of power or justly implied within such express grant as proper and
necessary to its exercise," Taft wrote. "There is no undefined residuum
of power which he can exercise because it seems to him to be in the
public interest."[14]

The evidence from the framers' debates probably favors Madison.
Some scholars of the Constitutional Convention state flatly that the
wording difference in the congressional and presidential grants of power
is meaningless: "no delegate advanced a theory of inherent power,"
write David Gray Adler and Michael Genovese. Even James Wilson, the
most persuasive advocate of a strong new executive branch, assured del-

egates that the only strictly executive powers under the Constitution should be to carry out the laws and to choose personnel. Indeed, why bother, if the president was vested with vast executive authority, to point out the power of that president to obtain written opinions from his department heads?[15]

Others, however, have suggested other sources for inherent powers, whether called "prerogatives" or not. For example, does the commander-in-chief power carry with it broad authority over warfare? How does the president execute the law "faithfully" if a given statute is, as is so common, vague or inexact—or if the president believes it is unconstitutional? Does the power to execute the laws itself supplement the powers enumerated in Article II, as President Grover Cleveland suggested? Does the presidential oath of office—to "preserve, protect, and defend the Constitution"—likewise carry with it its own, perhaps ironic, extraconstitutional mandates? Is there an implied equivalent of the legislature's charge to do what is "necessary and proper" to implement presidential duties?[16]

Whatever the academic resolution of these debates, in practice, Hamilton's view has decisively won out. Thomas Jefferson, who urged Madison to attack the Pacificus letters, quickly adopted Hamilton's view of executive powers upon attaining them. He purchased the Louisiana Territory without prior congressional approval, ordered offensive naval action against the Barbary powers, and spent unappropriated funds to restock military stores when war with Britain seemed imminent after the U.S. frigate *Chesapeake* was seized in 1807. In an 1810 letter he argued that "to lose our country by a scrupulous adherence to written law, would be to lose the law itself, with life, liberty, property and all those who are enjoying them with us; thus absurdly sacrificing the end to the means." Presidents have long pointed out that they are the only nationally chosen elected official and that they therefore have special status as, in Theodore Roosevelt's phrase, a "steward of the people." Even a president as unassertive as James Buchanan once scolded the House of Representatives by stating that he was "the only direct representative on earth of the people of all and each of the sovereign states. To them, and them alone, is he responsible."[17]

Whether "stewardship" or not, certainly the unitary structure of the presidency helps its occupant vis-à-vis the other branches of government. As Hamilton pointed out in *Federalist* No. 70, the "energy" of the executive branch comes in part from a president's formal powers and independence from the legislature, but some comes from "unity" itself. The fact that Congress is a divided body run by collective choices gives presidents inherent advantages of "decision, activity, secrecy, and dispatch." Presidents can make decisions quickly and discreetly (unlike Congress) and can act on them without resort to other branches (unlike Congress or, for that matter, the judiciary). Even if they don't get the last say, presidents often get to make the first move—which itself may shape the landscape over which subsequent decisions are taken. Hamilton pointed out as Pacificus, for example, that "the executive, in the exercise of its constitutional powers, may establish an antecedent state of things, which ought to weigh in the legislative decision."[18]

THE CIVIL WAR & AFTER

It was, of course, Buchanan's successor who pushed these various questions to their limits—asking, for example, whether that "antecedent state of things" might be affected by a president's use of powers that clearly went beyond the Constitution's text. As the Civil War began, Abraham Lincoln expanded the volunteer and regular army far above the ceilings set by Congress. He authorized the construction of new warships, sent weapons to Union loyalists in western Virginia, and ordered a blockade of ports in the south. He spent $2 million of unappropriated funds to purchase military supplies. He censored the mail, imposed restrictions on foreign travel, suspended the constitutional right of habeas corpus (thus asserting the right to hold prisoners without charges or trial), undermined Fourth Amendment protections against warrantless searches and seizures, and instituted military tribunals in place of the civilian judiciary. "The process was so casual," note Christopher Pyle and Richard Pious, "that Secretary of State Seward could boast that whenever he wanted someone arrested, all he had to do was ring a little bell on his desk." Later, by executive order, Lincoln ordered that slaves be emancipated, without compensation for abrogating what the Supreme Court had, after all, determined was a personal property right.[19]

For Lincoln these actions were clearly justified by the crisis brought on by Southern secession and the later outbreak of overt warfare. Unlike

Buchanan, he never doubted that he had the duty, and power, to act to preserve the Union and the Constitution that governed it. He did not call Congress into session until July 1861. In so doing he famously asked, "are all the laws, *but one,* to go unexecuted, and the government itself go to pieces, lest that one be violated?" In 1864, with the Civil War raging on, Lincoln defended his actions more broadly still.

> My oath to preserve the constitution to the best of my ability, imposed upon me the duty of preserving, by every indispensable means, that government—that nation—of which that constitution was the organic law. Was it possible to lose the nation, and yet preserve the constitution? By general law life *and* limb must be protected; yet often a limb must be amputated to save a life; but a life is never wisely given to save a limb. I felt that measures, otherwise unconstitutional, might become lawful, by becoming indispensable to the preservation of the constitution, through the preservation of the nation.[20]

Lincoln did not claim that these were powers embodied in the presidency alone but rather that emergency compelled him to act quickly and decisively. His actions, from budgeting to blockade, were steps that Congress could have taken, and Congress later explicitly endorsed them. Nor did Lincoln suspend electoral processes, though he feared he would lose his bid for reelection in 1864. As Arthur Schlesinger Jr. put it, "Lincoln successfully demonstrated that, under indisputable crisis, temporary despotism was compatible with abiding democracy."[21]

In fact, with the crisis passed (and Lincoln dead), Congress soon reasserted itself. Andrew Johnson, who battled with Congress for control of Reconstruction policy, was impeached; his immediate successors were largely willing to allow the legislature to dictate terms. War hero Ulysses S. Grant proved surprisingly malleable as president. For a time, as legislator George Hoar wrote, if senators "visited the White House, it was to give, not to receive, advice."[22]

The Supreme Court, too, which in 1863 had upheld Lincoln's naval blockade and subsequent seizure of foreign merchant ships, decided later that the president had not possessed the power to bypass civilian courts and institute nonjury, military trials in Union territory. The idea that the Constitution could be suspended by some "theory of necessity" was "pernicious" and "false," Justice Davis wrote in *Ex Parte Milligan*. Indeed, Davis argued, "it could be well said that a country, preserved at the sacrifice of all the cardinal provisions of liberty, is not worth the cost of preservation." Tribunals might be necessary behind enemy lines, but "martial rule can never exist where the courts are open, and in the proper and unobstructed exercise of their jurisdiction," loyal to the United States and actively hearing criminal cases.[23]

Still, this judicial rebuke came in 1866, after the war was safely resolved. Davis admitted that "during the late wicked Rebellion, the temper of the times" made it difficult to separate "considerations of safety" from judicial decision making. As Chief Justice William Rehnquist has written, "there remains a sense that there is some truth to the maxim *Inter arma silent leges*"—that the laws are silent during wartime.[24] And even on the legislative side of the ledger, the shorthand convention of presidential torpor is rather underdrawn. Presidents Rutherford B. Hayes, James Garfield, Chester Arthur, and Grover Cleveland, for example, strongly defended presidential appointment and administrative powers against congressional incursion, to popular acclaim. Far from taking legislative advice, Cleveland protested, "I am not responsible to the Senate, and I am unwilling to submit my actions and official conduct to them for judgment."[25]

In short, presidents continued to claim the right to act unilaterally— and did so. In *In re Neagle* (1890), the attorney general argued that the presidential oath must, "by necessary implication," be read to "invest the President with self-executing powers; that is, powers independent of statute." While a dissenting opinion noted that such an oath might perhaps pledge presidential fealty to Article I, Section 8 ("the Congress shall have powers . . . to make all laws"), the Court majority stood with the president, focusing on the requirement that he faithfully *execute* the laws. Could that mandate, the Court asked, be "limited to the enforcement of acts of Congress or of treaties . . . according to their *express terms,* or does it include the rights, duties and obligations growing out of the Constitution itself, our international relations, and all the protection implied by the nature of the government under the Constitution?" The answer, said the majority, without undue specificity, must be closer to the latter than the former. In like fashion, the Court held in *In re Debs* that the federal government's power to control interstate commerce and regulate the mails could not be limited to legislation punishing interference with those processes after the fact. That extra power—the residual between the power utilized by congressional legislation and "the entire strength of the nation"—could be used by the president proactively, in the absence of contrary law, when federal functions were threatened. The post–World War I "Palmer Raids," where supposed communist subversives were searched, detained, and even deported without warrant, provided an example of how far this power could be stretched.[26]

In 1909 President Taft (who had evidently not yet drafted his memoirs) sought to regulate oil exploration on public lands by executive order, effectively amending the statute governing such exploration. When Taft's action was challenged, the Supreme Court held that the president's regulatory power in this area had been accepted frequently over time by Congress and that such historical precedent might govern executive-legislative relations as much as constitutional doctrine. Practice, then, may carry its own weight in "determining the meaning of a statute or the existence of a power."[27] As the twentieth century continued, that practice provided a wide menu of precedent for presidents seeking to exert unilateral power; and presidents continued to add to the selection.

TRIBUNE OF THE PEOPLE?

The resort to inherent executive power was only one aspect of presidents' efforts to overcome their constitutionally weak position. Another stems from the status of presidents (with their vice presidents), noted earlier, as the only nationally elected officials. Most presidents since at least Andrew Jackson have thus claimed a special legitimacy as "tribunes" of the national interest, as opposed to the sectional interests arrayed in Congress. Jacksonian democracy put direct representation of the people at its heart—and the presidency at the heart of that process.[28]

Over time, history, strategy, and technology combined to allow presidents to leverage this credo into capital for leadership. Jackson's own claims were enhanced by developments in the presidential election process, for any notion of the Electoral College as an independent body of deliberative elites never took hold.[29] The framers had not expected presidential selection to provide the president with the powers of public mandate; as James Ceaser has written, "Without any additional authority deriving from the selection process, the Founders believed that there was little to fear in the way of an imperial presidency." The indirectly elected president was supposed to be able to *resist* public pressures to act if need be. But by 1832 the members of the Electoral College were chosen by direct election in all but one state. Further, the electorate itself within each state had expanded quite dramatically in the early nineteenth century as property restrictions on voting eligibility were gradually dropped. By Jackson's time most white adult males in the United States had the right to vote—a sad fraction of universal suffrage by current standards, to be sure, but impressive for its day. Jackson and his successors could thus claim wide popular support.[30]

That claim was not unconstrained. The mass political organizations that grew during the 1820s and 1830s were premised on making loyalties to party, not person, paramount. One result was that party leaders often chose candidates who were uncontroversial rather than gifted or, at best, gifted at being uncontroversial. British observer Lord Bryce complained that this meant that "great men are not elected president."[31] By the twentieth century, though, the Progressive movement, frustrated by the continuing grip of reform-averse party machines on American politics, urged a wide range of changes to the electoral process. State by state, secret ballots, "Australian ballots" (with all candidates listed together), and primary elections began to appear. These reforms loosened the parties' choke hold on ballot access and nominations and encouraged the creation of candidate-centered campaign organizations. While their success was only partial—it did not reach full bloom until after the 1968 election and the Democratic rules changes it inspired— the Progressives did provide voters with the mechanics to split their tickets and the theoretical justification for so doing: the candidate, not the party label, was what mattered most. Parties were necessary to provide clear policy choice and to bridge the constitutional chasms between the branches. But for Woodrow Wilson and his followers, public opinion was the key to government's legitimacy. For them, a party system was not a goal in itself but rather the means by which the president could exercise popular leadership, translating the will of the people directly through him as its direct representative. Instead of constraining the president, the party "would now form around him and adopt his program or 'vision' as its own."[32] This effort to lay a parliamentary system over the actual structure of the federal government met with mixed success. But popular appeals over the head of Congress became a key element in governing.

Such a strategy became even more attractive as new technology for mass communication developed. As railroads carried newspapers (and presidents) across the expanding United States, as the telegraph spawned near-instant transmission of information, and as—perhaps most crucially—the radio gave presidents a direct, unmediated link to the public ear, presidents mated Wilson's theory with ever more ambitious strategies for outreach. The availability of the technology, in turn, encouraged the strategy. The expectation that presidents would communicate with the public directly, and would translate public support into political capital, became a basic part of the office. The scholar Jeffrey Tulis has suggested that the result is nothing less than a "second constitution" for presidents.[33]

LEVERAGING FORMAL POWERS

At the same time presidents learned to use what they had, or claimed to have, in the "first" Constitution. If the formal powers listed in Article II were a bit sparse, presidents nonetheless could use them creatively. In some cases, such a strategy coincided with the notion of "going public" noted previously. For example, presidents are required to give a State of the Union message to Congress and are invited to suggest policy proposals. At first such efforts were resented: Jeffersonian members of Congress who had cooperated with the president were cursed as collaborators, as "toads that live upon the vapor of the palace."[34] But in the twentieth century this began slowly to change. Theodore Roosevelt had a program, if one he kept purposefully general; William Howard Taft sent Congress a series of specific policy proposals and even legislative drafts. In 1913 Wilson became the first president since Jefferson to turn the State of the Union message into a State of the Union *address,* setting the legislative agenda by gathering a joint session of Congress together to hear his programmatic plans. Unlike Jefferson a century before, Wilson did not stay to hear the congressional reply, much less to reply to that reply. For the first time the press began to mention "administration bills."[35]

Presidents also weighed in at the other end of the legislative process, utilizing their veto power to shape public policy. George Washington had feared that if he let the veto slide into disuse a potentially harmful precedent would be set. He and his immediate successors nonetheless used the tool sparingly and reserved it for laws they felt were unconstitutional. Andrew Jackson, on the other hand, vetoed bills—most notably the reauthorization of the Bank of the United States—with little restraint and because he thought they were bad policy. His twelve vetoes more than doubled the number issued together by the six presidents before him. Though the Senate, outraged, censured Jackson, the president was well within his constitutional rights, and the censure was later expunged. Other presidents followed suit until the veto became a generally accepted part of the legislative routine. John Tyler, with his own vetoes of banking legislation, established that even politically weak presidents could shape policy through the use of executive powers. In the late nineteenth century Grover Cleveland vetoed nearly six hundred bills over his eight years in office, many of them Civil War pension "pork," and was overridden barely 1 percent of the time.[36]

Administrative powers, likewise, were strategically deployed. Article II makes it clear that the president is the head of the executive branch, in charge of his department heads, but the specifics of those departments were left vague. As early as the 1790s, "all major decisions in matters of administration, and many minor ones, were made by the President."[37] James K. Polk, who held office from 1845 to 1849, has been lauded as "the first president to exercise close, day-to-day supervision over the executive departments," even over fiscal matters.[38] In the latter area he was ahead of his time, but by the 1920s the president was required to create a coordinated executive budget to submit to Congress.

"Coordination" in this and other instances really meant "control," and this in turn meant relying on the loyalty of one's executive appointees. Back in the first Congress, James Madison had fought to get presidents the right to fire members of the executive branch without Senate approval, overcoming those who felt that the Senate power of confirming nominees in office should mean similar confirmation upon their removal from office. For Madison and his allies control of personnel was crucial to presidential accountability. Since the president's appointments were key to helping him carry out his constitutional duty of "taking care that the laws be faithfully executed," they fell within the executive power itself.

As political parties developed and matured, patronage became a critical part of the government. "To the victors belong the spoils" went the Jacksonian slogan; and Jackson again made a mark by removing Treasury Secretary William Duane when Duane refused to follow the president's order to withdraw the federal government's deposits in the Bank of the United States. Jackson then appointed Roger Taney, his attorney general, as treasury secretary, and Taney did Jackson's bidding. Other presidents, notably Abraham Lincoln, continued to play the patronage card, if with a defter hand.

At that point the fight was not yet over, as the Tenure of Office Act aimed at Andrew Johnson indicated. But presidents largely resisted any control over their discretion; as noted earlier, even the oft-maligned post-Reconstruction presidents were quite aggressive, and usually successful, in this area. In the 1926 case *Myers v. U.S.,* the Supreme Court finally confirmed that presidents did indeed hold the power of removal—and thus of controlling the behavior of executive branch officials even when they were confirmed by the Senate.

Administrative strategies were, unsurprisingly, far more salient in a government of six hundred thousand civilian employees (the figure in 1930) than of eleven thousand (the total a century before).[39] Growth in government made power over appointments and removals more critical; it also forced Congress to delegate more powers to the president through statute. Each time an executive agency was created with the power to promulgate regulations, presidential power expanded. While Congress could not constitutionally delegate its legislative powers, the delegation of regulatory authority sometimes amounted to something close, especially when Congress passed vague statutory standards or neglected to conduct adequate oversight of administrative behavior. During wartime, as noted later, delegation reached new heights. For example, the Palmer Raids of 1919 and postal censorship of the left-wing press were carried out under authority granted the executive in the 1917 Espionage and Trading with the Enemy Acts and the 1918 Sedition Act.[40]

Even before the New Deal and World War II exploded the size of government, presidents also managed executive branch behavior through executive orders, proclamations, and other administrative directives. Properly speaking, these regulatory devices are an extension of formal powers, not prerogative powers, since (like appointments) they are a tool for executing the law; thus, authority to issue a given order must be rooted in the Constitution or in statute.[41] While they were not tracked formally until 1895, some fifty thousand executive orders and proclamations may have been issued over time. Many of them have dealt with minor personnel matters. But many others have had substantive impact. Washington's Neutrality Proclamation set off the Pacificus-Helvidius debate. The Louisiana Purchase was consummated by proclamation, as was emancipation of the slaves during the Civil War. Public lands were an especially popular topic, as the *Midwest Oil* case suggests: presidents used executive orders to create Indian reservations, grazing areas, lighthouses, military reservations, and (under Theodore Roosevelt) millions of acres of conservation land. More than seventeen hundred executive orders were issued by Woodrow Wilson alone in the years around World War I.[42]

As this last observation suggests, many of the most important executive orders are those issued in the president's role as commander in chief. The broader point is that war enhances executive authority. Madison happily told Jefferson that the Constitution, "with studied care, vested the question of war in the Legislature." But throughout American history armed conflict has expanded presidential power; each war president, to borrow Corwin's description of FDR, has been "happily free of any mistrust of power when it was wielded by himself."[43]

It is not clear from the Constitution whether the president's formal status as commander in chief carries with it any power outside of a state of war. But presidents have long acted as if it provided a separate grant of authority. From the Barbary Pirates to the Boxer Rebellion to an array of excursions into Mexico and Latin America, presidents have often justified the unilateral use of troops as presidential prerogative—sometimes as a defensive effort to "repel sudden attacks" or to protect American lives or property. James K. Polk's deployment of troops near the border between Mexico and Texas, which successfully aimed to provoke an armed clash leading to broader war, was not unusual except in the unexpected length of the conflict that ensued. Abraham Lincoln famously denounced Polk's action; but, as noted previously, Lincoln himself was hardly shy in asserting power. "I think the Constitution invests its commander-in-chief clause with the law of war, in time of war," he argued in 1863, later adding, "As commander-in-chief . . . I suppose I have a right to take any measure which may best subdue the enemy," even if this included "things on military grounds which cannot constitutionally be done by Congress." Other presidents agreed. Interestingly, where Lincoln's claims have been justified by the evident crisis of the Civil War, other military actions have been justified by their *lack* of severity, by their supposed standing as police actions rather than as a "real" use of force that would constitute acts of war. William McKinley, Theodore Roosevelt, Taft, Wilson, and Calvin Coolidge, for example, used U.S. troops to rule Cuba, Nicaragua, Haiti, and the Dominican Republic and even to occupy Veracruz, Mexico. Wilson also ordered in March 1917 that all American merchant ships crossing the Atlantic be accompanied by protective armed convoys, despite Congress's rejection of this measure.[44]

In these aspects, the administrative power of the executive reflects and reinforces the importance of presidential initiative, even in areas of congressional authority. As with any first mover in a game where sequence counts, a president's initiatives may reshape in his favor the landscape on which political actors move. While hardly helpless, Congress does in such cases necessarily confront presidential power on less than favorable ground. When the Senate balked at Theodore Roosevelt's cherished plan to have the American battle fleet circumnavigate the globe, TR simply pointed out that he had enough funding to send them halfway and that if Congress chose not to appropriate the remaining amount the fleet would just stay in the Pacific. "There was," he noted, "no further difficulty about the money."[45]

CONSOLIDATING PRESIDENTIAL POWER:
THE MODERN PRESIDENCY TO 1965

Even before Franklin Roosevelt took office, then, ambitious presidents could choose from an array of precedential actions that pushed against congressional power and, finding insufficient resistance, expanded the scope of presidential power. The story confirms the importance of the "living Constitution," a collection of historical experience overlaying the text of the Constitution itself. Not all presidents were strong. But as Woodrow Wilson put it, "the President [was] at liberty both in law and conscience to be as big a man as he can."[46]

From FDR's time forward, these tools became expectations rather than possibilities. They became part of the nature of the office rather than optional instruments. The Great Depression and, on its heels, World War II, followed by the cold war, dramatically raised Americans' expectations of their government and especially of their presidents. The size, scope, and reach of the federal government grew immensely in the forty years after FDR defeated Herbert Hoover in 1932. Richard E. Neustadt, in a play on Wilson's observation, noted that the president could certainly still be big, "but nowadays he cannot be as small as he might like."[47]

As this comment suggests, our current conception of the presidential office was largely shaped by the administration of Franklin Roosevelt and his immediate successors. Changes in the presidency since the New Deal, the political scientist Fred Greenstein concludes, "added up to so thorough a transformation that a modifier such as 'modern' is needed to characterize the post-1932 manifestations of the institution that had evolved from the far more circumscribed traditional presidency." That modern presidency has played out, in the historian William Leuchtenburg's well-known phrase, "in the shadow of FDR."[48]

Greenstein suggests four characteristics by which "modern" presidents can be contrasted with "traditional" presidents: in their ability to use formal and informal powers on their own initiative; in their agenda-setting powers for federal policy-making; in their enhanced staff capacity, adding up to a "presidential bureaucracy"; and in their immense visibility.[49] These areas parallel the discussion of the pre-FDR presidents in the previous section, but Greenstein is right to see a change in kind as well as quantity—what a physical scientist might call a "shift change," as from ice to water—in the post–New Deal, World War II age. Thus the narrative that follows, rather than tracing the history of each administration since FDR, will utilize Greenstein's categories, in reverse order, to organize the discussion.

The "Bully Pulpit" in a Broadcast Age

If Theodore Roosevelt foresaw the use of the presidency as a "bully pulpit," it was his cousin Franklin who spread the good news across the airwaves. By the 1920s, the invention of radio transformed the president's ability to send an unmediated message to the American public. Even the notably laconic Calvin Coolidge took advantage of the novel technology. As radio spread to half of all U.S. households by 1935 and closer to 80 percent by 1940, Franklin Roosevelt proved to be the first master of the medium. His first "fireside chat" a week after his inauguration discussed banking, as he sought to reassure Americans that their financial system was secure: not only did runs on the banks end, but deposits streamed back in from under mattresses and floorboards. Subsequent chats, which Roosevelt delivered at well-spaced intervals during the remainder of his presidency, were likewise reassuring, folksy, and, to the modern ear, relentlessly substantive. The presidency, he commented, is "pre-eminently a place of moral leadership" for "leaders of thought" seeking to clarify big ideas; and he sought to lead by educating the public so that they would see the issues the same way he did.[50]

Reporters were another communicative tool FDR used with brio. Woodrow Wilson was the first president to bring the White House press into his office and to brief them personally, but his relationship with journalists was strained: he considered them "dullards," as Samuel Kernell notes, "and they sensed his condescension." After Harding, Coolidge, and Hoover tightened press access, Franklin Roosevelt opened it wide, holding what he called "delightful family conferences" to provide reporters with a wide range of hard news: his first press conference (of the nearly one thousand he would hold over twelve years) ended with applause from the gathered correspondents. While future presidents were not always as skilled in badinage as FDR, the door to the Oval Office, once unbarred, could not be completely shut.[51]

Television's arrival on the mass market in the 1950s upped the ante further. Truman had already allowed radio broadcasts of his news conferences—thus it was hard for him to talk off the record, as Roosevelt had often done. But now presidents could appear in one's living room in person, and in 1955 Dwight Eisenhower began to allow TV cameras into press conferences. The story of the impact of TV on the 1960 debates between John Kennedy and Richard Nixon is well known: those listening to the first debate on the radio judged Nixon the winner, while those watching on TV overwhelmingly thought the vigorous JFK had beaten the pallid vice president. Soon television was shaping presidential agendas—in the area of civil rights, for example—but also serving as a means for presidents to seize the public's agenda through what Kennedy aide Ted Sorensen called "direct communication" without "alteration or omission." The mechanics of the broadcast industry helped too. It was far easier for the media to focus on one person than on the inchoate multitudes in Congress.[52]

Certainly Kennedy was confident enough in his broadcast presence to allow live coverage of his press conferences in prime time; 65 million Americans watched the first one. With the concurrent shift to a half-hour nightly newscast, suddenly the president's presence was not a treat but an expectation. It was an expectation Kennedy lived up to, rounding out Jackson's notion of "tribune" or TR's idea of "steward" of the people with not just policy but personality. Alexander Hamilton had claimed in the *Federalist* that presidents would have no "spiritual jurisdiction"—but the outpouring of emotion at Kennedy's (televised) funeral suggested the success he had in forging a faith in the personal presidency.

These developments of technology and strategy gave presidents an advantage in visibility that underlay the other powers traced earlier. If Nixon later aimed at a plebiscitary presidency, the idea was hardly new.

THE INSTITUTIONAL PRESIDENCY

The forging of a public yet personal presidency was itself supported by a rather impersonal growth in White House bureaucracy. From one secretary in 1933, the White House press office has grown to at least thirty paid staff, themselves part of a much larger White House Office of Communications.[53]

This development exemplifies the general growth of the executive office staff. Until the 1870s presidents had to pay any assistants out of their own pockets and were thus often limited to the services of their unemployed nephews. They had almost nothing in the way of substantive staff help and scarcely enough secretarial help to keep up with the incoming mail. As late as the 1930s, White House staff could barely be described in the plural.

During his first term, Roosevelt relied largely on his so-called Brains Trust, recruited from the private sector and academia, and on staff borrowed from other executive agencies and "detailed" to the White House. In 1936, worried about his capacity for policy development and management, Roosevelt appointed the President's Committee on Administrative Management under public administration luminary Louis Brownlow. The Brownlow Committee famously concluded that "the President needs help." In accordance with the best principles of contemporary administrative science, the committee called unapologetically for strengthening the executive: it proposed new personal staff aides—for a grand total of nine—and tools to enhance the president's coordination of the executive branch, starting with the creation of an Executive Office of the President (EOP) to house presidential staff agencies such as the Bureau of the Budget (BoB). Brownlow also recommended that the president gain much more control over executive branch organization and personnel. While Congress resisted giving the president unbridled control over departmental structure and civil service, in 1939 it did allow the president the authority to hire additional staff and to create the EOP. The "institutional presidency" was born.

The EOP quickly gained in staff and stature. While the White House staff proper remained limited in number for some years, the BoB grew enormously—quintupling in the decade after 1939—and served in many respects as an extension of the president's staff. The two blue-ribbon commissions headed by former president Herbert Hoover in the late 1940s and early 1950s took a tack quite similar to the earlier Brownlow Committee, endorsing increased managerial authority for presidents and spurring executive-centered organizational changes in the departments and regulatory agencies.[54]

Congress also added to the president's institutional resources. In 1946 the Employment Act required the submission of an annual Economic Report and, in principle at least, made the president single-handedly responsible for the American economy; but the statute also created a Council of Economic Advisers (CEA) to gather information for the president on the state of economic policy-making. In 1947 the National

Security Act created a National Security Council (NSC) as well as the Central Intelligence Agency (CIA) and the first unification of the armed services into what would become the Department of Defense. While the NSC as a formal forum for high-level deliberation would prove an intermittent tool of presidential advising, the staff serving the council—or more accurately, the president—became a critical part of the EOP infrastructure.

In the 1950s the CEA was strengthened and a plethora of specialized White House staff aides added, including a legislative liaison office, a science and technology adviser, and staffers devoted to such topics as cold war planning, atomic energy, and public works. In the 1960s the president's policy staff housed in his Special Counsel's office grew markedly. So did the NSC staff, especially after Kennedy aide McGeorge Bundy set up a Situation Room in the basement of the White House's West Wing after the 1961 Bay of Pigs debacle. This new office was staffed around the clock and could receive, transmit, and comment upon the range of classified cable traffic from State, Defense, and intelligence posts. The NSC staff was now located in the White House itself and took on responsibility for the president's day-to-day needs for security advice.[55]

The growth of centralized staffing was made more critical by the enormous growth of the federal establishment starting in the 1930s. The "alphabet soup" of New Deal agencies added thousands of employees and new substantive ingredients to government, rounded out by a new cabinet-level Department of Health, Education, and Welfare in 1953. Even before World War II started, more than a million civilians worked for the federal government, a number that would nearly quadruple by 1945. A larger Executive Office staff was a useful coordinator of this managerial mass, for purposes of policy and patronage both.

As the number of presidential staffers increased, so did the desire of presidents to keep their counsel confidential. "It is essential to efficient and effective administration that employees of the Executive Branch be completely candid in advising each other on official matters," Eisenhower argued in 1954; thus he deemed it "not in the public interest that any of their conversations or communications, or any documents or reproductions, concerning such advice be disclosed." Less formally, Ike noted, "Any man who testifies as to the advice he gave me won't be working for me that night." His attorney general, William P. Rogers, came up with the phrase *executive privilege* to justify the refusal of the administration to pass along information to Congress.[56]

In short, while American government had always had an executive branch, it now had a "presidential branch" as well. The development was considered, when it was noticed at all, to be a good thing. Given the demands of the job in the cold war era, staff was a presidential extension that would "giv[e] the incumbent a sporting chance," wrote one political scientist. Still another foresaw "salvation by staff," since, as a third noted, without additional resources the president would be unable to function without "overload and breakdown." The president still needed help—now more than ever.[57]

FORMAL POWERS & AGENDA SETTING

One of the things the president needed help in doing was setting the public agenda. One means was the public communications strategy sketched already; but for Greenstein, at least, the power of agenda setting is linked more closely to the role of the president in the legislative arena.

Into the 1920s the constitutional invitation to provide Congress with measures the president deemed "necessary and expedient" was not one that legislators thought should be often accepted. Forays by Theodore Roosevelt, Taft, and Wilson into that forum were important but not sustained, as members of Congress denounced the executive's encroachment on legislative prerogatives.

Franklin Roosevelt's approach to the 1933 banking crisis served as a dramatic announcement of new boundaries. On March 5, a day after taking office, Roosevelt issued an executive order temporarily closing the banks (the authority for which was rooted in a World War I law prohibiting trading with the enemy) and called Congress into special session. On March 9 he sent legislators an emergency banking bill, which was passed without having even been formally printed, after forty minutes of debate in the House and little more in the Senate. So began the famous "hundred days," which have become the inevitable, if unfortunate, benchmark for Roosevelt's successors. During this time a flood of proposals rolled out of the executive branch and into law, receiving remarkable legislative deference. In the House temporary "gag" rules even prevented members from amending administration proposals on the floor.

Yet it was under Harry Truman that the "president's program" truly took hold. Roosevelt's first term was by far his most productive in terms of legislative leadership, and even then Congress initiated much important reform; his second was tainted by the effort to "pack" the Supreme Court; his third and brief fourth were dominated by wartime concerns.[58] By the time Roosevelt died in 1945, the president's involvement in that process was no longer insult, but not yet institution.

However, by the end of 1947, the struggling Truman administration realized that, if the Republican "do-nothing" Congress was to be made a successful electoral foil in 1948, the president needed an affirmative and comprehensive marker of his own. Special legislative messages were therefore packaged for congressional consideration nearly weekly. After Truman's surprise victory this systematic presentation of presidential requests became routine. Indeed, by the time Dwight Eisenhower took office, legislators not only accepted but demanded a presidential agenda. When the new administration was slow in providing one in 1953, a House committee chair angrily admonished Ike: "Don't expect us to start from scratch on what you people want. That's not the way we do things here—*you* draft the bills, and *we* work them over." Eisenhower complied and even created a White House staff devoted to congressional liaison. By 1962 President Kennedy could comment matter-of-factly that "it is a responsibility of the President of the United States to have a program and to fight for it."[59]

Presidents in the 1949–65 period sent between fifty and ninety messages to Congress each year, containing anywhere from sixty-five to more than four hundred separate proposals for legislative consideration.[60] And once bills reached the president's desk, they faced a newly aggressive veto pen. FDR reportedly told members at a cabinet meeting to "find me something I can veto." Even the supposedly passive Eisenhower vetoed nearly two hundred bills in eight years. As he pointed out, the veto made him part of the legislative process. Presidents took full advantage of that.

They also asserted more influence over another critical element of the policy agenda, the budget. A 1921 statute requiring a unified executive budget finally gave presidents the chance to centralize control over agency spending requests. Upon arriving in the EOP, the BoB became a key instrument for presidents seeking to manage agencies' requests to Congress, both legislative and monetary. That included efforts to control monies on the other side of the budget process—after funds were appropriated. In lieu of a line-item veto, presidents had long withheld occasional spending they considered wasteful; before and during World War II, for example, Franklin Roosevelt annually deferred several hundred million dollars in nonmilitary construction appropriations. The broad practice, if not all its applications, was unchallenged by Congress; by 1950, in fact, statutory language authorized President Truman to impound funds if spending became unnecessary due to "changes in requirements" or "other developments."[61]

Those permissive conditions obviously had the potential for discretionary interpretation favoring presidential priorities. The growth of the executive establishment, however, made such discretion not only more powerful but more necessary. The rapidly expanding administrative state—and the tasks of economic revival, stabilization, and world war placed upon it—brought the need for organization and management to the fore. Thus Congress actively delegated presidents new powers in all areas of policy-making.

In the area of foreign affairs the Supreme Court not only upheld this delegation but endorsed it. The 1936 *Curtiss-Wright* decision famously backed the right of Congress to leave it to the president's discretion when to invoke and implement a neutrality act preventing arms sales to belligerents. It did so in extraordinarily broad language that presidents have come to cherish. This case, wrote Justice Sutherland for the Court, involved the "very delicate, plenary, and exclusive power of the President as the sole organ of the federal government in the field of international relations—a power which does not require as a basis for its exercise an act of Congress." Many have argued that Sutherland went too far, that the framers had no intention of giving the president exclusive power over much of anything. In that context *organ* is the right word only if by it is meant an instrument whose notes are defined by the other hands on its keys. Still, presidents to this day quote the opinion in their arguments to Congress or courts concerning foreign policy.[62]

The *Curtiss-Wright* decision appeared to be in sharp contrast to the

Court's tone in two cases decided the year before. Those cases had over-turned New Deal statutes giving the president discretion over domestic policy. Most famously in the *Schechter* decision, the Court had rejected the notion that Congress could delegate to the president the power to promulgate industrial codes regulating labor conditions such as mini-mum wages and maximum hours. "Extraordinary conditions may call for extraordinary remedies," wrote Chief Justice Hughes. "But . . . extraordinary conditions do not create or enlarge constitutional power" that would allow Congress to give presidents the authority to write statute. Justice Cardozo's concurrence put it this way: "The delegated power of legislation which has found expression in this code is not canalized within banks that keep it from overflowing."

But even here the Court was soon to switch gears. Though Roo-sevelt's efforts to "pack" the Court after the 1936 election failed in Con-gress, the Court's decisions on New Deal legislation nonetheless became markedly more sympathetic to presidential power and to the expansion of national governmental power generally (for example, through a gen-erous interpretation of the scope of what constituted interstate com-merce). The administrative presidency continued apace. As World War II encroached and then exploded, the First and Second War Power Acts granted FDR broad emergency powers that prompted the issuance of nearly three hundred executive orders, including the creation of more than fifty new agencies. Few of these had specific congressional sanction, and thus their operation depended on reflected executive authority rather than statutory authorization. This segues neatly to unilateral action less grounded—if at all—in legislative delegation.[63]

RELIANCE ON UNILATERAL AUTHORITY

"In the event Congress shall fail to act, and act adequately, I shall accept the responsibility, and I will act," proclaimed Franklin Roosevelt on Labor Day 1942. "The President has the powers, under the Constitu-tion, and under Congressional acts, to take measures necessary to avert a disaster."[64]

Roosevelt was seeking a law governing wage and price controls, and he got one. But the speech highlights his willingness to utilize executive authority, broadly defined, with or without congressional approval. The lead-up to World War II provides a number of dramatic illustrations.

With the fall of France in June 1940, Roosevelt declared an "unlimited national emergency" and utilized statutory authority to mobilize the economy, spending more than $15 billion appropriated for military preparedness measures. He also concluded a series of executive agreements, thus evading the Senate ratification needed for treaties. One created provisional governments in Latin America that kept French possessions in the region away from the Vichy government. Another formed a Permanent Joint Board of Defense linking the American and Canadian military staffs. A third, more dramatically, transferred fifty destroyers to Britain in return for eight Caribbean naval bases. Such a transaction violated a 1917 statute prohibiting the transfer of warships to a belligerent nation and also the 1940 Neutrality Act, since the ships were usable military equipment; however, the attorney general's opinion justifying the agreement grounded it in various principles, including the "plenary powers of the President as Commander in Chief of the Army and Navy and as the head of the State in its relations with foreign countries."[65] In January 1941, months before lend-lease legislation finally passed, FDR began to arrange $3 billion in supplies for the Soviet Union, a controversial partner given its earlier alliance with Hitler.

More was in store. An executive agreement with Denmark in April 1941 allowed American forces to occupy Greenland, followed in July by an agreement to defend Iceland as well. Since those U.S. troops needed provisions, the navy was ordered to protect the supply convoys and to sink Axis submarines threatening them. In September, after an American ship heading toward Iceland was attacked by a German U-boat, Roosevelt ordered the navy to shoot on sight. (The U.S. ship, FDR told the public, was simply carrying mail; in fact, it had tracked the submarine and reported its position to the British navy.) In October merchant ships were armed, and the navy was told to provide "neutrality patrols" and to sink Axis ships even if they were not near the convoys. British documents released later indicate that Roosevelt had very deliberately sought to force an incident in the North Atlantic.

All of this, of course, was retroactively legitimated by the Japanese attack on Hawaii and the sheer scale of the evils of the Axis. Congress had shortsightedly misread the stakes, passing arms embargos against England and France in 1939, nearly repealing the draft in 1941, waiting a year to pass lend-lease legislation, cutting funds for new arms, and even resisting naval construction in the Pacific. "The Lockean doctrine of emergency prerogative had endured," Schlesinger commented, "because it expressed a real, if rare, necessity in a free state. FDR was a Lockean without knowing it." As Richard Pious has concluded, something of a "frontlash" resulted, legitimating future presidents' likewise unilateral endeavors: "American foreign policy became a presidential prerogative as a reaction to presidential successes and the pathetic congressional performance prior to Pearl Harbor."[66]

Roosevelt's successors took full advantage of their new freedom of action. Harry Truman, for example, committed the nation to protecting southern Europe against communism as the cold war began, winning support, in part, by "scaring hell out of the country." He oversaw the creation within the new CIA of an Office of Special Operations, which immediately began covert operations in Italy; in 1949 the director of Central Intelligence saw his powers expanded to include broad spending discretion with little congressional oversight—"a secret arm of the executive, with a secret budget."[67]

When hostilities erupted on the Korean peninsula, Truman immediately committed American forces to the defense of South Korea. Korea would become the first great undeclared war, lasting three years and killing some thirty-seven thousand American servicemen. Truman not only refused to ask for congressional authorization for this action but refused a resolution when it was offered; he felt, as Secretary of State Dean Acheson put it, that to seek legislative support would weaken the presidency by setting a "precedent in derogation of presidential power to send our forces into battle." Extending the principle past the battlefield in 1951, Truman sent four combat divisions' worth of reinforcements to Europe, claiming that the commander-in-chief power allowed him to move troops wherever he liked without congressional approval, even in the absence of hostilities. After extended debate, Congress backed down.[68]

Dwight Eisenhower was more circumspect in committing American combat troops. He resisted pressures to involve the United States in Indochina in the wake of the French colonial collapse there. However, in the face of tensions between Taiwan and Communist China in 1955, he requested (and received) congressional authorization to deploy the armed forces "as he deem[ed] necessary" in the region. No enemy was named, nor limits set. A similar resolution was passed with regard to the Middle East in 1957.

Eisenhower never used this blank-check authority. He did, however, send some fourteen thousand troops to Jordan for a brief period in 1958, without requesting legislative sanction. And he was far less shy in initiating covert operations around the globe. Most notable were the overthrows of the governments of Iran, Guatemala, and Laos, where Eisenhower feared communist influence. The new Kennedy administration, swayed by these successes, quickly and rather thoughtlessly approved the ongoing planning for the overthrow of the Castro regime in Cuba. When Kennedy refused to add combat troops to the mix, the landing force was routed. The next year, in the wake of this fiasco, Kennedy revamped his advising system, but he did not go so far as to include Congress in those consultations. He also began to send soldiers—termed "advisers"—to an obscure nation called South Vietnam. There was, once again, no declaration of war and no congressional authorization.

The crisis atmosphere of the cold war drove these decisions, and congressional and public acquiescence to them, to the extent that they were known at all. The old battles of the balance of power intersected with the new logic of the nuclear age, with Americans hoping to win hearts and minds without assuring mutual destruction. In 1950 the secret government policy paper NSC-68 laid out the doctrine that "in the context of the current polarization of power a defeat of free institutions anywhere is a defeat everywhere." This expression of what would soon be called the "domino theory" justified initiatives up to and including Vietnam; much of the action it underlay, since secrecy was considered so important to its implementation, was presidential action.[69]

But in light of later events, it is worth noting that this philosophy did not apply only overseas. Six months before the attack on Pearl Harbor, Roosevelt used federal power to break a strike at the North American Aviation factory in California. He also ordered extensive wiretapping, even of his own staff: New Deal stalwarts Tommy Corcoran and Harry Hopkins were among the victims.[70] This sort of political espionage, relished by FBI director J. Edgar Hoover, became a regular tool of power, with a diverse cast of targets including columnist Drew Pearson, Roosevelt cabinet secretary Harold Ickes, and nuclear scientist J. Robert

Oppenheimer (as well as his lawyer). By the 1960s John F. Kennedy used wiretaps to gain information in his battle over steel price hikes and Robert Kennedy to track the press leaks of Justice staffers and the sex life of the Reverend Martin Luther King Jr.

Even though the Supreme Court had sought to limit the use of evidence obtained through wiretapping, FDR overrode this decision after failing to receive legislative authorization. "It is too late to do anything about it after sabotage, assassinations, and 'fifth column' activities are completed," Roosevelt wrote to Attorney General Robert H. Jackson in 1940. "You are, therefore, authorized and directed . . . to authorize the necessary investigating agents that they are at liberty to secure information by listening devices direct to the conversations or other communications of persons suspected of subversive activities against the Government of the United States, including suspected spies." He hoped Jackson would "limit these investigations so conducted to a minimum and"—also notable in retrospect—"limit them insofar as possible to aliens." But he did not require those restrictions, and he also sought ways to use the military to investigate suspected plots. Had large-scale domestic sabotage broken out during World War II, Jackson later wrote, "there is no doubt in my mind that President Roosevelt would have taken most ruthless methods to suppress it. He had no patience with treason, and he did not share the extreme position about civil rights that some of his followers have taken."[71]

The truth of that last clause is clear from Executive Order 9066, which spurred the detention of some 112,000 Japanese Americans on the West Coast in internment camps, for as long as four years. This decision, of course, was endorsed by Congress and (at least tacitly) by the Supreme Court. But even after hot war turned to cold, Roosevelt's successors continued to expand their capacity for domestic intelligence gathering. Truman expanded the 1940 order to include cases "vitally affecting the domestic security, or where human life is in jeopardy." In 1956 the FBI launched its counterintelligence program COINTELPRO, which included surveillance, forgery, and even the use of infiltrated agents to incite violence, especially by communist groups. This program expanded under the Kennedy administration to monitor civil rights groups, the Black Panthers, and the Ku Klux Klan. Over time, the FBI also became skilled at intercepting the mail and carrying out so-called black bag jobs—covert burglaries—against suspected individuals or organizations, functions implicitly endorsed by the Truman Justice Department and explicitly by Eisenhower's. By one estimate, between 1942 and 1968, the FBI committed more than 230 illegal entries.[72]

It is worth noting, in this context, the *Youngstown Sheet and Tube* decision of 1952 quoted in chapter 1. In striking down President Truman's seizure of steel mills during the Korean War, the Court did place some limits on executive authority. Wartime authority, the justices held, could not mean infinite executive power: it did not, for example, allow the president to unilaterally seize private property simply because the president did not want to follow the labor arbitration mechanism endorsed by Congress. But even Justice Jackson wrote that "the widest latitude" must be given the president's use of force "when turned against the outside world for the protection of our society"; and several of his colleagues saw no need for that caveat. In a period of permanent cold war, the outside and inside worlds seemed perilously permeable. And in any case, it was up to Congress to protect its own—and the people's—prerogatives.

THE "SAVIOR" PRESIDENCY

And so the story arrived in the 1960s far distant from its starting point in Philadelphia in 1787. Along the way presidents had acquired many tools to work around their constitutionally mandated weakness. They used their formal powers creatively and proactively; they built an executive branch in their own image, with an extensive "presidential branch" to oversee and control it; and they moved unilaterally to use vaguely defined executive powers to reshape the policy landscape, relying on a direct connection with the public to legitimize their actions. Arguably a new framework for American government had been created along the way.

Most mid-century observers welcomed such a development. If thirty years after Nixon's resignation there was concern about the eclipse of Congress, thirty years prior to Nixon most worry went the other way. Arguing that a strong president was a crucial force in overcoming the fragmentation of American democracy in a time of seemingly perpetual crisis—when "emergencies in policy," by prewar standards, became business as usual—scholars of politics and public administration hailed the rise of a vigorous chief executive.[73] A menacing world required the swift decision-making capacity of centralized leadership. In 1944, for example, Paul Appleby, later dean of Syracuse University's Maxwell School, approvingly noted "the trend to Presidential Government." After all, "what our Government needs most of all is greater unity, and it can have greater unity only around the leadership of the President. . . . [T]he time when Congress has been most in the saddle has been the time of most government inadequacy. I think that Congress has and should always have a veto power rather than a devising, formulating, originating function."[74]

There were some critics, notably Charles Beard, who argued vigorously in a 1948 book that FDR had greatly overstepped his bounds. But this "simply outraged many American intellectuals, including most historians," who stressed that deception of the public was necessary. The dean of the journalism establishment, Walter Lippmann, declared that the national interest was dangerously undermined when Congress and public opinion worked to "devitalize, to enfeeble, and to eviscerate the executive powers." But public opinion actually did little of the sort: a 1959 poll showed that 61 percent of those surveyed thought that presidents should have more power. Only 17 percent chose Congress.[75]

More rigorous scholarship came to the same conclusion. Clinton Rossiter's influential book *The American Presidency,* published in 1956, laid a host of duties at that president's feet, from his role as chief executive to those of chief of state, chief diplomat, chief legislator, commander in chief, chief of party, Voice of the People, Protector of the Peace, Manager of Prosperity, and international coalition leader. "Since Congress is no longer minded or organized to guide itself," Rossiter cautioned, "the refusal or inability of the President to serve as leader results in weak and disorganized government." Indeed, President Eisenhower was criticized for his seeming passivity, for his failure to exercise "the kind of leadership essential to survival." By contrast, "the verdict of history" concerning FDR "will surely be that he left the Presidency a more splendid instrument of democracy than he found it."[76]

Richard Neustadt's landmark book *Presidential Power,* published in 1960, certainly thought so. Using FDR as a template, Neustadt discussed how presidents could enhance their influence over governmental outcomes and stressed how important it was to the quality of American governance that they do so. "An expert search for presidential influence contributes to the energy of government and to the viability of public policy," Neustadt assured his readers, among them president-elect John F. Kennedy. "[W]hat is good for the country is good for the President, and vice versa." Indeed, in the nuclear age, he would later add, "when it comes to action risking war, technology has modified the Constitution."[77]

A third scholar, James MacGregor Burns, summed up the argument in two book titles. In 1963 he bemoaned *The Deadlock of Democracy;* in 1965 he argued that the solution had to be *Presidential Government.* Only the presidency could provide leadership that overcame fragmentation and indecision. "As a general proposition," he asserted, "the stronger we make the Presidency, the more we strengthen democratic procedures and can hope to realize modern liberal democratic goals." To be sure, he argued, it was important to have a "vigorous, coherent, creative" opposition that could promote an alternative platform—this was all the more important, in fact, as presidential power grew. But in the end, "presidential government, far from being a threat to American democracy, has become the major single institution sustaining it—a bulwark of individual liberty, an agency of popular representation, and a magnet for political talent and leadership."[78]

As of the mid-1960s, then, worry about an "imperial" presidency fell far behind worry about a Congress seemingly unwilling or unable to meet the challenges of the postwar era. The president, as Erwin Hargrove and Michael Nelson conclude, was largely seen as a "savior." Legislators' failure to prepare for World War II; their reluctance to commit to an expanded American role in the wider world after 1945; their slow deliberations in a nuclear age that required dispatch; their fragmented, seniority-dominated committee system that brought dullards to power; their tacit (and often not so tacit) defense of institutionalized racism; their short-sighted, sectional demands for local pork at the expense of wider public goods—looking at all this, many felt that leadership must be vested instead in the executive branch. If, as Edward Corwin summed up long before Watergate, "the history of the presidency has been a history of aggrandizement," that aggrandizement was generally

well received and even applauded. If presidents of the past had sometimes overstepped, a sense of "all's well that ends well" nonetheless prevailed.[79] And for 175 years after the ratification of the Constitution,
America's ventures had, by and large, ended well.

But in the spring of 1965, Lyndon Johnson sent U.S. marines ashore
in South Vietnam. Soon he asked for $700 million to continue military
operations there and announced the deployment of fifty thousand additional servicemen, with more to follow. At the time, fewer than one in
five Americans listed Vietnam as an important issue; fewer still, it is safe
to say, could locate the place on a map.[80] For presidents, though, it
would become an indelible landmark on the panorama of power.

III. THE "OLD"
IMPERIAL PRESIDENCY

The events of the last chapter described the building blocks of executive unilateralism being put in position; from the mid-1960s to the early 1970s they were cemented together. By the time Richard Nixon won reelection, scholarly acclamation for a strong executive branch had been replaced largely by horror.

In 1973 the historian Arthur M. Schlesinger Jr.—previously an advocate of an energetic executive, at least in the persons of Andrew Jackson, FDR, and John F. Kennedy—laid down an enduring marker. Schlesinger's iconic book, *The Imperial Presidency,* gave Cato's anti-Federalist forecasts of ancient Rome's reincarnation on the Potomac a twentieth-century twist. By "imperial" was meant the absolute power of modern presidents but also their relative power, as altered by the office's predilection for expansion across the constitutional map. Schlesinger still claimed to favor presidential strength. But Nixon, he argued, sought instead presidential supremacy,

> a new balance of constitutional powers, an audacious and imaginative reconstruction of the American Constitution. He did indeed contemplate, as he said in his 1971 State of the Union message, a New American Revolution. But the essence of this revolution was not, as he said at the time, power to the people. The essence was power to the presidency.

Schlesinger devoted most of his focus to the war powers and "the rise of presidential war." However, he also criticized the efforts of the Nixon administration to centralize budgeting powers and unilaterally shape policy outcomes via impoundment; to manage the press; to build up a large, politicized staff; to greatly expand the "secrecy system"; and, relatedly, to broaden the notion of executive privilege.[1]

Schlesinger was not alone, and the assessments of other contemporary observers were, if anything, even harsher. One 1968 piece suggested the office was "defective," a "Frankenstein monster." George Reedy, a longtime staffer to Lyndon Johnson, suggested that patriotic reverence had become "idolatry" compounded by presidents' isolation from "the company of lesser breeds." Unfortunately, Reedy continued, "divinity is a better basis for inspiration than it is for government." By 1973 some even rued the rise of Roosevelt: liberal senator Alan Cranston (D-CA), for example, lamented that "those who tried to warn us back at the beginnings of the New Deal of the dangers of one-man rule that lay ahead on the path that we were taking . . . may not have been so wrong." Political scientists Hargrove and Nelson artfully combined these threads when they observed that the presidential image after Nixon had taken on a whiff of brimstone—shifting from "Savior" to "Satan."[2] The "presidential government" that seemed imminent and desirable in 1944 and even 1964 seemed horrifying in 1974.

What lay behind the presidency's rather abrupt drop through the circles of paradise? This chapter will explore and update the charges brought by Schlesinger and others, with specific attention to the decade or so leading up to the resignation of Richard Nixon. The main focus will be on the Johnson and Nixon policies in Vietnam—especially their political impact—and on the Watergate scandal, broadly defined.

Enough years have passed that many do not remember why people were so exercised at the time or why "gate" has become a standard suffix to scandal. But even a cursory list of the relevant events shows how sweeping the indictment against the presidency had become. The counts start with petty (and not so petty) campaign sabotage and quickly ratchet up to burglary, bribery, extortion, fraud, destruction of evidence, domestic espionage, obstruction of justice, and abuse of various aspects of executive power—from efforts to inflict punitive tax audits on political opponents to refusal to spend money appropriated by Congress to secret aerial and ground warfare against a neutral nation.[3] Stephen Ambrose rightly observes that, "had there never been a Watergate, there still would have been a war between Nixon and Congress" over policy issues ranging across domestic, economic, and foreign affairs.[4] But my use of the term *Watergate* will follow common practice in encompassing the various battles of that war under its broad label, a collection of transgressions that rose past the confines of the building that lent its name to the era and landed right in the Oval Office.

What follows is not a comprehensive history of the key "imperial" decade, 1965–74, given how carefully these events have been chronicled elsewhere. The books on Vietnam alone could fill a small library, and Watergate is not far behind.[5] Instead, the idea is to give a sense of the developments in executive power that so alarmed scholarly observers—and, more important, political actors—by the early 1970s. If the post-Watergate era is one of reaction, to what were people reacting?

This chapter will answer that question in the context of four substantive areas of presidential behavior and authority: unilateral executive action and executive privilege; budgetary powers and politics; foreign policy, focusing on the war powers and intelligence gathering; and ethics. Together, these categories cover the scope of executive powers whose history was discussed in chapter 2. They will be used to organize the discussion in the following three chapters as well.

EXECUTIVE AUTHORITY & GOVERNMENTAL SECRECY

Lyndon Johnson, it is said, was reviewing marines bound for Vietnam. As he walked across the tarmac toward a departing helicopter, an officer caught up and pointed another way: "Sir, that's your helicopter over there." Johnson stopped him. "Son," he replied, "they're *all* my helicopters."[6]

Such was Johnson's view of executive authority, and possessiveness began at home. If the Brownlow Committee had found in 1937 that "the President needs help," by the 1960s he had help to spare. The president's White House staff had risen from Roosevelt's handful of administrative assistants with a "passion for anonymity" to a large bureaucracy in its own right, frequently taking a very visible center stage in policymaking and serving as a buffer to and sometime substitute for the cabinet secretaries. Johnson had some four hundred staff in the White House Office, allowing him to build capacity for domestic policy formulation through aides such as Joseph Califano, who oversaw a series of task forces aimed at bypassing the cabinet departments. He also continued and expanded Kennedy's reliance on the NSC staff. Some analysts have laid the blame for Johnson's Vietnam decision making at the feet of an insular advising process that wallowed in "groupthink," providing a forum for railing against opponents rather than testing the policy's assumptions and seeking contradictory opinions.[7]

Still, when Nixon arrived in the White House he dramatically accelerated these developments. While pledging fealty to "cabinet government," especially in domestic policy, Nixon expanded and empowered the White House staff. A small but telling point concerns lunch: in the Eisenhower administration, there was one White House mess. In the Johnson administration there was one mess, but two servings. Under Nixon, a second dining area had to be added.

Whatever else that action may imply about the new administration's hungers, recent scholarship has established the Nixon years as a clear "tipping point" for White House staff organization. Both its size and the range of its responsibilities expanded greatly.[8]

This was not accidental. Nixon liked an orderly, hierarchical system, and properly staffing issues out required more people. Further, the growth of the presidential branch was intended to counter, and substitute for, the civil service-dominated executive branch, by then nearly 3 million employees strong. Johnson wanted control of that bureaucracy, but Nixon felt he needed it. He feared (not without reason) that the permanent bureaucracy, after spending twenty-eight of thirty-six years under Democratic presidents, opposed him and would subvert his programs.

Thus Nixon sought to build up a counterbureaucracy in the Executive Office. While raw numbers should be read with some caution, the trend is clear: by 1972 the White House Office employed close to six hundred people and the EOP had grown to fifty-six hundred employees (compared to fourteen hundred in 1952). In the first Nixon term alone the EOP budget nearly doubled, to $54 million per year. Managing all this required resurrecting and expanding upon the Eisenhower innovation of a full-time chief of staff, a role filled by H. R. Haldeman with ruthless efficiency through his own West Wing mini-secretariat.[9]

The president's men also became far more functionally specialized, both in domestic and foreign policy. Under Henry Kissinger, the NSC staff was to be the main source of foreign policy advice and even operations; most of Nixon's foreign policy endeavors—Vietnam, detente, the opening to China—ran through the NSC, not the State Department. The NSC staff went from eighteen professionals to fifty, and its budget tripled. Kissinger himself took over the chair of most of the upper-level interdepartmental committees (and, not coincidentally, a prestigious office just down the hall from the president's); one new assignment even gave Kissinger budget review power over the State Department and Pentagon.[10] Kissinger was also given the authority to order background research studies without going through the cabinet-level membership of the NSC itself, aiding Nixon's predilection for back-channel diplomacy.

In 1970 Nixon created the Domestic Council to parallel the NSC: like the NSC, the Domestic Council came with an executive director (John Ehrlichman) and a sizeable staff that could act independently of the putative council membership. One aide told an interviewer, "there isn't anything in the domestic area that we don't handle, and when we set this up we defined domestic as anything that wasn't obviously foreign. So there's quite a range." Though this boast perhaps overstated the case, at the same time Nixon transformed the BoB into the Office of Management and Budget (OMB). The new emphasis on the "M" in OMB was designed to facilitate Nixon's efforts to shape the way executive agencies created and implemented policy. As Ehrlichman put it in a 1972 memo to Caspar Weinberger, then OMB's director, "I'm for whatever will strengthen the President's hand vs. the bureaucracy." This meant focusing on management—so long as it wasn't boring public administration theory but rather "management in the get-the-Secretary-to-do-what-the-President-needs-and-wants-him-to-do-whether-he-likes-it-or-not sense." The goal was to gain for Nixon the ability to control bureaucratic structures, personnel, processes, and, thereby, outcomes.[11]

Nixon also paid significant attention to public relations and outreach; indeed, "public opinion was a guiding concern of the Nixon White House." While Johnson established polling as a stand-alone operation within the White House, Nixon expanded in-house polling quite dramatically, both in terms of its capacity and its political orientation. He commissioned nearly twice as many private polls (230 in all) between

1969 and 1972 as LBJ did between 1963 and 1968, and those polls were qualitatively superior—more detailed, more sophisticated, and more precisely timed and targeted. The White House polled not just on election trial heats but on multiple policy issues, from Vietnam to busing to the environment.[12] With results in hand, Nixon formed a nascent office of public liaison to reach out to organized interest groups (and to help organize those that might be helpful). And he created an Office of Communications to coordinate press relations, including efforts to bypass the White House press corps by releasing material directly to local media outlets deemed more sympathetic to the administration's programs than the national networks.

Another segment of Nixon's strategy to get a handle on the wider executive branch was organizational. Unhappy with cabinet-level loyalty—Ehrlichman commented that the secretaries only appeared at the White House for Christmas parties, since they had gone off and "married the natives"—Nixon used his appointment power to seed the bureaucracy at the operational level with those personally loyal to his programmatic initiatives and to fire at least some of those who resisted the Nixon line. He also sought to reorganize the cabinet into a smaller group of more functionally consistent departments; failing in this, he briefly implemented an experiment in which certain departments would report through others via so-called supersecretaries, who also held White House staff appointments. For example, Treasury Secretary George Shultz became the assistant for economic resources, overseeing the Treasury and Commerce Departments, the U.S. Trade Representative, and the Federal Reserve. (This double appointment also meant that the new assistant could claim executive privilege regarding his communications with the president.)

By 1976, then, former Eisenhower and Nixon staffer Stephen Hess could charge that "the modern Presidency has moved toward creating all policy at the White House, overseeing the operations of government from the White House, using White House staff to operate programs of high presidential priority, and representing in the White House all interests that are demographically separable."[13]

Given Nixon's fears about bureaucratic unresponsiveness, his "administrative presidency" strategy had potential.[14] However, a large, far-flung White House staff brings with it managerial costs as well as benefits, since it is inherently harder to monitor. Nixon largely relied on his staff structure to manage for him: he preferred to meet regularly with only a few advisers (especially Haldeman, Ehrlichman, and Kissinger, who became known collectively as the "Berlin Wall"), relying on written memos instead of personal encounters and scheduling large blocks of time for private thinking and writing. Large staffs also tend to bring non-presidential problems into the White House orbit. And they become a tempting center of resources for Executive Office end runs around what the president sees as bureaucratic intransigence but what the bureaucracy sees as strict adherence to the law.

This temptation was too infrequently resisted, resulting in broad claims of presidential power. One theme was the selective enforcement of the laws. In 1969, for example, the administration ordered the Department of Health, Education, and Welfare to ignore the portions of the 1964 Civil Rights Act that required the federal government to cut off funds to colleges that had not desegregated. "Appellants insist that the enforcement of [this statute] is committed to agency discretion," the circuit court noted, finding instead that enforcement was specifically required by the law. Likewise, in 1971 Congress passed a defense authorization act stating it was now U.S. policy to "terminate at the earliest practicable date" American involvement in Vietnam. Nixon, when he signed the bill, declared this language "without binding force or effect" since "it does not reflect my judgment about the way in which the war should be brought to a conclusion" and (despite its presumed status as the law of the land) "will not change the policies I have pursued and that I shall continue to pursue toward this end." Prospective impoundments, discussed in more detail later, provide another example. As the district court observed in one such case, the administration was arguing that "the Constitution confers the discretionary power upon the President to refuse to execute laws passed by Congress with which he disagrees." This, the court ruled, could not stand.[15]

Such broad claims to discretionary power permeated the administration. In late 1971 the White House launched what became known as the "Responsiveness Program," designed to capitalize on what Nixon aide Fred Malek called "the President's unique asset in the forthcoming campaign," namely, "his control of the executive branch." Various grant programs were targeted toward Nixon supporters and away from likely opponents; a Cleveland recreation program, among others, lost funding because its beneficiaries, urban blacks, were unlikely to vote Republican.[16]

Sometimes responsiveness pushed in more sinister directions. As early as 1969 the administration sought to use the Internal Revenue Service (IRS) to curtail the activities of left-leaning groups: "what we cannot do in a courtroom via criminal prosecutions," suggested a White House memo, "IRS could do by administrative action." The agency eventually created a Special Services Staff, which collected information on some eleven thousand organizations and individuals and conducted more than two hundred audits. Other targeted audit requests—for example, of hostile reporters—were also passed down from the White House; *Washington Post* lawyer Edward Bennett Williams was audited for three consecutive years. In 1972 Ehrlichman demanded information on the tax records of the Democratic National Committee chairman, Lawrence F. O'Brien. Later that year White House counsel John Dean gave IRS commissioner Johnnie Walters a list of nearly five hundred people active in Democratic senator McGovern's presidential campaign, insisting they be investigated. Walters complained to Treasury Secretary Shultz, who told him to ignore the request.[17]

Such recalcitrance only aggravated the president and his men. As early as 1971 Dean wrote a memo discussing the "use of the available federal machinery to screw our political enemies."[18] In September 1972, Dean told the president, "One of the things I've tried to do, is just keep notes on a lot of the people who are emerging as less than our friends." Nixon replied, "I want the most comprehensive notes on all of those that have tried to do us in. Because they didn't have to do it. . . ."

> But now [the President went on] they are doing this quite deliberately and they are asking for it and they are going to get it. . . . We, we have not used the power in this first four years, as you know.

Dean: That's true.

President: We have never used it. We haven't used the [FBI] and we haven't used the Justice Department, but things are going to change now. And they're going to change, and, and they're going to get it right—

Dean: That's an exciting prospect.

President: It's got to be done. It's the only thing to do.

Haldeman: We've got to.[19]

Dean was not the only one taking notes. At the same time White House political aide Charles Colson was busy putting together an "Opponents List" as part of the "Political Enemies Project." This compilation—to which others in the White House also contributed names—became later known simply as the "enemies list," running to some two hundred people, including entertainers, journalists, and academics along with Democratic politicians and militant activist groups like the Black Panthers. The list underscores how the administration transmuted "opponents" into "enemies" in a manner that pervaded its policies and politics.[20]

In other areas the administration received more cooperation against its "enemies" than Shultz and the IRS had provided.

One was in using emergency and military forces to control the antiwar demonstrations that convulsed Washington throughout the late 1960s and early 1970s. In May 1971, for example, several thousand people were arrested in dragnets and then detained; in 1975 more than a thousand of those detainees were awarded monetary damages as recognition that their civil rights had been violated.[21]

Even more ominously, government agencies were working to provide more systematic intelligence on "subversive" organizations and individuals the president saw as threatening domestic tranquility and national security. The FBI's COINTELPRO (Counterintelligence Program), begun in 1956, did not end until 1971. It was truncated not because of presidential regret but because of bad publicity accrued when antiwar activists broke into an FBI office, stole COINTELPRO documentation, and distributed it to the media. The stolen memos, and documents obtained later through lawsuits against the bureau, laid out a wide range of surveillance techniques, including infiltration but also warrantless wiretapping, searches (thus, in English, "break-ins"), examination of financial records, and interception of the mail. One 1970 memo recommended making clear to "New Left" circles that "there is an FBI agent behind every mailbox."[22] Field agents forged letters to various groups, hoping, in the words of a 1968 memo, to "create factionalism between not only the national leaders but also local leaders, . . . to neutralize all organizational efforts . . . [and] to create suspicion amongst the leaders" about each other's motives, finances, and loyalty to the cause; in some cases they hoped to incite violence between the groups. One such letter, purportedly from a branch of the Students for a Democratic Society, mocked Black Panthers leader Huey Newton as "Huey the Homo" and urged Panthers to "get high on wine and dream your alcoholic dreams of conquest." Other calls or notes to reporters passed along, under false names, "facts" about financial links and even sexual liaisons between public figures and antiwar or black militants. The FBI alone had some two thousand agents and one thousand paid informants keeping track of the New Left. It should be stressed that this aggressive undermining of lives and careers rarely stemmed from suspicion of actual criminal activity.[23]

Other agencies got in on the action, too, even after COINTELPRO was formally terminated. The National Security Agency (NSA), with its state-of-the-art spy equipment, had begun conducting electronic surveillance of civil rights and antiwar activists in 1967. In July 1969 Project MINARET was formalized in order to provide "information on U.S. organizations or individuals who are engaged in activities which may result in civil disturbances or otherwise subvert the national security of the U.S." and on any efforts of foreign governments to influence or aid those activities.[24] This last issue was of great concern to Presidents Johnson and Nixon, who also ordered the CIA to investigate foreign links to domestic protesters, despite the legal ban on such CIA operations within the United States. The CIA's domestic surveillance program, code-named CHAOS, ran from 1967 to 1974, when investigative journalist Seymour Hersh broke the story in the *New York Times*. During its heyday, more than fifty staffers compiled dossiers on some seventy-two hundred American citizens, conducted their own break-ins (or contracted them out), opened mail (some 380,000 letters, between the CIA's and FBI's combined efforts), and tapped phones. The program's computer files had some three hundred thousand names in them, neatly cross-indexed; however, the CIA could not find the links Johnson and Nixon so urgently sought, and it said so in three separate reports.[25] The agency nonetheless went on to aid the Nixon "Plumbers" (discussed later) by providing them with disguises, false identity documents, and electronic equipment as well as providing the White House with a psychological profile of Daniel Ellsberg, who leaked the Pentagon Papers to the press in 1971.

To be sure, and as should be clear from chapter 2, these methods of operation were not invented by Nixon but have roots back to the 1940s. Lyndon Johnson was an especially enthusiastic consumer of both domestic surveillance and what might be called personal intelligence (that is to say, intimate gossip). In 1968, suspicious of Nixon's contacts with South Vietnam, LBJ had the FBI bug Nixon's campaign plane; Nixon claimed the same had been done even in 1962 when he ran for governor in California. In this sense, then, as noted earlier, Nixon was not without justification when he periodically complained that "everybody does it." And if Nixon read political opposition as personal enmity, there too he was not always wrong. The vicious attacks on the president's character that sprang up as the Johnson administration wound down and that continued unabated through Watergate were often simple denigration without any element of constructive deliberation.

It is also worth stressing the context of the times and their resonance in our own. Various organizations were involved in what can only be called domestic terrorism: planting bombs, robbing banks, inciting riots. The assassinations of Martin Luther King Jr. and Robert F. Kennedy, the provocations and subsequent "police riot" of the Democratic National Convention in Chicago, the widespread unrest (a comforting euphemism for vandalism, looting, and assault) both in inner cities and on college campuses—all this, in 1968 alone, led many to wonder whether the country was coming apart. In 1969 a clash in Berkeley, California, left one dead and thirty wounded; the Center for Advanced Study in the Behavioral Sciences in Stanford, California, was firebombed in the spring of 1970. During the fifteen months ending in April 1970, some 37,000 real and threatened bombings were recorded, causing forty-one deaths; Rutgers University was shut down 175 times in 1970 alone by bomb threats. "Never in our history has this country been confronted with so many revolutionary elements determined to destroy by force the government and the society it stands for," declared the attorney general. In May 1973, thinking back on the various intelligence efforts detailed in this chapter, Nixon argued to Chief of Staff Al

Haig that they "involve[d] groups that were engaging in violence, dis-
ruption and unbelievable hell around this place. . . . I don't think the
country is going to get excited about a damn plan that was drawn up by
agencies to control the goddamn riots." Haig replied, "In fact, most
people will say 'thank God.' Again, if we had done less, we would have
been irresponsible."[26]

Haig's first point probably had merit; however, his second was on less
solid ground. Despite the context, the Nixon administration's domestic
intelligence efforts, and the claims put forth to justify them, ultimately
went beyond the defensible to the self-serving. The sweeping language
that sought to redefine the "inherent" executive power is rather chilling
in retrospect (as, indeed, at the time). In June 1969, for example, Attorney General John Mitchell claimed that unilateral presidential power
extended to wiretapping any group investigators believed was seeking
"to attack and subvert the government by unlawful means." In 1973
John Ehrlichman testified that the Plumbers' activities, including their
burglaries, were "well within the President's inherent constitutional
powers" because they were conducted as a response to national security
concerns.[27] Combined with the breadth of the Nixonian definition of
"enemy" and his self-identification with "the government," such for-
mulations led quickly to unbounded presidential authority—if all opponents of the administration were enemies attacking the government,
then any action was justified.

While the era's domestic dissent was periodically harrowing, it was
closer to a particularly virulent crime wave than a systematic threat to
national security. Nixon knew this. While as late as 1973 he would argue
that "some of the disruptive activities were receiving foreign support," a
long litany of reports (whether from the CIA or Nixon's handpicked
Commission on Campus Unrest) had found no support for that claim;
John Dean later testified that "we never found a scintilla of viable evidence indicating that these demonstrators were part of a master plan."[28]
They represented instead deep dissatisfaction with government policies,
at home and especially abroad.

The administration placed little credence in the notion that changes in
policy would result in changes of attitude. As Nixon aide Tom Huston
wrote, "Perhaps lowered voices and peace in Vietnam will defuse the
tense situation we face, but I wouldn't want to rely on it exclusively."[29]

Nor did the president. And the other tools he sought extended far enough past those of previous administrations to represent a shift in kind as well as degree.

A key piece of evidence for that argument is the extent to which the administration sought to use internal security as just another tool for enforcing a political agenda. By the spring of 1970, the White House was dissatisfied with the quality and focus of domestic intelligence efforts. The FBI, Ehrlichman aide Bud Krogh wrote to his boss, was "almost blind to opportunities which could help us" politically; top-level direction was needed to make sure that the Justice Department would "work for the President" instead of in its own bureaucratic interests. FBI head J. Edgar Hoover had grown more cautious, refusing both Johnson and Nixon White House requests to expand COINTELPRO for fear it might lead to bad publicity for the bureau (as indeed it soon would). White House staffer Tom Huston, who had worked on the team preparing Washington for the massive antiwar demonstrations of November 1969, was tasked with enlarging and coordinating internal security matters. As the historian Stanley I. Kutler summarizes, "Huston's implicit instruction was to bypass the recalcitrant Hoover and provide an intelligence-gathering apparatus that would serve the President's will more effectively."[30]

In June 1970 Nixon convened a working group designed to do just that. After complaining that the agencies' lack of cooperation was obstructing domestic intelligence gathering, the president instructed the group—made up of the FBI, CIA, Defense Intelligence Agency (DIA), NSA, and the White House—to prepare a "threat assessment" and a "range of options" for dealing with its findings. Less than three weeks later, it reported back, arguing that the leftist student groups had "revolutionary aims," which were "apparent when their identification with Marxism-Leninism is examined." As a result, a number of options to relax restraints on intelligence gathering were considered. Huston, in transmitting the report to the president, attached a memo stating that "the need for increased coordination, joint estimates, and responsiveness to the White House is obvious to the intelligence community." He recommended that Nixon choose the most aggressive option in nearly every case. The core of the "Huston Plan" thus provided for increasing electronic surveillance of "domestic security threats" as well as foreign diplomats; opening and reading the mails; lifting restrictions on "surreptitious entry"; recruiting more campus informants; and creating a permanent Interagency Group on Domestic Intelligence and Internal Security, representing the FBI, CIA, NSA, DIA, and other military counterintelligence units, that would be staffed—thus, run—by the White House. Huston argued that the benefits outweighed the costs, since "existing coverage is grossly inadequate." He noted that "surreptitious entry" was, well, "clearly illegal," not to mention "highly risky." But it was worth it: "it is also the most fruitful tool and can produce the type of intelligence which cannot be obtained in any other fashion." Nixon approved the report.[31]

Huston's plan didn't last, at least not in its original form. Hoover, jealous of ceding ground to the White House, had put himself on record as dissenting from Huston's recommendations on civil liberties grounds. Nixon, while presumably bemused by Hoover's arguments, given their author, feared that the FBI chief might expose the plan. By late July Haldeman ordered that the decision memoranda be withdrawn.

However, as the discussion of COINTELPRO, CHAOS, MINARET, and their ilk makes clear, most of the elements of the plan were still implemented: each of these programs was intensified after a new Intelligence Evaluation Committee was activated within the Justice Department in late 1970, bringing together the Huston groups plus the Secret Service and Treasury.

Further, the Nixon White House decided it needed to supplement these official efforts. To do so it created its own private secret police force—in fact, two of them. One, termed the White House "Investigations Unit," was started in April 1969, when John Ehrlichman put former New York detective John Caulfield on the White House payroll; Caulfield's assistant, another former New York policeman named Anthony Ulasewicz, was paid out of surplus campaign funds by Herbert Kalmbach, Nixon's personal attorney and fundraiser. The two investigated a variety of happenings that caught the attention of the White House, from the background of a comedian named Richard M. Dixon, who did impersonations of the president, to a nightclub that counted Speaker of the House Carl Albert (D-OK) among its clients. But the unit's bread and butter was Sen. Edward M. Kennedy. Nixon's history with the Kennedy family went back to 1947, when he entered the House with John F. Kennedy, and since his 1960 defeat to JFK he had been "preoccupied—even obsessed"—with the Massachusetts clan. When the news of Edward Kennedy's automobile accident at Chappaquiddick broke in July 1969, Ulasewicz was quickly dispatched to Martha's Vineyard. There he posed as an investigative reporter in an effort to dig up details on the fatal crash. In August Caulfield flew to Hawaii to trail Kennedy as he vacationed there after a trip to India; "no evidence was developed," Caulfield had to report, "to indicate that his conduct was improper." As Kennedy's criticism of Nixon's Vietnam policy continued that fall, Nixon ordered increased attention to the "Teddy Kennedy fight," and Haldeman had to be talked out of ordering round-the-clock surveillance.[32]

The Kennedy harassment paled, however, in contrast to the duties of the White House's second "Special Investigations Unit," better known as the "Plumbers." This group, led by Ehrlichman aide Krogh and Kissinger staffer David Young, was named after its major assignment: to plug leaks.

Leaks of sensitive—classified, or merely untimely—information are a staple of Washington life. They are often strategic and are used for many purposes. Nixon was a master leaker himself, going back to his days of investigating Alger Hiss on the House Un-American Affairs Committee.

As president, however, he found them less palatable. Both Nixon and Kissinger, seeking to control the flow of information concerning Vietnam and other foreign policy, were angered when the *New York Times* printed a number of stories about troop withdrawals, the Strategic Arms Limitation Treaty (SALT) talks, and North Korea in the spring of 1969. On May 8 the *Times* reported that U.S. bombers had been raiding Vietcong and North Vietnamese camps in Cambodia—a story that attracted surprisingly little attention at the time, though it would become wildly controversial a year later. Certainly Kissinger recognized its significance at once. Through his then-deputy Al Haig, he asked the FBI to find the story's source, and eventually wiretaps were placed on *Times* reporter William Beecher, three other reporters, and thirteen members of the White House staff, from NSC aide Morton Halperin (Kissinger's prime suspect) to speechwriter William Safire. The tap on the latter, as well as another on deputy counsel John Sears, had nothing to do with national security and everything to do with friendly relations with reporters and others on the Georgetown social circuit. The taps on Halperin and his colleague Anthony Lake continued even after they left the NSC staff, since they went to work for Sen. Ed Muskie's campaign and thus became potential sources of political intelligence. Summary transcripts of the taps—which went on for nearly two years—were distributed around the upper levels of the White House staff, to Haldeman, Ehrlichman, Kissinger, Haig, and the president himself.[33]

Still, as shown by its resistance to the Huston Plan, the FBI was not always so amenable to White House requests. In 1969 Nixon ordered Ehrlichman to create "a little group right here in the White House. Have them . . . find out what's going on and how to stop it."[34] If Hoover would not help the president, the president would help himself. And when in June 1971 the Defense Department's encyclopedic secret history of American involvement in Vietnam, the Pentagon Papers, began appearing in print, Nixon came to decide that an aggressive response was in order. This was not his first reaction; after all, the Pentagon Papers largely incriminated the Johnson and Kennedy administrations, demonstrating that the American public had long been deceived about the scope and success of U.S. efforts in the region. Few of the documents, if any, jeopardized current military operations. (Nixon would later describe another leak by saying, "this does affect the national security—this particular one. This isn't like the Pentagon Papers.")[35] But other things, including governmental credibility, were at stake. With so many secret negotiations under way around the globe—with North Vietnam, with China, with the USSR—Nixon and Kissinger feared that the leak would undercut other nations' faith in the American ability to keep such talks confidential; "the era of negotiations can't succeed without secrecy," Nixon told Defense Secretary Melvin Laird. They also worried that the leak might inspire others within the national security bureaucracy to release other, more damaging, information. Further, they were hardly unaware that exposing their predecessors' deceptions would set a dangerous precedent for their successors to exploit.[36]

Nixon therefore first sought an injunction to prevent publication of the Pentagon Papers; this request for prior restraint, rare in American history, was denied by the Supreme Court. With former NSC staffer Daniel Ellsberg soon identified as the leaker, Nixon's attention turned to ways in which Ellsberg could be made an example. "Convict the son of a bitch in the press," he told his staff at various times. "If you can get him tied in to some communist groups, that would be good."[37]

Other leaks around this time, regarding U.S. intelligence on Soviet-Indian relations and the SALT negotiations, further infuriated Nixon. "I don't care how it is to be done, do whatever has to be done to stop these leaks and prevent further unauthorized disclosures," Nixon told Charles Colson. "I want it done, whatever the cost." In another conversation he asked, "Does that bother you as being repressive?" Colson replied, "Oh, hell, no," to which Haldeman added: "We've got to be repressive."[38]

Enter the Plumbers, with an assignment to find out all they could about Ellsberg's life, motives, and associates. Their main operatives were former FBI agent G. Gordon Liddy and former CIA operative E. Howard Hunt. For Hunt the new assignment was more of the same. On the White House payroll since the summer of 1970, largely as a consultant to Colson, he had worked on forging cables purporting to show that the Kennedy White House had provoked the assassination of South Vietnamese president Ngo Dinh Diem in 1963. He had also dug further both into the Bay of Pigs operation (using files ordered from the CIA by Ehrlichman and, ultimately, Nixon) and into Chappaquiddick and other aspects of Ted Kennedy's personal life (often using an identity, equipment, and disguises helpfully provided by the CIA).

The Plumbers' first formal assignment was to work on the "neutralization of Ellsberg," as Hunt put it in a July 1971 memo. He laid out at least two ethically dubious maneuvers: obtaining a CIA psychological profile of Ellsberg and seeking "to obtain Ellsberg's files from his psychiatric analyst."[39] The CIA proved compliant, despite the rules ostensibly barring it from performing such evaluations on American citizens at home; but the Plumbers were unhappy with the profile's conclusion that Ellsberg was sane. They sent it back, demanding revisions, and obtained a slightly juicier conclusion (the leaks were "an act of aggression at his analyst, as well as at the President and his father"). Still unsatisfied, and seeking a jackpot of incriminating information, Krogh and Young wrote to Ehrlichman proposing a "covert operation" that would "examine the medical files still held by" Dr. Lewis Fielding, Ellsberg's psychiatrist. Ehrlichman agreed, so long as it would be "done under your assurance that it is not traceable." He later claimed Nixon himself approved the plan; Nixon in his memoirs denies prior knowledge, but he admits that "it was at least in part an outgrowth of my sense of urgency about discrediting what Ellsberg had done and finding out what he might do next. Given . . . the peril I perceived, I cannot say that had I been informed of it beforehand . . . I would have automatically considered it unprecedented, unwarranted, or unthinkable."[40]

Hunt and Liddy thus recruited a team of burglars, largely made up of Cuban exiles trained by Hunt during his CIA days on the Bay of Pigs operation; the project was paid for (unwittingly) by money obtained from the dairy lobby by Colson. The duo, supplied once more with false identities and disguises from the CIA, cased the Fielding office building. But the subsequent operation was not a success. It was supposed to leave no trace but instead left so many that the office had to be trashed in order to make the entry look like a run-of-the-mill robbery. Receiving little useful information, Hunt and Liddy urged a raid on Ellsberg's apartment as well.

This request was declined. Others were not—in May 1972, for example, the Plumbers team broke into the Chilean embassy in Washington, evidently to gain information about the plans of the socialist Allende government as well as to cover their other break-ins by making them appear to be CIA operations.[41] The Plumbers also installed wiretaps, most notably on a navy officer—who, rather bizarrely, had been spying on the Nixon NSC on behalf of the Joint Chiefs of Staff. As the election wore on, Hunt and Liddy found themselves over at the Committee to Re-elect the President (CRP or, irresistably, CREEP); their exploits there are discussed later in this chapter.

"At this point," concludes J. Anthony Lukas, "the White House [had] moved across the line from . . . prodding other agencies into direct operations more appropriate to a secret-police force." It is hard to reject the analogy. Indeed, one need only read the multiple references in the Nixon transcripts to the Brookings Institution. Not once but at least six times the president explicitly ordered that it be raided to obtain whatever information its staff had on Lyndon Johnson's late fall bombing halt in 1968: "You're to break into the place, rifle the files, and bring them in." Planning got under way before, in this case at least, Nixon's staff had the sense to ignore his commands.[42]

A CODA: EXECUTIVE PRIVILEGE

The Plumbers' job flowed from the avowed need to keep secrecy. Thus, the rise of "executive privilege" discussed in chapter 2—that is, the claim that information on these activities could be kept from Congress and even the courts—requires additional consideration here.[43] As noted earlier, the phrase itself arose only in the 1950s. But the behavior it described (and by its new name subtly legitimated) goes back to the Washington administration, which concluded it had the right to withhold information from Congress concerning military operations and diplomatic negotiations. More generally, over time presidents had claimed the right to determine what, in James Polk's phrase, was "compatible with the public interest to communicate." Largely these concerned sensitive issues of foreign relations.

Later, as the presidential branch grew, the claim expanded to provide for the confidentiality of advice to the president from his staff, using the model of lawyer-client privilege. As Nixon summed up the matter of confidentiality, "it is absolutely essential, if the President is to be able to do his job as the country expects, that he be able to talk openly and candidly with his advisers about issues and individuals. . . . This kind of frank discussion is only possible when those who take part in it can feel assured that what they say is in the strictest confidence."[44]

Some aspects of executive privilege had been generally accepted by Congress, with conflicts resolved case by case. Johnson relied more heavily on classification than on executive privilege, though his staff certainly claimed it from time to time, the more so as public criticism of Vietnam escalated. White House staffer DeVier Pierson would argue that "principle and precedents" excused "immediate staff assistants" from testifying about matters relating to their duties on behalf of the president.[45]

However, Nixon pushed the envelope much further. In March 1973 he claimed that executive privilege could be claimed on behalf of former as well as current staff; in May he applied it not just to information requested by Congress but to that subpoenaed by grand juries. He also extended it to "all documents, produced or received by the President or any member of the White House staff in connection with his official duties." After all, he claimed, "the manner in which the president exercises his assigned executive powers is not subject to questioning by another branch of the government. . . . [I]t is equally appropriate that members of his staff not be so questioned, for their roles are in effect an extension of the Presidency." The separation of powers, in this case, was to be absolute.[46]

This view was exemplified by Attorney General Richard Kleindienst in testimony before a Senate subcommittee in April 1973. Kleindienst argued that the president could direct any member of the executive branch to refuse information in response to congressional request. Sen. Ed Muskie couldn't quite believe it: "the Congress, in your view, has no power to command the production of testimony or information by anyone in the executive branch under any circumstances?" None, said Kleindienst, if the president says so. *Every* employee? Muskie asked. Right, said Kleindienst: "your power to get what the President knows is in the President's hands." Sen. Sam Ervin tried again: "Your position is the President has implied power under the Constitution to deny the Congress the testimony of any person working for the executive branch . . . or any document in [their] possession?" Yes, said Kleindienst. But, he suggested, "you have a remedy, all kinds of remedies—cut off appropriations." Or, he added, almost as a dare, you could "impeach the President."[47]

The battle over executive privilege would, of course, go down that very path.

WAR POWERS, INTELLIGENCE OVERSIGHT, & FOREIGN POLICY

On August 2, 1964, the U.S. destroyer *Maddox* reported it had been attacked by three North Vietnamese torpedo boats as it sailed in international waters some sixteen miles from North Vietnam's coast. It fired back, sinking one enemy vessel and damaging another.

Though it was not widely known, South Vietnamese ships and commandos backed by American ships and military advisers had since February been conducting a series of secret "34-A" raids against North Vietnamese coastal areas. They were designed to bolster Southern morale and put the North on notice of American steadfastness toward its ally. At the same time, American vessels were on patrol near Northern waters, gathering electronic intercepts and other intelligence and generally making a show of force. The *Maddox* was on such a mission when it was attacked, near where a 34-A operation had taken place two days before; presumably the North Vietnamese thought the ship had been part of the offensive and tried to counterpunch.

The Johnson administration, likewise, did not want to send a signal of weakness. Thus it ordered the continuation of the *Maddox*'s patrol, along with a reinforcing destroyer, the *C. Turner Joy*. On the evening of August 4, North Vietnamese orders to attack both ships were intercepted. In Washington, President Johnson decided that he would request congressional support for a retaliatory strike if such an attack occurred. Defense Secretary Robert McNamara argued that "we cannot sit still as a nation and let them attack us on the high seas and get away with it." Later that afternoon, Johnson ordered strikes on North Vietnamese torpedo boat bases and oil storage facilities. And he requested that Congress pass what would become known as the Tonkin Gulf Resolution.[48]

The language of the resolution was straightforward: "That the Congress approves and supports the determination of the President, as Commander in Chief, to take all necessary measures to repel any armed attack against the forces of the United States and to prevent further aggression." It noted that the United States was "prepared, as the President determines, to take all necessary steps, including the use of armed force, to assist any" Southeast Asia Treaty Organization (SEATO) member or protocol state (such as South Vietnam, Cambodia, or Laos) "requesting assistance in defense of its freedom." The resolution would expire when "the President shall determine that the peace and security of the area is reasonably assured by international conditions created by action of the United Nations or otherwise," or when Congress canceled it.[49]

As seen in chapter 2, the Tonkin Gulf Resolution was not the first blank-check delegation of power Congress had granted the president: the language was explicitly modeled by Johnson's staff to mirror the Formosa Resolution of 1955 and the Middle East Resolution of 1957. Nor was it drawn up in response to the Tonkin incidents, for as the Pentagon Papers later showed, drafts were ready as early as May 1964.

In early versions a dollar limitation was placed on military operations, but this was discarded by August, making the blank check literal as well as figurative.[50]

In presenting his case to the public and Congress, Johnson stressed the North's "open aggression on the high seas," arguing on August 5 that "the attacks were deliberate. The attacks were unprovoked." They were, he said, "aggression—deliberate, willful, and systematic aggression." Defense Secretary McNamara took a similar line, testifying before a Senate committee that the ships were engaged in a "routine patrol in international waters." Congress reacted quickly and nearly unanimously: the resolution passed the House by a vote of 416–0, the Senate, 88–2. Rep. Ross Adair's (R-IN) comment was typical of the debate: "the American flag has been fired upon," he argued. "We will not and cannot tolerate such things."[51]

It turned out, of course, that the facts were rather hazier than the administration's presentation of them. The patrol was not routine, nor was either attack entirely unprovoked. Indeed, the second may never have happened. As early as August 4, the commander of the *Maddox* telegraphed word that "many [of the] recorded contacts and torpedoes fired appear doubtful. Freak weather and over-eager sonarman may have accounted for many reports. No actual visual sightings by *Maddox*." Johnson later speculated disgustedly that the "stupid sailors were just shooting at flying fish." Other evidence suggests some attack did occur. But certainly the case for "systematic aggression" by the North was not strong.[52]

Sen. Jacob Javits (R-NY) would later write, backtracking a bit, that "the language of the Gulf of Tonkin resolution was far more sweeping than the congressional intent." However, as he added, "whatever President Johnson's position . . . Congress had the obligation to make an institutional judgment as to the wisdom and propriety of giving such a large grant of its own power to the Chief Executive."[53] That judgment was, apparently, positive. Nearly a year later, in July 1965, Johnson requested $700 million in supplemental appropriations for Vietnam, a clear up-or-down vote on administration policy: it passed by near unanimous votes in both chambers. The president took full advantage of this broad legislative support to expand troop operations in the region.

Still, even in 1965, the administration was not entirely candid about its plans. Operation Rolling Thunder, a massive bombing campaign of North Vietnamese targets, had kicked into gear in February. This was presented again as simple tit-for-tat, this time for an attack on a U.S. army barracks in Pleiku. But in fact it represented an important escalation and a new commitment by the United States to further escalation thereafter. By 1966 the State Department had asserted very expansively "the constitutional powers of the President" to repel sudden attacks on American interests. The president was to be the sole judge of what counted toward those interests—he could decide that Vietnam, for example, qualified. "Under this theory," Schlesinger commented, "it was hard to see why any future President would ever see any legal need to go to Congress before leading the nation into war."[54] The administration claimed in 1967 that the Tonkin Gulf Resolution was the "functional equivalent" of a declaration of war, but LBJ himself said he didn't need it then, or later, to go to war.[55]

Presumably such arguments also applied to events in the Dominican Republic in 1965. A military coup in 1963 had replaced elected president Juan Bosch, somewhat to the relief of American policymakers, who distrusted Bosch's anticommunist credentials. When a rebellion aimed at restoring Bosch was launched in the spring of 1965, Johnson sent in the marines. He argued that foreign nationals in the country were in danger and that the rebellion had communist, probably Cuban, backing ("people trained outside the Dominican Republic are seeking to gain control," he told the nation). Ultimately, more than twenty-five thousand troops were deployed, without congressional authorization. Notably, Congress did not object; the House even passed a resolution backing interventions aimed at preventing communist takeovers of Western Hemisphere governments. Still, Johnson's expansive rhetoric was just as notable. The president described the murders of some fifteen hundred civilians, "murdered and shot, and their heads cut off," for example. The U.S. ambassador, he claimed, was sheltered under an embassy desk while the bullets flew through the window above him and "a thousand American men, women, and children . . . were pleading with their President for help to preserve their lives." None of this, nor the extent of Cuban involvement in the rebellion, could be proved.[56]

The hyperbole involved soon raised grave doubts about Johnson's credibility. Indeed, by the time of the Tet Offensive in early 1968, the

Johnson administration had plunged into a "credibility gap" regarding the progress of the war. Johnson's case was not helped by ongoing hearings probing the attacks in the Gulf of Tonkin. Nor had the commitment of more and more troops (half a million by 1967) and the most massive aerial bombing in the history of warfare made discernible progress on the battlefield, despite the administration's repeated optimistic assertions. Even Johnson's stress on the international nature of the coalition fighting alongside the United States—including forces from the Philippines, South Korea, and Thailand—was undercut when it became known that those forces had been heavily subsidized with U.S. aid on a quid pro quo basis. The presence of one Thai division in South Vietnam cost the United States at least $260 million.

Tet proved to be a military victory for the United States, but it was a psychological disaster. In March 1968 Johnson announced he was limiting the bombing of North Vietnam as a way of encouraging peace talks to begin. And, stunning the nation, he announced he would not run for reelection that fall.[57]

"We will not make the same old mistakes," Henry Kissinger said in 1969 of the new Nixon administration and Vietnam. "We will make our own."[58] When it came to asserting executive power, the administration did both. "With Nixon as with Johnson," Schlesinger charged, "the central role for Congress in foreign affairs was to provide aid and comfort to the Commander in Chief. He never sought its advice before major initiatives."[59]

As already noted, secrecy was the watchword of the Nixon administration. Even the famous 1972 trip to China, while widely supported after the fact, was planned in secrecy and carried out without congressional—or the State Department's—involvement. Kissinger's first trip to Beijing involved a faked illness in Pakistan followed by supposed seclusion at the Pakistani president's private estate. "The P obviously is really cranked up about this whole Chinese thing," Haldeman wrote in his diary. "P even lied to Billy Graham."[60]

Still greater secrecy obtained in Vietnam, where the theater of war was expanded even as "Vietnamization" promised the gradual withdrawal of American combat forces. The Vietcong had long used the Ho Chi Minh Trail through neighboring—but neutral—Cambodia to move troops and supplies from North to South Vietnam. In March 1969 Nixon approved a plan to bomb enemy sanctuaries inside Cambodia. The new front (code-named MENU) was a closely held secret; "knowledge of the operation," its official military history notes, "was limited to individuals essential to its successful execution, and a procedure was carefully devised to conceal the bombing." That procedure involved briefing pilots on night missions over Vietnam, then diverting them via ground control instructions over Cambodia; false reports on each mission were filed through regular channels, while real reports were filed separately and secretly. "While the MENU attacks were taking place," the official history concludes, "only a few United States officials were aware of the B-52 operations in Cambodia, and the U.S. public had no knowledge of the attacks at all." Nearly four thousand sorties were flown, lasting until late May 1970.[61]

By then another Nixon initiative in Cambodia was convulsing American public opinion. After a March 1970 coup brought a pro-American faction to power there—removing the neutral regime of Prince Sihanouk—Nixon approved the use of South Vietnamese troops on the ground in Cambodia to attack Northern sanctuaries and drive the North Vietnamese into the arms of Cambodian troops. Instead, as its troops moved farther into Cambodia, North Vietnam began full-scale support for the murderous Khmer Rouge guerrillas fighting the new Cambodian government. In late April Nixon decided to up the ante by secretly ordering the use of thirty-two thousand U.S. ground troops in assaults inside Cambodia. In an address from the Oval Office on April 30, he claimed that American policy since 1954 "has been to scrupulously respect the neutrality of the Cambodian people" but that the North Vietnamese forces in that country were "building up to launch massive attacks on our forces and those of South Vietnam" as well as to attack the Cambodian capital. The operation was not an "invasion," he stressed, since Cambodia itself was not being attacked—it was an incursion for Cambodia's benefit as well as for the longer-term safety of American and South Vietnamese troops.[62]

Nixon ended his speech by acknowledging that public opinion would be against his decision. If anything, he underestimated the reaction: widespread demonstrations broke out, and at Kent State and Jackson State protesters were killed by nervous National Guardsmen and police.

Congress reacted angrily as well. Even Senate Minority Leader Hugh Scott (R-PA) reproached Nixon for having kept him in the dark. In June the Senate voted to repeal the Tonkin Gulf Resolution and to pass the Cooper-Church amendment denying funding to military operations in Cambodia, though the amendment was carefully circumscribed to allow the president, as commander in chief, to "protect the lives of U.S. armed forces wherever deployed." The House did not go along, rejecting even the modified amendment.[63]

In the short term, Nixon defused the political crisis by removing most American troops from Cambodia by the end of June; privately, he reacted to domestic criticism by beginning work on the Huston Plan. But the frenzy had little effect on long-term policy. Nixon would continue to refuse to accept congressional declarations of policy regarding Southeast Asia. Nixon's theory of the war power, as an influential 1972 law review article by Francis Wormuth stressed, was one that highlighted the president's ability to act unilaterally. The administration argued that the president's constitutional authority included "the power to deploy American forces abroad and commit them to military operations when the President deems such action necessary to maintain the security and defense of the United States." In defending the Cambodian incursion Assistant Attorney General William Rehnquist cited authority under Supreme Court precedent as well as the "tactical" decision-making power granted the commander in chief.[64]

Such tactics continued. In May 1972 Nixon announced he had approved a naval blockade of North Vietnam and the mining of Haiphong Harbor, to go along with a renewed escalation of the bombing campaign. A week before the 1972 election, Kissinger famously declared that "peace is at hand": the public, and Congress, were therefore rather surprised to find that the most massive bombing of the war had begun on December 18, after Nixon's landslide electoral victory. The so-called Christmas bombings of Hanoi and other northern cities dropped thirty-six thousand tons of bombs in ten days, more than had been dropped during the entirety of 1969, 1970, and 1971 combined.

Legislation seeking to end the war began to move through Congress as soon as it convened in January 1973. Later that month, however, a peace agreement was announced. The war was not over for the Vietnamese, but American involvement was effectively over. Some fifty-eight thousand American servicemen had died—more than one-third of them since Nixon took office in 1969.[65]

The end of the war did not end the use of unilateral power, in that region and elsewhere. For example, though military action in Cambodia was by now forbidden by law, in early 1973 American bombing resumed (this time against rebels battling the Lon Nol government). Further, covert actions continued unabated around the globe. Indeed, the unimpeded use of intelligence agencies is another aspect of the "imperial presidency." As noted in chapter 2, throughout the cold war covert operations were utilized by presidents to extend the reach of the United States in areas ranging from Iran to Guatemala to the Congo to Cuba. Kirsten Lundberg estimates that between 1951 and 1975 the CIA engaged in some nine hundred major "projects."[66]

Some of these were in Southeast Asia. Within Vietnam, the Phoenix Program of pacification within South Vietnam sought to weed out Vietcong sympathizers lurking in the general population. Military, State Department, and CIA personnel set up interrogation centers in all 235 districts of the country—during 1969 alone some 19,534 Vietcong suspects were "neutralized," over 6,000 of them killed. In 1971 the CIA's William Colby said the program had killed 20,587 South Vietnamese since its inception in 1968, with an additional 30,000 jailed. A program of assassination, though officially denied, was by many accounts part of the Phoenix repertoire.[67]

In Cambodia, U.S. special forces had been quietly crossing the border in conjunction with South Vietnamese troops since at least mid-1967—some four hundred such missions in 1967–68 and more than a thousand in 1969–70 before the "official" invasion. Whether the CIA helped to underwrite the overthrow of Prince Sihanouk is still disputed. Certainly Lon Nol knew he would have immediate U.S. support; and it is intriguing that a memo from Kissinger to Nixon discussing Nol's plan for expanding the Cambodian military was dated the day *before* the coup. Efforts in Laos went back even further, to the 1950s, and took off under the Kennedy administration, aiding Meo tribes against communist Pathet Lao guerillas. Later efforts, less successful, involved crossings from South Vietnam in attempts to cut off the Laotian portion of the Ho Chi Minh Trail. By the mid-1960s the CIA was, in the words of the agency's Richard Helms, "flat out in its effort to keep the tribes viable militarily";

some $300 million a year was budgeted for these covert operations. The CIA's own proprietary air force, Air America, had more than fifty planes and twenty helicopters, moving freight and carrying out rescues; six bases and forty-five thousand troops were in neighboring Thailand, supporting Laotian operations. Operations in Laos continued into 1973.[68]

These were not the only notable covert operations of the Nixon years. One, particularly intriguing in light of later events, included $16 million in aid to the Kurds of Iraq, who were supporting the Shah of Iran. That aid was cut off abruptly under President Ford in 1975, much to the Kurds' chagrin. Most notoriously, in 1970 Nixon personally ordered efforts to prevent Salvador Allende, a socialist, from becoming president of Chile. Chile to that point was "one of the CIA's outstanding success stories,"[69] democratic and very friendly to American multinational corporations. The 1964 runoff election, which Allende lost, was influenced in part by $20 million in U.S. subsidies (the equivalent of eight dollars per voter) to organizations supportive of his opponent's candidacy. When Allende was elected after all in 1970, Nixon authorized "Track II," assigning the CIA to induce a military coup and even to support assassination. Immediate efforts failed, but continuing initiatives to destabilize the regime and aid sympathetic figures in the military paid off in 1973, when General Augusto Pinochet—who would go on to lead one of the most repressive regimes in history—led a coup in which Allende was murdered. By some accounts American military attaches were in the field with some of the Chilean troops participating. Richard Helms would later be convicted of perjury for his role in covering up the CIA's involvement.[70]

Again, these sorts of activities go back some time. But what shifted during the Nixon years was that many of the bureaucratic safeguards for oversight of covert action—for example, the "Special Group" of the NSC—were evaded. The "40 Committee," which replaced the Special Group in 1970, had putative representation from across the executive branch. But the 40 Committee was not consulted about Cambodia, the Kurds, or Track II in Chile. Kissinger, the chair, held very few meetings, preferring one-on-one phone polls that diminished the chance for the give-and-take of debate and made sure he alone had full information. The Cambodian operation is a good example. Rather than go through the Defense and State Departments, the CIA alone was utilized for the planning, complete with a back channel direct to Saigon. A CIA analysis, completed in April 1970, concluded that the invasion would be unsuccessful in preventing further use of Cambodia by North Vietnam, even if American troops were used; that report never made it to the White House, as Director Helms refused to consider it until early June. By then the incursion had become an excursion.[71]

To the end, Nixon remained unrepentant in his exercise of unilateral foreign policy powers. His veto of the War Powers Resolution (WPR) claimed that its restrictions "upon the authority of the President" were "both unconstitutional and dangerous to the best interests of our nation." And a White House "Vietnam White Paper," touting the peace agreement and distributed to members of Congress in January 1973, eschewed graciousness. Instead, it flayed the "incessant attacks from the United States Congress. . . . No president has been under more constant and unremitting harassment by men who should drop to their knees each night to thank the Almighty that they do not have to make the same decisions that Richard Nixon did."[72]

But by then, legislators seemed more inclined to bring Richard Nixon to his knees instead.

THE BATTLE OF THE BUDGET, PART I: DEFICIT POLITICS

A leading student of American fiscal policy has termed the period 1966–73 the "seven years' budget war."[73] To be sure, the technicalities of budgeting rarely excite as much popular passion as the news from the front. But the distribution of public resources is at the very heart of politics: it determines who gets what.[74] There are some $2.5 trillion of "what" to distribute in the contemporary federal budget.

Doing so is clearly a congressional prerogative. After all, the Constitution states that no money shall be spent by the federal government that is not appropriated, and the power to tax and appropriate is clearly given in Article I to the Congress. "The power of the purse," James Madison noted in Federalist No. 58, represents "the most complete and effectual weapon with which any constitution can arm the immediate representatives of the people."[75]

However, the fragmented nature of a bicameral Congress makes efficient budget planning and coordination difficult at best, shrinking the range and firepower of Madison's "weapon." That didn't matter much while government was small and the scope of its functions limited, since the House and Senate could consider spending and revenue measures without too much internal division of labor. But as government grew, especially with and after the Civil War, appropriations responsibilities were widely distributed across multiple legislative committees. At the same time, executive budgeting was decentralized: most departments and agencies sent their spending requests directly to Congress, without coordination by, or the approval of, the president's office. Arriving on Capitol Hill, the requests were considered in isolation both of each other and of available revenues. The usual results were duplicative or contradictory policy—and overspending.

The 1921 Budget and Accounting Act addressed one side of the problem by requiring a unified, coherent executive budget and creating the BoB as presidential enforcer. But it did nothing to require a coherent process for its consideration. Instead, the revenue and expenditure sides of the budget were split off and handled separately. Then the expenditures were further separated, sent to a host of different subcommittees and treated as independent measures throughout their legislative gauntlet. Combined with entitlement spending—on Social Security, Medicare, pensions, farm supports, interest on the national debt, and the like—no one could predict in advance what government spending might actually be in a given year. As the *New York Times* commented, the United States did "not have a fiscal policy but a fiscal result."[76]

The result was to empower the president, even to the point of what some observers called "presidential dominance." The budget economies required by the Depression set in motion a process of central legislative clearance, which used the BoB to gain presidential control over agencies' fiscal needs (and eventually over their legislative policy proposals as well). When Congress and the president were of the same party, legislators tended to defer to the president's spending requests, keeping variation within a reasonable range; when Congress and the president were of different parties—which was relatively rare until 1969—presidents waved their veto pen. Dwight Eisenhower, for example, frequently set aside budget bills he thought showed insufficient economies. "As a result," James Sundquist has observed, "even an opposition Congress was not able to break freely from the bounds the president set for it and put into effect its own independent fiscal policy." Presidents used budgets to reinforce their programs and vice versa; this culminated in the outburst of new domestic programs from 1964 to 1966.[77]

But the Great Society was an expensive proposition. As the real war in Vietnam expanded, it became a casus belli of the budget war: it was costly and, many in Congress thought, unjustified. Thus legislators balked at raising taxes to pay for it. At the same time Lyndon Johnson pushed for both Vietnam guns *and* Great Society butter. "Both of these commitments involve great costs," he admitted in his fiscal 1967 budget. But "they are costs we can and will meet."[78] That course, combined with already promised New Deal entitlement spending and a soft economy, caused deficits to rise from $1.6 billion in fiscal 1965 to over $25 billion by fiscal 1968.

Impoundment—the refusal to spend money appropriated by Congress—was one of the strategies followed by Johnson to bridge the gap. This was not a new tool. And as noted in chapter 2, Congress had even endorsed it at times, specifically giving presidents starting with Theodore Roosevelt the authority to withhold funds under certain circumstances. Normally the power was used to defer, or spread out, spending rather than to make cuts in a particular program. Where presidents pushed the point, as Franklin Roosevelt did in the 1940s by refusing to release infrastructure appropriations he considered detrimental to the war effort, other political actors usually pushed back. Indeed, when Johnson announced he would withhold highway trust fund monies, Congress amended the 1958 Highway Act to make clear that "no part of any sums" under the law "shall be impounded or withheld from obligation." But Johnson was able to implement other unilateral cuts. In 1966 (after Congress added $312 million to a farm bill) he announced he would cut agriculture expenditures that exceeded his requests; later that year he directed that savings be found in programs ranging from housing to parklands and that the "excess" spending be canceled.[79]

During this period, Congress was consistently unable to take decisive action to reconcile spending and revenues. Always politically painful, specific programmatic cuts were made even harder by the 1960s explosion in the number of protective interest groups watching over every sliver of the federal pie. Congress chose to let the president make the calls, in fiscal 1968 pairing a new income surtax with spending ceilings on nonentitlement (and non-Vietnam) expenditures. Johnson was given the power to withhold monies beyond the ceilings.[80]

The new tax and impoundment powers balanced the budget in fiscal 1969. But to achieve that result, Congress had delegated the power of the purse. And the first full year of the Nixon administration, fiscal year 1970, marked the start of the modern era of budget deficits: surpluses would not return until fiscal year 1998. Entitlement spending quickly rose at more than twice the level allowed under the rather pliable budget ceilings, adding billions to the deficit. Further, the economy's performance continued to sink, with GDP growing less than 2 percent a year, inflation nudging 9 percent by 1974, and unemployment rising 60 percent between 1969 and 1974. High inflation and high unemployment were two bad things the dominant Keynesian economic model said weren't supposed to go together. Yet as they did they spurred more spending, especially on social programs.

President Nixon, facing a Democratic Congress, saw both fiscal and political ground to gain in calling for lower spending. "Just because Congress passes the buck doesn't mean the president has to spend it" went one joke pushed into speeches by White House communications staffers. Nixon and his aides lost no occasion to run down legislative spending habits, attacking the "hoary and traditional procedure" of the "credit-card" Congress. As will be discussed in a moment, Nixon called for budget caps and aggressively impounded funds. It is worth noting, however, that he was perfectly happy to spend money where it would help politically. As the 1972 election approached, Nixon pushed not a balanced budget but a "balanced full employment budget," supported stimulative tax cuts without offsetting decreases in spending, and signed into law 20 percent benefit hikes for Social Security recipients.[81]

At the same time, he sought tighter control of departmental administration, helped by the transformation in 1970 of the Bureau of the Budget into the Office of Management and Budget. OMB, as its future director told Nixon, will "act as your principal agent for improving the management and responsiveness of the Executive Branch." To do so it was given a new layer of political appointees above its civil service employees working on budget analysis, and new OMB director George Shultz moved from the Old Executive Office Building into an office in the White House itself. Nixon's OMB, especially later under director Roy Ash, took a very aggressive stand on the "battle of the budget," a phrase Ash used in memos to the president. One handwritten note assured Nixon, "Don't worry—we're hanging tough." In another memo Ash concluded that, while "[i]n the process we have reached an impasse with the Congress on many matters . . . the Hill still seems to have considerable respect for Executive strength."[82]

Even if so, Congress was certainly aggrieved by Nixon's version of the impoundment strategy, which was far more aggressive than his predecessors'—"unprecedented in scope, severity, and truculence," as one scholar observed.[83] Here, as in other areas, Nixon upped the ante at the outset by defining his powers as inherent and nonnegotiable. In 1971 Caspar Weinberger, then Nixon's deputy budget director, conceded to a Senate panel that Congress had the power to *appropriate*. But he continued that it "does not follow from this, however, that the *expenditure* of government funds involves an exclusively legislative function." Indeed, "a law appropriating funds is permissive and not mandatory in nature." Deputy Attorney General Joseph Sneed argued that "substantial latitude to refuse to spend" derived from the "'executive power' vested in [the president] by the Constitution," since good administration implied a duty to avoid fiscal instability. Nixon himself put it plainly: "The Constitutional right of the President of the United States to impound funds . . . is absolutely clear."[84]

The president's actions in this area were correspondingly grandiose, especially after a 1972 election campaign during which he made Congress and its budgetary irresponsibility major themes. In January 1973 Nixon announced that he would put "restraining Federal expenditures at the top of the list of economic policies." He proposed a spending ceiling of $250 billion and soon announced he would impose it administratively, "with or without the cooperation of the Congress." The amounts subsequently impounded were enormous, encompassing as much as $15 billion by 1973—an astonishing 20 percent of discretionary spending.

Nixon also used targeted impoundments as a way to eliminate entire programs he didn't like, whether loans for rural electrification or funds for wetlands protection. Some programs were actually canceled prospectively: because they were not in the president's budget request, they were zeroed out, even though their current authorization had not expired and they were funded to the end of the fiscal year. In one case, the Office of Economic Opportunity (OEO)—the onetime cornerstone of Johnson's War on Poverty—was eliminated in the president's pro- posed budget. The agency's acting director, Howard Phillips, started to dismantle the agency's Community Action Agencies immediately, even before Congress had acted on the new budget.

This amounted to what Sen. Hubert Humphrey (D-MN) termed "policy impoundment," the modification or even elimination of laws passed by Congress. Impoundments came even when large majorities of legislators made their will clear. In 1972, for example, even though Nixon's veto of the Federal Water Pollution Control Act Amendments was overridden, the president impounded more than half of the funds committed through the law. His constitutional claim was thus effectively one encompassing absolute veto power. It was, at the least, line-item veto authority by another name. A federal court, overturning the OEO impoundment, pointed out the implications for executive power: "if the power sought here were found valid, no barrier would remain to the executive ignoring any and all Congressional authorizations if he deemed them . . . to be contrary to the needs of the nation."[85]

In that instance, of course, the power was not found valid. Still, Ash's claim that the president had asserted himself successfully had some merit. Certainly as regarded economic policy-making, Congress was very def- erential, if very calculating. "The vast and influential powers of the Office of the President must be brought to bear against these sharply ris- ing price increases," demanded then majority leader Carl Albert. Want- ing to make absolutely clear that it was the president, not Congress, who was responsible (and thus blameworthy) for the state of the economy, Banking Committee chair Wright Patman (D-TX) likewise argued it was the "duty" of the legislature to give Nixon "all the power he needs when he needs it to protect the people against inflation."[86] Thus the Economic Stabilization Act of 1970, responding to that winter's reces- sion, gave Nixon immense discretionary powers to impose wage, price, and rent controls. Nixon had denied any interest in using this authority, but on August 15, 1971, he announced a new economic program that included ninety-day wage and price freezes along with tax and expendi- ture cuts and a historic shift from the gold standard set up at Bretton

Woods after World War II. This was the first time price and salary controls had been imposed in peacetime. Two additional phases would follow, with decidedly mixed success in battling inflation.[87]

Even in the realm of impoundment, despite its heated rhetoric, Congress often seemed eager enough to pass on the political hot potato. As OMB's Weinberger pointed out in 1971, Congress had passed any number of conflicting statutes—the 1946 Employment Act, which opposed inflationary policy; a 1970 expenditure ceiling; and the ongoing statutory ceiling on the national debt—at the same time as it approved higher spending levels. In this view, presidents were forced to impound in order to mediate between contradictory congressional directives. And not all legislators disagreed, as much as they chafed under Nixon's tactics. Sen. Lawton Chiles (D-FL) argued that "Congressional power . . . has been not so much usurped by the Presidency as given up to the Presidency by Congress." The bottom line, as Sen. Sam Ervin (D-NC) put it later that year, was that "many of us have found it more comfortable to have somebody else—the President—make the hard decisions and relieve us of responsibility."[88]

In budgeting as elsewhere, Nixon was very happy to do just that.

ETHICS: THE "WHITE HOUSE HORRORS"

The Watergate crisis centered on executive ethics: those of the president's men—and those of the president. Much of the chapter so far could be replicated in this section, given that wiretapping, forgery, and abuse of power are normally not considered ethical behaviors. But as Nixon later conceded, "I brought myself down. I gave them a sword. And they stuck it in."[89] It was the break-in of the Watergate office complex and the subsequent cover-up that gave Nixon's opponents the "sword" they needed.

On June 17, 1972, such an outcome was hard to foresee. The issues of executive overreach traced previously were not well known to the public or even hugely salient within Washington. Richard Nixon was running a methodical, well-funded reelection campaign, while the Democratic opponent the Nixon camp most preferred, dovish South Dakota senator George McGovern, was on the verge of clinching the nomination. The president's electoral vital signs were solid—his approval ratings from late May to mid-June hovered around 60 percent.

Still, Nixon had won just 43 percent of the popular vote in 1968, and the Democratic Party retained a solid edge nationally in voter registration. Polls throughout 1971 had shown Nixon consistently behind potential challenger Sen. Ed Muskie of Maine. Another survey in early May 1972 showed Nixon just five points ahead of McGovern, with former Alabama governor George Wallace a credible third. Thus, while in retrospect Nixon's landslide victory seems inevitable, at the time the White House was uneasy.[90]

Those around Nixon were nothing if not true believers. White House operative Charles Colson wrote his staff a memo that summer: "There are only seventy-one days left and every one counts. Ask yourself every morning what you are going to do to help re-elect the President today!" John Mitchell, who had gone from the Justice Department to run CRP, later told congressional investigators, "The most important thing to this country was the reelection of Richard Nixon and I was not about to countenance anything that would stand in the way of that reelection."[91] In this context, the administration's attention to the campaign took on a ruthless edge.

Nixon was especially eager for expanded campaign intelligence that might be used against McGovern and DNC chair Lawrence F. O'Brien. Under pressure from the White House, CRP therefore implemented Project Gemstone, a surveillance plan conceived by former Plumber G. Gordon Liddy, now a CRP lawyer, and approved by campaign manager Mitchell and his deputy, Jeb Magruder.

The fixation with targeting McGovern was ironic, for in surveying the Democratic primary field the Nixon White House had identified the liberal senator as its weakest potential opponent. It had implemented at least three efforts to help him win the nomination by undermining the campaigns of his opponents, especially Muskie and former vice president Hubert Humphrey. White House aides Dwight Chapin and Gordon Strachan recruited college friend Donald Segretti to conduct "dirty tricks" ranging from setting off stinkbombs to mailing fabricated campaign literature (claiming, for example, in the name of Muskie, that Humphrey had been arrested for drunk driving while in the company of a prostitute). Other operatives, working directly through CRP, also disrupted campaign events and canvassing endeavors; and from the White House itself Charles Colson spearheaded yet another set of tricks, including the famous "Canuck" letter that drove Muskie to a tearful denunciation of *Manchester Union-Leader* publisher William Loeb.[92]

Project Gemstone was of a different order of magnitude. In its original formulation, presented to Mitchell and White House counsel Dean in a meeting held at the attorney general's office in the Justice Department, it had a million-dollar budget and included kidnaping, sabotage, wiretapping, and entrapment: delegates to the Democratic National Convention were to be lured by call girls to a houseboat wired for pictures and sound. As finally approved, the houseboat was left in dry dock. But the budget was still $250,000, focusing on electronic surveillance. It was decided that O'Brien's office at the DNC's Watergate suite was the first priority.

The team formed to bug the DNC was made up of many of those responsible for the break-in of Daniel Ellsberg's psychiatrist's office: the core group was Liddy, his fellow ex-Plumber Howard Hunt, and Hunt's Cuban connections, augmented by former FBI and CIA agent James McCord, an electronics expert working as head of security for CRP. Their skills had not improved much since the Ellsberg operation. The first Watergate break-in occurred over the Memorial Day weekend; one of the phone taps didn't work and another gave little useful information about politics (though much about the victim's personal life). As a result the burglars returned on the night of June 17. That night, they were caught.

It is unlikely that the break-in, by itself, could have brought down the president. But Nixon's reaction was not remorse, except perhaps at his staff's inability to do things right, and it was not to cut his losses by coming clean about CRP involvement. Instead, he told Haldeman within a week of the break-in, "Play it tough. That's the way they play it and that's the way we are going to play it." By June 23 he had already approved a plan to have the CIA obstruct the FBI investigation into the burglary. The CIA was to tell the FBI that any further inquiry would lead into sensitive territory: " 'this will open the whole Bay of Pigs thing . . .'—just say this is sort of a comedy of errors, bizarre, without getting into it," the president urged. "They should call the FBI in and say that

'we wish, for the country, don't go any further into this case, period.'"
A week later, on June 30, he mused to Haldeman about another means
of turning off the investigation: "I'm not at all sure if Mitchell shouldn't
call [Attorney General Richard] Kleindienst and [acting FBI director
L. Patrick] Gray and say . . . to halt the investigation." As one account
of the scandal observes, "obstruction of justice could hardly be more
explicit."[93]

The CIA only briefly complied with the White House directive, soon
informing the FBI's Gray that the agency had no interest in the Watergate. John Dean's request that the CIA pay the burglars' bail and salaries
was summarily rejected. Gray wavered but restarted the investigation in
early July.

The cover-up thus shifted tracks. The burglars were to be kept silent,
and relevant CRP and White House staff were to mislead investigators,
shredding files and committing perjury if need be. Hunt's White House
safe was cleaned out by Ehrlichman and Dean, who delivered its materials on Ellsberg and other Plumbing operations to Gray himself, hinting
it should be destroyed. Gray did so. Meanwhile CRP staffers questioned
by investigators sought to play down the amount spent on Project Gemstone and to implicate Liddy as the lone perpetrator. Colson assured the
burglars that they would receive pardons or commutations from the
president. At the same time, the president's personal lawyer, Herbert
Kalmbach, was tasked with raising funds to support the families of the
burglary team and to keep them silent. A cloak-and-dagger operation
ensued, with cash passed to Howard Hunt's wife through bus station
lockers and telephone booths.

Eventually the scale of the hush money began to frighten Dean, who
in his famous "cancer on the presidency" conversation with Nixon on
March 21, 1973, discussed how White House aides had decided "there
was no price too high to pay" to prevent disclosure before the 1972 election. This led to the criminal liability of various White House aides:
"Bob [Haldeman] is involved in that; John [Ehrlichman] is involved in
that; I am involved in that; Mitchell is involved in that. And that's an
obstruction of justice." He told the president that White House staff
were simply not capable of "cleaning" sufficient cash. "This is the sort of
thing Mafia people can do." Nixon cut to the chase: "how much money
do you need?" Dean hesitated. "I would say these people are going to

cost, uh, a million dollars over the next, uh, two years." Another pause ensued, followed by the president's reply: "We could get that." The conversation continued at some length, identifying sources of funding and the possibilities of clemency for the burglars after the 1974 midterms (rejected, if rather wistfully, as "too hot").[94]

The corrupting role of money is a key element in Watergate and what Mitchell memorably termed the "White House horrors." One reason the burglars were so readily tracked back to CRP was that they possessed not only sequential bundles of hundred-dollar bills given to the campaign but a $25,000 check originally sent to the campaign from a donor in Minnesota and then endorsed directly to the burglars. Not only were the payoffs to the burglars raised from Nixon campaign donors, but the funds came in part from a $350,000 slush fund kept by Haldeman in a White House safe in order to pay for private polling. Another $200,000 was raised directly by Kalmbach, who testified later that he solicited $75,000 of it, in a package of hundred-dollar bills, in a single donation from the president of the Northrop Corporation.[95]

Beyond the obvious lesson (avoid transferring large amounts of money to criminals), the 1972 campaign set other negative standards for campaign finance as well. All told, Nixon and McGovern spent over $90 million in their campaigns, with Nixon outspending McGovern two to one. Nixon's $61 million eclipsed prior records—it was more than both campaigns had spent in 1968. A number of donors gave the campaign upward of $100,000; Ray Kroc of McDonald's fame gave $250,000; Chicago businessman Clement Stone gave over $2 million (after nearly $3 million in 1968). And when the dust cleared, it became clear how aggressively the money had been raised. A new campaign finance law requiring disclosure of contributors' names kicked in on April 7, 1972. CRP's finance director therefore encouraged big donors to pony up before then: in the sixty days leading up to April 7 some $20 million was collected. Doing so was quite legal, depending on the money's source; later allegations suggested, however, that some of it had come from corporations or from abroad. It didn't help matters that, six days after the break-in, the records of the pre–April 7 contributions were destroyed— or that some donations that arrived after this date were backdated by CRP.

The administration did like one thing about the disclosure law.

"Those lists there, are we looking over McGovern's financial contributors?" Nixon asked in the summer of 1972. "Are we looking over the financial contributors to the Democratic National Committee? Are we running their income tax returns? Is the Justice Department checking . . . ? . . . . [W]ith all the agencies of government, what in the name of God are we doing about the McGovern contributors?" When he was told "nothing," Nixon exploded: "We have all this power and we're not using it."[96]

As should be clear by now, this was a little pessimistic. Further, CRP was working wonders, of sorts, in its own realm. Herbert Kalmbach later received jail time for tutoring donors in how to bypass campaign finance laws. Florida shipbuilder George Steinbrenner, for example, was advised to break his $100,000 donation into thirty-three smaller chunks purportedly from various employees. A pledging system instituted by CRP for companies doing business with the government, especially defense contractors, raked in some $840,000, with twenty-one corporations ranging from American Airlines to Phillips Petroleum later found guilty of making illegal donations. (They also donated another $120,000 to five Democratic candidates.) Firms drew on slush funds; laundered their contributions through dummy accounts, home and abroad; and even created fake bonus schemes for employees that sent the "bonus" in the employee's name to the campaign treasury. Chrysler Corporation noted that Kalmbach asked for money just as Chrysler was about to file for a delay in implementing auto emission controls.[97] In other cases, donations were traded for jobs, in direct contravention of federal law; in 1971 Nixon declared, "anybody who wants to be an ambassador must at least give $250,000," and CRP received $1.3 million from willing diplomats-in-waiting. One woman became ambassador to Luxembourg after complaining she had given too much ($300,000) to be sent to Costa Rica.[98]

Two other events helped cement the public belief that the executive branch would trade policy outcomes for campaign income. In 1969 the Associated Milk Producers (AMP) had given the Nixon campaign an illegal cash gift of $100,000 direct from its treasury. In 1970 they offered to raise some $2 million. But in mid-March 1971, the Agriculture Department announced that price supports for milk would remain unchanged, and AMP angrily withdrew its fund-raising promise. Two weeks later, after Nixon met with dairy lobbyists and then huddled with his staff about ways to get political credit for the change, the original announcement was amended—prices would go up. AMP was told to reaffirm its $2 million commitment. Within weeks, over $300,000 flowed into CRP coffers from the milk industry; nearly $700,000 would eventually be raised. It should be noted that AMP also covered its bases with congressional Democrats, donating some $200,000 to House Ways and Means chair Wilbur Mills and $40,000 to Hubert Humphrey, Nixon's 1968 opponent.[99]

Another case involved telecommunications giant ITT, the target of a series of Justice Department antitrust suits. In February 1972 an internal ITT memo was published by columnist Jack Anderson. The memo, by ITT lobbyist Dita Beard, described a deal to contribute $400,000 to the Republican National Committee (RNC)—offering to underwrite the Republican National Convention in exchange for favorable Justice Department disposition of the lawsuits. The administration claimed the memo was a fake, and Plumber Howard Hunt was dispatched to Denver—as ever, in disguise—to get Beard to disavow it. But a memo by Colson to Haldeman reviewing administration actions on ITT going back to April 1969 told a different story. Most damningly, it noted, "there is a Klein to Haldeman memo dated June 30, 1971, which of course precedes the date of the ITT settlement, setting forth the $400,000 arrangement with ITT." Both the attorney general and the campaign had received copies of this as "constructive notice . . . of the ITT commitment at that time and before the settlement, facts which [Mitchell] has denied under oath. We don't know," Colson gloomily added, "whether we have recovered all the copies." Worse still was the transcript of a 1971 conversation Nixon held with then deputy attorney general Kleindienst, ordering the Justice Department to drop the suit and to fire the head of the antitrust division if he did not comply. Kleindienst, having denied all this to Congress, would later plead guilty to perjury.[100]

In an August 1972 conversation with Nixon, Ehrlichman sighed, "we do have a knack for doing this stuff ineptly."[101] And by late April 1973, Ehrlichman and Haldeman were forced to resign when John Dean began to cooperate with investigators. At the same time Richard Kleindienst was fired and replaced as attorney general by Elliot Richardson, who appointed Archibald Cox as special prosecutor to begin yet another investigation of Watergate matters. In July 1973 Nixon aide Alexander Butterfield was asked, almost in passing, whether he knew of any recording systems in the White House. Butterfield told the truth: that the Oval Office and other presidential office spaces were consistently taped using voice-activated microphones.

From that point Nixon waged a long and ultimately unsuccessful battle to keep control of the tapes. In late October he ordered Richardson to fire Cox, who was aggressively pursuing release of the tapes. Richardson refused, choosing to resign instead, as did his deputy, William Ruckelshaus. Solicitor General Robert Bork, third in command at Justice, finally consented to follow the president's wishes, closing down the special prosecutor's offices and turning Cox into an instant folk hero. Nixon had miscalculated: in the wake of the fallout from the firings, quickly dubbed the "Saturday Night Massacre," he was forced to appoint a new special prosecutor and promise him the right to conduct an autonomous investigation.

Over time other events ate away at the president's credibility. There came the revelation of an eighteen-and-a-half-minute gap on one of the requested tapes; the resignation of Vice President Spiro Agnew on bribery charges unrelated to Watergate; and charges that Nixon had used government funds to make improvements on his private property. But what hurt most was the court-ordered release of the tapes after a last-ditch effort to release generously edited transcripts was rejected. On July 24, 1974, the Supreme Court ruled unanimously that Nixon must comply with the special prosecutor's subpoenas; that same day the House Judiciary Committee began formal impeachment proceedings. Even before Nixon had fully obeyed the Supreme Court's order, the House Judiciary Committee had approved three articles of impeachment. The first listed nine counts of obstruction of justice; the second, abuses of power, including the use of the IRS, CIA, and FBI so as to be "subversive of constitutional government"; the third, failure to comply with congressional subpoenas during the investigation.[102]

On August 5 Nixon released the transcript of the "smoking gun": the conversation with Haldeman on June 23, 1972, that ordered the misuse of the CIA and showed his early knowledge of the details of the break-in. "I am not a crook," Nixon had declared nine months before, but few now believed him. On August 6 the members of the Judiciary Committee who had voted against impeachment announced they would change their vote on the House floor. On August 7 the Republican leadership of Congress visited the Oval Office and told Nixon that impeachment was certain and that he would receive at most a dozen votes in a Senate trial. On August 8 Nixon told the American people he would resign the next day. His resignation letter was to the point, one sentence long. But his rambling, emotional farewell to the White House staff the morning of August 9 was more revealing.

"Others may hate you," he said. "But those who hate you don't win unless you hate them.

"And then," he added, "you destroy yourself."

CONCLUSIONS

The powers of the presidency were built up over time less by usurpation than by accretion and often as a matter of law or even congressional initiative.[103] But by the mid-1970s, presidents had pushed their luck too far. If presidents before Nixon showed imperial ambition, it was under his administration that overreach led to the empire's fall. In 1973, before Nixon resigned, Arthur Schlesinger had already broadened the importance of the Watergate break-in, making it a symbol and a symptom of a broader disease that enervated trust in government—in 1960 more than 70 percent of respondents said they felt the government did "what is right" all or most of the time, but fewer than 30 percent said this was true by 1980[104]—and eroded the body politic. "Watergate's importance," he wrote, "was not simply in itself. Its importance was in the way it brought to the surface, symbolized and made politically accessible the great question posed by the Nixon administration in every sector— the question of presidential power. The unwarranted and unprecedented expansion of presidential power, because it ran through the whole Nixon system, was bound, if repressed at one point, to break out at another. This, not Watergate, was the central issue."[105]

And so was the romantic glow of Camelot dispersed in the harsh glare of Vietnamese rice paddies and the klieg lights of congressional committee hearing rooms. The unilateral use of troops and covert operatives, the Responsiveness Program—the White House counter-bureaucracy—the civil liberties violations—all these were ideas and abuses that predated the Nixon administration. But they became uniquely his in the extent of their execution. "When the President does it, that means that it is not illegal," Nixon famously remarked in 1977.[106] Congress, having battled Nixon the president, was now ready to turn its attention to the institution of the presidency. They were ready, in short, to *make* it illegal.

IV. THE WORLD
AFTER WATERGATE

The Resurgence Regime Takes Shape

Richard Nixon's resignation took effect at noon on August 9, 1974. There was one last walk across the White House lawn, a last clenched grin and V-for-victory wave. Marine One whirred to life, lifted off, and faded from sight.

With that, as new president Gerald Ford remarked upon taking the oath of office that afternoon, "our long national nightmare" was over. "Our Constitution works," Ford exulted. "Our great Republic is a government of laws and not of men. Here the people rule."

Congress was soon circling warily around the body of the imperial presidency, seeking to forestall its resurrection. Throughout the 1970s legislators erected a latticework of statutes that aimed to imprison the president and to strengthen the legislative hand in interbranch relations. From war powers to public records to executive ethics, from intelligence oversight to impoundment, this wide-ranging array of new laws reshaped executive-legislative relationships in the substantive areas where congressional prerogative had been slighted. The congressional show of strength, at times abetted and sometimes altered by the judiciary, would profoundly affect American politics for the next thirty years.

Indeed, it is not going too far to call this new, overarching institutional framework a "regime," as scholars of international relations have used the term: as a comprehensive "set of implicit or explicit principles, norms, rules, and decision making procedures around which the expectations of actors converge for a given issue area."[1] The intent and extent of the 1970s legislative regime were as complex and far-reaching in some ways as the network of multinational agreements and organizations that formed the postwar world. The post-Watergate enactments were very much intended to shape politics, and policy, by laying out the formal and informal mechanisms through which the players in the great game of governance were supposed to interact and come to decisions.

It is not surprising that the framers of the regime foresaw a much greater role for congressional input—for both advice and consent—than recent presidents had desired or allowed. "The President has over-stepped the authority of his office in the actions he has taken," warned Rep. Gillis Long (D-LA) in April 1973. "Congress will not stand by idly as the President reaches for more and more power. . . . Our message to the President is that he is risking retaliation for his power grabs, that sup-port for the counter-offensive is found in the whole range of congres-sional membership—old members and new, liberal and conservative, Democratic and Republican."[2] Congress intended to reclaim control over the nation's bottom line and to forbid presidential impoundments; to have a key role in authorizing and overseeing America's military deployments and covert adventures; and to keep a close eye on execu-tive corruption. James L. Sundquist notes that, after a "Congress at nadir," by 1973 or so legislators had achieved "a collective resolve—a firmness and unity of purpose extraordinarily difficult to attain in a body as diffuse as the Congress—to restore the balance between the executive and legislative branches. . . . A period of resurgence had begun."[3]

This chapter details the construction of the resurgence regime. The narrative that follows tracks the four broad categories already intro-duced: executive authority and secrecy; war powers and intelligence; budgetary politics; and ethics. The enactments and developments in each of these areas add up to an impressive whole—so much so that by the late 1970s many argued that the wave of legislation had flooded the Oval Office. That conclusion, as we shall see later, was incomplete and premature. But at the time it seemed far from unfounded.

EXECUTIVE AUTHORITY & GOVERNMENTAL SECRECY: NO "PALACE GUARD"

One prominent symbol of the Nixon White House was the "Berlin Wall" of top staffers Haldeman, Ehrlichman, and Kissinger, who were blamed for sealing Nixon off from both wider sources of advice and the consequences of his decisions. Gerald Ford took office vowing to tear down that wall. "We will have an open, we will have a candid administration," the new president told reporters an hour after taking office. Ford said he would have no chief of staff; he intended to set up a collegial White House personnel system in which he would be the hub of a wheel, with a number of spokes leading directly to him. The cabinet was not to work through the Domestic Council staff or holdover Nixon chief of staff Al Haig but through Ford directly. As Ford wrote in his memoirs, "A Watergate was made possible by a strong chief of staff and ambitious White House aides who were more powerful than members of the Cabinet. . . . I decided to give my Cabinet a lot more control." He was generally given credit for fulfilling that promise, though at some cost to the coherence of his policy-making. Indeed, far from being rigidly hierarchical, Ford's staff melded Nixon veterans with Ford's own congressional and vice presidential staffs, as well as those loyal to new vice president Nelson Rockefeller. It had a "staff coordinator"—but no full-blown chief of staff. (The staff coordinators were Donald Rumsfeld and then Dick Cheney, who both clearly drew some lessons about presidential management from the experience.) In December 1974, trying to establish his own dramatic mark on the White House, Ford pledged to cut his staff an additional 10 percent.[4]

Carter repeated and expanded Ford's pledges during his 1976 campaign, which suggests there was still political capital to be gained by attacking the Nixon White House two years after the fact. In an interview before the election, he said he would require "much heavier dependence on the Cabinet members to run their departments than we've had in the past. I would not establish a 'palace guard' in the White House." His aide, Hamilton Jordan, made the comparison even more explicit. "I don't think you'll have a Haldeman or Ehrlichman in the Carter Administration," he said soon after the election. "The concept of a chief of staff is alien to Governor Carter and those of us around him." Jordan was first among equals, but Carter was to be his own chief of staff.[5]

Upon taking office, Carter dismantled a variety of advisory groups centered in the EOP and supported by presidential staff, from the Economic Opportunity Council to the Energy Resources Council. The Domestic Council staff remained in place, renamed the Domestic Policy

Staff (DPS), but shrank from seventy to twenty-odd members. In all the White House staff was reduced by close to 25 percent, from the nearly 500 that Carter criticized during the campaign to about 360 in 1978. "Although still in the embryonic stage, the organizational and proce-dural modifications could reverse the trend toward centralization of authority within the White House, dating back to the Administration of Franklin D. Roosevelt," the *National Journal* reported in February 1977.[6]

Carter's staff organization evolved sharply over time, most dramati-cally in 1979, as will be detailed in chapter 6. Some of the reduction in staff size was arguably an accounting trick, such as Carter's transfer of the Office of Administration from the White House Office to the also cen-tralized, but less visible, EOP. All in all, the stated differences among Nixon, Ford, and Carter may have been more for public consumption than anything else: the Nixon staff organization, after all, actually worked quite efficiently to serve the president's needs in many instances.[7]

Nonetheless, that Ford and Carter decided they had to make such pledges—Carter went so far as to give a televised address on the topic within two weeks of taking office—speaks volumes to the general atti-tude of the public and Congress toward the way the institutional presi-dency had developed.

Executive Privilege

That attitude carried over to other areas, for instance to the governmen-tal secrecy that was a hallmark of the Vietnam/Watergate era. David Halberstam, in *The Best and the Brightest,* claimed that Lyndon Johnson had an "almost neurotic desire for secrecy." This especially pervaded military decision making, tightly held in order to maintain confidential-ity; but even in other areas, Johnson demanded that he control access to information and the administration's outgoing message. He went so far as to change substantive policy decisions after they had been leaked to the press in order to undermine the leaker and embarrass the leakee.[8] The Nixon White House, as we have seen in some detail, was even less forthcoming.

One aspect of the secrecy "neurosis" was the assertion of executive privilege. As discussed in chapter 3, Nixon claimed that executive priv-ilege extended to past and former aides, to all executive branch employees, and to deliberations on virtually any topic. Eventually his efforts to withhold from the special prosecutor taped conversations with his aides facing criminal charges stemming from the Watergate cover-up brought these claims before the Supreme Court. Special prosecutor Leon Jaworski argued that the tapes were evidence necessary for the prosecution (and defense, for that matter) of Haldeman, Ehrlichman, John Mitchell, and the rest. Nixon, in turn, argued that he was the sole judge of what the executive branch needed to disclose: "In the exercise of his discretion to claim executive privilege the president is answerable to the Nation, but not to the courts." The question, as Jaworski then put it, was, "shall the evidence from the White House be confined to what a single person, highly interested in the outcome, is willing to make available?" In 1974's *U.S. v. Nixon,* a unanimous Supreme Court said the answer was no.

The Court's opinion first affirmed its own relevance, overturning Nixon's claim of absolute separation of powers. Next, the justices held that Nixon's claim in this case could not be upheld: "neither the doctrine of separation of powers, nor the need for confidentiality of high-level communications, without more, can sustain an absolute, unqualified Presidential privilege of immunity from judicial process under all circumstances," since to allow executive privilege to circumscribe a criminal trial would "cut deeply into the guarantee of due process of law and gravely impair the function of the courts" and their own constitutional duties. After all, "in designing the structure of our Government and dividing and allocating the sovereign power among three co-equal branches, the Framers of the Constitution sought to provide a comprehensive system, but the separate powers were not intended to operate with absolute independence."[9]

The judiciary had thus expressed its own "ambition" (in *The Federalist*'s sense of the word), counteracting that of the presidency. And the presidency was forced to yield. Though Nixon had pondered resisting the Court's opinion, its unanimous nature made that untenable. The tapes were released; and what was thereon did the rest, galvanizing impeachment proceedings on Capitol Hill. In the circumstances it seemed for the moment less important that the Court had gone further than it needed to by holding for the first time that executive privilege, when legitimately exercised, was in fact constitutionally grounded.

Certainly that ruling was little comfort to Nixon's immediate successors. The doctrine of executive privilege had been painted as a mechanism of cover-up, "a ploy to deceive or to conceal wrongdoing," and reclaiming it seemed a losing cause. Ford never even issued guidelines on the topic, as his predecessors had generally done, seeking, it seems, to avoid even mentioning the term. A White House memo pointed out the obvious: executive privilege, bound up as it was with Watergate, had "unfavorable connotations" that, when combined with "the present mood of Congress, dictated "a sharp break from traditional practice." As a result, the few times that the Ford administration declined to provide sensitive information to legislative overseers, the doctrine was never formally invoked and compromise was usually reached. In general, Ford felt he had little choice but to provide Congress with virtually all it requested, even on the very sensitive topic of FBI and CIA abuses.

Nor did things change much under Jimmy Carter. Like Ford, Carter never endorsed a formal policy on executive privilege and almost never invoked it. The hopeful declaration of one 1977 memo—"We hope to find a sound legal basis to answer the subpoena without using the term 'executive privilege'"—was the post-Watergate formula of choice. But as proponents of the "open" presidency, Ford and Carter had little leeway to withhold secrets, by whatever name for secrecy their lawyers devised. Carter even toned down the rules for classifying documents as secret, ordering a balancing test so that "the public's interest in access to government information" would be considered against the need to keep certain items confidential.[10]

OPEN GOVERNMENT: PRIVACY AND FREEDOM OF INFORMATION

Congress also stepped into the question of secrecy more directly. In one area, legislators actually encouraged more government discretion, namely, where personal records were concerned. The 1974 Privacy Act restricted disclosure of personally identifiable information about individuals to people not authorized to get that information (e.g., White House staffers hoping to see tax returns) and gave the affected individual the right to sue if private information was revealed. At the same time the law expanded disclosure by giving individuals the right to see what information the government had collected pertaining to them (outside of criminal investigations or the like) and to amend those records if they were inaccurate.[11]

The latter provisions dovetailed with a sweeping reworking of the Freedom of Information Act, passed originally in 1966. Before then, under the Administrative Procedure Act, agencies had wide discretion to keep records closed. FOIA, on the other hand, declared that openness was in the public interest. President Johnson was unenthusiastic, reaffirming his right to exercise executive privilege and noting contingently that "a democracy works best when the people have all the information that the security of the nation permits." The implication was that it did not permit much. Johnson's concern was written into the act itself, which provided for nine expansive categories of documents to be exempted. Most notably, it allowed presidents, by executive order, to keep information "secret in the interest of the national defense or foreign policy."

This last phrase contributed to a 1973 decision in which the Supreme Court upheld the Nixon administration's decision to keep secret a series of classified reports concerning the environmental impact of nuclear testing in the Pacific. The Court reasoned that FOIA as drafted did not allow the judiciary to determine whether something had been rightly classified, merely that it had been classified at all. Once the president decided that a document contained sensitive information, judges could go no further.[12]

In 1974 Congress responded to this decision and to agency recalcitrance under the law by substantially broadening FOIA, over President Ford's veto. Judicial review of executive determinations that something needed to be kept secret was now authorized, even for national security materials: information could be withheld only if it was "in fact properly classified." The original law had allowed law enforcement agencies to withhold investigative files; the new version changed "files" to particular "records," broadening the possible release and allowing withholding only when releasing given records would harm an active investigation or jeopardize an investigator.

Access was eased in other ways as well. Applicants' requests for documents, for example, could now be less specifically targeted, solving the chicken-or-the-egg problem posed when agencies had required details about a file an applicant would rarely have without the file already in hand. Fees could now be charged only for the direct costs of search and duplication (not for time spent reading and redacting relevant documents) and were to be waived if the information released could be considered in the public interest. Agencies had strict time limits—normally just ten working days—to make a decision about the provision of documents, and requesters were immediately granted court standing to sue if the agency missed its deadlines. The costs of any litigation would be paid by the government if a court determined that documents had been improperly withheld. Indeed, personnel who wrongfully withheld records could be subject to disciplinary action. In 1975 the number of requests made under FOIA quadrupled.[13]

In the 1970s presidential records themselves were, for the first time, deemed public records. Until the Nixon years, White House papers and memos had been considered the personal property of the individuals involved. Presidents had set up libraries, to be sure, but they donated their materials to the government through a deed of gift, which could restrict access for a certain period of time or to certain researchers. (For a long while they also received a hefty tax deduction for this, which brought Nixon more grief when the deduction he claimed for the donation of his vice presidential papers made his later tax burden embarrassingly low.)

Immediately after Nixon resigned, he arranged for his papers to be shipped to his home in California. President Ford signed off on the agreement. But since it was still possible that Nixon would be criminally charged, the special prosecutor's office objected, worried that Nixon's staff would remove crucial evidence documenting the administration's abuses of power. Congress quickly passed the Presidential Materials and Preservation Act, effectively setting aside Nixon's claims, and the papers made another cross-country flight, eastward to the National Archives. The Supreme Court upheld the act in 1977's *Nixon v. Administrator of General Services*.[14]

The PMPA procedure was made prospective instead of retroactive with the passage of the Presidential Records Act in 1978. The PRA decreed that documents created during a presidency were government property and that, like other executive branch records, they should be made public in a reasonable time. The law set this marker at twelve years after a president left office: thus, for example, Ronald Reagan's papers were to become public in January 2001, twelve years after his term's conclusion in January 1989. Some restrictions, including the relevant FOIA exemptions, still obtained, so as to protect personal privacy and national security. But the principle that records would be released on a timely basis without undue obstruction by past or current presidents was absolutely clear.

The same principle carried over to ongoing government decision-making processes. Congress passed the Government in the Sunshine Act in 1976 to require that most decision making by the fifty or so independent agencies run by boards or commissions be conducted in open meetings. The Federal Communications Commission, the Securities and Exchange Commission, and the Occupational Safety and Health Administration were among those included.[15] Another effort at greater disclosure was aimed at presidential task forces, which are often created by executive order without congressional input. Congress feared that such advisory groups—which grew in number and importance in the 1960s—were increasingly powerful and unrepresentative; prior legislative efforts to control them had tried to limit their funding, a constraint presidents evaded by shifting money from other EOP accounts. The Federal Advisory Committee Act (FACA), passed in 1972, took a different tack. Nongovernmental groups (that is, those including at least one person who was not a full-time federal employee) advising the executive branch, whether newly created or preexisting and merely "utilized" by the president, were now required to hold open meetings and to issue public reports of their findings. The president in turn was required to compile a detailed annual report describing, among other things, the activities and reports of each of the advisory committees, the names and occupations of their members, their termination date, and their cost.[16]

Privacy and Due Process. Another aspect of the move toward open government concerned civil liberties: what due process protections against government intrusiveness were required? How would the needs of law enforcement balance against individuals' right to privacy?

As noted in chapter 3, the Nixon administration had wiretapped aggressively, even staking a claim to an inherent presidential power to conduct surveillance without a warrant when gathering intelligence about threats to the national security. Lower courts had tended to be deferential on this point, generally agreeing to presidential discretion so long as it was linked directly to such threats.[17] As we have seen, the Nixon administration was wont to use the national security umbrella to shield its own domestic political espionage; but this was not yet known when the wiretapping question finally reached the Supreme Court in the *Keith* case of 1972. The claim there concerned whether the president could set aside Fourth Amendment warrant requirements for suspects of crimes that he felt had national security ramifications. The *Keith* defendants were accused of bombing a Michigan CIA office, and the attorney general argued to the Court that the surveillance was "deemed necessary to protect the nation from attempts of domestic organizations to attack and subvert the existing structure of Government." There was, however, no indication of any foreign involvement.

The Court unanimously held that even this category of domestic case required a warrant. As Justice Lewis Powell wrote, "Fourth Amendment freedoms cannot properly be guaranteed if domestic security surveillances may be conducted solely within the discretion of the Executive Branch." The president's argument may have "pragmatic force," Powell conceded, but he added pointedly that executive branch officials are vested in any given case as investigators and prosecutors, not "neutral and disinterested magistrates. . . . We cannot accept the Government's argument that internal security matters are too subtle and complex for judicial evaluation." More broadly, and most crucially,

> Official surveillance, whether its purpose be criminal investigation or ongoing intelligence gathering, risks infringement of constitutionally protected privacy of speech. Security surveillances are especially sensitive because of the inherent vagueness of the domestic security concept, the necessarily broad and continuing nature of intelligence gathering, and the temptation to utilize such surveillances to oversee political dissent. . . . The price of lawful public dissent must not be a dread of subjection to an unchecked surveillance power. . . . Given the difficulty of defining the domestic security interest, the danger of abuse in acting to protect that interest becomes apparent.[18]

The Court did not address the question of the president's ability to order wiretaps where the activities in question *did* involve foreign powers or their agents. But it suggested that Congress pass more specific statutory guidance for prosecution of such cases. And as more of Watergate was revealed, from the NSC intra–White House wiretapping to the Plumbers to Operations CHAOS and MINARET, addressing both domestic and foreign intelligence gathering became a salient legislative priority. Even Henry Kissinger, largely untouched by Watergate fallout to this point, was buffeted by criticism during and after his confirmation as secretary of state over his role in the NSC wiretaps.[19] Rep. William Cohen (R-ME) put legislative options in rather dire terms later in 1974: "When the chief executive of the country starts to investigate private citizens who criticize his policies or authorizes his subordinates to do such things, then I think the rattle of the chains that would bind up our constitutional freedoms can be heard, and it is against this rattle that we should awake and say 'no.'"[20]

In 1976 the executive woke first, when Attorney General Edward Levi instituted a series of strong regulatory restrictions on FBI "domestic security" surveillance. Under the Levi guidelines, the bureau could open a preliminary investigation only when it had information that an individual or group was, first, violating federal law and, second, engaged in force or violence. The preliminary investigation had to turn up additional factual evidence before a full investigation was launched, and it had to do so without using methods such as electronic surveillance, infiltration, or mail intercepts. A full investigation could "only be authorized on the basis of specific and articulable facts giving reason to believe that an individual or a group is or may be engaged in activities which involve the use of force or violence and which involve or will involve the violation of federal law."[21] No investigations were to take place where the offense was simply to advocate controversial or offensive stands, without threat of violence. The Justice Department was to review all full investigations annually to make sure they met these standards and to decide whether the FBI should continue a given investigation.

Jimmy Carter followed up with a 1978 executive order regulating both domestic and foreign intelligence gathering. A long section entitled "Restrictions on Intelligence Activities" required that all domestic investigations move through a procedure approved by the attorney general to "protect constitutional rights and privacy, ensure that information is gathered by the least intrusive means possible, and limit use of such information to lawful governmental purposes." The CIA was explicitly barred from "internal security," electronic surveillance or physical searches within the United States; any domestic counterintelligence had to be approved by the attorney general. Further, intelligence agencies were not allowed to subcontract such work to others for the purposes of plausible deniability. In March 1976 the FBI had 4,868 domestic security investigations under way. By the end of 1981 that number had plummeted to 26.[22]

Cases involving foreign counterintelligence were subject to less rigorous standards under the Levi and Carter guidelines but even here could only be pursued upon "reasonable suspicion" that the suspect was a "conscious member of a hostile foreign intelligence network." Electronic surveillance could only be approved upon showing probable cause that the suspect was involved in the "clandestine transmission of information to a hostile intelligence service."[23]

Despite these executive initiatives, though, Congress did step in as the Court had suggested in *Keith,* goaded by the Nixon administration's use of warrantless wiretaps on war and civil rights dissidents. The Foreign Intelligence Surveillance Act (FISA) of 1978 sought to provide oversight of what presidents had claimed as inherent authority for four decades. FISA limited "foreign intelligence information" to information related to clandestine intelligence activities, sabotage, terrorism, or other hostile actions carried out by a foreign power or its agent. It then created a special court—the Foreign Intelligence Surveillance Court (FISC)—to review applications for surveillance linked to such investigations and required that the attorney general personally sign off on each application. The standard for issuing FISA "warrants" was relatively low, especially where Americans were not the targets: the Justice Department merely had to establish that the target of surveillance was a foreign power or an agent thereof. For "U.S. persons," on the other hand, there had to be evidence that the suspect was working on behalf of a foreign power in ways that might violate criminal statutes, not merely advocating in ways protected by the First Amendment. Further, a "wall" was erected between FISA investigations and regular criminal investigations of the same suspect. Foreign intelligence, not criminal prosecution, had to be the primary purpose of the surveillance. The idea was to make it hard, though not impossible, to use information obtained through a FISA warrant in a criminal prosecution—at the least, to minimize the temptation to use counterintelligence as an easy end run around Fourth

Amendment constraints. To this end, the attorney general had to submit an annual report on FISA activities. In 1980 a federal appeals court ruling further limited Justice's ability to influence intelligence surveillance, forbidding it to make FISA-related recommendations to intelligence officials. "The FBI and the Criminal Division [of the Justice Department] shall ensure that law enforcement officials do not direct or control the use of the FISA procedures to enhance criminal prosecution," the court held. To enforce this the decision also created what the FBI came to call a "chaperone requirement," mandating that the Justice Department's Office of Intelligence Policy and Review sit in on meetings between the FBI and the Criminal Division seeking to coordinate investigation or prevention of "foreign attack or other grave hostile acts, sabotage, international terrorism, or clandestine intelligence activities by foreign powers."

That "wall," or at least the way it was interpreted by subsequent administrations, would engender great controversy after the September 2001 terrorist attacks as a structural constraint burdening life-or-death investigations. But at the time, it was hailed—by legislators at least—as "a landmark in the development of effective legal safeguards for constitutional rights . . . a triumph for our Constitutional system of checks and balances."24

EXECUTIVE POWER & CONGRESSIONAL OVERSIGHT

In 1974 the United States had been in a continuous state of emergency since 1933. During that time, Congress had delegated a wide array of powers to the president to meet various exigencies. Thus the forty years of "emergency," beyond diluting the meaning of the term, meant that presidents had accumulated nearly five hundred discretionary powers ready at hand as "standby" authority. Those powers had been activated in 1933, 1950, 1970 (to deal with a postal strike), and 1971 (to deal with the balance of payments crisis) but never rescinded. A Senate committee examining the question found that "this vast range of powers, taken together, confer[s] enough authority to rule the country without reference to normal constitutional procedures." Indeed, presidents could seize property, limit travel or communications, declare martial law, and nationalize various industries; they could suspend publication of their own orders in the Federal Register (as Nixon did during the bombing of Cambodia) or (as in World War II) order the detention of suspect groups.[25]

In response, the Emergency Detention Act—which had allowed the president, in case of an "internal security emergency," to detain anyone suspected on "reasonable" grounds of spying or sabotage—was repealed. The new statute declared that no citizen "shall be imprisoned or otherwise detained in the United States except pursuant to an Act of Congress." More broadly, the National Emergencies Act of 1974 terminated standing emergencies as of 1976. It then set a two-year limit on future states of emergency, providing further that they could be terminated earlier by passage of a concurrent resolution. Another refinement came with the International Emergency Economic Powers Act (IEEPA) of 1977, designed to constrain executive emergency powers over the regulation of international and domestic financial transactions and to limit the latter to periods of declared war.[26]

With the emergencies housekeeping perhaps in mind, Congress sought to commit itself more generally to conducting rigorous, ongoing oversight of the executive branch. Oversight had long taken a backseat to other legislative duties—despite its importance to checking executive excess, it is rarely a political lucrative endeavor. One 1970s innovation was the creation of a cadre of statutorily grounded, Senate-confirmed inspectors general (IG) within most executive departments and agencies. The IG were to probe into agency operations, conducting audits to detect waste, fraud, and corruption and reviewing pending statutes and regulations with an eye toward agency efficiency.

Inspectors general had existed on an ad hoc basis before this time but were subject to presidential manipulation or punishment, as the abolition of the Agriculture Department's IG in 1974 made abundantly clear. The Inspector General Act of 1978 reacted by systematizing the office and prohibiting agency heads from interfering in a given audit or investigation. Both chambers of Congress had to be notified whenever an IG was removed by the president. And each IG's findings would be communicated not just to the agency head but directly to Congress and the public. This last provision was strongly opposed by the attorney general at the time; indeed, all twelve agencies covered by the 1978 act testified against it. Nonetheless, as Sundquist notes, "In signing the bill, President

Carter did not protest this additional limitation on executive privacy and concealment."[27]

But oversight was not to be contained within the executive branch. Congress sought to bind itself to the task as well by requiring that new authorizations be time limited (thus closing down nonrenewed programs) and shortening existing multiyear authorizations. The State and Justice Departments and the CIA were authorized for only a single budget cycle by 1976; by 1980 this was true of nearly 15 percent of all federal spending.[28] Congress also amended the GAO's authorizing legislation in 1980 to allow that office, as Congress's auditing arm, to bring civil suits against agencies that failed to provide records it requested during its audits and investigations.

At the same time, Congress began to write more and more "legislative vetoes" into law. These were to provide "a more timely and authoritative means of intervention in the administrative process" than after-the-fact oversight could exert. While they varied in form and stringency, legislative vetoes enabled all or part of Congress to review the executive branch's use of a given power statutorily delegated to it, before the executive decision took final effect. Sometimes this just meant that an agency would "report and wait," giving Congress time to review and to take affirmative action if so desired. More often the action could be vetoed— sometimes merely by a committee, sometimes by one chamber, sometimes by both. From 1932 to 1972, one study shows, fifty-one laws containing some form of legislative veto were passed. But from 1972 to 1979 another sixty-two were added. A study defining the veto more broadly (for example, to include Congress's use of concurrent resolutions to terminate programs) found there were 132 provisions passed from 1932 to 1969—sometimes more than one per law—but 423 between 1970 and 1980. More than half of these were passed after 1975.[29]

A few examples make the scope of the new requirements clear. One new provision gave Congress the power to veto arms sales valued at over $25 million. Another allowed one chamber the power to revoke budget deferrals, as discussed in the next section. Others provided for potential veto of all regulations issued by the Federal Election Commission and Federal Trade Commission and of the guidelines issued by the Department of Health, Education, and Welfare to local school districts. A 1976 House measure that would have made all regulations promulgated by all administrative agencies subject to legislative veto eventually attracted two hundred cosponsors. While it did not pass, individual provisions continued to be written into law, "the most forceful continuing expression of the congressional resurgence."[30]

"By the end of the decade," Sundquist concludes, "the Congress appeared to have won its point. There could be no more secret wars, no more secret covert operations, not even secret scandals."[31]

Even in the wake of Watergate, of course, presidents could still utilize their constitutional powers. Ford frequently exercised the veto, for example, in a largely successful effort to block the policy priorities of the Democratic legislative majority. His pardon of former president Nixon in September 1974, massively unpopular at the time, was not subject to congressional check.

But where Congress could act, it did. And in many other areas, the law of anticipated reactions helped govern presidential behavior. After Ford pardoned Nixon, he felt compelled to appear in person before a congressional committee to justify his actions. It is hard to imagine a more resonant tribute to the state of executive power in the resurgence regime.

WAR POWERS, INTELLIGENCE OVERSIGHT, & FOREIGN POLICY

"The Constitution assumed that democratic control of foreign policy was a possibility," Schlesinger wrote in *The Imperial Presidency*. "The Indochina War proved it to be a necessity."[32] During the 1970s, Congress tried to write that control into law.

RESOLVING WAR POWERS

The Tonkin Gulf Resolution was not the first blank check, but subsequent doubts about the way its authority was used and misused made it the last—for a while, at least.

Doubts about the veracity of the events in the Tonkin Gulf, and thus the solvency of the account on which the resolution's check drew, had been raised in Congress as early as 1966 and renewed with force in a series of hearings in 1968. In 1969 the Senate held hearings on the issue of "national commitments," which produced nothing in the way of binding legislation but did prompt some interesting debate. "Crisis has been chronic" since the start of World War II, the Senate Foreign Relations Committee opined, and choices had often been made "in an atmosphere of real or contrived urgency," leading to a premium on speed and decisiveness—parameters favoring executive authority. Congress's failure to challenge executive claims to the war powers, the committee's report warned, was "probably the single fact most accounting for the speed and virtual completeness of the transfer" of authority and initiative. But in doing so it "is giving away that which is not its to give, notably the war power, which the framers of the Constitution vested not in the executive but, deliberately and almost exclusively, in the Congress."[33]

It took more time for Congress to act on these sentiments. As noted in chapter 3, the Cambodia incursions of April 1970 prompted a wave of angry debate but no unified legislative action: here, as elsewhere, those who agreed with Nixon's tactical objectives felt unable to criticize their constitutional underpinnings. The Tonkin Gulf Resolution was finally repealed in 1971, but, like Johnson, Nixon had never felt the resolution was as necessary as it was convenient.

The 1972 "Christmas bombings" finally stirred Congress to seriously debate proposals aimed at reining in presidents' abilities to wage unilateral warfare. Various versions of such legislation had been floated since 1970 or so, along with attempts to cut off funding for military operations in Southeast Asia. The two debates overlapped; the continuing bombing of Cambodia in the spring of 1973, after legislative disapproval, prompted a vehement reaction from those who, like Sen. William Fulbright (D-AR), raged that "the Nixon administration has shown that it will not be gotten the better of by anything so trivial as a law." When Nixon vetoed a ban on further funding for the bombing, a new version was subsequently attached to a critical debt limit measure. This forced Nixon to cut a deal: military operations in the region would end by August 15.[34] Still, the power of the purse was a blunt instrument for influencing military action. And it was politically unwieldy. After all, it would be difficult to pass a funding cutoff during an ongoing operation, when a lack of resources might endanger troops under fire.

The two chambers had different ideas of how to check the president's ability to send those troops into battle in the first place. Both wanted to make sure that Congress would be consulted before military action ever began. But the House allowed some wiggle room, requiring that the president consult in "every possible instance" before sending forces into imminent or ongoing hostilities; if unable to do so, he had to give a detailed report within seventy-two hours. The Senate version required legislative approval in advance, except in very specific circumstances: namely, if troops were deployed to repel an attack on the United States or its armed forces (wherever stationed), to forestall the imminent threat of such an attack, or to rescue endangered Americans abroad or at sea. Even under these circumstances military engagement would have to end after a month unless Congress voted to authorize it—again different from the House requirement, which gave the president 120 days. In either case, if Congress did not act within the stated time frame, the military engagement was terminated; it could also be terminated earlier if Congress so directed by concurrent resolution (a procedure that meant presidents could not veto the order).

The different drafts went to conference committee. The House had doubts about exactly specifying presidential powers, given the difficulty in interpreting terms such as *imminent threat*. The Senate in turn feared giving the president power to commit troops even for four months without a tighter leash than the House provided. In the end, the resolution merged the two approaches, and the War Powers Resolution (WPR) was finally passed in November 1973, over President Nixon's veto. Nixon claimed it would limit flexibility in foreign policy; members of Congress responded that "flexibility has become a euphemism for presidential domination." The *nation's* ability to make decisive choices, they stressed, was not equivalent to the *president's* ability to do so.[35]

As finally approved, the resolution started with a statement of purpose and policy that included a version of the Senate's list of conditions. It held that presidents' "constitutional powers . . . as Commander-in-Chief" applied only after a declaration of war or some other formal authorization by Congress or if the United States or its armed forces were attacked. The next section included the House requirement that presidents "shall consult with Congress" before the use of force "in every possible instance" and shall continue consultations until troops are out of harm's way. Consultation with Congress was not intended to be optional; the president, explained Senate sponsor Jacob Javits (R–NY), would now be "obliged by law to consult before the introduction of forces into hostilities and to continue consultations so long as the troops are engaged."[36]

Unless war had been declared, presidents were further required to report on each troop deployment within forty-eight hours of that deployment, justifying the circumstances of the decision and "the constitutional and legislative authority under which such introduction took place," along with the likely duration of the hostilities. Choices triggering disclosure included the introduction of new troops into hostilities or into the "territory, airspace or waters of a foreign nation, while equipped for combat" and also any deployments that would "substantially enlarge" existing force levels. Periodic reports were to follow at least once every six months.

With this information in hand, Congress retained the right to require at any time by concurrent resolution that the engagement cease. And without affirmative congressional authorization in the meantime, troops were in any case to be removed from hostilities within sixty days (up from the thirty-day window the Senate had passed). This period could be extended either by congressional action or by the president, if he certified in writing that the additional time was a matter of "unavoidable military necessity" to ensure their safe withdrawal. But in the latter case the extension could last no more than an additional thirty days. Treaties and alliances were explicitly ruled out as a justification for military action unless implementing legislation specifically authorized that action.

As will be discussed in the next chapter, the wording of the resolution as it combined the House and Senate versions led to complications for interpretation and enforcement. But if the WPR was partly symbolic, even the symbol was substantial: it epitomized the idea that Congress was an indispensable actor in all areas of policy-making. "It is the purpose of this joint resolution," the text began, "to fulfill the intent of the framers of the Constitution and the United States and insure that the collective judgment of the Congress and the President will apply to the introduction of United States Armed Forces into hostilities." Even Henry Kissinger was moved to assert that "Congress is a coequal branch of government . . . [and] foreign policy must be a shared enterprise."

Javits went further. There would be no more "Presidential war," he asserted, for Congress had at last moved to "codif[y] the implementation of the most awesome power in the possession of every sovereignty."[37]

INTELLIGENCE OVERSIGHT

With the massive CIA efforts in Laos and Thailand and the Operation 34-A adventures in Vietnam in mind, some lawmakers hoped to include covert operations within the consultation and reporting functions of the WPR. These efforts were unsuccessful. However, the CIA began to come under further scrutiny as early as 1973, when the agency's support of various White House Plumbers' efforts (providing false identities, electronic equipment, and the like, as well as the Ellsberg psychological profile) came to light through the Watergate investigations. Further, it was noted, there had been no objection to the excesses of the Huston Plan from Langley's side of the table.

Soon thereafter U.S. involvement in the dismantling of Chile's Allende government came under suspicion. A House Armed Services subcommittee held oversight hearings that by 1974 led to an effort to ban altogether covert actions undertaken for "the purpose of undermining or destabilizing" any foreign government. While this failed, in December 1974 the Hughes-Ryan Amendment was added to a foreign aid bill. Hughes-Ryan put into statute important new reporting requirements: the CIA would have to brief six (later eight) separate committees on what specific actions were under way outside of "activities intended solely for obtaining necessary intelligence." To get even that far, the president would have to make a finding, in writing, that each operation was "important to the national security of the United States." Otherwise, no funds could be expended for the operation. Congress thus reinserted itself into the intelligence oversight process; and the president, further, was stripped of the "plausible deniability" behind which so many prior operations had been shielded. Interestingly, President Ford did not fight the amendment very hard: administration officials, one Republican negotiator noted, were demoralized, "shell-shocked from the Chilean exposé." What the scholar Kathryn Olmsted has called "a historic erosion of [executive] foreign policy powers" thus took place without much publicity or resistance.[38]

It should be noted that Hughes–Ryan only required notification, not permission. But worse was to come for the agency. Just before Christmas in 1974, Seymour Hersh's blockbuster reporting on the CIA's Operation CHAOS—its program of domestic surveillance and harassment—alerted Washington to a new scandal quickly dubbed "son of Watergate."[39] In 1973 new CIA director James Schlesinger, wanting to know his liabilities in light of the revelations of CIA-Plumber relations, had directed that all potentially embarrassing agency actions be compiled into a single report. The result—693 pages of the CIA's "family jewels"—detailed some nine hundred major covert projects and several thousand lesser ones since 1961. Those projects included plots to assassinate foreign leaders and overthrow governments; programs examining the effects of illicit drugs by testing them on unsuspecting American citizens; and the wiretaps, mail opening, and black bag jobs of Operation CHAOS.

Not all of this was in Hersh's story. But enough was there that a firestorm of legislative recrimination (some self-directed) ensued, fueled by ongoing media reports about the CIA and, soon, the FBI's COINTELPRO. By mid-January the CIA's Bill Colby had been called to testify before the Senate Armed Services Committee and President Ford had been pressured into appointing a blue-ribbon commission on domestic abuses by the CIA. Led by Vice President Nelson Rockefeller, members included the AFL-CIO's Lane Kirkland, Eisenhower and Kennedy cabinet member Douglas Dillon, and former California governor Ronald Reagan. While finding that the "great majority of the CIA's domestic activities comply with its statutory authority," the commission concluded that "some were plainly unlawful." However, it claimed, "the Agency's own recent actions . . . have gone far to terminate the activities upon which this investigation has focused."[40]

Congress wasn't so sure and began conducting its own hearings. After February 1975, when Daniel Schorr of CBS broke the news of CIA-sponsored assassination attempts, public interest in the investigations exploded. The Rockefeller Commission began looking into the assassination allegations, but the Ford administration shelved those efforts, prompting renewed accusations of cover-up. The field was open for the Senate's new Church Committee and its House counterpart, led by Rep. Otis Pike (D-NY).[41]

Looking into the controversy proved a tad problematic for the Democratic majority, since, as noted earlier, a number of the abuses had taken place under Democratic administrations. Conservatives on the committee who felt that presidents should have wide unilateral power in foreign affairs were less conflicted. Sen. Barry Goldwater (R-AZ) defended JFK and LBJ and suggested that, had he won the 1964 election, he too would have ordered assassinations: in a war, even a cold one, ruthless methods were required. One comforting Democratic response was to charge the CIA with "rogue" status, acting outside the bounds of presidential knowledge and approval; but as Sen. Walter Mondale (D-MN) concluded, the problem was, rather, "presidential unaccountability to the law," given that "the grant of power to the CIA and these other agencies is, above all, a grant of power to the President." Since the president could exercise that power in secret, the question of reform was a difficult one.[42]

In April 1976 the final Church Committee report was released, six hefty volumes comprising several thousand pages of detailed information on foreign and military intelligence, domestic operations, the organization and historical evolution of American intelligence agencies, and (as a sop to conspiracy theorists) the performance of those agencies in investigating JFK's assassination. Its conclusions condemned the FBI much more strongly than the CIA, which was odd, since even the conservative Rockefeller Commission had called much of Operation CHAOS illegal and all of it "improper."[43] Still, Presidents Ford and Carter were pressured to do their own housecleaning of the agency. Anticipating the Church Committee report, Ford issued a February 1976 executive order that banned political assassination, created an Intelligence Oversight Board, channeled the CIA out of the domestic arena, and prevented human subjects research—policies continued under the Carter administration, when former Church Committee stalwart Mondale became vice president. Further, in 1977 new director of central intelligence Stansfield Turner purged the agency by demoting or dismissing some eight hundred espionage officers, even renaming the Directorate of Intelligence the National Foreign Assessment Center. Covert operations were limited by executive order to activities "designed to further official [i.e., overt] United States programs and policies abroad." Such operations continued, to be sure, especially after the Soviet invasion of Afghanistan in 1979, but the CIA's capability for carrying them out had been significantly weakened by the agency's trials since 1973.[44]

The Church Committee's final report reflected the ambivalence many members of Congress had about the necessity for covert actions and the likely efficacy of their own body in directing such actions when necessary. Keeping secrets comes hard to a legislative body, as the repeated inquiries into leaks during the Church and Pike investigations attested.

This debate was resolved in two related ways. First, if Congress was conflicted about the need for secret operations, it did at least want to be kept informed. "If CIA had been acting as the President's agent in many of its improper actions," longtime agency hand (and later director) Robert M. Gates later wrote, "then the way to control CIA was to dilute the President's heretofore nearly absolute control over the Agency. And that would be done by a much more aggressive congressional oversight mechanism." The eventual result, in 1976 and 1977, was the creation of permanent Select Committees on Intelligence in each chamber, with membership rotating after six to eight years. The idea was to reduce the number of committees with jurisdiction over covert action, thus making information less prone to leaks and forging a more effective oversight relationship with the administration. The Intelligence Oversight Act, passed in 1980, added punch to that process, making sure required disclosure was limited to the intelligence committees and expanding the Hughes-Ryan mandates by requiring that those committees be "fully and currently informed" of *all* intelligence activities run out of the CIA or elsewhere in the government. This included intelligence collection and counterintelligence operations as well as covert action. Further, the committees were to receive information on "any significant anticipated intelligence activity," that is, they were to be notified in advance. If the president did not give advance notice, briefings still had to occur quickly thereafter ("in a timely fashion," as under Hughes-Ryan) and fully explain the lapse. And the president still had to make specific findings that covert activities were required by national security.

There were some concessions to demands of speed and secrecy. Under "extraordinary circumstances affecting vital interests of the United States," for example, notice could be restricted to eight members of Congress: the chair and ranking minority members of the intelligence committees, the Speaker and minority leader of the House, and the majority and minority leaders of the Senate. Nevertheless, as Loch Johnson wrote in 1984, the Intelligence Oversight Act was a "benchmark in congressional efforts to enhance the participation of elected representatives in the making of international agreements. It achieves—in law— equal access to information, and makes that information available to legislators before it is too late for them to use it."[45] Whether it achieved that goal in fact as well as law was, of course, a matter to be decided in practice. In the short run, at least, the Senate and House Intelligence Committees did prove to be aggressive interlocutors.[46]

A second avenue for legislative assertiveness was via the power of the purse. Hughes-Ryan had already banned funding for covert activities that went unreported to Congress, and Ford administration efforts to take sides in the Angolan civil war prompted further such efforts. The CIA had been shipping millions of dollars' worth of arms, communications gear, and cash to a faction fighting another backed by Cuba and the Soviet Union. The administration's efforts to hide this aid prompted statutory language in 1976 limiting CIA activities in Angola to intelligence gathering. The Clark Amendment passed later that year prohibited any assistance to any side in the Angolan war "unless and until the Congress expressly authorizes such assistance by law"; in separate action, Congress refused to provide any funding. In other areas, though, presidents were able to gain support for what Louis Fisher calls "covert action in the open"; enormous funding was provided, for example, to the Mujahedeen resistance to the Soviet Union after the latter's invasion of Afghanistan in 1979.[47]

EXECUTIVE AGREEMENTS

During the 1970s Congress also tried to gain information about another area of executive-directed foreign policy: agreements with other countries that do not conclude in treaties. Treaties, of course, must be ratified by a two-thirds vote of the Senate. "Executive agreements," however, need no such sanction, and, indeed, the commitments they make have not always even been disclosed to Congress. By the mid-1920s the number of executive agreements began consistently to outpace the number of treaties, a trend accelerated by World War II; President Truman concluded more than 1,300 agreements while submitting just 145 treaties for ratification. One calculation suggests that between 75 and 80 percent of significant military commitments abroad were conducted via executive agreement rather than by treaty between 1953 and 1972.[48] These included, in the mid-1960s, major commitments to the defense of such nations as Ethiopia, Thailand, and Spain. In the last case the United States pledged to protect Spain (which did not join NATO until 1982) against attack in exchange for the right to use Spanish soil for military bases.

Such a relationship linked directly to war powers and to the issue of national commitments debated as early as 1969. Legislators' concerns were exacerbated by the "obsessive secrecy," in Sen. Henry Jackson's (D-WA) phrase, of Nixon-Kissinger back-channel diplomacy in the Middle East, Southeast Asia, China, and the USSR. What commitments were being made, what understandings reached? Hearings in 1972 led to the Case-Zablocki Act, which required that "the text of any international agreement, other than a treaty," be submitted to Congress "as soon as is practicable" but in any case within sixty days after the agreement took effect. If an agreement was deemed too sensitive for release to the full Congress, it could be sent to the foreign relations committees under seal.

Oral agreements were soon added to the mix, along with a requirement that presidents explain in writing any delays in reporting agreements to Congress.[49] Later proposals were even stronger, recommending that all executive agreements have a waiting period before going into effect, so that they could be legislatively reviewed. Some required both House and Senate participation in that process, others just the Senate; arguments over this question ultimately stalled various versions of the language in mid-1970s conference committees. Sen. Dick Clark (D-IA) tried to limit presidential discretion further with the Treaty Powers Resolution, which would prohibit presidents from reaching "significant" agreements without seeking their ratification. If presidents evaded this, in the judgment of the Senate, the Senate rules would henceforth make it out of order to consider any funding to implement the agreement. Definitional problems soon arose: what triggered "significance," after all? However, the cumulative debate had an effect on executive behavior: when the Spanish base agreement came up for renewal in 1975, the Ford administration submitted it as a treaty.[50]

In general, then, Congress throughout the 1970s took dramatic new stands affirming the legislative role in matters of war and peace. Even so, the previous account is truncated: Congress also used foreign aid and trade as instruments for asserting a proactive place in the making of foreign policy more generally. A new office in the State Department was created and charged with preparing annual reports on the human rights observances of all nations seeking military assistance, and Chile, Uruguay, and South Korea saw their U.S. aid cut over similar concerns. The Jackson-Vanik Amendment, seeking the right of Jews to emigrate freely from the Soviet Union in exchange for granting Russia favorable trade status, became law in 1974. Congress withdrew the United States from the International Labor Organization; cut its contribution to the United Nations Educational, Scientific, and Cultural Organization (UNESCO) over UNESCO's exclusion of Israel; and then cut funding to the United Nations itself. Congress placed conditions on arms sales and attempted to place a total ceiling on overall weapons sales. All this, President Ford warned in 1976, placed "impermissible shackles on the President's ability to . . . conduct the foreign relations of the United States."[51] For many in Congress, though, that was their job too—and for them the president's shackles had been very belatedly fastened.

THE BATTLES OF THE BUDGET RESUME

The budget battles of the early 1970s were less amenable to dramatic television than were many of the other fronts of the Watergate wars. Yet they were arguably the most critical from the point of view of legislative prerogative, given how fundamental the power of the purse is to congressional authority.

IMPOUNDMENT CONTROL

Because of this, perhaps, the congressional reaction to Nixon's assertions of power came earlier in this area than in others. As early as March 1971, Sen. Sam Ervin (D-NC) blasted impoundments by declaring that Nixon had "no authority under the Constitution to decide which laws will be executed or to what extent they will be enforced." The selective nature of impoundment, he argued, did just that. A half dozen bills were filed requiring the president to at least notify Congress when he planned to withhold funds.[52]

In the interim, a number of court actions were brought that challenged the president's impoundment authority. It was not obvious that the courts would step in: Was this a "political question" between the branches? Were the suits "ripe" for judicial determination? While some cases were set aside on these grounds, most were heard. Where they were heard, the president nearly always lost.[53] By mid-1973 a memo from budget director Roy Ash to Nixon referenced some forty-five ongoing lawsuits resulting from impoundment. "The volume and variety of these legal challenges were clearly unanticipated at the time the budgetary decisions were made," Ash admitted. He continued, with some understatement: "Defending them continues to be a difficult proposition, and some setbacks in the courts have occurred."[54]

By the end of that year, two cases had reached the circuit courts of appeal, and these were consolidated for appeal to the Supreme Court in April 1974 as *Train v. City of New York*.[55] The cases involved $23 billion passed over Nixon's veto in 1972 to ameliorate water pollution but withheld; only 55 percent of the specified funds were allotted. The circuit court had held that "the executive trespasse[d] beyond the range of its legal discretion" in so doing, since such a strategy would "make impossible the attainment of the legislative goals" explicit in the statute. The Supreme Court's unanimous ruling was more narrowly drawn, but still a clear defeat for the administration: "The legislation was intended to provide a firm commitment of substantial sums within a relatively limited period of time in an effort to achieve an early solution of what was deemed an urgent problem," wrote Justice Byron White for the Court. "We cannot believe that Congress at the last minute scuttled the entire effort by providing the Executive with the seemingly limitless power to withhold funds from allotment and obligation." Such a holding rejects, at least by implication, the Nixon claim to an inherent power of impoundment—since if such a power were constitutional, statutory language could not have set it aside.[56]

The *Train* decision was not handed down until February 1975, and in the meantime Congress took action of its own. After the 1972 campaign and Nixon's escalation of impoundments in 1973, the debate over anti-impoundment legislation had rekindled. Senator Ervin again was at the center of the argument and put the case starkly: unless Congress responded, he claimed, "the current trend toward the executive use of legislative power is to continue unabated until we have arrived at a presidential form of government." Congress itself would cease to be a "viable institution."[57]

The Impoundment Control Act, which ultimately passed in 1974, put Congress back in charge of spending. The act divided impoundments into two main categories, deferrals and rescissions. A rescission reflected a president's intent to rescind, or cancel, the appropriation in question. By contrast, deferrals were monies held aside temporarily for use later in the fiscal year. The comptroller general, who heads Congress's GAO, was put in charge of ensuring that requests were properly classified.

Under the Impoundment Control Act, both deferrals and rescissions had to be sent to Congress for evaluation. Deferrals could be vetoed by the majority disapproval of one chamber of Congress but became effective if neither House nor Senate disapproved. However, rescission requests would only take effect, and thus actually cancel spending, if they were affirmatively adopted by both chambers within forty-five days of continuous session. There was no requirement that the president's proposals receive a vote or even debate. Thus, while presidents could delay spending somewhat, Congress could readily ensure that its fiscal wishes were carried out on a case-by-case basis.

Nixon left office before the Impoundment Control Act became effective. President Ford briefly pressed the point by repeatedly seeking to withhold all appropriations that came in higher than his own recommendations. However, Congress just as regularly overturned his decisions (just 12 percent of Ford's $3.3 billion in rescission requests were approved), and the administration eventually gave up. There were fifty rescissions proposed in 1976, twenty-one in 1977, and just eight in 1978.[58]

THE CONGRESSIONAL BUDGET ACT

The impoundment debate kick-started another one over the larger process followed by Congress in formulating a budget. The administration argued that impoundments were necessary in part because of legislative irresponsibility. Members wanted expenditures cut—but while they did not want the president to choose where those cuts would come, they did not want to act themselves either. The basic problem was the so-called tragedy of the commons, where the aggregate of individually rational acts is problematic for the whole community. It is not surprising that each member of Congress seeks gains for his or her own district and seeks to lower the costs imposed on his or her own constituents. And while those goals make individual sense, when pursued by 535 legislators, they add up to fiscal disaster. The body needed centralized discipline to ensure that the body could see the forest for the trees, that overall goals and balance were not nibbled away by particularistic self-interest. Thus in late 1972 a Joint Study Committee was created to suggest ways to address these institutional shortcomings.

The Congressional Budget Act was the result. Signed into law in July 1974 in conjunction with the Impoundment Control Act, it represented a complete reshaping of the legislative budget process.

Three provisions in particular are worth exposition. First, the CBA created new Budget Committees in each legislative chamber whose job it was to formulate an overall budget ceiling—revenues and expenditures both—and broad funding allocations by governmental function, within which the existing Appropriations Committees would be constrained to work.

Second, a series of deadlines were set up for completion of various stages of the process. These came complete with rules protecting the process from various strategies of delay, privileging the budget for debate and guarding it from Senate filibuster.

A resolution agreeing to the overall Budget Committee determinations was to be passed by May 15, giving the Appropriations subcommittees the summer to determine spending on particular items within each allocation. A second resolution reconciling the first with any legislative changes made during the year would follow by September 15. This was to match spending levels with statutory requirements: to cut spending on entitlements, for example, Congress might need to change the conditions for eligibility in various entitlement programs. By October 1, which now marked the start of the fiscal year, the thirteen different appropriations bills funding the entire federal government were to be passed and signed into law.

Third, the CBA created the Congressional Budget Office (CBO) to provide Congress as a whole with its own source of budget expertise. CBO was to "score" the fiscal impact of legislative initiatives and to vet the assumptions of the president's budget as a check against the Office of Management and Budget (OMB).

Relatedly, Congress sought to dilute presidential partisanship at OMB itself. One tack was to undercut executive unity in the budget formulation process. Legislators required that certain agencies send their desired funding levels to Congress at the same time they submitted them to OMB and even mandated that the president include the unedited requests of select other agencies in his own budget, next to his own recommendations.[59]

Congress also required that OMB's top two appointees, who had served since 1921 as purely presidential staff, receive Senate confirmation. The original draft of the bill sought to make this requirement retroactive—in order to get at controversial Nixon appointees Roy Ash and Fred Malek. However, Nixon's veto of this power play was sustained by the House. A proactive version of the bill became law in February 1974.[60]

All told, by the mid-1970s the budget battle had come to temporary truce on congressional terms. In 1975 Senate Budget Committee chair Brock Adams (D-WA) could declare that "for the first time in its history the Congress . . . had developed and operated a comprehensive national budget"; had formulated "an economic policy that is distinctly that of the Congress, not the President"; and had thus "recaptured from the executive its constitutional role in controlling the power of the purse." Even OMB's deputy director, Paul O'Neill, gave the act credit for moderating congressional spending inclinations. By 1980 the president and Congress were working together on a balanced budget resolution, so closely that House Speaker Tip O'Neill (D-MA) declared, "consultation of this type I've never seen in all my years in Congress." Using the discipline of the new process, the standing committees quickly produced changes in law to make the needed cuts. While declining economic conditions put balance out of reach, Sundquist concludes that, "in the sixth year of the budget process, the great potential of that process was beginning to be realized."[61]

If Congress wanted to exercise detailed oversight and coordination of fiscal policy, it was now equipped to do so without reliance on the president. The question was no longer capacity but determination. And during the remainder of the 1970s, at least, Congress seemed committed to making the process work.

ETHICS: BUILDING THE "ETHICS EDIFICE"

Given the breathtaking scope of the ethical lapses uncovered by the Watergate investigations, by 1974 few members of the public admitted to having much faith in any segment of government. Efforts to restore public trust led Congress to act in a number of areas designed to deter official corruption and to systematically prosecute it when it occurred. In 1976 the Public Integrity Section was established in the Criminal Division of the Justice Department to consolidate efforts to investigate "criminal abuses of the public trust." The Federal Election Campaign Act of 1974 and the Ethics in Government Act of 1978 sought to institutionalize guardianship of governmental integrity. As G. Calvin Mackenzie has concluded, "the effort to protect the public from its own leaders became one of the fastest-growing sectors of government in the years after Vietnam and Watergate."[62]

CAMPAIGN FINANCE REFORM

As noted earlier, the Federal Election Campaign Act (FECA) of 1971 was violated in every particular by the subsequent campaigns of 1972. Nixon campaign money flowed from corporate coffers into slush funds and thence into the accounts of burgling ex-Plumbers. For large donors, *quid* seemed to lead quickly to *quo*. The 1971 act seemed quickly and wholly inadequate. "Watergate is not primarily a story of political espionage, nor even of White House intrigue," argued John Gardner, head of the good-government group Common Cause. "It is a particularly malodorous chapter in the annals of campaign financing."[63]

In response, Congress passed extensive amendments to FECA in 1974. The new law required that each candidate be limited to one campaign committee: this was to eliminate the various coordinated "volunteer" committees commonly used to evade spending limits and to provide off-budget aid to campaigns. Contributions would be capped: for each election, individuals could give just $1,000 to candidates, $5,000 to political action committees (PACs) or state parties, and $20,000 to national party committees, with the total across all recipients limited to $25,000. Even if running for office themselves, individuals were constrained: presidential candidates could give just $50,000 to their own campaigns and congressional candidates even less. PACs and, in most cases, parties could themselves contribute $5,000 to any given candidate. In-kind donations uncoordinated with a campaign, but de facto on its behalf, were limited to $1,000 per candidate.

Spending was limited too. House campaigns were capped at $70,000 in expenditures, Senate races at $100,000, except for the largest states, though even there spending could not exceed eight cents per potential voter. Party committees could spend another $10,000 on behalf of their House candidates, $26,500 in the Senate.

On the presidential side, the excesses of 1972 were to be stemmed by making elections publicly funded. If a candidate became eligible by raising a threshold amount of money in small contributions ($250 or less) across twenty different states, those donations would become eligible for federal matching funds until the candidate faltered and received less than 10 percent of the vote in consecutive primaries. Primary season spending limits were set in each state based on population, starting at just $10,000. Overall expenditures on primary elections were also capped. To avoid the temptation of corporate underwriting of the national conventions (à la ITT in 1972), $4 million in federal funding was provided for each party's grand party. And full public funding was instituted for the general election season after the conventions, with $20 million for each major party candidate. The Senate version of FECA had included federal financing of congressional races as well; but even without that, FECA's mechanisms for election funding were "heralded as the most significant reform of the campaign finance system in American history."[64] Capping them off was a permanent enforcement mechanism in the form of the new Federal Election Commission (FEC). The FEC was to develop electoral regulations and to enforce them, as well as to serve as the public clearinghouse for the periodic reports on contributions and expenses each campaign now had to compile and file.[65]

The intent of the new FECA was, like so many of the post-Watergate enactments, to restore the public's faith in the electoral process. The idea was to strike back at big money's influence in politics, real and perceived, clearing the field for small and presumably more virtuous donors. FECA, Sen. Edward Kennedy (D-MA) argued, would "guarantee that the political influence of any citizen is measured only by his voice and vote, not by the thickness of his pocketbook." Even PACs, quickly seen as perfidious, were viewed positively at the time as mechanisms that allowed the pooling of small contributions for big impact and that required those contributions to be disclosed instead of slipped under the table.

Soon enough, of course, the Supreme Court would strike the first blow at this new framework; purveyors of "soft money" would inflict the fatal wounds. But in 1974 Sen. Howard Cannon (D-NV) could claim that the "new law will constitute the most significant step ever taken in the area of election reform." Kennedy went further: the bill's passage was "one of the finest hours of the Senate in this or any other Congress." Even President Ford, no fan of public financing, could not resist the pressure to sign FECA into law. The fact was, he conceded, "The times demand this legislation."[66]

The Ethics in Government Act & the Independent Counsel

The Ethics in Government Act (EGA) of 1978, as President Carter noted in his signing statement, likewise "respond[ed] to problems that developed at the highest level of Government in the 1970's." The president added, probably sincerely, that he was "very pleased" with "this milestone in the history of safeguards against abuse of the public trust by Government officials."[67]

The EGA, under various labels, had been in the works long before it became law. Early versions dating back to 1974 and 1975 included requirements for financial disclosure by the president and vice president, enhanced limitations on political activity by government employees, and the creation of a "congressional legal service" able to advise legislators on the legality of executive practices and to initiate civil actions on Congress's behalf.

By the time the EGA became law, the bill had changed substantially. It contained a variety of requirements designed to stem malfeasance and to deter conflicts of interest, largely by making them more transparent: all elected federal officials, senior staff, Senate-confirmed appointees (including judges), and presidential candidates would be required to file public financial disclosure forms laying out income and investment information. Any gifts valued over thirty-five dollars—or cumulating to more than one hundred dollars in a given year—also had to be disclosed. To jam the "revolving door" between government and the regulated private sector, formal and informal lobbying contacts between ex–federal employees and their former agencies were forbidden for two years. An Office of Government Ethics was created to monitor executive branch compliance with these requirements; GAO was to enforce legislative compliance.[68]

But by far the best-known provision of the EGA was Title VI, the special prosecutor provisions, which would later be known as the Independent Counsel Act (ICA).[69] Title VI hearkened to the aftermath of the 1973 "Saturday Night Massacre," when Nixon removed Archibald Cox from office. Within days, legislation to create a permanent, independent special prosecutor's office had been introduced and attracted wide support in both chambers.

In the short run, the White House undercut the bills' momentum by quickly naming a successor to Cox, Leon Jaworski and granting him a large degree of independence from the executive branch proper. The Justice Department went so far as to publish new regulations specifying that "the Special Prosecutor will determine whether and to what extent he will inform or consult with the Attorney General about the conduct of his duties and responsibilities." Indeed,

> In accordance with assurances given by the President to the Attorney General that the President will not exercise his Constitutional powers to effect the discharge of the Special Prosecutor or to limit the independence that he is hereby given, the Special Prosecutor will not be removed from his duties except for extraordinary improprieties on his part and without the President's first consulting the Majority and the Minority Leaders and Chairmen and ranking Minority Members of the Judiciary Committees of the Senate and House of Representatives and ascertaining that their consensus is in accord with his proposed action.[70]

Congress nonetheless pushed to institutionalize the independence that Jaworski had negotiated. While some members persistently argued that the ultimate result of Watergate indicated that no new procedures were required—that, after all, the "system worked"—many more thought an impartial mechanism needed to be put in place as a concession to an era of burgeoning polarization. Senate Judiciary Committee hearings were entitled "Removing Politics From the Administration of Justice."[71] After all, even if one trusted Congress to do the right thing instead of the partisan thing, the executive branch could not be trusted to police itself. Over time, attorneys general had tended to be appointed on the basis of their loyalty to the president rather than on their legal expertise;[72] and in any case, the president, as chief executive, is likewise the nation's chief prosecutor. Cox's firing (later combined with the revelation of the smoking gun evidence that the president had sought to quash the FBI investigation) suggested that a president determined to protect himself would use that authority ruthlessly. In a 1987 debate over amending the act to provide for presidential appointment of the independent counsel, Sen. Carl Levin (D-MI) accused the administration of amnesia: "What you want to do is say let's just forget about what has happened in the 1970s with that Saturday Night Massacre. . . . I think you are going to find the Congress resisting that advice."[73]

Substantive conflicts over the structure of the special prosecutor's office (How should a prosecutor be chosen? Should it be a permanent appointment?) delayed enactment of the law until Ford was defeated by Jimmy Carter in the 1976 elections. As finally passed, with Carter's support, the independent counsel law provided a three-stage process for setting an investigation in motion after the attorney general received information alleging that a high-level federal official had committed a violation of federal law. First, the attorney general was to conduct a preliminary investigation. Second, unless the attorney general found that "no reasonable grounds exist to warrant further investigation," she was to apply to a Special Division of the United States Court of Appeals, a panel of three judges serving two-year terms on the panel.[74] The panel would then name and appoint the independent counsel and define his jurisdiction. The counsel was then to have "full power and independent authority to exercise all investigative and prosecutorial functions and powers of the Department of Justice." There was no time limit or spending limit binding the investigation.[75] At the outset, the counsel could only be removed for "extraordinary impropriety," though this standard was changed to the still daunting requirement of "good cause" in 1982.

The ICA had widespread support among Washingtonians. Indeed, Katy Harriger's authoritative book on the topic suggests that "the strength of elite support for the institution of the special prosecutor is perhaps the arrangement's greatest contribution to American politics. . . . The confidence of elites in the impartiality of independent counsel investigations helped to defuse the animosities and limit the conflict among the branches and between the parties."[76] The use of independent counsels quickly became a routine part of Washington life—the first was appointed almost immediately, in 1979, followed by another in 1980 and a third in 1981. Before the act's expiration in 1999, twenty cases were brought, employing twenty-five independent counsels at a cost of over $175 million. Charges ranged from allegations of drug use by White House aides to perjury, bribery, fraud, and influence peddling by cabinet secretaries.[77] Some fifty convictions resulted. Many investigations did not lead to the filing of any criminal charges, a fact that the statute's defenders argued showed its basic impartiality; on the other end of the scale were the immense Iran-contra investigation of 1986–93 and the wide-ranging 1994–2000 probe that began with the Whitewater land deal. These are described in more detail in the next chapter, but both had far-reaching impact. The Iran-contra investigation led to eleven convictions and two pretrial pardons; the Whitewater probe, through the tortuous expansion of the independent counsel's authority into areas ranging from suicide to sex, led to some fifteen convictions and the impeachment of the president of the United States.

In 1988 the Supreme Court decisively upheld the ICA's constitutionality, despite its odd amalgamation of a judicial appointee into the executive branch. In general, the Court accepted the contention made by the Senate in its 1978 committee report on the act: that a court's appointment of the prosecutor was required "in order to have the maximum degree of independence and public confidence in the investigation conducted by that special prosecutor." The Court agreed that Congress had not tried to usurp executive functions but simply sought a workable mechanism for dealing with allegations of executive corruption.[78]

Not everyone bought that argument. While only Justice Antonin Scalia demurred from the Court's opinion, his vigorous dissent pointed out that the ICA went past simple workability to mark yet another institutional resurgence against the executive branch. The act, Scalia claimed, "deeply wounds the President, by substantially reducing the President's ability to protect himself and his staff. That is the whole object of the law, of course, and I cannot imagine why the Court believes it does not succeed."

In this view, both the courts and Congress grabbed power. On the one hand, Scalia took the position that executive power could not be qualified: Article II did not give the president "some of the executive power, but all of the executive power." Thus the Court's judgment that it had the power to determine when infringement on executive authority was "substantial" was itself pretentious, since the Court had no right to overlay shades of gray on black-and-white boundaries.

On the other hand, Congress also gained at the president's expense. The trigger mechanism of the law was so low that attorneys general had little standing to resist the appointment of independent counsels; presidential accusers were thereby empowered to bring criminal charges with little evidence but much potential for damaging the White House. In Scalia's opinion,

> The institution of the independent counsel enfeebles him more directly in his constant confrontations with Congress, by eroding his public support. Nothing is so politically effective as the ability to charge that one's opponent and his associates are not merely wrongheaded, naive, ineffective, but, in all probability, "crooks." And nothing so effectively gives an appearance of validity to such charges as a Justice Department investigation and, even better, prosecution. The present statute provides ample means for that sort of attack.[79]

Whether or not they were as weakened as much as Scalia argued, presidents could not welcome the *Morrison* decision. The ICA was in place, and, at least on constitutional grounds, the issue seemed settled. For Congress, the institution of the independent counsel was "the grandest monument to its victory over Richard Nixon and the Imperial Presidency."[80] It was the cornerstone of a new "ethics edifice" erected to gild the resurgence regime.[81]

CONCLUSIONS

The resurgence regime was undergirded by what the legal scholar Gerhard Casper has called "framework statutes": laws designed not to solve a particular policy problem but "to support the organizational skeleton of the Constitution by developing a more detailed framework for governmental decisionmaking . . . and attempt[ing] to stabilize expectations about the ways in which governmental power is exercised."[82] Statutes ranging from the Congressional Budget and Impoundment Control Acts to the National Emergencies Act to the War Powers Resolution were aimed at channeling information—and authority—through new procedures and veto points. Court decisions added their own constraints.

A critical motive was to enhance public trust and confidence in government. Proponents of resurgence argued that trust could only be built through more open, less secret government.

Still, it was no coincidence that public confidence was also deemed to require increased legislative assertiveness. The frameworks enacted in the 1970s were hardly neutral in their approach to the constitutional balance of power. Both court and, especially, Congress pushed back against the presidency's two-century-long expansion of prerogative authority. Throughout the 1970s the efforts by Congress to regain the powers of the purse and the sword, along with its general institutional standing, were extensive and ambitious. Already by 1976 journalists were keeping track of "the score since Watergate" in a running battle of "the President versus Congress"; and Congress was ahead.[83]

By the 1980s some argued that the truly imperial branch was not the presidency but Congress. The resurgence regime, they felt, set too many limits, thus undercutting national security, effective administration, and even the constitutional order. "America faces a constitutional crisis," wrote Gordon S. Jones and John A. Marini, settling on two causes: "the congressional failure to observe traditional limits on its power, and the acquiescence of the other two branches of government in the resulting arrogation of power." They urged a restoration of presidential power.[84] But that, as we will see, was already under way.

V. THE RESURGENCE
RECEDES, PART I

Money & Morals

The resurgence regime was both extraordinarily ambitious and, it appeared, quite successful. Richard Nixon himself wrote in 1990 that, "in view of all these restraints, the periodic talk about the 'imperial Presidency' is ludicrous." Some complained the "imperial" presidency was now "imperiled" (President Ford's claim), or "impossible," or, at best, "tethered."[1]

But in retrospect these claims were overblown. Some parts of the broad statutory framework put in place in the 1970s had holes from the outset that grew, and grew more obvious, over time. The War Powers Resolution (WPR) is a good example. Other parts were lacerated by third parties—as with the Supreme Court's *Buckley v. Valeo* decision regarding campaign finance. Ronald Reagan's aggressive use of executive tools, adopted by his successors as well, frayed yet other elements. And Congress itself backed away from using the tools it had created to challenge the president—or failed to make them work. By the mid-1990s, even in the face of a new Republican majority in both chambers of Congress, journalists could write angrily of an "out-of-control presidency." President Clinton might have had his troubles, Michael Lind suggested, but "the presidency is still on top. . . . Like a black hole, the presidency grows by absorbing ever more power and light."[2]

To be sure, not every piece of the regime crumbled at once or for all time. The Iran-contra scandal gave rise to endless investigation and calls for congressional action. The end of the cold war in the early 1990s emboldened some legislators to press for a "peace dividend" and to become more activist in foreign affairs—for if no external threat existed (or seemed to), then politics no longer needed to stop at the water's edge. And, most obviously, the impeachment and trial of Bill Clinton in 1998–99 were the first since 1868 and the first ever of an elected president. It seems strange to talk about congressional deference in that context.

Still, even this period in the late 1990s highlighted the presumed unilateral powers of the president and renewed legislative acquiescence to their use. "Clinton Perfects the Art of Go-Alone Governing" read one 1998 headline. That summer, cruise missiles were fired at the Sudan and Afghanistan at the president's order even as the House debated his fate. Clinton's success in achieving his preferred policy outcomes in this period by taking advantage of the congressional budget process and his veto power is also notable. Further, the fervent partisanship that motivated the impeachment—in spite of hostile public opinion and even hostile midterm election returns—helped to discredit it and undercut the independent counsel process.[3]

By the time George W. Bush took office in January 2001, the "resurgence regime" was on its last legs. Across the board, the laws passed to reshape executive-legislative relations in the 1970s had failed to channel those relations in the manner foreseen by their framers. Part of the problem was that legislation proved an inadequate substitute for concerted political will. Further, "efforts to check presidential power through legislative restrictions often have had the counterproductive effect of legitimizing the very powers that Congress has tried to limit."[4] That is, by providing a process, however constrained, for exercising power, legislators have formalized presidential authority, giving presidents a statutory foothold where they previously had inserted themselves mainly by force of will.

This chapter and the next trace this renewed expansion of presidential power, dividing between them the topic areas traced in earlier chapters. This chapter examines the ongoing battles of the budget and the developments in campaign finance and ethics laws. Chapter 6, in turn, looks at broader claims of executive authority in both war and peace. Claims spurred directly by the terrorist attacks of September 11, 2001, and the responses to those attacks receive separate treatment in chapter 7.

THE BATTLE OF THE BUDGET:
THE RISE, FALL, & RISE OF THE "ROSY SCENARIO"

The Congressional Budget and Impoundment Control Acts provided a framework rather than guaranteed a result. Congress was as free to let presidents dominate the budget process after the acts as before them, but it had new resources—the Budget Committees, the Congressional Budget Office (CBO), the reconciliation process—that allowed it to drive that process in collectively beneficial ways.

In the 1970s, as noted earlier, Congress largely accepted the responsibility the new process implied. Such a development was rather impressive, given that both institutional and individual incentives frequently ran in the other direction, toward piecemeal strategies. Even after the Congressional Budget Act (CBA) was passed, there was no collective enforcement mechanism save moral suasion and party discipline to stick to budget resolution targets—and even that resolution could be overturned by a later one at any time in the fiscal year. Rather than wipe out the existing process, after all, the CBA "layered over" it with the new committees and deadlines, meaning that many different power centers within the legislature retained the ability to balk at fiscal demands. Further, members could easily vote for increased spending, then vote against the budget as a whole on the grounds of its fiscal profligacy, selling both votes to different groups of interested constituents. By consolidating a variety of decisions, the new process made any given vote more consequential and thus harder to build a majority around. Despite all this, Allen Schick could observe in 1980 that, "considering the temptation to 'cheap shot' the budget process, Members have engaged in remarkably little of this practice."[5]

A NEW AGE OF DEFICIT POLITICS: 1981–98

During the 1980s, though, events outpaced that assessment. Members would soon fail to resist temptation. They would be led there by new president Ronald Reagan. But they would stay there of their own volition.

Ronald Reagan took office in January 1981 after a surprisingly large victory over incumbent Jimmy Carter. Much of his appeal to voters centered around economic circumstance: "Are you better off than you were four years ago?" his campaign had asked. For many Americans, continuing inflation, unemployment, and high interest rates (thirty-year mortgages topped 15 percent in early 1980) meant the answer was "no." Further, in the face of the lengthy Iranian hostage crisis and the Soviet invasion of Afghanistan, Reagan urged that American military might and credibility abroad be restored. Domestically, he argued, "government is not the solution to our problem, government is the problem."

The Reagan platform was correspondingly concise: it promised tax cuts, increased defense spending (to achieve "peace through strength"), and big cuts in other programs. The Program for Economic Recovery, presented in February 1981, was to rein in deficit spending through some $50 billion in on- and off-budget savings, a renewed attack on "waste and fraud" to save $25 billion more, a 10 percent reduction in individual tax rates for each of the next three years, fewer regulations, and lowered taxes on investments. The approach assumed that lowered tax rates would lead to an increase in investment and productivity that would generate *increased* tax revenues.

Congress proved willing to buy that assumption, though it had doubters among Congress, the public (polls showed that adding to the deficit was a greater concern than tax rates), and even the White House (including OMB director David Stockman and, presumably, Vice President Bush, who had derided the plan as "voodoo economics" before being added to the ticket). An impassioned televised speech by Reagan in late July helped put pressure on Congress; members received hundreds of calls, telegrams, and letters supporting the plan. Reagan bargained aggressively with holdout legislators, promising not to campaign against Democrats who voted with him and offering substantive district-based concessions. He took full advantage of members' willingness to duck: House Ways and Means chair Dan Rostenkowski (D-IL) discovered that "liberal Democrats . . . preferred to let the president win and be held responsible." Ultimately, the Economic Recovery Tax Act (ERTA) of 1981 contained most of what Reagan had sought.[6]

On the spending side, Reagan showed how the presidency could take advantage of the 1974 budget process. Using a strategy developed by Stockman and the Senate Budget Committee, Reagan was able to force a single up-or-down vote on a wide array of cuts that probably could not have survived individual votes. The trick was to use the reconciliation process called for by the CBA not at the end of the budgeting cycle but at the start. Thus, instead of using it to force recalcitrant committees to come to terms after disagreement, the Reagan reconciliation proposal bound those committees from the beginning to making cuts they would otherwise have shirked. It required congressmen to take just one tough vote instead of dozens. And it had the further advantage of procedural protection: by rule, the reconciliation bill could only be debated for fifty hours in the Senate and could only be amended by proposals deemed germane to the budget.

As Stockman put it later, the budget was based on a "rosy scenario" of future revenues and present-day cuts. As such it represented a clear test of presidential power. "The Gramm-Latta [reconciliation bill] and the Reagan Revolution had all along required . . . one thing: surrender," Stockman recalled. "The Congress had to forfeit its independence and accept the role of a rubber-stamping parliament if the whole plan was to work." Majority Leader Jim Wright (D-TX) agreed: Reagan was trying to "dictate every last scintilla, every last phrase" of the budget. But members seemed happy enough to take dictation. Allowing the executive to take control was comforting and good politics to boot, especially after Reagan took to the airwaves that spring. Riding a wave of good feeling after his courageous response to an attempted assassination, Reagan made his budget not only an institutional referendum but a personal one. As the constituent calls and mail rolled in, minds changed; "they say they're voting for it because they're afraid," said Rep. Toby Moffett (D-CT). The House Rules Committee tried to break up the bill into several votes, but this effort was defeated on the floor. As Reagan correctly observed, the budget and tax wins together made up "the greatest political win in half a century."[7]

However impressive the political victory, the result of the 1981 votes was to rejoin deficit politics at a higher plane. Red ink was nothing new; it had underlain the impoundment debate, and between 1975 and 1980 annual shortfalls continued to range between $41 and $74 billion. Supply-side economics promised a new math that would cure structural imbalances. But the aftermath of ERTA proved that the old math still works: lower revenue plus higher spending equals bigger deficits. Much bigger deficits, in fact: from $79 billion in 1981 to $128 billion in 1982 to $208 billion in 1983. For the next decade deficits of at least $150 billion were standard fare, with the imbalance peaking (for the moment) at $290 billion in 1992, the last year of the first Bush administration. None of these figures included the IOUs written to the Social Security trust fund, which was in surplus pending the coming retirement of the baby boom generation but which had been spent to offset on-budget operating deficits.

At the same time, naturally, the aggregate of those annual deficits—the national debt—also grew rapidly. The gross debt doubled from $909 billion in 1980 to $1.8 trillion five years later to $3.2 trillion in 1990 to $5.4 trillion at the end of fiscal 1998. This meant that, in 1998 alone, $243 billion had to be put in the budget simply to pay interest on the debt.[8]

The debt figure gained special public salience, since it made for ready conversion to per capita figures and to conveniently shocking mathematical calculations. With a U.S. population of 260 million, for example, the debt in 1998 was about twenty thousand dollars per resident. A huge electronic billboard on New York's Avenue of the Americas informed passersby of the national debt at each moment, the figure's right-hand columns blurred from the rapidity of their additive motion—some ten thousand dollars per second.

Economists differ on whether an exactly balanced budget matters for economic performance. But the public had few such doubts, and elected officials took heed. "The deficit," wrote budgeting expert Aaron Wildavsky in the late 1980s, "has become both an obsession and a weapon." In the second presidential debate in 1992, that weapon was unsheathed; perhaps prompted by independent candidate H. Ross Perot's proselytizing on the deficit issue, an audience questioner used the national debt as a synonym for all economic woes. By April 1995 82 percent of respondents told the Gallup Poll that reducing the deficit was a "major concern," with just 3 percent indicating that it was of no concern. In House debate that year Rep. Gerald Solomon (R-NY) provided the appropriate rhetorical flourish. "Mr. Chairman," he cried, "this nation is at war!"[9]

During the 1980s Congress experimented with different ways to fight that war. The most direct method was to raise taxes; it is often forgotten that President Reagan signed tax increases in 1982, 1984, 1985, 1986, and 1987.[10] But all five together offset only about one-third of the cost to the Treasury of the 1981 tax cuts; while the 1986 law represented a major change in the tax code, it was designed to be largely revenue neutral. Further, effective in 1985 long-term revenues were additionally reduced by tying tax brackets to inflation and thus eliminating "bracket creep."

It was hardly surprising that Congress found raising taxes much harder than slashing them. A more attractive option was to implement mechanisms designed to force spending cuts. In 1985, for example, the Gramm-Rudman-Hollings legislation was passed. Gramm-Rudman (as it was usually called; Sen. Ernest Hollings [D-SC] good-naturedly accepted that everything had to be cut) made some changes to the budget process itself, but most attention focused on its deficit reduction procedures. It required that deficit targets be set each year, successively smaller until the budget was in balance. If the annual target was not met, the dollar figure needed to reach it would be set aside and cut, or "sequestered," from all programs not separately exempted from that process. A deficit of $171.9 billion was to be allowed for fiscal 1986, then $144 billion, and so on, until a zero deficit was achieved in 1991. Gramm-Rudman-Hollings II was passed in 1987 to delay the government's arrival in the black to fiscal 1993.[11]

This automatic process was supposed to deter political actors from avoiding hard choices over their collective priorities, since no one would see across-the-board cuts as a better solution. But the reaction instead was to come up with various accounting tricks that made the current year's deficit look better at the expense of future years, then annually repeating those tricks. If budget projections, however unrealistic, met the Gramm-Rudman targets, then the budget was in compliance, even if actual spending wildly outpaced the projections. The president still presented his budget first. So if he included fanciful assumptions about revenue or spending discipline, Congress had little incentive to come up with more honest ones, since it would appear that legislative action had increased the projected deficit and required painful cuts. Congressional autonomy was thus truncated, albeit by choice.[12]

Further limiting legislative power was the decision in Gramm-Rudman to give the power to make sequesters not to its own members but to OMB and the CBO—which were to determine when and where sequesters were required—and to the comptroller general at the GAO, who would certify those results and require the president to issue an order canceling the requisite spending. This authority was shifted out of the legislative branch altogether after the Supreme Court ruled in 1986 that a legislative employee (as at GAO) could not carry out the executive function of enforcing the laws.[13]

In 1990, as it became clear that Gramm-Rudman was not working and deficits were continuing to rise, President George H. W. Bush and legislative leaders agreed on the Budget Enforcement Act (BEA). The BEA cut spending but also raised taxes; Bush's gutsy acceptance of the latter in violation of a campaign pledge may have cost him reelection, a result that did not make members of Congress more willing to assume a real, rather than rhetorical, mantle of fiscal responsibility. More broadly, and crucial to longer-term budgeting, BEA set up new rules for dealing with the deficit. Replacing the Gramm-Rudman deficit targets would be spending caps, set well in advance in a number of different areas. Each area—generally, defense, nondefense, and entitlement spending—had to stay within its specified bounds or face sequesters on all accounts in that area. This discipline was backed up by another principle, "pay as you go" (PAYGO). Any new proposal or expansion of an old law was examined for its fiscal impact. If the proposal would cost money, its sponsor needed to identify a source of revenue or an offsetting reduction in spending. The massive 1993 Omnibus Budget Reconciliation Act in the first year of the Clinton administration renewed caps and PAYGO.

Some members scorned these types of procedures as "government by automatic pilot," as Rep. Henry Waxman (D-CA) put it in debate on Gramm-Rudman. "We are establishing a financial doomsday machine that will make our choices for us," he went on. "We are betraying [the public] trust by handing our jobs over to bureaucrats, triggers, and automatic decisions." The PAYGO rules also led to constrained choices over policy alternatives, since what one CBO staffer called "the balkanization of the budget" meant that discretionary and mandatory spending were walled off from each other during debate. Further, myopic obsession with how spending was "scored" by CBO replaced long-term thinking about what would actually constitute good public policy. On the whole, the various spending ceiling laws indicated a certain lack of confidence in Congress's ability to make good budget choices generally.[14]

Be that as it may, the automation of the process was no accident. The idea was to bind Congress to prevent it from action, as Odysseus bound himself to the mast in order to resist the Sirens' lovely song ("spend more, spend more"). As one member later put it: "Let us face it. . . . we in Congress cannot help ourselves." Another added, "the Congress as an institution has proven itself to be incapable of fiscal restraint when it polices itself."[15]

And, for all this, the fact that the "war" cited by Representative Solomon was ongoing as late as 1995 highlights the fact that the budget was still well out of balance. The actual deficit figure for fiscal 1986 was $221 billion; for fiscal 1993, $255 billion; and for fiscal 1995, down a bit, but still $164 billion.

One result was to seek other binding mechanisms. In 1995 the House passed a Balanced Budget Amendment to the Constitution, with the Senate falling just one vote short of the two-thirds majority needed to send it to the states for ratification. Meanwhile, legislators revisited the impoundment issue. Article I of the Constitution requires that the president sign or veto legislative measures in their entirety; but in his 1986 State of the Union address Reagan had renewed the old presidential call for a line-item veto. "I'll make the cuts, I'll take the heat," he boasted. As deficits continued to rise, lawmakers began to find this approach rather attractive, given its potential for shifting blame for the deficit onto the executive branch.

Much gnashing of legislative teeth ensued. As Sen. William Cohen (R-ME) argued, "We have reached the point of 'Stop us before we spend again!' The power of the purse . . . is a power we have abused too often, and too often, I might add, to the applause of our constituents. For too long, we have been rewarded for bringing home the bacon while condemning the presence and prevalence of trichinosis in Congress. We cannot continue to have it both ways." Only an item veto, he argued, would impose the needed discipline. House Minority Leader Bob Michel (R-IL) put it this way: if asked, "'Bob, why would you give up your legislative authority to an all-powerful chief executive?'" he suggested his response would be simple: "Because we have loused it up here in the Congress. That is why."[16]

Some members of Congress urged Presidents Reagan, Bush, and Clinton to claim an item veto even without legislative action; they argued that vetoing individual appropriations items might be inherent in the veto power. In 1993, for example, Sen. Arlen Specter (R-PA) said he believed "there is constitutional authority" for an item veto "without a constitutional amendment or without any other statutory authorization."[17] Successive attorneys general, however, advised their presidents that such authority was doubtful. And thus long debate ensued as to how to transfer it to the president. The extant rescission process, as chapter 4 noted, was simple enough: presidents proposed spending cuts, and if Congress voted to pass them they went into effect. A number of different approaches—ranging from simply requiring that Congress actually vote up or down the president's rescission requests to a procedure that would break up budget bills into thousands of "bill-ettes" that could be signed or vetoed—gained growing support during the first half of the 1990s.[18]

Passing item veto authority had been part of the 1994 Republican campaign platform, the "Contract with America," and the House passed it in February 1995—on Ronald Reagan's birthday. The Line-Item Veto Act of 1996 ultimately negotiated with the Senate provided the president with an "enhanced rescission" power that reversed the burden of action between the branches. That is, the president's proposed vetoes of specific spending or revenue items would go into effect unless Congress took affirmative action to stop them by passing a bill that reinstated the spending. That bill would, of course, itself be subject to presidential veto, requiring the constitutional two-thirds majority of each chamber to override. As a result, the president could make his rescissions contingent on the support of just one-third plus one member of either the House or the Senate.

President Clinton thus became the first president with legal item veto power—"the most significant delegation of authority by the Congress to the President since the Constitution was ratified," as Senate Appropriations chair Ted Stevens (R-AK), who supported the law, put it. After the law survived an initial court challenge, Clinton used the item veto to propose cancellation of some forty tax and budget items in August and October 1997. However, in June 1998 the Supreme Court ruled on a lawsuit brought by New York City, which had lost health-care funding through one of the Clinton vetoes. The Court held, in a vote of 6 to 3, that the item veto procedure was unconstitutional. The majority observed that the new law, as altered by the president, might well be a better law than the one first passed by Congress. But it was not the one passed by following the constitutional procedure dictating how a bill becomes a law.

Richard Nixon commented in 1990 that the item veto was "a surefire cheer line before conservative audiences" but felt sure "it will never happen. Congress will jump at the chance to curb the power of the executive but it will never limit its own power." Yet just the opposite proved true. The power of the purse was retained by Congress, but only because of the Court's decision—"not," as congressional scholar Louis Fisher sardonically commented, "because legislators were willing to defend their own institution."[19]

SURPLUS POLITICS: A SHORT STORY

By fiscal 1998 the tax increases of 1990 and 1993 on the highest-income Americans had converged with an economic boom and stock market surge that brought those same Americans more income than ever. Revenues leaped, even as the PAYGO and cap rules kept spending increases relatively low. The result was a return to surplus in the year ending September 30, 1998—the first surplus in twenty-nine years.

The brief era of surplus politics proved little more responsible than that of deficit politics. President Clinton tried to seize the high ground by arguing that Social Security should be the first priority into which the new black ink should flow. Instead, in 1998 and 1999, the budget caps were broken by nearly $60 billion as legislators identified various "emergency spending" priorities as a way to evade spending limits. These "emergencies" ranged from provisions preventing Haitian refugees from attaining American citizenship to the authorization of new roads in Alaskan wildlife sanctuaries. Even the 2000 census, which one might understandably identify as a predictable cost, was deemed an emergency requiring uncapped funds. This charade ended when the caps themselves were allowed to expire in 2002.

The 2000 election was in part a referendum on how to spend the surplus—on the Social Security "lockbox" endorsed by Vice President Al Gore or on the tax cuts promised by Texas governor George W. Bush. With Bush's narrow victory, tax cuts became the first priority of 2001. A massive package estimated at $1.35 trillion but in fact certain to cost much more, given the accounting sleight of hand used in that calculation, was signed into law on June 7. Economic conditions rapidly worsened, and other tax revenues sank too with the end of the "dot-com" boom and the impact of the September 11 attacks. At the same time, spending rose, both for reasons related to 9/11 (such as homeland security and the war in Afghanistan) and not (such as the $250 billion farm bill passed in 2002). After a $313 billion projected surplus in fiscal 2001 withered to $127 billion, the fiscal 2002 deficit stood at $158 billion—a $285 billion turnaround in one year.

"Our Due": Deficit Spending, 2002–?

Two years later the federal deficit and national debt had reached record levels. The fiscal 2004 deficit was $412 billion, the largest federal deficit in history in nominal terms—and giving the inflation-adjusted record set at the height of World War II a run for its money, so to speak. Eight percent of the federal budget was already dedicated to the interest on the national debt, which leapfrogged the $7.5 trillion mark in 2004, requiring the statutory debt limit to be raised three times in three years. The $160 billion needed for annual debt service exceeded the amount spent by the federal government on education, homeland security, and law enforcement combined.[20]

In the face of these developments legislators nonetheless expressed little interest in exercising serious control over the power of the purse. President Bush's proposed fiscal 2005 budget was by the administration's own admission at least $360 billion out of balance. That proposal omitted spending for continuing military operations in Iraq or Afghanistan, then running at some $5 billion per month; by January 2005 the projected deficit topped $425 billion. Further, additional large costs loomed on the horizon. Needed reform of the Alternative Minimum Tax would add another half trillion dollars to the bottom line over the next decade. Entitlement reforms ensuring the solvency of Medicare and Social Security would cost tens of billions more. And wrangling over reauthorization of the nation's transportation programs was already under way. The new bill was expected to cost at least $250 billion over six years, funding thousands of loyal partisans' pet projects.[21]

By July 2003 more than three-quarters of those polled by Gallup rated the deficit as a "crisis" or "major problem" for the United States. As the salience of the deficit grew, the president repeatedly requested a return to the 1990s in the form of a new line-item veto that "passed Constitutional muster."²² Some in Congress sought instead to reinstate that decade's PAYGO rules and budgetary caps. The idea, as then, was to require offsets or supermajority approval for legislation that increased the deficit, whether it added spending or subtracted revenue.

While the Senate temporarily approved such rules—targeting, most immediately, the extension of the tax cuts passed in 2001—the House, with strong presidential backing, refused to do so. Its version, though entitled the "Spending Control Act," placed caps only on new spending initiatives and not on new tax reductions. Since, as House Majority Leader Tom DeLay (R-TX) claimed, sufficient legislators still believed "as a matter of philosophy" that cutting taxes would create sufficient economic growth to make "revenues to the government grow," tax cuts should not be considered as foregone revenue and thus as a net cost to the budget. As a result, administration assertions that the deficit would be halved within five years—a projection that curtailed the usual ten-year projection so as to avoid including rapidly increasing entitlement costs and the likely costs of extending the 2001 tax cuts past 2010—were left largely unchallenged. Even the revelation that a $400 billion expansion of Medicare's prescription drug program, passed only after immense pressure from the president and House leadership, would actually cost hundreds of billions more aroused more sputtering than substantive response. As the 2004 election approached, the Senate gave up its argument for the PAYGO rules in order to pass a $146 billion extension of the most popular elements of the 2001 tax package, adding it directly to the deficit. Legislators also approved another law spreading $137 billion in corporate tax breaks to industries ranging from Chinese ceiling-fan producers (at a time of record trade deficits) to energy companies (at a time of record oil prices). The presidential campaign, while paying verbal homage to fiscal discipline and PAYGO rules, nonetheless spurred calls for new spending on the military, education, health care, border protection, and Social Security.²³

All this could be justified, politically if not substantively. For those whose math skills were not dulled by DeLay's supply-side elixir, Vice

President Dick Cheney provided the more pragmatic medicine. "Reagan proved deficits don't matter," he told the cabinet in pressing for the 2003 round of tax cuts. "This is our due."[24] Congress was happy to ask future generations to pay the tab.

BUDGET ENDGAMES & PRESIDENTIAL POWER:
IS THE BUDGET PROCESS "DEAD"?

Deficits do not themselves represent evidence of a shift in the balance of power between the branches; after all, Congress might want to run a deficit over presidential objections, or the two might agree that a deficit is necessary. But as the item veto debate indicates, Congress has been eager to shift power, and thus blame, down Pennsylvania Avenue. Nor did the rest of the budgetary portion of the resurgence regime fare much better. The litmus test is simple—and disturbing: Congress failed most years to pass a budget on time. And after 1999 it never kept spending below the level mandated by its own budget resolution, when it could pass such a resolution at all.

Beginning in fiscal 1990 and continuing through fiscal 2005, Congress managed only twice to enact all the appropriations bills used to fund the federal government by the start of the new fiscal year on October 1. More common is the example of fiscal 1999, when just one of the requisite thirteen bills was passed on schedule and six "continuing resolutions" carrying over government funding into the new year had to be passed in order to buy time to finalize the budget on November 21. In fiscal 2001 it took twenty-one continuing resolutions. In fiscal 2003 the last appropriations bill was not passed until February 3, 2003—a full third of the way into the fiscal year. The delays and, to a lesser extent, the size of the deficit were blamed largely on partisan gridlock between the Republican House and the Democratic Senate. But in fiscal 2004—despite the return of unified government to Capitol Hill after the 2002 midterm elections—only three of thirteen appropriations measures were passed on time, and continuing resolutions once again carried government spending well into January 2004. In fiscal 2005 no budget resolution was ever passed to guide spending, and just one appropriations bill was approved by October 1. The lame-duck session this necessitated meant, as *Congressional Quarterly* dispassionately reported, that "Deci-

more terrorism." Reagan was right: by the end of the arms transfers, the three American hostages in the region released had been replaced by three others and another hostage had been murdered.[34]

The other side of the scandal violated specific congressional prohibitions on aid to the contra rebels. Further, in channeling some $18 million from the Iran arms sales away from the Treasury and direct to Nicaragua, and in soliciting millions more in private donations for contra support, NSC and CIA staff violated the clear constitutional demand that all money spent by the government be appropriated by Congress. Nor (as discussed in chapter 6) was Congress notified of the covert action, despite the strictures of the Intelligence Oversight Act.

No criminal charges were brought against President Reagan himself. Nor did Congress seriously consider direct disciplinary action against him. However, six Reagan staffers, CIA officers, and professional fundraisers pled guilty to charges such as fraud and perjury. Five others, including national security adviser John Poindexter and NSC staffer Oliver North, were convicted of conspiracy, obstruction, and theft of government property. The Poindexter and North convictions were overturned when higher courts found the verdicts had been tainted by the defendants' congressional testimony, for which they had been granted immunity; three other trials were preempted by presidential pardon or the administration's refusal to release classified information. But most Americans shared Walsh's view that the president's men "skirted the law, some of them broke the law, and almost all of them tried to cover up the President's willful activities."[35]

Still, as the investigation spiraled up and around the executive branch, Republicans soured on Walsh and the Independent Counsel Act (ICA). The first President Bush blamed his reelection defeat partly on the continuing investigation, which periodically raised suspicions that the then vice president had been "in the loop" as the contra plans were hatched. Most notably, diary notes long concealed by Caspar Weinberger and released by Walsh in October 1992 suggested that Bush had participated in a key 1986 meeting concerning the arms-for-hostages exchange. As a bitter parting shot at Walsh, Bush pardoned Weinberger and five others on Christmas Eve in 1992. In the pardons' wake, Senate Minority Leader Bob Dole (R-KS) accused Walsh of a "partisan crusade" and attacked him as a "persecutor, not a prosecutor." Reagan attorney general Edwin Meese said Walsh's final report was "an unconscionable act of deception intended to cover up Walsh's own unethical and illegal conduct, divert attention from Walsh's years of prosecutorial incompetence, and abuse and smear the Reagan Administration." Even more neutral observers gently suggested that, "by the time it concluded, Walsh's probe offered a primer on the ills of the law—undue length, unwise prosecutions, excessive zeal on the part of the prosecutors."[36]

Up to that point, Republicans had been the overwhelming targets of independent counsel investigations, for the simple reason that the GOP had controlled the presidency for all but four years since Watergate. Still, it was hard to argue that Iran-contra had not involved serious crimes or that no investigation had been needed. Nor was Walsh himself, as a retired Nixon appointee and lifelong Republican, a noncredible accuser. Nonetheless, the ICA was allowed to expire for a time in 1992 as Republicans angry at Walsh refused to support its extension. Documents in the George H. W. Bush Library suggest that the president was prepared to veto any renewal act that came to his desk. "Independent counsels under the act are, for all practical purposes, completely unaccountable in their exercise of prosecutorial power," the Justice Department concluded in a draft veto message circulated at the White House. Fiscal controls, the department argued, were likewise lacking. And, in any case, "history demonstrates that the Department of Justice is fully capable of performing this function."[37]

But soon the GOP changed its mind, as accusations arose concerning Commerce Secretary Ron Brown's financial dealings and, more tantalizingly, President Clinton himself. Clinton and his wife, Hillary, had invested some $70,000 in an Ozark real estate development called Whitewater starting in the late 1970s, winding up $40,000 in the red on the deal. Their partner in this venture, James McDougal, ran a savings and loan institution that failed in the 1980s S&L collapse, at a cost to taxpayers of some $49 million. Media organizations queried whether the bank had been sufficiently regulated, with attention focusing on the Resolution Trust Corporation (which looked at bankrupt savings and loans), on Hillary Clinton's legal work for the bank (the records for which vanished but then oddly reappeared in the White House residence), and on a loan to McDougal's wife, Susan. With vague but persistent Whitewater allegations making constant headlines in the fall of

1993, President Clinton was pressured to announce support for renewing the ICA. And even before the act was reauthorized in June 1994, Attorney General Janet Reno appointed a special prosecutor to begin moving forward.[38]

An array of independent counsels would soon litter the 1990s political landscape. Five Clinton cabinet officials, among others, were investigated. Brown was killed in a plane crash in Croatia, short-circuiting the probe into his business dealings; but the inquiry into allegations that Agriculture Secretary Mike Espy took bribes from Tyson Foods dragged on for four years and cost $23 million before he was acquitted on thirty counts by a federal jury in late 1998. Housing and Urban Development Secretary Henry Cisneros was investigated on charges that he lied to the FBI in his background check about payments to a former mistress. More than four years after independent counsel David Barrett took the case in May 1995, Cisneros pled guilty to a misdemeanor and paid a fine. No charges were brought after additional investigations of Interior Secretary Bruce Babbitt or Labor Secretary Alexis Herman. The huge expenditure of resource and reputation these probes represented led many Democrats to turn against the independent counsel process.

But it was the Whitewater investigation that eventually swelled into the biggest political scandal since Watergate, threatening to swallow up the president and succeeding in swallowing up the ICA. With the reauthorization of the act in 1994, Attorney General Reno had requested the Special Division to appoint a counsel. Rather than keep Reno's original appointee, Robert Fiske, on the job, the panel chose former solicitor general Kenneth Starr. White House counsel Bernard Nussbaum proved prescient in predicting that the new ICA would be "a roving searchlight,"[39] for Starr's investigation would encompass not just Whitewater but "Fostergate," "Travelgate," "Filegate," and eventually "Monicagate." That is, it included exploration of the conspiracy theory holding that White House staffer Vince Foster's suicide was a cover for his murder by the Clintons; of the firing of White House Travel Office employees in 1993; and of the acquisition by White House staffers of confidential FBI files concerning prominent Republicans, raising shades of the Nixon "enemies list." In each of these, the president was cleared of personal wrongdoing; but not so in the intensely personal case of Monica Lewinsky. Clinton's affair with Lewinsky beginning in late 1995 became tangled in his defense against a sexual harassment civil suit brought by former Arkansas state employee Paula Jones. In a deposition Clinton denied any relationship with Lewinsky. Later he allegedly sought to have Lewinsky lie about their affair. These actions ultimately led to his impeachment by the House on near-perfect party lines. Clinton's ordeal ended only when he was acquitted in the Senate, which did not muster even a majority on either article of impeachment.

The path to that point requires more explication than space here allows.[40] But along the way, the Starr investigation became nearly as reviled as Clinton's behavior. As a Reagan judicial appointee, Starr had solidly partisan credentials. During his investigations he continued to work for outside clients (some clearly linked to anti-Clinton organizations), earning over $1 million in 1997 from his private law firm. Pre-Lewinsky, he even offered professional advice to Paula Jones's legal team.[41] The decision of the House to pursue impeachment despite clear public opinion against that course—the votes were taken in lame duck session, after the extraordinarily rare gain of seats by the president's party in the 1998 midterm election—led to still further charges of rabid partisanship against Clinton's pursuers.

Clearly the ICA had not ended executive corruption; but nor had it done a particularly good job in investigating it. Many became newly sympathetic to Justice Scalia's dissent in *Morrison v. Olson* suggesting that the structure of the statute made it a better tool for political vitriol than for impartial, accountable law enforcement. The ICA was faulted for its cost, its scope, and its zeal. The Clinton administration investigations alone cost some $100 million, more than half of it for the Whitewater (et al.) investigation, which ran through four independent counsels before finally closing down in March 2004. At the same time, nearly five years after the expiration of the ICA, the long-defunct Cisneros case was still costing taxpayers $1.6 million per year. It was clear that independent counsels had few constraints against digging deep into even unpromising prosecutorial seams. Indeed, their incentives ran the other way. As *Morrison v. Olson*'s Ted Olson put it, "If you are given a fishing license which has the name of the fish on it, and you don't come back with that fish, you've failed."[42]

In a long letter to the House Judiciary subcommittee considering reauthorization of the ICA, the Justice Department concluded in April 1999 that "public confidence has not been materially enhanced by the process set out in the Independent Counsel Act. . . . The decisions of whether and when to turn to an outside Special Counsel to handle a matter is one that is best left to the discretion of the Attorney General."[43] These outcomes were in plain contradiction to the expectations of the statute's framers. And later that year, the statute was allowed to expire. The circle had come full.

THE BEST PRESIDENT MONEY CAN BUY?

"The [campaign finance reform] system we created in the 1970s essentially collapsed" in 1996, concluded the political scientist Anthony Corrado after that year's election. Five years later, Sen. Zell Miller (D-GA) came to the same conclusion, albeit more colorfully. After a day of fundraising calls, he wrote, "I always left that room feeling like a cheap prostitute who'd had a busy day."[44]

How had the hopes of campaign finance reform slid so far so fast?

The first push came quickly. The 1974 Federal Election Campaign Act (FECA) amendments were immediately challenged in court, and by January 1976 the Supreme Court's landmark ruling in *Buckley v. Valeo* had reshaped the regulatory landscape. To attack corruption was a legitimate goal, the Court held, and thus some constraints could be placed on campaigns and campaigners. Most notably, contributions could be limited (unless they were to one's own campaign, since presumably that sort of donation could not make one more corrupt than one already was). Spending on presidential campaigns could also be limited—so long as candidates for the presidency opted into the new system of federal financing. However, most of the other spending limits were declared to be unconstitutional. To limit spending was to violate candidates' right to free speech, since the Court held that money used in campaigning was tantamount to speech. The majority opinion argued:

> The First Amendment denies government the power to determine that spending to promote one's political views is wasteful, excessive, or unwise. In the free society ordained by our Constitution, it is not

the government but the people, individually as citizens and candidates and collectively as associations and political committees, who must retain control over the quantity and range of debate on public issues in a political campaign.[45]

Truncating spending would truncate that debate.

Since in the wake of *Buckley* spending continued to rise but individual contributions remained limited to one thousand dollars per election, funding from PACs became more appealing. An individual could give five thousand dollars to a PAC, which could give that much to a candidate, five times the limit otherwise. Thus the PAC population exploded, doubling by 1977 and expanding sixfold, to over four thousand, by 1990. In 1974 labor accounted for half of PAC spending; by 1984, with corporate interests catching on, labor's share had fallen below 20 percent. PAC influence was enhanced all the more by the rapidly increasing costs of campaigning, as television advertising became the communication of choice for candidates and as computer technology, pollsters, and consultants became standard features of professional campaigns. In 1960 federal candidates spent $14 million on advertising—thirty years later the figure was close to $1 billion.[46] Fund-raising took increasing amounts of candidates' time and energy.

Independent expenditures, supposedly unaffiliated with campaigns, also skyrocketed during this time. *Buckley v. Valeo* had held that so long as organizations pressing a cause did not use the so-called magic words (e.g., "vote for" or "vote against") advocating a candidate's election or defeat, they could spend whatever they wanted on political advertising. The famous "Willie Horton" ad from 1988 attacking Democratic candidate Michael Dukakis was run not by the Bush campaign but by the National Security Political Action Committee. The "Harry and Louise" ads opposing Clinton's 1993 health-care plan were run not by the RNC but by the Health Insurance Association of America. In 1996 the AFL-CIO spent $35 million on ads attacking the labor stands of Republican candidates.[47]

Perhaps unintentionally, the FEC soon opened up another source of funding. In 1978 it approved regulations that allowed donations to state political parties for "party building" expenditures to be regulated by state law, not by the federal government. Since most states had far looser limits on contributions than FECA did, hugely increased amounts of money could suddenly be given in the name of voter registration drives or for the purchase of buttons and bumper stickers. Building on this, new amendments to FECA in 1979 allowed state parties to support the campaign activities of federal candidates. Thus was born the "soft money" loophole. Money given to the state parties under state rules could now be spent in those states to promote presidential candidates, outside the federal "hard" caps on contributions. Until 1991 such "soft" donations did not even have to be disclosed.[48]

In 1988 the Dukakis campaign raised over $40 million in this manner, outpacing George H. W. Bush's Team 100 effort (named for those raising more than one hundred thousand dollars) more than two to one. By the 1996 election both parties had effectively co-opted this money for their national candidates. State parties funded "issue advocacy" advertisements, which were supposed to build the party by, coincidentally, promoting its presidential candidate. Bill Clinton, who had promised during the 1992 campaign to end soft money, proposed a new campaign finance law in 1993 that would have imposed voluntary spending caps in congressional races in return for free television time; this went nowhere. After the 1994 election proved disastrous for Democrats, Clinton instead became extraordinarily aggressive in raising soft money, hosting a series of White House coffees, movies, and overnight stays for big donors. A DNC pamphlet offered various options for those seeking presidential access: one hundred thousand dollars, for example, was worth a dinner invitation.[49]

Clinton was the beneficiary of $40 million worth of soft money ads starting in the fall of 1995 as he sought both to bolster his cause during the budget shutdown and to link his likely opponent, Sen. Bob Dole, to increasingly unpopular House Speaker Newt Gingrich. ("The Dole-Gingrich budget tried to cut Medicare $270 billion," intoned one ad, complete with grainy black-and-white footage of the two Republicans looking appropriately disdainful of senior citizens.) Given that they were scripted in the White House, it was hard to claim the ads constituted bottom-up party building by the state parties. "For all intents and purposes," wrote the *Washington Post,* "the DNC became an extension of the Clinton-Gore campaign, . . . effectively obliterating the spending cap." The White House itself proved an effective tool in the reelection campaign. Nor did the RNC follow a much different strategy, even though without the trappings of the presidency it was ultimately less successful. The parties between them spent $260 million in soft money in 1996.[50]

By 2000 that figure had nearly doubled to $495 million. And the overall amount of hard money spent on campaigns also spiraled ever upward: in 2000 and 2004 presidential candidate George W. Bush opted out of public financing and its spending limits altogether during his primary runs. This enabled him to spend over $90 million in the prenomination period of 2000. Just four years later he compiled an astonishing $263 million war chest for the primaries in 2004—primaries in which he was unopposed. This allowed ads attacking the presumptive Democratic nominee, Sen. John Kerry (D-MA), to begin running eight months before the general election. Indeed, Bush spent approximately $50 million on his campaign in March 2004 alone, more than $40 million of it on advertising. But Kerry also opted out of public financing in 2004 (as did Democratic rival Howard Dean), compounding the blow to the FECA regime in the name of staying competitive with the president's reelection effort. Kerry himself raised $236 million—by far a new Democratic record—in the preconvention period. Thus the candidates combined collected nearly half a billion dollars, not including party spending or factoring in another $150 million in public financing for the general election. Recall that in 1972 the figure that so shocked observers was a combined total of $90 million.

The FEC, evenly divided between Democratic and Republican commissioners, usually stalemated, unable to take action when charges of campaign malfeasance arose. Sen. Mitch McConnell (R-KY), a strong opponent of campaign finance regulation, charged that FECA had, quite simply, created a "regulatory disaster—where grassroots volunteers have been replaced by lawyers and accountants, candidates break the law with impunity, and wealthy contributors feed millions of dollars through innumerable backdoor accounts."[51]

One response was the Bipartisan Campaign Reform Act (BCRA) of 2002, more popularly known as the McCain-Feingold Act, after its Senate sponsors. BCRA marked a major shift in the post-Watergate campaign finance regime. It banned soft money, or sought to. National parties and federal candidates could not solicit or spend funds that did not comply with federal contribution limits and source prohibitions; state parties could spend only hard money on activities that affected federal elections. Further, contribution caps were adjusted upward: these were doubled to two thousand dollars per candidate per election and thereafter tied to inflation. Under the so-called millionaire's amendment, if a candidate faced an opponent financing his or her own campaign and spending over a certain amount, contribution caps could be dramatically higher.

Controversially, BCRA also cracked down on independent expenditures. All ads aired within a month of a primary election or two months of a general election that mentioned a federal candidate were deemed to be devoted not to issues but to getting that candidate into or out of office. Only hard money could be used to pay for such ads: this meant that issue advocacy groups could not run them unless their funding was disclosed and from sources allowed by federal law (i.e., not union or corporate treasuries).

Unimpressed by these changes, Senator McConnell was among the first to sue. But when the Supreme Court ruled on the matter in December 2003, it surprised many by largely upholding the law, including the First Amendment implications of the issue ad ban (the "magic words" test, held the Court, "is functionally meaningless," finding that the ads in question were clearly designed to influence election outcomes). By a 5–4 vote, the Court held that soft money indebted officeholders even if no obvious trade of money for policy—à la the "milk money" scandal—was enacted. A visible quid pro quo standard, the majority held, was a "crabbed view of corruption, and particularly of the appearance of corruption" that ignored "common sense, and the realities of political fundraising. . . . The best means of prevention is to identify and to remove the temptation."[52]

Yet, even before the ink was dry on the Court's opinion, candidates had devised ways of undercutting the soft money ban. The political parties—long shorn of their monopoly over nominations, now seemingly denied much of their ability to fund campaigns—found themselves handicapped, unable to sanction or reward candidates aligned with their collective philosophy and thus unable to plausibly bridge the chasm between Congress and White House. They sought, with some success, to raise new hard money, using Internet appeals and sophisticated market research technology. But important new players arose too—most notably the so-called 527 committees, named after their designation in the Internal Revenue Code. Independent of parties and candidates and not subject to rules of transparency or disclosure, 527 groups sprang up during 2003 and began collecting soft money in large amounts to be used for voter registration and "education" drives as well as for advertisements. The FEC declined to regulate these groups, at least for 2004, angering proponents of the new law and laying the groundwork for what the RNC chair called a "free-for-all."[53]

Further, while the 1972 ITT scandal helped prompt public financing of the national party conventions, by 2000 the DNC had raised more than $35 million in private donations to support its convention activities in Los Angeles. In 2004 the Republican party raised more than double that. In both cases funds came largely from corporate interests that could not otherwise have legally made sizable contributions to the parties.

In 2000, scholars concluded, "the financing of the 2000 elections bore a greater resemblance to campaign funding prior to the passage of the FECA than to the patterns that were supposed to prevail after it." The same could be said for the 2004 campaign. As the Court itself admitted in *McConnell:* "We are under no illusion that BCRA will be the last congressional statement on the matter. Money, like water, will always find an outlet."[54] By the time the Court wrote, it already had.

VI. THE RESURGENCE RECEDES, PART II

Peace & War

Developments in the areas of budgeting and executive ethics were parallel to those in the other areas under study. Indeed, as the resurgence regime receded, presidential power over matters both of peace (in unilateral expressions of executive authority) and war (in military and intelligence operations) was enhanced. The result, by the start of the twenty-first century, was inter-branch terrain altered from the Watergate era, but still recognizable, after Congress's intervening surge and decline.

EXECUTIVE AUTHORITY & GOVERNMENTAL SECRECY

President Ronald Reagan's White House counselor and attorney general Edwin Meese recalled in his memoirs that one "major threat to constitutional government" faced by the Reagan administration "was the legislative opportunism that arose out of the Watergate controversies during the early 1970s. Congress had used this episode to expand its power in various ways vis-a-vis the executive branch."[1] Reagan intended to turn this around.

By his second term, many academic observers believed he had succeeded. "More than any other modern president," one wrote, "Ronald Reagan has moved with dedication and comprehensiveness to take hold of the administrative machinery of government." Another concluded that Reagan's presidency was "postmodern" in that it had accelerated and consolidated trends of the post-FDR "modern" presidency discussed in chapter 2 in ways that added up to a newly empowered office.

The development was praised by some as a realistic approach to the varied constraints on presidential power; others decried it as an arrogation of power.[2]

BUILDING EXECUTIVE CAPACITY

Responsiveness & Centralization

Presidents starting with Reagan paid renewed attention to controlling appointments throughout the executive branch. With an eye toward what former OMB staffer Richard Nathan called the "ideological purity of the cabinet and subcabinet," Reagan and his staff put significant effort into placing hundreds of well-vetted loyalists across the bureaucracy. New appointees in 1980–81 were oriented to their departments not by the departmental staff but by conservative think tanks. Civil service reform passed in 1978 had given presidents more leeway over high-level appointments to what was now called the Senior Executive Service: Reagan used this tool to remove numerous career officials from key positions and to replace them with his own partisans, while using staffing cuts to eliminate entire offices of civil servants. Reagan also aggressively used his power to make recess appointments to evade Senate confirmation of nominees—doing so nearly 250 times in eight years. After failing to abolish the Legal Services Corporation, for example, he appointed its entire board in this manner.[3] Judicial appointments followed a like path. The merit-based judicial screening process established in the Carter administration was replaced in 1981 by a President's Committee on Federal Judicial Selection, which institutionalized close ideological review of candidates for the bench.[4]

Future presidents took note. They stressed "responsive competence" over the old public administration ideal of "neutral competence"—and responsiveness over competence generally. The Iran-contra projects of the NSC staff, discussed in the last chapter, serve as a case in point; but this level of loyalty was hardly considered a fatal flaw on a White House résumé. As Clinton staffer George Stephanopoulos put it, "doing the president's bidding was my reason for being; his favor was my fuel." George W. Bush cabinet secretary Paul O'Neill, with his long background in policy analysis, chafed under the White House's demands for "personal loyalty" and that staffers "stick together, *no matter what,*" even if empirical analysis dictated a different policy path. True presidential control of the bureaucracy remained elusive, but presidents kept trying, as the 1994 reorganization of the OMB and the 2001 "President's Management Agenda" made clear. Under the latter, President Bush sought to privatize as many as 850,000 jobs in the federal bureaucracy while utilizing a new Program Assessment Rating Tool to link funding levels to agency performance.[5]

As ever, managerial efficiency was usually perceived to flow from increased attention to the priorities of the current administration. And thus appointment strategies remained a critical tool. By the mid-1990s, what Paul Light has termed "thickening government" gave presidents some 2,400 high-ranking positions to fill—up by a third even from 1980—reaching down into the middle management ranks of most federal agencies. In 2001 incoming president George W. Bush controlled nearly 500 slots from the deputy assistant secretary level up, as well as 185 ambassadors, 200 U.S. attorneys and marshals, more than 700+ non-career senior executive service managers, and 1,400 lower-level political appointees scattered around the bureaucracy. Presidents built up the White House Personnel Office so as to maintain strict control over the responsiveness of their appointees, often drawing them from lobbies or industries sympathetic to the administration and deeply interested in a given substantive area. The Bush personnel office worked in close conjunction with political adviser Karl Rove and the Office of Political Affairs. While the slow pace of the confirmation process for those nominees requiring Senate approbation was decried, in the end few nominees were denied.[6]

Sometimes presidents don't want to fill a vacancy—George W. Bush indicated his feelings about the Environmental Protection Agency's (EPA) Office of Regulatory Enforcement by leaving it vacant for more than a year and a half.[7] But where presidents did grow tired of waiting, acting and recess appointments were common. Clinton, while more reluctant to use recess appointments than Reagan (or George H. W. Bush), did so in several high-profile cases that angered senators, including the appointment of the openly gay ambassador James Hormel in 1999. Clinton also made a recess appointment to the federal judiciary in late 2000, only the second time since the 1950s that strategy had been utilized; he resubmitted the judge's name, successfully, for regular confirmation in 2001. George W. Bush pushed the recess strategy much further in early 2004 by using it to appoint two contested circuit court nominees whose pending nominations had been filibustered on the Senate floor. Democratic senators complained that the move was "questionably legal and politically shabby," but they had little recourse. Later Bush was able to trade a promise not to make further recess appointments in 2004 in exchange for the quick confirmation of twenty-five less controversial nominees.[8]

Another fundamental piece of this strategy was the use of centralization, as described earlier: the shift of policy-making capacity out of the wider executive bureaucracy into the White House itself. One indicator of this trend was that the size of the White House staff largely bounced back from its early pruning by Carter. As noted in chapter 4, some of that decline had reflected accounting shifts rather than changes in the actual personnel available to the president; in 1980, for example, the number of authorized personnel was held constant, but under the pressures of the reelection campaign a large number of staff were detailed from other agencies to the White House. Carter's commitment to cabinet government, so fervent in 1976, waned throughout his term. As early as 1977—and most visibly after 1979, when he fired five members of his cabinet—he began to give White House aides more say in the policy-making process. That same summer, Carter also abandoned the idea of operating without a chief of staff, naming Hamilton Jordan to that post; all subsequent presidents have utilized one. The Nixon White House has, in a real sense, become the "normal" model for presidential staff organization.[9]

This development both meant and reflected a larger and more hierarchical White House. As important as the "general secretariat"[10] centered in the chief of staff's office was the increasing functional specialization and layering within its various staff units. The EOP housed aides—and aides to aides—devoted to policy-making (domestic, economic, and national security), communications (with the public, the bureaucracy, Congress, and interest groups), and internal coordination and administration. One study found that an index combining the number of titles, levels of hierarchy, and topics of specialization within the White House staff more than doubled between the 1970s and 1990s.[11] New staff units sprang up to reflect salient presidential or simply societal concerns, from the drug czar to an AIDS outreach office to one exploring faith-based initiatives. The Domestic Policy Council was restored; like other cabinet-level councils it has been important largely for its White House staff secretariat. The importance of the National Security Council (NSC) staff, especially its head, is well known. Less prominently, the National Economic Council was created in 1993 to integrate foreign and domestic policies with economic implications; its workings were likewise dominated by its directors, Democrats Robert Rubin and Gene Sperling and Republicans Larry Lindsey and Stephen Friedman. The various pledges during the 1992 campaign to cut the size of the White House staff—by a quarter, Clinton promised—suggest the continuing resonance of the issue, but it proved a promise not worth keeping and only briefly kept.[12] While questions remained as to whether centralization always provided presidents with the resources they needed for effective policy deliberation, as a source of resources and capacity for exercising authority the White House at the dawn of the twenty-first century seemed undiminished by Watergate.

Another facet of centralization was the use of direct executive action—executive orders, presidential decision memoranda, and the like—as a means of implementing policy preferences by directing bureaucratic action without explicit legislative authorization. With Congress at least partly in opposition hands for most post-Watergate presidents, this strategy became increasingly tempting. As Clinton aide Rahm Emanuel put it in 1998, "sometimes we use [an executive order] in reaction to legislative delay or setbacks. Obviously, you'd rather pass legislation that can do X, but you're willing to make whatever progress you can on an agenda item." Orders could be used to issue binding directives to members of the executive branch; to shape regulatory action; to reorganize agencies or decision-making processes; to control the military; or even to make new policy, especially in areas where Congress had not acted or where presidential initiative was generally accepted. Whether or not divided government was the cause, and scholars disagree on this point, the number of significant executive orders issued by presidents has risen dramatically over time. One exhaustive survey of the executive orders issued between 1936 and 1999 found that, after a World War II–induced surge in their use in the 1940s, the proportion of substantively significant orders tripled from the 1950s to the

1990s. Another study similarly concluded that the number and scope of substantive orders have risen impressively since the Reagan administration, aimed at "efficient, effective, prompt, and controlled action within the executive branch."[13] Recent examples include the Clinton set-aside, by proclamation, of nearly 2 million acres of land in Utah as a national monument and George W. Bush's faith-based social services initiative.

In 1994 the Supreme Court held that presidential executive orders were not subject to the Administrative Procedures Act—thus no public comment or balanced research process is required in their development. Such orders are, however, supposed to be grounded in statutory authority. Where so—and at times they rely instead on the happily vague "executive power" of the Constitution—they often show the unintended consequences of congressional delegation. Clinton's Utah proclamation, for example, rested on a 1906 statute long forgotten by Congress but not by presidents. Further, as noted earlier, congressional efforts to constrain executive authority sometimes legitimate it. A good example is the International Emergency Economic Powers Act. The IEEPA was passed in 1977 to rein in the use of its titular powers by carefully specifying when they might be used. But by providing a process for declaring emergencies as a means of preventing economic transactions with disfavored regimes, Congress formalized a previously shadowy claim to power. Presidents took advantage: between 1979 and 2000 nearly thirty "national emergencies" were invoked to seize the assets of and prohibit trade with countries ranging from Iran (1979) to Libya (1986) to Afghanistan (1999). Sometimes these "emergencies" simply provided a means for unilateral implementation of policy preferences, as when President Reagan applied IEEPA sanctions against Nicaragua in 1985 as a substitute for those Congress had refused to enact.[14]

Executive orders are hardly unfettered. For one thing, they can be overturned by court or Congress. But outright negation is relatively rare. And in the interim they can give the president power to shape or reshape the policy landscape, often under the political radar screen.[15]

For example, take the rise of "central clearance" within the OMB in the 1940s (discussed in chapter 2). OMB had grown to be a powerful tool of presidential control over the executive branch; as we have seen, Congress eventually responded by requiring Senate confirmation of its top two positions and creating the CBO as a legislative analogue. But in the 1980s, using executive orders, President Reagan expanded OMB's functions in another direction. Now the agency was to review department-issued regulations.

This sounds dull. But agency rule making is extraordinarily powerful, turning vague statutes into specific mandates on individuals and businesses. The substance of any law is in many ways determined by the regulations issued in its name.[16] Thus as Reagan sought to expand presidential power over the bureaucracy, as a way of enforcing bureaucratic responsiveness, the implications were far-reaching. If nothing else, it was hoped the exercise would limit the number of new regulations published, itself a Reagan policy goal.

President Nixon, perhaps not surprisingly, had been the first to assert a regulatory approval power within OMB; Ford and Carter had directed agencies to consider the inflationary impact and cost-benefit ratio of new regulations. But Nixon's strategem never took hold, and the Ford and Carter directives applied no sanctions. Reagan, on the other hand, aimed to stop regulations that imposed any net cost at all, to anyone. In February 1981 he issued an order grounded rather vaguely in "the authority vested in me as President by the Constitution and laws of the United States," stating flatly that "regulatory action shall not be undertaken unless the potential benefits to society for the regulation outweigh the potential costs to society." OMB had the power to recommend that regulations be withdrawn if they could not "be reformulated to meet its objections."

The process as it developed was largely off the record—over the phone or via confidential comments—which served to shield it from legislative or judicial review. Further, since (under the Paperwork Reduction Act of 1979) all the forms bureaus wanted to use for research had to be cleared through OMB, that agency's staff announced it would not approve departmental efforts to collect the information needed to justify the costs of new regulations. By 1985 a more direct route—simply denying bureaus the funds for regulatory research—had been chosen; that year also marked the issuance of a new executive order requiring agencies to create an annual list of "anticipated regulatory actions" for OMB review. One legal analysis concluded that this meant OMB had "virtually unbridled power to supervise or veto almost any agency's activity without public scrutiny." Despite congressional grumbling, there was little legislative reaction; and regulatory review remained in place through the Bush, Clinton, and Bush presidencies. Upon taking office, President Clinton placed a moratorium on George H. W. Bush's pending regulations; George W. Bush, in turn, did the same to Clinton's.[17] The latter Bush's desire for regulatory responsiveness in environmental policy attracted perhaps the most attention, as scientists charged that scholarly, technical review was being shunted aside in favor of political considerations, usually favoring development over preservation.[18] Nonetheless, regulatory review had become a fixture, if not one with any statutory approbation.

Executive orders were not the only presidential tool used to centralize authority over policy: the use of presidential memoranda also increased dramatically. Memoranda direct departments to act in a certain way. They are similar to executive orders and may supplement them, but they do not, unlike those orders, need to be published in the *Federal Register*. President Reagan signed a memorandum freezing federal hiring on his Inauguration Day, even before he had left the Capitol. George H. W. Bush used memoranda to extend the Reagan regime by imposing a moratorium on all rule making and by shifting regulatory oversight to an aggressively deregulatory Council on Competitiveness headed by Vice President Dan Quayle, whose authority was to extend even to independent regulatory commissions (and which, as an executive creation, could claim executive privilege when asked for records of its deliberations). President Clinton used a memorandum to overturn the Reagan/Bush "Mexico City" policy banning funds for foreign organizations advising family planning, a decision itself reversed by George W. Bush immediately upon his own accession to the presidency in 2001. Indeed, according to one scholar Clinton "transformed" the use of memoranda, issuing more than 530 of them during his eight years in office; other controversial examples from the 1990s include decisions to direct the Food and Drug Administration to reconsider imports of the abortion-related drug RU-486, to order the secretary of defense to draft language "ending discrimination on the basis of sexual orientation" within the armed forces, and to declare a patients' "bill of rights" within federal health-care programs. By their nature, memoranda are hard to challenge—harder than executive orders, though they may have almost identical effects.[19]

Another variant of memoranda deals with national security issues and is normally drafted through the NSC staffing process. National security directives—given different names by different administrations[20]—are normally classified, and thus no good overall count can be made. But in the mid-1980s such directives underlay the policies in Iran and Nicaragua that ran afoul of the statutory bans on arms sales to terrorists and aid to the contras. They provided negotiation instructions to diplomats working on nuclear arms control and shaped the Strategic Defense Initiative. They even implemented the "Plan for Economic Warfare Against the USSR," which laid out aggressive plans for hindering Soviet commerce. Needless to say, this plan did not receive congressional review or approval. Legislative efforts in the late 1980s to obtain a list of national security directives failed, even after the Iran-contra investigation had presumably weakened the president's hand. Rep. Lee Hamilton (D-IN) complained in 1988 that such directives "are revealed to Congress only under irregular, arbitrary, or even accidental circumstances, if at all."[21]

Signing Statements

Chapter 3 noted several examples of President Nixon's use of signing statements, designed to make clear that the president had no intention of implementing part of a bill he was signing into law. But President Reagan far surpassed the Nixon record in this regard. The goal was to direct executive agencies in their interpretation of the law as they drafted rules or made other decisions about implementation—including whether to do so in the first place. Secondarily, presidents hoped to influence judicial readings of a given statute by putting executive office views into its legislative history. Either way, Reagan and his successors made frequent use of the tactic.

One Reagan-era example harkened back to the questions of secrecy raised earlier (and renewed later). Reagan had issued a national security directive with strict enforcement provisions governing the disclosure of information deemed sensitive. When Congress passed a bill forbidding the administration from enforcing those provisions, Reagan signed it— but wrote that "this provision raises profound constitutional concerns," since it "impermissibly interfered with my ability to prevent unauthorized disclosures of our most sensitive diplomatic, military, and intelligence activities." Thus, "in accordance with my sworn obligation to preserve, protect, and defend the Constitution, [this section] will be considered of no force or effect." Reagan likewise refused to enforce language requiring that reports by the CIA inspector general be submitted to the legislative intelligence committees.

Presidents throughout this period routinely included language in signing statements that would in their view "unconstitutionally constrain my authority regarding the conduct of diplomacy and my authority as Commander-in-Chief." And, when signing authorizations of force, they uniformly asserted their refusal to concede the constitutionality of the War Powers Resolution (WPR).[22]

These claims to constitutional interpretation have gone beyond national security issues. George H. W. Bush, for instance, used a signing statement to direct the Energy Department to administer language requiring affirmative action contracting "in a constitutional manner"—that is, so as not to include affirmative action contracting. Reagan and both Bushes argued that Congress cannot interfere with any processes leading to the potential proposal of measures that presidents might deem "necessary and expedient," as Article II puts it, for legislators to enact; for instance, in spring 2001 George W. Bush asserted that a section directing the administration to submit legislation concerning mad-cow and foot-and-mouth diseases would be interpreted instead as a suggestion. Clinton added the appointment power to the list. In October 1999 he filled a newly created National Nuclear Security Administration with extant Energy Department staff in defiance of congressional dictates. George W. Bush in 2001 followed his example, rejecting legislative specification of the pool of potential appointees for a Defense Department post.[23]

Such signing statements, claiming the right to selective execution of the laws, are a form of line-item veto dressed up as constitutional commentary. They have not gone entirely uncontested—a circuit court once scolded the Reagan administration's effort to avoid parts of a contracting act by saying that "this claim of right for the President to declare statutes unconstitutional and to declare his refusal to execute them . . . is dubious at best." But in other cases the Supreme Court has at least implicitly endorsed the practice; at the least, such presidential assertions have proven hard to overturn, and more often than not Congress has not tried. Presidents, in turn, have tended to act in accord with the Justice Department's Office of Legal Counsel (OLC) guidance drafted in 1994: "where the President believes that an enactment unconstitutionally limits his powers, he has the authority to defend his office and decline to abide by it, unless he is convinced that the Court would disagree with his assessment."[24] On that last score, they have proven hard to convince.

Overlooked Oversight

Meanwhile, the Supreme Court's landmark 1983 decision in *INS v. Chadha* made it harder for Congress to conduct oversight over other aspects of the administrative presidency. Recall that the use of the legislative veto, checking the executive's use of delegated powers, had exploded in the 1970s as a pragmatic means of dealing with the explosion of the regulatory state. It had become, as Justice Byron White put it, "a central means by which Congress secure[d] the accountability of executive and independent agencies."

The *Chadha* case came about when Mr. Jagdish Chadha sued the government after the attorney general's suspension of his deportation was vetoed by the House. Though the circuit court had found narrower grounds for ruling in Chadha's favor, the Supreme Court declared that the legislative veto mechanism was itself unconstitutional. In so doing, it set aside some two hundred statutory provisions. The core rationale was that the legislative veto violated the presentment clause of the Constitution, that is, the portion of Article I laying out how a bill becomes a law. That "step-by-step, deliberate and deliberative" process requires both chambers of Congress to pass the same measure and to present it to the president for his signature. Thus, extending the process to require that the measure return to Congress in some manner for reconsideration and action "essentially legislative in purpose and effect" was not acceptable. That the act allowed for a one-chamber veto only made things worse, since this violated the principle of bicameralism as well.

In a lengthy, peeved dissent, Justice White argued that there was a good case for the legislative veto's basic constitutionality, since its exercise did not write new law but merely fulfilled the terms of the original statute. Overturning all such vetoes, he thought, went much too far and did damage to Congress's practical ability to rein in "the modern administrative state." The result was to empower presidents—who had no such presentment limitations placed on their use of executive orders and proclamations and the new law those tools created.[25]

Some have argued that the overturning of the legislative veto mattered little substantively, because Congress didn't really want the responsibility that came with its aggressive use. This has the ring of truth to it. Either way, there is little doubt that congressional oversight has decreased dramatically from the mid-1970s. Vigorous hearings on matters of policy, as opposed to allegations of wrongdoing, have dropped off sharply: one political scientist found that congressional committees met, in aggregate, only half as many days in 1997 as in 1975 and that fewer of those days were devoted to oversight activities. Instead of agency-by-agency review during authorization hearings, governmental functions were increasingly reauthorized in huge omnibus legislation (or quite frequently not at all, relying on recurring waivers of authorization authority through the annual budget appropriation). "Lately," one 2004 analysis concluded, "the watchdog is getting a reputation for sleeping on the job."[26]

Proxy overseers, such as the inspectors general, have also been criticized. Some complain that Congress no longer used the inspector general process effectively; others were more concerned that inspectors general, like their 1978 counterparts the independent counsels, had too many incentives to find abuse and wasteful spending even where little objectively existed. Still others accused presidents of politicizing the inspector general corps. For example, George W. Bush, upon taking office, dismissed a number of agency inspectors general and also appointed the daughter of Supreme Court Chief Justice William Rehnquist as inspector general at Health and Human Services. An ex-Whitewater investigator later became chief of staff of the Defense Department's inspector general staff. Former congressional counsel Stephen Ryan argued in 2003 that inspectors general were "pushing their conception of what's good public policy" instead of auditing the efficient implementation of established policy.[27] But from the presidential vantage, this may not be a bad thing.

Responsiveness & Law Enforcement

Despite its kinship to the Nixon Responsiveness Program—indeed, it has been judged by most to be more successful—the reborn "administrative presidency" was not extended to law enforcement agencies as vigorously as its predecessor. No credible analogue to Operation CHAOS, or COINTELPRO, or the Huston Plan emerged in the 1980s or 1990s. Still, even here the resurgence against executive discretion in law enforcement came under fire. The Carter Justice Department had prosecuted and convicted two top Nixon-era FBI officials for their role in authorizing COINTELPRO break-ins; Reagan pardoned them. A 1981 executive order superseded Carter's more stringent constraints on the FBI's use of infiltration techniques. And in 1983 Attorney General William French Smith issued domestic security guidelines that significantly amended the Levi guidelines of 1976.

Smith eliminated Levi's earlier requirement for a preliminary investigation to prove the need for a full-blown investigation. Further, where a full investigation could previously be justified only if "specific and articulable facts" showed that an individual or group was breaking the law, and in a violent way, the Smith guidelines allowed domestic security investigations if "facts or circumstances reasonably indicate that two or more persons are engaged in an enterprise for the purpose of furthering political or social goals wholly or in part through activities that involve force or violence." Beyond weakening the evidentiary requirement (from "articulable fact" to "reasonable indication"), the language allowed the FBI to investigate groups that "knowingly support" another group that is violent, even if they did not themselves commit criminal acts. And, where the resurgence regime guidelines had considered activities to be conducted under the First Amendment unless shown otherwise, the new rules stress that an organization's rhetoric inciting violence or criminal activity is fair game for investigation "unless it is apparent . . . that there is no prospect of harm." While such inquiries could not be based solely on activities reflecting free speech, infiltration of organizations could be authorized even if it occurred "in a manner that may influence the exercise of rights protected by the First Amendment." An appeal court ruled in 1984 that this was good enough: the FBI "need not wait till the bombs begin to go off, or even till the bomb factory is found."[28]

As protest grew over Reagan's foreign policies, especially in Central America, the bureau was used to monitor and infiltrate groups that opposed those policies. The Committee in Solidarity with the People of El Salvador (CISPES), the Central America Solidarity Association, the Inter-Religious Task Force, and other groups were the target of lengthy investigations, which accelerated after a small bomb exploded in the U.S. Capitol in 1983. As with earlier antiwar groups, the FBI hoped to show that CISPES and the rest were both violent and directed from abroad, thus undercutting the legitimacy of their protests against administration policy. Yet there was little evidence for either accusation.[29] On the foreign intelligence side, the 1987 case of the Palestinian "L.A. Eight" highlighted the possibility, at least, of abusing FISA authority, even of non-"U.S. persons," by focusing on a group's political activities and associations rather than on its support for violence or terrorism.[30]

The CIA also got back into the act. "Reagan's men in early 1981 believed deeply that CIA was dominated by political liberals very much out of touch with the real world and the worldview of the president," recalled future agency director Robert Gates. For the first time in memory, an outside transition team was commissioned to evaluate the CIA, and Reagan's campaign manager, William Casey, became director of central intelligence.[31] Tellingly, Reagan's intelligence activities directive of December 1981 (Executive Order 12333) reworked the section previously entitled "Restrictions on Intelligence Activities" into one called simply "Conduct of Intelligence Activities." While some of Carter's language was retained, the tone of the document reflected the retitling: constraints were no longer the rule but the exception to a broad authorization of authority. Where the Carter order stressed legal boundaries, Reagan's focused on the ability to do anything not strictly prohibited. The ban on assassinations remained in effect, for example, but the ban on using or even encouraging third parties to conduct operations ruled out in the order did not. In the Carter order, the Intelligence Oversight Board was to probe not just illegality but "impropriety"; this instruction was deleted in 1981. The agency was, further, given additional freedom from White House oversight (and accountability), shifting review responsibility from the national security advisor to the director of central intelligence himself.[32]

There seemed to be some willingness too to have the CIA reenter the domestic sphere. The agency was specifically authorized to "conduct counterintelligence activities within the United States in coordination with the FBI," so long as they did not perform any "internal security functions." The CIA passed on to the FBI information on Salvadoran leftists in the United States, much of it provided by the National Guard of El Salvador, to aid in its investigations; in return, by some accounts, the FBI provided the National Guard information about refugees who had fled to the United States illegally and had been deported back to El Salvador. On neither side was their welcome a warm one.[33]

Further, the new definition of "special activities," aka covert operations, was expanded. First, the Carter requirement that such actions be consistent with overt operations, "designed to further official United States programs and policies abroad," was deleted. And until the 1991 amendments to the Intelligence Oversight Act in the wake of the Iran-contra affair, the Justice Department held that the written findings used by the president to authorize covert action were "merely procedures instituted for the 'internal use' of the president and his intelligence advisers and could not legally bind him"; after all, the assistant attorney general wrote, "activities authorized by the President cannot 'violate' an executive order in any legally meaningful sense."[34] Given the broadening importance, as discussed previously, of executive action, such a claim suggested a distinct absence of boundaries for executive power.

The rise of terrorism both as a rising global concern and as a domestic phenomenon—made painfully clear by the 1993 World Trade Center and 1995 Oklahoma City bombings and the 1996 attacks on U.S. bases in Saudi Arabia—enhanced those claims. In 1995 FBI director Louis Freeh announced that the 1983 Smith guidelines would be "reinterpreted" to allow expanded investigations into terror cases, arguing that investigations previously requiring "imminent" commission of a crime could now be conducted against groups that had the potential for carrying out violence, advocated it, and acted in a way that "might violate" federal law. From 1995 to 1997 the number of open security investigations shot up from about one hundred to as many as eight hundred.[35]

These unilateral expansions of surveillance and investigation reflected in part the Republican-led Congress's temporary unwillingness to enhance the president's legal tool kit, even though President Clinton had proposed doing just that as early as February 1995—before the

Oklahoma City bombing that April. Much of the delay owed to conservative outrage at the 1992 Ruby Ridge, Idaho, and 1993 Waco, Texas, incidents where standoffs with well-armed suspects turned into deadly shootouts with federal law enforcement personnel. But legislative recalcitrance changed in 1996 with the Antiterrorism and Effective Death Penalty Act, which awkwardly tied new barriers to appealing capital sentences to new presidential powers. At the time, as much attention was paid to what was not included in the bill—roving wiretap authority, for example (which would be partially granted in 1998 and fully in the 2001 Patriot Act), and chemical "taggants" in gunpowder (to allow it to be traced)—as to what was. But its contents were quite extensive. The secretary of state, in conjunction with Treasury and Justice, was given authority to designate given groups as terrorist organizations; individuals associated with such groups could be denied visas and more readily deported (whether or not they had themselves participated in any terrorist activities). Treasury received new power to block designated groups' fund-raising, to freeze their assets, and to ban transactions between countries supporting them and U.S. citizens. Terrorism became a federal crime, as did the use of biological and chemical weapons. The FBI received new authority to obtain financial records from consumer reporting agencies. And $1 billion was provided (about half of it to the FBI) for improving counterterrorism tools; that fall, with the election looming, Clinton demanded and received another $1.1 billion for securing overseas military and intelligence operations.[36]

GOVERNMENTAL SECRECY: EXECUTIVE PRIVILEGE & BEYOND

Executive Privilege

Starting in the 1980s executive privilege received new life, if not immediately in name then in deed. President Reagan was the first president since Nixon to issue administration-wide guidance on executive privilege, arguing that it had "legitimate and appropriate" uses, though only if specifically invoked by the president himself. And early in the administration Attorney General Smith produced a memo strongly supporting invocation of the doctrine against a pending congressional subpoena. Smith pointed out that U.S. v. Nixon placed executive privilege squarely within the Constitution. "A President and those who assist him must be free to explore alternatives in the process of shaping policies and making decisions and to do so in a way many would be unwilling to express except privately," Chief Justice Burger had written, adding that some sort of communications "privilege is fundamental to the operation of government and inextricably rooted in the separation of powers under the Constitution." The privilege was not absolute, and in the Nixon case it was trumped by the Court's duty to safeguard the judicial process. But in other areas, especially when "military, diplomatic, or sensitive national security secrets" were at stake, the Court owed the president "great deference." Smith recommended that the president use this decision to withhold Interior Department documents pertaining to foreign ownership of mineral leases that contained information from Canadian officials. Besides the documents' diplomatic and deliberative protections, he argued, Congress did not have a presumptive right to executive branch information during its investigations. Smith wrote:

> The interest of Congress in obtaining information for oversight purposes is, I believe, considerably weaker than its interest when specific legislative proposals are in question. . . . [T]he congressional oversight interest will support a demand for predecisional, deliberative documents . . . only in the most unusual circumstances.[37]

In the end, Reagan did not hold fast to the doctrine in this conflict or several others; during the Iran-contra investigation, he even consented to turning over portions of his personal diary. Ironically, George H. W. Bush, the consummate Washington insider (and close observer of the effects of Watergate as the chair of the RNC), ultimately was more successful than Reagan at keeping information from Congress. One scholar concluded that "Bush's strategy was to further the cause of withholding information by *not* invoking executive privilege" and thus not calling attention to the doctrine. This approach was similar to Ford's and Carter's—but different in that Bush contended that executive privilege by any other name did, indeed, smell as sweet. Under the rubric of "deliberative process privilege," "attorney work product" and "attorney-client privilege," "internal departmental deliberations," "secret opinions policy," "deliberations of another agency," and the like, the Bush administration was frequently able to win the point while not engaging the larger argument. One House Judiciary Committee staffer complained in 1992 that the president "knew how to work the system. . . . In reality, executive privilege was in full force and effect during the Bush years."[38]

But it was Bill Clinton who brought the term itself back to life, prompted by his battles with independent counsel Kenneth Starr and Congress. Clinton took a broad view of the doctrine; the administration renewed the Reagan-era distinction between oversight and legislation, arguing that Congress's rights to access information concerning the former were weak. The presumption was that White House communications were privileged and that nothing would be released that was "subject to a claim" of privilege, even if that claim was not actually made.

The doctrine was accordingly used aggressively—it was officially asserted fourteen times, in the end, compared to once by George H. W. Bush and three times by Ronald Reagan—to the point that journalists began drawing parallels to the 1970s. "What's the difference," Clinton was asked, "between your case and Richard Nixon's effort to stop the Watergate investigation?"[39] The proximate cause was the aggressive legislative investigations into administration actions and ethics, especially after 1994. For example, the president claimed executive privilege in an effort to withhold documents relating to the firing of White House Travel Office staff from a House committee; if successful this would have extended privilege to the First Lady's discussions with White House staffers. In 1994 the White House was forced by a circuit court to release documents relating to the independent counsel investigation of Agriculture Secretary Mike Espy. And Clinton's extended efforts to exert executive privilege over materials relating to the Whitewater investigation and its extended progeny, the Lewinsky affair, were also unsuccessful; the Lewinsky case, the courts held, had little to do with official government business.

But the administration also successfully invoked executive privilege in a number of instances as well, even where it made broad claims. For example, refusing a congressional request for documents concerning the administration's policies in Haiti, Attorney General Janet Reno made the startling claim that Congress had no power to conduct oversight of foreign affairs, due in part to the "sole organ" doctrine of the 1936 *Curtiss-Wright* case. The investigating committee backed down.

Further, in the Espy case, the presidency achieved some broadening of judicial doctrine regarding executive privilege even as President Clinton suffered a tactical defeat. The court's careful opinion divided executive privilege into "deliberative process privilege" and "presidential communications privilege." The former, while valid, could be "overcome by a sufficient showing of need" and denied "where there is reason to believe the documents sought may shed light on government misconduct." But the latter, following *U.S. v. Nixon,* was grounded in the separation of powers—thus "congressional or judicial negation of the presidential communications privilege is subject to greater scrutiny than denial of the deliberative privilege"—and, when invoked, "the documents become presumptively privileged." That presumption was qualified by the needs of the court system to be able to guarantee full access to evidence (like the *Nixon* court, the Espy decision focused on judicial needs, and it specifically avoided most questions peculiar to the balance between the president's need for confidentiality and legislators' need for information). And in this case, the court held that the independent counsel's need for the evidence outweighed presidential prerogative, especially since the evidence was not available elsewhere.

Where this was not so, though, the court noted that "the critical role that confidentiality plays in ensuring an adequate exploration of alternatives cannot be gainsaid." Thus the presidential communications privilege applied to "final and post-decisional materials as well as pre-deliberative ones"; and it applied to "communications made by presidential advisers in the course of preparing advice for the President . . . even when these communications are not made directly to the President," so long as they were "in the course of performing their function of advising the President on official government matters" on issues arising from the president's constitutional duties.[40] Documents concerning the president's controversial decision in 1999 to grant clemency to members of a Puerto Rican terrorist group fell into this category, given the absolute nature of the pardon power.

Clinton's extensive use of executive privilege, associated in the public mind with the Lewinsky scandal, did little to bring the doctrine back into good repute. But George W. Bush was, if anything, even more aggressive in shielding information from the legislative gaze, even before the tragedies of September 11, 2001, vaulted national security to the forefront of the policy process. The rationale, argued Bush press secretary Ari Fleischer, was that "these are vital matters dealing with constitutional prerogatives vested in the presidency. They should not be whittled down over time as a result of the actions of the previous administration."[41]

Bush rarely made formal claims of privilege, preferring like most of his post-Watergate predecessors the pragmatic practice of utilizing its substance while avoiding its nomenclature. One exception came in response to a subpoena seeking information on FBI investigations of Boston mobsters; releasing such documents would, Bush wrote to the attorney general, "inhibit the candor necessary" for executive deliberation. Indeed, "Congressional pressure on executive branch prosecutorial decisionmaking," he continued, "is inconsistent with separation of powers and threatens individual liberty."[42] The administration never did release all of the requested documents, despite angry rhetoric from legislators of both parties. Nor did it hand over records relating to alleged campaign finance violations from the 1996 campaign. This last, obviously, shielded the records of former president Clinton still held by the Justice Department.

More systematically, Bush sought to extend privilege to all former presidents even after their records moved into the National Archives system. After delaying the planned release of records from the Ronald Reagan Library in early 2001 for more than eight months, Bush issued an executive order restricting access to historical documents subject to the Presidential Records Act (PRA).

In 1989 Reagan's own executive order had identified three areas (national security, law enforcement, and a much broader "deliberative process" category) in which a former president could claim executive privilege over his records due for release by presidential libraries. However, the National Archives were not bound by that claim after a thirty-day review period expired; unless the incumbent president made a formal assertion of his own executive privilege, the records would be automatically released after the thirty days.[43]

The 2001 order added new categories to Reagan's list (including the "presidential communications privilege" and one for legal work) and granted both former and incumbent presidents joint claims of privilege over documents in those categories. That is, a current president could assert privilege even if the former president objected—and vice versa. Vice presidents, and presidents' and vice presidents' estates, were also given the ability to make binding claims of privilege, an unprecedented grant of power making executive privilege something to be bequeathed to one's heirs, presumably in perpetuity. Further, in contrast to the PRA, the burden of proof for the records' release was ratcheted up and placed squarely on the researcher, who was required to have a "demonstrated, specific need" for a given record. (This was in addition to the requirements already in the PRA safeguarding the release of national security information.) Thus, while the order was entitled "Further Implementation of the Presidential Records Act," the result was actually to amend that act quite dramatically.[44]

In the brief furor that followed the order's issuance, the White House did agree to release, more than a year late, most of the first batch of Reagan documents cleared by the National Archives. This gesture was sufficient to forestall a half-hearted effort in Congress to overturn the order. And in 2004 a court case over the breadth of the executive order was dismissed, despite the order's inconsistency with the Supreme Court's 1977 decision in the Nixon papers case. Because the researcher bringing the suit had died during its long gestation, he could no longer be said to have been harmed by his failure to get access to the papers.

Government in the Sunshine?

If the Reagan administration had limited success in its formal claims to executive privilege, it nevertheless showed little compunction in trying to evade public oversight more generally. The *Los Angeles Times* went so far as to complain that Reagan "set a policy and tone for secrecy in government that exceeds anything since Watergate. In fact, not even during the Nixon years were so many steps taken to establish secrecy as government policy."[45]

This conclusion was partly driven by administration efforts to manage the press. During the invasion of Grenada, for example, journalists were kept more than 150 miles from the fighting. Reagan tried aggressively to curb leaks of sensitive information to the press, authorizing the use of lie detector tests on employees handling such information and seeking to impose White House advance approval for any contact with reporters if classified materials might be discussed.

Further, starting in 1981 Reagan proposed rolling back parts of the Freedom of Information Act (FOIA); as Attorney General Meese argued the administration brief, Congress had "overcorrected" in 1974 and "seriously impaired . . . the effective functioning of law enforcement agencies" by limiting their ability to withhold "FOIA-ed" information. In 1982 Reagan issued an executive order modifying Carter's requirement that only information causing "identifiable damage" to national security could be withheld; automatic declassification of documents was suspended and the standard duration of classification extended. Restrictions on access to additional information (e.g., at the Energy Department) were also expanded, by departmental regulation. All this mattered for FOIA since one of the exemptions in the law provides that information otherwise legally secret—no matter how it gets that way—cannot be released.

In 1984 a new exemption allowing the CIA director to withhold "operational files" from release was approved. In 1986, as part of legislation designed to fight the war on drugs, Congress acquiesced to other changes. Reasonably enough, the new amendments protected undercover informants and confidential sources and prevented pending investigations from being revealed to potential targets. But the revised language went beyond this to substantially broaden existing FOIA exemptions for law enforcement records and to create a new one. Among other things, instead of protecting just "investigatory records," FOIA now covered any "records or information compiled for law enforcement purposes." (Meese's memoranda interpreting the amendments for federal agencies broadened this still further, telling them to "carefully consider the extent to which any of their records, even though not compiled for a specific investigation, are so directly related to the enforcement of civil or criminal laws that they might reasonably meet [the] revised threshold standard.") The new exemption allowed the FBI not just to withhold, but to deny the existence of, certain restricted records, most notably those "pertaining to foreign intelligence or counterintelligence, or international terrorism."[46]

Another change in FOIA was enacted in 1996, when the Electronic FOIA Act doubled, and in some cases tripled, agencies' original ten-day window for their original responses to requests for information.[47] By then, the number of classified documents immune from FOIA had also risen exponentially. Still, President Clinton had ordered agencies generally to release documents under FOIA unless banned from doing so by statute. He also issued an executive order streamlining declassification of older material and reversing extant policy by providing that in unclear cases the government's basic stance should be against classification.

The George W. Bush administration, however, reversed the burden of proof in both instances. In 2001 Attorney General John Ashcroft announced a new policy directing federal agencies to withhold responses to FOIA requests if any legal basis existed to do so. And an executive order amending Clinton's policy, in the works since mid-2001, was issued in March 2003. The new order removed the default stance of declassification and gave the CIA new power to resist declassification decisions; other information, such as that pertaining to weapons of mass destruction or "current vulnerabilities" in security, was exempted from the automatic declassification process. Another section made it possible to reclassify previously declassified information. Even before this, notably, the number of documents marked as classified rose by more than 40 percent during the first (and predominantly pre–September 11) fiscal year of the Bush administration. Future classification was abetted by complementary low-profile administrative orders that gave three new cabinet officers—at Agriculture, at Health and Human Services, and at the EPA—the right to designate documents as "secret."[48]

These developments were consistent with the Bush administration's overall attitude toward the release of information: "a matter of theology . . . that we the people have made the White House too open and too accountable," as one close observer put it.[49] That faith was exemplified, perhaps, by the administration's actions and claims in the energy task force saga.

In early 2001 Vice President Richard Cheney was asked by the president to develop energy policy for the administration. The task force subsequently appointed did not count among its formal membership any nongovernmental actors but rather consisted of fifteen or so cabinet secretaries, agency heads, and White House aides. It was therefore presumably not subject to the Federal Advisory Committee Act (FACA), described in chapter 4.

However, two Democratic congressmen, intrigued by press reports suggesting that Cheney's most meaningful consultations were with representatives of various groups and companies pushing for increased extraction of fossil fuels, asked the GAO to find out more. The request was joined by others, including two Senate chairmen. The GAO attempted to comply and requested extensive information about who attended the task force meetings and what was said. Their request was refused, on the grounds that the GAO had no authority to investigate program development. While this was news to most agencies in the executive branch, the GAO subsequently limited its request so as to seek only meeting dates and the names of attendees. The vice president's office refused again. The GAO decided to bring suit.

However, a district court judge upheld the vice president's refusal to turn over the names of his task force members. The decision rested largely on the fact that Congress as a whole, or even as a full committee, had not directed the GAO to gather this information or issued a subpoena requiring Cheney to comply. Thus the merits of the case could not be decided. Further, since the head of GAO had suffered no harm from Cheney's refusal, he thus had no standing (despite the 1980 statute directly authorizing him to sue) to get the court involved in "a clear constitutional confrontation between the political branches." The agency, while protesting that its governing statute required it to respond to committee requests (and that the Senate chairs involved were speaking for their entire committee), nevertheless decided not to appeal the decision. By this time, the Senate had returned to Republican control, and the legislative leadership now strongly opposed pursuing the suit further. Indeed, at least one Capitol Hill news agency reported that GAO was warned its budget would be jeopardized if it appealed the district court decision.[50]

Meanwhile, a parallel case had been pursued by a pair of interest groups on different grounds. Their argument was that the industry sources consulted by the vice president were so important to the task force's deliberations as to make them de facto members of the group: if so, FACA—and its requirements to hold public meetings, to release minutes, and so forth—should apply. The plaintiffs asked that the courts require the Bush administration to produce documents that would establish the role that industry contacts had played. The administration, in turn, argued that to do so—even if the court wound up agreeing that FACA should not apply—would disclose the information the plaintiffs wanted in the first place.

For Bush, though, the core question was not this limited excursion into court procedure, or even the definition of statutory terms; rather, it was grounded in the separation of powers. The Constitution, the solicitor general told the Supreme Court, grants the president "a zone of autonomy in obtaining advice, including with respect to formulating proposals for legislation." Congress can do what it will with those proposals; but "Congress does not have the power to inhibit, confine, or control the process though which the President formulates the legislative measures he proposes or the administrative actions he orders." If FACA did permit this sort of intrusive inquiry, it interfered with the president's constitutional rights and duties and was "plainly unconstitutional."[51]

The plaintiffs in turn argued that this set of claims represented a "startling bid for effective immunity from judicial process." At the least, the administration should have to make a specific claim of executive privilege to protect a given document from release. But the Supreme Court, which considered this impasse in the spring of 2004, ruled instead that those seeking information bore the burden of specificity, so as to protect the president from "unbounded" requests. It was a "mistaken assumption" that the *Nixon* decision required presidents to explicitly invoke executive privilege, the Court held, for doing so set "coequal branches of Government . . . on a collision course" that "should be avoided whenever possible." Since the civil matter presented by the Cheney task force did not have the same constitutional "urgency or significance" presented by the criminal case wrapped up in *Nixon,* the lower courts would have to revisit the matter with a more deferential eye toward protecting executive prerogatives. The Court did not address the broader point of FACA's constitutionality.[52]

The result, at the start of the twenty-first century, was a transformation of Congress's admittedly self-serving presumption, post-Watergate, that executive processes and deliberations would be transparent. If Congress has been frustrated by the shift, it has rarely acted on this frustration. Executive privilege can be overcome by sufficient political pressure, as the Bush administration would find out with the 9/11 Commission (more formally, the National Commission on Terrorist

Attacks Upon the United States), but legislators have found it difficult to mount that pressure. Nor will the courts usually come to Congress's defense: over time they have been very reluctant to use their authority under the 1974 FOIA amendments to overrule executive decisions about classification. The principle, as one opinion put it, is one of "utmost deference" to administration determinations.[53]

This combination of legislative lassitude and judicial deference undercut Congress's ability to breach the "zone of autonomy" and conduct effective oversight in the face of aggressive administrative policy implementation. In this sense the secrecy debates serve as useful summary for arguments over executive authority more broadly conceived.

WAR POWERS, INTELLIGENCE OVERSIGHT, & FOREIGN POLICY

WAR POWERS, UNRESOLVED

On the twenty-fifth anniversary of the War Power Resolution (WPR), in 1998, the legal scholars Louis Fisher and David Gray Adler suggested that the statute had overstayed its welcome. Rather than the lauded "high-water mark of congressional reassertion in national security affairs," the WPR was instead "ill conceived and badly compromised from the start, replete with tortured ambiguity and self-contradiction." It was, they wrote, "time to say good-bye."[54]

Note that it was not the administration of George W. Bush that had raised so much scholarly ire but that of Bill Clinton. Elsewhere, indeed, Adler accused Clinton of "one of the most flagrant acts of usurpation of the war power in the history of the republic," namely, the NATO air war against Serbia on behalf of ethnic Albanians in Kosovo.[55]

Kosovo is just one entry on a long list of presidential uses of force since passage of the WPR that occurred without benefit of congressional authorization. Even an abbreviated litany would have to include Lebanon, Iran, Grenada, the Persian Gulf (in 1987–88), Libya, Panama, Somalia, Iraq (in 1993 and throughout the "no-fly zone" period), Haiti, Bosnia, Sudan, and Afghanistan (in 1998).[56] Only once has the formal notification process required under the resolution been invoked, by

President Gerald Ford after he ordered American forces to rescue the crew of the *Mayaguez,* a ship seized by Khmer Rouge guerrillas off the Cambodian coast. And even he reported only after the operation was over. Every president since Nixon has resisted the WPR's constitutionality (without quite daring to challenge it in court) and has refused explicit adherence to its provisions.

None of this is surprising, perhaps, given the language of the resolution. There are at least five problematic aspects to the drafting—which itself, it will be remembered, was a product of the amalgamation of divergent House and Senate approaches to the issue. Presidents have exploited each of these ambiguities.

The first comes with the resolution's effort to define when the commander-in-chief powers to introduce troops into imminent or actual hostilities may be exercised. Two cases are intended: in the event of sudden attack on U.S. troops or territory or when Congress gives specific statutory authorization, as in a declaration of war. As written, these conditions are rather narrow, not including, for example, the protection of American embassies abroad or even the suppression of civil insurrection at home. Presidents have felt free to define "self-defense" more generously. The 1983 invasion of Grenada or the extensive naval operations in the Persian Gulf later in the 1980s, for example, were not cases where U.S. territory or servicemen had been attacked.

Presidential autonomy on this score is enhanced by the structure of the WPR. The conditions are not contained in the operational parts of the resolution but rather in Section 2(c), the "purpose and policy" section. This placement effectively makes them advisory rather than binding, a fact that sponsor Senate Jacob Javits played down at the time of passage but later conceded.[57]

Second, though consultation with Congress was meant to come when a "decision is pending," according to the 1973 House report accompanying the resolution, the WPR leaves the president a clear out: he must consult in advance only in "every possible instance." Though politics is the art of the possible, presidents have proven adept at finding such instances to be impossible. What "consultation" itself requires is left hazy. It has been defined in practice by presidents as "notification"—not asking what to do, but saying what was about to be done, or, more often, what already had been done. President Carter decided to tell lawmakers about his attempted rescue of the hostages held in Iran only after it was too late to turn back; likewise, President Reagan called congressional leaders to the White House in 1986 only as U.S. bombers approached Tripoli. President Bush did not consult Congress regarding the long buildup to the Gulf War in 1991. Nor did President Clinton consult before ordering air strikes on Baghdad in June 1993, which he justified under the right of the United States to self-defense under the UN charter.[58]

In any event, who, specifically, should be consulted? The whole membership of Congress? Party leaders? At the time of the *Mayaguez* incident, Congress was in recess; Ford complained that legislators were scattered around the nation and the globe and that he could not find anyone with whom to consult. Proposals designating "consultation groups" or even some congressional body parallel to the NSC have been suggested but not adopted.

Third, the resolution itself seems to override the Section 2(c) "purpose and policy" limits mentioned previously by requiring the president to report on a variety of circumstances where armed forces might be introduced—but assuming that he has the unilateral right to do such introducing in the first place. The section in question (Section 4) is in the passive voice: "in any case in which United States Armed Forces are introduced . . . the president shall submit" such a report.

Further, troops are to be withdrawn after sixty days—or ninety if the president certifies that more time is needed to ensure their safety—unless Congress has authorized them to stay longer. But this means the president is given a clear opportunity to commit U.S. forces at his discretion within the sixty- to ninety-day window. As Sen. Thomas Eagleton (D-MO) argued—in support of sustaining President Nixon's veto of the WPR—suddenly the president had "unilateral authority to commit American troops anywhere in the world, under any conditions he decides, for sixty to ninety days. He gets a free sixty days and a self-executing option."[59] As this suggests, presidents have certainly not sought prior authorization for troop deployments. Assistant Attorney General (and later Solicitor General) Walter Dellinger claimed in 1994 that the resolution's structure "makes sense only if the President may introduce troops into hostilities or potential hostilities without prior authorization by Congress." This logic was used by the Clinton administration in

Haiti and the former Yugoslavia, operations that received not congressional approval but antipathy. In Haiti the Senate voted 100–0 to stress that the UN Security Council resolution sanctioning force did not give the president any power to deploy troops. But the president said he could invade anyway: "Like my predecessors in both parties, I have not agreed I was Constitutionally mandated to get [approval from Congress]."[60]

One of those predecessors had taken the argument to an extreme, at least temporarily, just a few years before. After Iraq invaded Kuwait in August 1990, President George H. W. Bush claimed he could fight the Gulf War without legislative sanction. At first, the American troop buildup was defensive, to prevent further Iraqi aggression. As the size of the deployment grew past four hundred thousand in late 1990, though, and the Bush administration spent much effort obtaining support from the UN Security Council for the use of offensive force, members of Congress demanded that no military action begin without their approval. Still the administration resisted. Dick Cheney, then secretary of defense, testified in December 1990 that the president did not need "any additional authorization from the Congress," while the Justice Department held that "war making" and "offensive actions" should be distinguished, with power over the latter vested solely in the president.[61] Even when he asked for congressional authorization in January 1991, Bush said, "I don't think I need it." After the war, he explained, "I felt after studying the question that I had the inherent power to commit our forces to battle after the U.N. resolution." Put another way: "I didn't have to get permission from some old goat in the United States Congress to kick Saddam Hussein out of Kuwait."[62]

Further, and fourth, the sixty- to ninety-day "clock" only starts ticking when the president reports under Section 4(a)(1) of the resolution. Presidents have therefore avoided mentioning Section 4(a)(1) when communicating with Congress. Instead, they report "consistent with" the requirements of the WPR rather than "subject to" it, without citing any particular provision.[63] As noted, George H. W. Bush did ultimately ask for authorization in 1991 and received it, thus obviating the need to start the clock. Yet his request asked only that Congress "express its support" for him, and he never filed a report specifically linked to the WPR. Even when President Reagan sent marines to Lebanon in 1982, a place where "imminent hostilities" could not have been more clearly presented, he declined to trigger WPR provisions. Instead, he said the troops had been deployed under his "constitutional authority with respect to the conduct of foreign relations and as Commander-in-Chief." Later, he argued that "the initiation of isolated or infrequent acts of violence against the United States Armed Forces does not necessarily constitute actual or imminent involvement in hostilities, even if casualties to those forces result." (Shortly thereafter, 241 marines were killed by a massive car bomb at their barracks near Beirut.) The NATO war in Kosovo utilized some eight hundred U.S. aircraft; two months into the war, more than twenty thousand air sorties had been flown over nearly two thousand targets throughout Yugoslavia. Again, President Clinton did not deem that troops had, in the language of the WPR, been "introduced into hostilities or into situations where imminent involvement in hostilities is clearly indicated by the circumstances."[64]

The notion of a ticking clock is also undercut by the mechanics of shorter engagements. Many of the uses of force after 1973 have been so short as to make a sixty-day limit a nullity. Sixty hours, indeed, would be a huge window for swift attacks via cruise missiles or bombing runs. Cruise missile launches, further, are certainly "hostilities," but they may not place U.S. troops in harm's way.

The fifth potential problem is relevant to the clock too. Section 5(c) of the WPR provides that Congress can pass a concurrent resolution to remove troops at any time, even before the sixty days are up. But even before the 1983 decision in *INS v. Chadha* traced previously, many scholars (and all presidents) argued that such a resolution would not be constitutionally valid since it would not be presented to the president for signature and thus would not become law in the sense of Article I, Section 7, of the Constitution. *Chadha* strengthened this argument by striking down the legislative veto. Still, though this aspect of the WPR has never been tested in court, some analysts have provided thoughtful arguments for the concurrent resolution's constitutionality. For example, Louis Fisher notes that *Chadha* centers on the ways Congress tried to delegate legislative authority, but the WPR was not meant to delegate; its last section specifies that it does not confer new power on the president. Further, using a mechanism that allows a veto means that presidents' unilateral war making could be stopped only if two-thirds of both chambers disagreed with him. "It does violence to the Constitution to place that burden on Congress."[65]

While presidents have thus taken advantage of every inch of slack in the WPR's text, the key questions are actually less legal than political, for both presidents and legislators. After all, even if the WPR is badly written, does that sufficiently explain Congress's failure to get involved in most deployments of American force after 1973? One way to see if a concurrent resolution would work is to actually pass one. Or to take another example, if presidents seek to avoid reporting via Section 4(a)(1), Congress could start the clock itself. (Indeed, since the language of the section says the clock starts on the date military action is reported or is "required to be [reported]," Congress could presumably do this simply by stating on what date the president *should* have reported.) Presidents have tried to use UN Security Council resolutions as a substitute for U.S. constitutional procedure. But the WPR specifically prohibits the use of treaty obligations as authorization for war and requires additional implementing legislation referencing the WPR itself.[66] Again, Congress has not pressed this point.

It is worth noting that presidents do seem to have felt constrained at times by the resolution. Through 2000 they submitted eighty-six reports "consistent with" its requirements. And when they contemplated major, long-term applications of force, they largely sought authorization—even if they claimed not to have to do so. In 1983 President Reagan eventually asked for support for the Lebanon peacekeeping mission; in 1991 President George H. W. Bush reluctantly sought approval for the Gulf War. It is hard to know whether the Kosovo war in 1999 was the exception that proves the rule—or the template for a new rule. Notably, in that conflict U.S. ground troops were not used, and active combat ended within ninety days; there were no American casualties during this period.[67]

Still, technical compliance might not equal practical utility. Even in the cases just specified, legislative assertiveness varied with political context. In October 1983, most notably, legislators did start the WPR clock. But they did so as of late August 1983, though marines had arrived in Lebanon in the fall of 1982; and they set it not at sixty days but at eighteen months—safely past the 1984 elections. After the barracks bombing, even this stand may have seemed too strong, as members worried that their very debate over the issue gave them unwelcome accountability for a disastrous intervention.[68]

In late 1990 and 1991 lawmakers also pressured the president to seek approval for offensive action in Iraq. Here, even though the WPR did not function as its framers intended—to the point it was deemed by some observers to be an "archaic joke"—the resolution does seem to have provided antiwar legislators with useful leverage. It was a way, as various members of Congress put it, to "get in the game," serving as a "framework for the debate that took place"; "we couldn't ignore it with any good conscience."[69] Congress didn't fully implement the resolution—it never started the clock ticking, for example, even while passing unsolicited resolutions in the early fall approving the troop buildup. But in January 1991 the House voted overwhelmingly to affirm that "the Constitution of the United States vests all power to declare war in the Congress. . . . Any offensive action taken against Iraq must be approved by the Congress of the United States before such action may be initiated." Legislative debate was extensive and serious about the merits of the war, and the final vote was quite close, especially in the Senate. Of course, having done the work in this case, the House could not resist a bit of self-congratulation after the fact. In a March 1991 resolution, it voted to commend the performance of the troops, the president, and, well, itself: "Whereas the House of Representatives, by means of its historic debate and courageous passage of H.J. Res 77 . . . authorized the President to use United States Armed Forces."[70]

In 1993, lawmakers (and public opinion) pressured President Clinton to withdraw the peacekeeping troops sent to Somalia by his predecessor. In 1999, on the other hand, Congress was wildly divided over Clinton's Kosovo actions and could come to no coherent conclusion. Legislation that would have authorized the war was defeated when a Senate-passed measure failed in the House on a tie vote. But the House also defeated, by a lopsided 139–290 vote, a concurrent resolution requiring termination of the Kosovo effort. Congress did not start the WPR clock. Further, it appropriated money specifically for ongoing Kosovo operations—twice as much, in fact, as the president had requested—while rejecting an attempt to limit presidential use of ground troops there. And in 2000 the Senate voted down another effort to terminate the peacekeeping deployment by then under way.[71]

Despite periodic suits brought by those in Congress who have opposed specific military actions, the courts have stayed out of this arena of legislative-executive relations. When Rep. Tom Campbell (R-CO) and twenty-five colleagues filed suit at the sixty-day mark of the Kosovo engagement, the case was dismissed; among other reasons, the district court held that Congress had not exercised its WPR authority and thus the president had not acted to nullify a clear legislative imperative. In short, as Justice Powell had written in 1979, "If the Congress chooses not to confront the President, it is not our task to do so."[72]

The massive gains by the GOP in the 1994 election may have made that sort of confrontation less likely. By 1995 prominent members of the new Republican majority had come to the same conclusion as Fisher and Adler, but from the opposite direction. The academic view was one of horror at the failure of the WPR to rein in presidential uses of force; but in some quarters of Capitol Hill, the horror was at the constricting nature of the resolution on presidential authority. Republican House Speaker Newt Gingrich himself supported efforts to repeal the resolution in 1995 even if, "at least on paper," that increased Democratic president Bill Clinton's power. Gingrich suggested that "the President of the United States on a bipartisan basis deserves to be strengthened in foreign affairs and strengthened in national security." As Clinton ordered troops to Bosnia in 1995, Senate majority leader Bob Dole—who opposed the action—nonetheless claimed he had a constitutional duty to acquiesce and to seek approval of authorizing legislation. Later, Rep. Benjamin Gilman (R-NY), chair of the House International Relations Committee, would argue that utilizing the WPR over the peacekeeping troops dispatched to Bosnia would "undermine . . . the morale of our young men and women who served" there.[73]

Even in 1998, as Clinton's adultery scandal dominated the news—his widely panned "apology" speech to the nation was just three days behind him—the president fired off missile strikes at suspected terrorist sites in Afghanistan and the Sudan. While some members of Congress accused Clinton of distracting attention from his personal problems, more suggested that "we have to support the President as commander-in-chief," as Rep. Peter King (R-NY) put it. Sen. Fred Thompson (R-TN), who had served as minority counsel to the Ervin Committee during Watergate, said that Clinton's attacks were "exactly the right response."[74]

Indeed, even during the impeachment debate itself in December 1998, Clinton ordered the firing of more than four hundred cruise missiles and six thousand air sorties aimed at Iraq after the UN reported that Saddam Hussein was not complying with inspection requirements. The result was what *New York Times* reporter R. W. Apple called a "surreal split-screen frenzy" in the Capitol. While a number of Republicans questioned the motives and timing of the action, few doubted the president's right to take action. Rep. Gerald Solomon (R–NY) griped that Clinton "deliberately ignored the Congress," but the House quickly passed a resolution supporting the troops in the Persian Gulf.[75] The nasty rhetoric, in some ways, only underscored legislative passivity in the face of the aggressive presidential claim to the war powers.

The election of George W. Bush seemed likely, then, to make the Congress, still narrowly controlled by the GOP, more supportive of presidential initiative. After September 11, as chapter 7 details, Congress reverted to blank check resolutions reminiscent of the Gulf of Tonkin. Had the story come full circle?

INTELLIGENCE OVERSIGHT

The arc was not quite so smooth in intelligence oversight, but here too Congress tended to cede back ground to the executive. As early as 1979 the so-called Canadian caper gave grist to those who felt notifying Congress about covert action could be counterproductive. In that case, President Carter authorized the CIA to extract from Tehran six Americans who had taken refuge in the Canadian embassy when the U.S. embassy there was seized. Any leak would have made the operation impossible, pro-presidential forces argued. The 1986–87 Iran-contra scandal, which spawned a congressional inquiry and an independent counsel investigation, did spotlight one corner of the covert intelligence world (showing too how it could be directed straight from the White House) and lead to new amendments to the Intelligence Oversight Act. In another sense, though, Iran-contra showed both the vast scope of such activities and how little of it members of Congress find out, or choose to know, about.

The Intelligence Oversight Act of 1980 had streamlined congressional oversight and mandated that the president notify the intelligence committees about covert operations. But despite the "strong sword" the act provided, scholarly observers worried by the mid-1980s that the intelligence committees had "lately chosen to return to the pre-1974 'know-nothing' era."[76] In 1986 Leslie Gelb concluded that the new regime had produced a "decade of support" for the CIA in Congress. Sen. Daniel Patrick Moynihan (D-NY) conceded, "Like other legislative committees, ours came to be an advocate for the agency it was overseeing." Congress gave the president nearly everything he asked for in intelligence budget requests and accepted that the administration would make the key choices as to how to allocate that spending. The committees, largely staffed by former CIA officers, forged a cooperative partnership with the agency; as Sen. David Durenberger (R-MN), chair of the Senate Intelligence Committee during the Iran-contra investigation, put it, "The purpose [of oversight] is to help intelligence, not to have an audit team sitting on the back of the [CIA]." His predecessor as chair, Barry Goldwater, was even franker. "I don't even like to have an intelligence oversight committee," he said. "I don't think it's any of our business."[77]

Congressional cooperation with the intelligence community does not in itself indicate less legislative power. Oversight could help grant legitimacy to covert policy by requiring that Congress assert accountability for it. But intelligence committees needed to be willing to search for knowledge beyond what they were told by the executive branch. When faced with a president committed to an aggressive campaign against communism, by both overt and covert means, and an equally aggressive CIA chief in William Casey, the oversight structure was not up to the challenge. Casey was determined to free the CIA from its Church Committee constraints; Reagan, for his part, stressed that "covert actions have been a part of government, and a part of government's responsibilities, for as long as there's been a government." Any number of administration actors held that the president had unilateral—even universal—authority in foreign policy, many of them citing the 1936 *Curtiss-Wright* case discussed in chapter 2.[78]

The tangible results of this philosophy came to a head in Central America. During the 1980s U.S. military advisers were used to support the government of El Salvador and were often involved on that nation's many battlefields; congressional efforts to cut aid to El Salvador because of its human rights record (sixty thousand civilians died during the bloody civil war) were evaded by presidential use of a military emergency fund that kept the cash flowing. In Honduras, the administration used a Pentagon "operations and maintenance" fund to train and equip Honduran forces and maintained a deployment of several thousand U.S. military personnel in Honduras and offshore in a series of exercises and maneuvers that soon proved permanent.[79]

The key battleground was Nicaragua, where the Somoza dictatorial dynasty had been deposed in 1979. As the new Sandinista government grew increasingly close to the Soviet Union and began funneling arms to rebels fighting against the El Salvadoran government, the United States grew hostile, and the CIA presented a plan for covert action to President Reagan in March 1981. Soon rebel armies known as the contras began to grow, first trained by Argentina and then by the CIA itself. The cover of *Newsweek* blared "America's Secret War" in November 1982, ensuring that the "secret" part was no longer accurate.

Newsweek did more than the CIA to identify the issue for Congress. But that said, Congress acted aggressively—it thought—to end the CIA's proxy war. Rep. Edward Boland (D-MA), House Intelligence Committee chair, proposed a budget amendment for fiscal 1983 to prohibit the CIA or Defense Department from using any funds to overthrow the government of Nicaragua. This passed the House by a vote of 411–0. In response, CIA funding was directed to activities that could be claimed were not aimed at direct overthrow, such as the sabotage of ports and oil supplies; and the agency sought to build up a stockpile of arms to be given to the contras in case Congress continued to be recalcitrant.

The prohibition expired in October 1983. In January and February 1984, with presidential approval, the CIA mined three Nicaraguan harbors. When this became public in April, Senate Intelligence Committee chair Goldwater changed his mind about his committee's relevance. "Dear Bill," he wrote to CIA head Casey, " . . . I am pissed off! . . . The President has asked us to back his foreign policy. Bill, how can we back his foreign policy when we don't know what the hell he is doing?" Ultimately Casey had to promise that the CIA would give the committee presidential findings in advance of covert action and to keep legislators updated on the progress of each operation. And in mid-1984 Congress passed a second Boland Amendment, flatly prohibiting the use of any funds by any government agency "which would have the effect of supporting, directly or indirectly, military or paramilitary operations in Nicaragua."[80]

The administration, however, was committed to just that support. One result was to seek funding for the contras from other governments and even private citizens. Saudi Arabia and Taiwan, among others, thus helped to create a small force of mercenaries and pilots helping to resupply the contras (including, ironically, at least one Cuban veteran of the Bay of Pigs invasion). When one of their planes was shot down over Nicaragua in 1986 the entire operation began to unravel.[81]

Another result was to shift control of contra operations away from the CIA and into the White House itself, to the NSC staff. This way, when the intelligence committees asked the CIA for information, they could be told the agency had none; this went on for almost two years.[82] But since the NSC staff was considered by the president to be his personal staff and thus shielded from congressional oversight, other information was hard to come by. Nor was it aggressively sought. NSC staff, when they did speak with the committees, were at best evasive; in one 1986 briefing, Lt. Col. Oliver North flatly lied about his involvement with the contras. But he was not pushed to give more information or to clarify a number of loose ends already evident. One account concludes, "Oversight was the right designation for the committee in more than one sense."[83]

At the same time, another series of covert actions run by North and the NSC staff was under way in Iran. Here the idea was to free American hostages held in the Middle East by selling weaponry, directly and via Israel, to the Iranian government—which had of course only recently released its own large group of American hostages after 444 days in captivity. This operation was authorized by a retroactive presidential finding in January 1986, a decision also withheld from the intelligence committees.

The denouement of these operations, and how they became intertwined as "Iran-contra," has already been discussed. But it seems clear that, at best, congressional oversight was incomplete and overly dependent on presidential good faith.[84] In 1986, even as the scandal broke, Assistant Attorney General Charles Cooper claimed that the "timely notice" phrase in the Intelligence Oversight Act "should be read to leave the president with virtually unfettered discretion" as to when to notify. In 1987 President Reagan issued a National Security Decision Directive prohibiting the NSC from conducting covert action but continuing to allow the president to avoid notifying Congress in advance of such operations.

Congress began drafting legislation as early as 1987 to tighten these requirements—aiming to require notification, at worst, within forty-eight hours of the commencement of an operation. For four years, however, legislators could come to no agreement. The president continued to insist that Congress could not be trusted to keep secrets; the House and Senate continued to argue about whether notification had to be time limited. Meanwhile, in 1989 President Bush vetoed a bill prohibiting the president from soliciting funds to get around a congressional ban on a particular policy; his veto was not overridden. And in 1990 he pocket vetoed a version of the Intelligence Oversight Act that omitted a specific notification requirement but added a broad definition of "covert action" itself that would have included the use of foreign governments as proxies for U.S. action.

The Intelligence Oversight Act of 1991 was finally signed into law the next August. The president was required to put his findings of a need for covert action in writing, and they could not be retroactive; they had to specify all parties involved, and the action contemplated could not violate American law or influence domestic affairs. But once again, notification would only be "in a timely fashion." Thus the likelihood of Congress getting in on the takeoff still depended on presidential discretion. As the Republican staff director of the Senate Intelligence Committee put it, "protecting the prerogatives of the Presidency overrode everything."[85]

In 2004, the 9/11 Commission investigation would conclude that Congress had done little after 1991 to contribute to the intelligence debate. It found that "the legislative branch adjusted little and did not restructure itself to meet changing threats." Military intelligence (and its large budget) remained the purview of the Armed Services Committees throughout this period, hampering the ability of the intelligence committees to serve as a central forum for coordination. Nor did legislators do much to focus sustained governmental attention on the rising issue of global terrorism. Indeed, as a subject for oversight, terrorism came under the jurisdiction of at least fourteen House committees, dropping it straight between the cracks.

In short, legislators asked few hard questions about what American intelligence did and didn't do—or about what it knew and didn't know. They did little to shape executive policy or reshape executive organization and appropriated some 98 percent of presidential intelligence budget requests from 1995 to 2000. Since intelligence spending was classified and channeled through various "black" accounts in different spending bills, even most members of Congress did not know how much was being spent on what.

At best, legislators outsourced the issue. Several outside commissions (three in 1998 alone) were created to explore issues of counterintelligence and homeland security. But in September 2001, those commissions' recommendations were sitting largely unread on office bookshelves all over Capitol Hill.[86]

TREATIES & EXECUTIVE AGREEMENTS

A last set of issues in foreign policy concerns treaties—both their making and their breaking—and executive agreements. Recall that executive agreements are reached with foreign leaders and have the force of law. But they do not require Senate ratification, and they are frequently not made public. The Case-Zablocki Act of 1972 had required that, at the least, presidents should submit all such agreements to Congress. But nearly immediately presidents began to toy with semantics: even the Ford administration, terming some "agreements" to be only "accords," refused to comply fully. In 1978 new amendments to the Case-Zablocki Act allowed the secretary of state to determine whether an agreement counted, though also requiring presidential explanation for all agreements reported late. Certainly the making of executive agreements continued apace. President Reagan concluded three thousand such agreements between 1981 and 1988, compared to only 125 treaties. Agreements likewise outnumbered treaties by more than nine to one under Presidents Bush and Clinton.

The 1981 Supreme Court decision in *Danes & Moore v. Regan* upheld the complex executive agreement that ended the Iran hostage ordeal, allowing the president to restore to Iran assets in the United States that had been frozen during the crisis and subsequently awarded by courts to American citizens. Congress, the Court suggested, had given the president broad discretionary powers in related areas. The president had thus been "invited" to act, even if his action resulted in the cancellation of court procedures and the transfer of assets without explicit legislative authorization.

Scholars agreed that Congress had not, in the Court's phrase, "resisted the exercise of presidential authority." As early as 1984 Loch Johnson concluded that presidents consistently reported their agreements late (when at all) but that Congress had settled for "submissive acceptance . . . of ex post facto notifications." Another study covering developments through 1996 reached largely the same conclusion. It noted that while statutory authority was most often the basis for presidential negotiations over executive agreements, thus implying legislative involvement, the statutes cited were nearly always decades old—popular choices included the 1961 Foreign Assistance Act and the 1954 Atomic Energy Act. As a result legislators were not in a position to take a partnership role in overseeing American commitments abroad. But neither did they act to put themselves in such a position.[87]

If making agreements remained a presidential prerogative, two very different presidents also came to the same conclusion about breaking them. While the Senate has to ratify treaties, it is less clear whether Senate (or wider congressional) involvement is necessary for their cancellation. Presidents, naturally, argue it is not. Thus, in late 1978 Jimmy Carter gave notice that the United States was going to withdraw from the 1954 Mutual Defense Treaty with Taiwan. This would enable the United States to establish formal diplomatic relations with the People's Republic of China, which still claimed sovereignty over Taiwan. And in December 2001, after a year of broad hints that he would do so, Bush informed Russian president Vladimir Putin that the United States would withdraw from the 1972 Anti-Ballistic Missile (ABM) Treaty with the Soviet Union. The prompt this time came from internal policy debates: the administration wanted to implement a missile defense program prohibited by the ABM Treaty (which defined such defenses as an impediment to the deterrence imposed by mutually assured nuclear destruction). In neither case did Congress as a whole act to block the presidential action, though the Senate voted to protest Carter's move.

Back in the early 1800s, however, Thomas Jefferson had written, "Treaties being declared equally with the laws of the United States, to be the supreme law of the land, it is understood that an act of the legislature alone can declare them infringed and rescinded." Using this logic, members of Congress filed suit against the president in 1979 and again in 2001. In the Taiwan case, Barry Goldwater led the charge for Senate participation, claiming that presidential unilateralism marked "a dangerous precedent for executive usurpation of Congress's historically and constitutionally based powers." While a district court judge agreed, the D.C. Circuit Court reversed that ruling, holding that since a president could decide whether or not to move forward with a treaty even after ratification, he had "the constitutional initiative in the treaty-making field." Upon appeal, the Supreme Court refused to comment on the merits. Instead, it dismissed the suit as a political question not subject to resolution by the judiciary. The 2001 suit brought by more than thirty House members was dismissed on like grounds: if Congress did not act to challenge the president, the court saw no reason to get involved and do work that was properly the legislature's.[88] In any case congressional ire seemed to be driven more by policy preference than by constitutional consistency. In 1979 Goldwater's suit was opposed by liberal senator Ted Kennedy and joined by conservative senators Strom Thurmond (R-SC), Jesse Helms (R-NC), and Orrin Hatch (R-UT). In 2001 Kennedy supported continued compliance with the ABM Treaty, while Hatch prevented a Senate resolution asserting that body's role in treaty termination from coming to a vote.

By 2001, then, presidents found themselves in a comfortably familiar spot: if not the "sole organ" of foreign policy, then certainly the maestro of a powerfully amplified orchestra. To be sure, this narrative should not lead one to conclude that Congress is inactive or overwhelmed in all areas of foreign affairs. Legislators were particularly active in trade policy and foreign aid, for example, during the Clinton years (though while Clinton was denied renewed "fast track" tariff negotiation authority, George W. Bush was soon granted it). Nor does it imply that congressional dominance in the exercise of the war powers represents an ideal balance of responsibilities. Many legislators, as noted, opposed the WPR, and even some supporters of the resolution came to feel over time that Congress should or even could not lead in foreign policy. As a House foreign affairs aide noted in 1981, "The general feeling is that the president is justified in asking for more flexibility"; and one academic review of the Clinton years suggests that, when congressional intervention into foreign policy occurred, it was largely irresponsible. Javits himself, distressed over the Senate's failure to extend the SALT I accords in 1977, noted, "I have been in the Senate 21 years, and I have spent all that time trying to bring Congress into a real partnership with the President on foreign policy. . . . Why have we not been successful? Precisely for this kind of performance."[89]

Still, flexibility is not the same thing as "unfettered discretion." And activation on constituencies' trade issues is different from institutional involvement in matters of war and peace. On the latter front, longtime senator Robert Byrd (D-WV) may be given the last word (at least for now). Asked to comment on the withdrawal from the ABM Treaty in December 2001, he replied that he thought the president's act was legal. But he added, even so, "I am sorry that the Senate apparently is willing to just lie down, be quiet, and not ask any questions."[90] It is an appropriate epitaph to the era.

CONCLUSIONS

As the next chapter describes, George W. Bush took office with an eye toward restoring presidential power and prerogative. Already, though, the ground lost by the presidency after Watergate seemed largely to have been retaken: as the twenty-first century dawned, the institutional landscape no longer reflected the vision of those who had sought to rein in presidential unilateralism. Consider the presidency as of 2001:

- It had a wide array of unilateral administrative tools, from executive orders to regulatory review, at its disposal.
- It had extensively exercised executive privilege, if not always by name, to withhold information from the public, Congress, and (less successfully) the courts.
- It had expanded its law enforcement authority to overcome many of the post-Vietnam limits on surveillance of suspicious groups and activities.

- It had never been formally limited by the WPR and resisted most effective oversight over intelligence activities.
- It had been granted, if temporarily, unprecedented item veto authority over spending, and Congress had proven unable or unwilling to abide by the deadlines and discipline of the CBA.
- The Independent Counsel Act had expired, leaving no independent mechanism for investigating criminal behavior within the executive branch (and executive office).

If the 1970s seemed a delayed affirmation of Bob Dylan's famous observation that "the times, they are a-changin'," the state of the presidency now was better described by the satirical observation of the fictional folk singer Bob Roberts in the 1992 film of the same name: "The times they are a-changin'—back."

To be sure, this period of presidential-congressional relations culminated in the impeachment and Senate trial of William Jefferson Clinton, the first elected president ever to have been impeached. The irony is that presidents regained their initiative even so. Old precedents were cemented and new ones established even as Clinton's critics bemoaned "the death of outrage." The 2003 edition of a leading compilation of essays on the president for classroom use mentioned impeachment only in passing. Two political scientists observed that, despite dire predictions, "one year later, the legacy of Clinton's impeachment is scarcely debatable"; its "main consequence," they noted, only partly tongue-in-cheek, was that two Republican House Speakers were deposed.[91] In any case, the impeachment debate never seemed to reach the structural level or to grapple with issues of separation of powers. One never got the sense that, because Congress had been unable to fight back on other fronts, it channeled its institutional pride into one grand extra-legislative battle. Instead, impeachment was directed at Clinton the individual, not at the office of the presidency. The articles of impeachment from 1974 and 1998 are instructive in this regard. Nixon's were about the abuse of presidential powers, while Clinton's were personal. Both were accused of obstructing justice, but Nixon's mechanism was to use one federal investigating agency to block another, while Clinton's was to try to get a former lover to lie about their affair.

Claiming as a result that Clinton was "imperial" went too far. Presidents had not been humbled; and certainly the office had rebounded since Watergate and Vietnam. But that process had further to go, as the events after September 11, 2001, would clearly show. Discussing those developments is the task of the next chapter.

Further, it is worth prospectively raising a question that is largely deferred to the final chapter: Was this increase in presidential power a bad thing? Was it, instead, necessary? After all, the 1980s were marked by nuclear uncertainty and the cementing of terrorism as an "-ism" in its own right, a strategy as well as a tactic. Both politicians and academics argued that presidents hampered by FISA, the Church Committee reforms, and the like would be hamstrung in dealing with issues quite literally of life and death. September 11 would bring that question to the forefront of American political discourse.

VII. TIDAL WAVE

The World after September 11

During the 2000 election campaign, then governor George W. Bush spoke frequently of the diminution of presidential authority. He meant, it seemed, moral authority: his administration, he argued, would "restore honor and dignity to the White House." But it soon became clear he had in mind a broader conception of presidential power. "I have an obligation to make sure that the Presidency remains robust," Bush noted. "I'm not going to let Congress erode the power of the executive branch. I have a duty to protect the executive branch from legislative encroachment." Chief of Staff Andrew Card later said this meant Bush "wanted to restore . . . the executive authority that presidents had traditionally been able to exercise." And Vice President Dick Cheney—who got started in political life as a staffer in the Nixon White House—put the aim more bluntly: "For the 35 years that I've been in this town, there's been a constant, steady erosion of the prerogatives and the powers of the president of the United States, and I don't want to be a part of that." He cited the War Powers Resolution (WPR) and Congressional Budget Act (CBA) as examples.[1] Thus even before the terrorist attacks of September 11, 2001, the Bush administration asserted a wide range of unilateral claims with the stated goal of rolling back the resurgence regime.

By late 2002, after the surprising Republican victories in that year's midterm elections, Bush seemed to have succeeded. A front-page headline in the *New York Times* trumpeted, "Shift of Power to White House Reshapes Political Landscape," with longtime Democratic power broker Robert Strauss quoted as saying, "George Bush . . . [has] made the

White House a power center in ways that I haven't seen in a long, long time—all the way back to Lyndon Johnson." The flip side, as a *National Journal* cover story proclaimed it, was a "Congress in Eclipse." Sen. Chuck Hagel (R–NE) concluded that "[this] administration. . . . treats Congress as an appendage, a Constitutional nuisance." House Democrat David Obey went further. "This administration," he groused, "thinks that Article I of the Constitution was a fundamental mistake."[2]

As chapters 5 and 6 suggest, the steady erosion noted by Cheney and Card was perhaps in the other direction—that the shifting sands of inter-branch interaction built up the presidency rather than wearing it down. Still, September 11 and its aftermath was a tidal wave accelerating this process, bringing enhanced visibility and leverage to the presidential office. And by suddenly placing the United States on a war footing, at least in some respects, the attacks prompted a range of executive claims that otherwise would not have been credible. Critics of the president were quick to charge that he used the "war on terror" as cover for things the administration wanted to do anyway. This is at best exaggerated and often simply malicious: in the absence of the attacks, for instance, it is hard to imagine the designation of "enemy combatants" or the creation of military tribunals. It is true, however, that the president's strategies for fighting the newly joined battle were consistent with his broader view of presidential-congressional relations. Two things seem clear: that the aftermath of the attacks gave the administration the opportunity to greatly expand presidential power; and that the other branches of government largely failed to check its exercise.

This chapter endeavors to trace those developments through the fall of 2004, leaving off with the presidential election that narrowly returned President Bush to office. To remain consistent the discussion here utilizes the subject-matter categories used in previous chapters, though given the common roots of the actions under review there is more spillover between categories than in the earlier narrative.

However, before turning to the additional powers claimed by, and granted to, the Bush administration in the wake of September 11, the chapter starts with a reminder of the events of that day. After all, neither the Bush administration nor Congress was acting in a vacuum. Rather, from the fall of 2001, events unwound in an environment of constant uncertainty and often, quite legitimately, of fear. The context does not necessarily justify the choices that were made; but those choices cannot be untethered from that context.

SEPTEMBER 11 & THE AUTUMN OF 2001

At 8:00 a.m. on September 11, 2001, American Airlines flight 11 left Boston for Los Angeles. Somewhere over the Adirondacks it was hijacked, reversed course, and headed toward New York City. At 8:48 a.m. it was flown directly into the north tower of the World Trade Center in Lower Manhattan. Fifteen minutes later, United Airlines flight 175, also originally bound from Boston to Los Angeles, impaled the south tower.

At 9:41 a.m. American flight 77 slammed into the west side of the Pentagon shortly after taking off from Virginia's Dulles Airport. At 10:03 United flight 93, headed toward another target in Washington—the Capitol Dome? the White House?—crashed in a field in western Pennsylvania after its passengers attempted to regain control of the plane from the hijackers.

The bad news came fast and furious. A little before 10:00 a.m., the south Trade Center tower collapsed, its 110 stories falling onto one another like a rapidly shuffled deck of cards as the structural steel within melted from the white-hot burning jet fuel. A half hour later the north tower did the same. All that was left of the twin towers were massive piles of rubble at what was immediately dubbed "Ground Zero." Under the mockingly beautiful blue skies, over 2,700 people from eighty nations lay dead—the single bloodiest day on American soil since the Civil War battle of Antietam. Nearly 200 more were dead in Washington and another 40 in Pennsylvania. In total, 2,976 people were killed and at least 6,000 more injured.[3]

Rumors flew as people stayed glued to their television sets and their cell phones, watching endless replays of the crumbling towers—of the desperate people on the upper floors leaping to their deaths—of doomed firefighters marching into the doomed buildings—of the crowds swarming out of Manhattan across the Brooklyn Bridge as soot and debris continued to rain down. Shocked news anchors knew little more than the general public, and speculation was reported as widely as fact. Were there more targets? Was Washington burning? Media reports suggested car bombs at the State Department and fires on the Mall, with tens of thousands dead in New York—a reasonable guess, given the daytime population of the World Trade Center. Government buildings, museums, and businesses were evacuated; the armed services went to DEF-CON Delta, the highest state of military alert. The entire passenger airline network was grounded for the first time in history, stranding frightened travelers around the globe. World reaction was immediate and immense: "Nous sommes tous americains," proclaimed Paris's *Le Monde;* and the "Star Spangled Banner" played at Buckingham Palace.

As days went on, and rescuers continued to probe the Ground Zero destruction, more details of the attacks were revealed. There had been nineteen hijackers, all originally from the Arab world, many of them trained at U.S. flight schools. Their allegiance was to the al Qaeda terrorist movement headed by Osama bin Laden and linked to a number of prior killings around the world, including the 1998 bombing of U.S. embassies in East Africa and the 2000 attack on the USS *Cole.* Bin Laden was a Saudi national believed to be resident in Afghanistan, sheltered there by the repressive Taliban regime.

Another threat soon emerged to keep Americans on edge. In October and November letters filled with a powdery form of the deadly bacterium anthrax were discovered in newsrooms and on Capitol Hill; one contained enough of the poison to kill one hundred thousand people. Congressional office buildings were shut down so that they could be sterilized; the Hart Senate Office Building did not reopen until late January 2002. Post offices in New Jersey and Washington that had handled the letters were also contaminated, and two postal workers from the D.C. branch later died. Government buildings cracked down on mail and visitors. The Capitol was suddenly off-limits to the American people.

On September 14 President Bush proclaimed a state of national emergency. On September 20 he addressed a joint session of Congress and the American people. The president urged the public to "be calm and resolute, even in the face of a continuing threat." He announced the creation of a new Office of Homeland Security (OHS), to be headed by Pennsylvania governor Tom Ridge. He asked for tolerance for those of Arab descent or the Muslim faith targeted by ignorant hate crimes. He asked "every nation to join us" in the battle against terror: "this is the

world's fight. This is . . . the fight of all who believe in progress and plu-
ralism." And he delivered an ultimatum to the Taliban regime: "They
will hand over the terrorists, or they will share in their fate."

"I will not forget the wound to our country and those who inflicted
it," Bush declared. "I will not yield, I will not rest, I will not relent in
waging this struggle for freedom and security for the American people."

From a 50–50 split just the week before, the president's approval ratings quickly brushed 90 percent. The speech was a "home run, a ten,"
said Rep. Maxine Waters (D-CA), one of the most liberal members of
the House. "Right now," she added, "the president of the United States
has support for almost anything he wants to do."[4]

PRESIDENTIAL POWER AFTER SEPTEMBER 11

WAR POWERS & INTELLIGENCE OVERSIGHT

Even before the president spoke, Congress had given him immense discretionary authority to act. Three days after the attacks, with just one
dissenting vote in the House and with none in the Senate—most Senate
discussion of the bill took place *after* the vote—Congress passed a joint
resolution authorizing President Bush to use "all necessary and appropriate force against those nations, organizations, or persons he determines planned, authorized, committed, or aided the terrorist attacks that
occurred on September 11, 2001, or harbored such organizations or persons, in order to prevent any future acts of international terrorism against
the United States by such nations, organizations, or persons."

Given the unprecedented events that were unfolding, such a resolution was hardly unwarranted. The language was toned down somewhat
from the draft prepared by the White House, which would have given
the president power to "deter and pre-empt any future acts of terrorism
or aggression against the United States." Further, the language
specifically invoked the WPR, stating that it was to serve as congressional authorization for military action subject to the WPR's provisions.

Nevertheless, the language of the resolution remained notably broad.
Sen. Carl Levin (D-MI), even in urging unanimous support for its passage, noted that "this joint resolution would authorize the use of force

even before the President or the Congress knows with certainty which nations, organizations, or persons were involved in the September 11 terrorist acts." But no language was added requiring the president to certify that targets of the use of force authorized by the resolution were actually connected to the September 11 attacks. War was declared but without a specified enemy; that choice was left to the president. As Levin conceded, "This is a truly noteworthy action and a demonstration of our faith in the ability of our Government to determine the facts and in the President to act upon them."

Further, the resolution found that "the President has authority under the Constitution to take action to deter and prevent acts of international terrorism against the United States." The source of this authority was not stated, but presumably it referred to the Madisonian argument that the president could "repel sudden attacks." Where deterrence or proactive prevention fit into this was not obvious. But congressional action was designed to be supportive rather than permissive in any case: many legislators claimed that Bush could act without an authorizing vote. Sen. Russell Feingold (D-WI) stressed that "Congress owns the war power"—but also argued that "there is no reason to suggest that the action we take here today is required in advance of any immediate military response by the President."

Nor was the WPR of abiding concern, given the circumstances. Responding to a tentative effort in the House to add specific reporting requirements to the resolution, Rep. Henry Hyde (R-IL) retorted:

> [T]he whole point of the joint resolution we are considering this evening is to clear away legal underbrush that might otherwise interfere with the ability of our President to respond to the treacherous attack on our Nation that took place three days ago. Most importantly, we are stripping away the restrictions of the War Powers Resolution. It hardly makes sense to reimpose and, in one case, tighten the restrictions of the War Powers Resolution, if our larger purpose is to make it easier for the President to respond to terrorism.

"In any other case," Hyde continued, "I might understand and sympathize with the interest of the gentleman in keeping the President on a short leash as he goes about exercising the authority we give him tonight. But this is not any other case. This is a situation in which our Nation has been attacked by a sinister enemy, and thousands of our fellow citizens have been killed. I, for one, do not want to restrain our President as he goes about responding to this heinous attack."[5]

That response, in the sense of exerting presidential power, had already begun: the air force rules of engagement had been revised by the president to allow the military to shoot down hijacked planes that posed a direct threat to targets on the ground.[6] The response abroad began almost immediately, too, as Army Special Forces troops were introduced to the remoter regions of Afghanistan to begin preparations for a war against the Taliban regime. The UN Security Council demanded on September 18 that Osama bin Laden be remanded to the United States or a third country; the Taliban refused. On October 7 an American and British air assault commenced, focusing on Kabul, Kandahar, and suspected terrorist training camps. The anti-Taliban warlords of the "Northern Alliance" gathered their troops and, in conjunction with American troops and airpower, advanced on Taliban lines. The Northern Alliance marched into Mazar-i-Sharif on November 9 and took Kabul on November 12. By the end of the year, the Taliban had been driven from power.

Neither Taliban leader Mullah Omar nor Osama bin Laden was captured during the offensive. But by early 2002 President Bush declared in his State of the Union address that "we are winning the war on terror. . . . The American flag flies again over our embassy in Kabul. Terrorists who once occupied Afghanistan now occupy cells at Guantánamo Bay." However, he went on, "What we have found in Afghanistan confirms that, far from ending there, our war against terror is only beginning."

Bush's speech would become most famous for his predictions of that war's future fronts. Naming Iran, Iraq, and North Korea, he warned,

States like these, and their terrorist allies, constitute an axis of evil, arming to threaten the peace of the world. By seeking weapons of mass destruction, these regimes pose a grave and growing danger. They could provide these arms to terrorists, giving them the means to match their hatred. They could attack our allies or attempt to blackmail the United States. In any of these cases, the price of indifference would be catastrophic.

Bush concluded by promising, "I will not wait on events, while dangers gather. I will not stand by, as peril draws closer and closer." In June 2002, in a commencement address to West Point cadets, he expanded on this theme. The war on terror, he argued, could "not be won on the defensive." Deterrence and containment, the mainstays of cold war security doctrine, were no longer adequate. Instead, as detailed in the administration's September policy paper, *The National Security Strategy of the United States,* proactive action might be necessary. The United States, it argued, could no longer be "reactive," given the undeterrable nature of potential attackers and the magnitude of harm that could result from their nuclear, chemical, or biological strikes. "We cannot let our enemies strike first. . . . To forestall or prevent such hostile acts by our adversaries, the United States will, if necessary, act preemptively."[7] As that language suggests, the notion of preemption in the document was very broad, moving beyond a surprise strike against an enemy clearly planning to attack nearly immediately—against an army massed on the borders, say—to "forestalling" well in advance developments that potentially pointed to future, and possibly more serious, attacks.

Quite clearly, the enemy the administration had first in mind was Iraq. Saddam Hussein remained in control of that country despite the Gulf War of 1991 and a decade of sanctions and sporadic American air strikes. Indeed, the oil-for-food program run by the UN had enriched him and his family (and various contractors) while doing little to bring his subjects food or medicine. He had failed to cooperate with UN weapons inspectors, causing inspection teams to be pulled from Iraq in 1998. The Iraq Liberation Act, passed that year, declared that it was American policy "to support efforts to remove the regime" there from power.[8] Most U.S. policymakers believed that Iraq retained weapons of mass destruction of some sort or at the very least the capacity to quickly reconstitute earlier programs.

Building on this history—and on a fervent belief that a free Iraq would help jump-start a positive chain reaction toward stability and liberal democracy across the Middle East—the Bush administration had started talking privately about the prospects for abetting (or creating) Iraqi regime change soon after the president took office. Immediately after September 11, planning expanded dramatically as the president ordered the preperation of invasion options. In early 2002 he signed a secret order giving the CIA authority to assassinate Saddam Hussein. It seems that the president had decided as early as that April that Saddam could not be allowed to remain in power. In late August Vice President Cheney put the case bluntly: "There is no doubt that Saddam Hussein now has weapons of mass destruction," he told the Veterans of Foreign Wars convention. "There is no doubt that he is amassing them to use against our friends, against our allies, and against us." Even if he didn't attack directly, as the "sworn enemy" of the United States Saddam might well pass along weapons or technology to terrorist groups.[9]

War was coming. Would it require legislative approval? The White House counsel's office advised the president that the answer was "no." The claim was threefold: that the president's commander-in-chief powers were themselves sufficient; that the September 14 resolution encompassed such action; and that the congressional resolution from the *first* Gulf War had already granted any necessary authority in any case, since Iraq had not lived up to the terms of the UN resolution ending—or, in this view, suspending—it. "We don't want to be in the legal position of asking Congress to authorize the use of force when the president already has that full authority," one senior official said. "We don't want, in getting a resolution, to have conceded that one was constitutionally necessary."[10]

Yet despite repeated high-level administration assertions—Secretary of Defense Donald Rumsfeld told an interviewer in September, for example, that, "as we sit here, there are senior al Qaeda in Iraq; they are there"—there was little evidence tying the Iraqi regime to al Qaeda and still less to September 11. This made using the 2001 resolution problematic. Using the 1991 resolution seemed even more dubious. The original resolution authorized the president to use force to implement UN demands that Iraq withdraw from Kuwait and restore the status quo ex ante. Using it to justify invasion and regime change was a stretch. Granted, U.S. and British air power continued to enforce the no-fly zones over northern and southern Iraq. But the legitimacy of the no-fly raids themselves was grounded in self-defense. (To the extent they were offensive operations, they probably should have had legislative authorization of their own.) Expanding those strikes to an invasion a decade later without renewed authorization would, as one scholar of international law put it, "completely contravene the spirit of the resolution and the constitutional values at stake."[11] After all, this was not a question of repelling a sudden attack on the United States or an ally; nor could it be argued that there was no time for congressional deliberation.

In any case, recalcitrance in going to Congress hardly seemed necessary, given the near certainty of legislative approval of the president's request. "The question we face today is not whether to go to war, for war was thrust upon us," House majority whip Tom DeLay (R-TX) declared. "Our only choice is between victory and defeat." Democrats were quick to stress that "we want to be helpful," as Senate Majority Leader Tom Daschle (D-SD) put it. "We do want to be supportive."[12]

Thus after an effective speech to the UN challenging that body to make its past resolutions relevant, the president turned to Congress and requested a resolution authorizing the use of force. The original administration draft was, once more, quite sweeping; "I don't want a resolution that ties my hands," President Bush cautioned.[13] His version authorized the president "to use all means that he determines to be appropriate" in order to "restore international peace and security in the region." Given the paucity of both those attributes in the Middle East, it represented a broad grant of power indeed.

Congressional negotiators did remove that phrase and added language making clear that the resolution was meant to serve as the approval required by the WPR. Reporting requirements parallel to the WPR were also imposed. But the bottom line changed little. President Bush had told members of Congress: "I want your vote. I'm not going to debate it with you," and he barely had to. The final language read: "the President is authorized to use the Armed Forces of the United States as he determines to be necessary and appropriate in order to defend the national security of the United States against the continuing threat posed by Iraq; and enforce all relevant UN Security Council resolutions regarding Iraq."[14]

Despite sometimes frantic efforts to build a "coalition of the willing," the only resolution ultimately passed by the UN Security Council was one declaring Iraq to be in breach of its obligations to disarm and demanding that weapons inspections restart. It noted that the Security Council had "repeatedly warned" Iraq of "serious consequences" but did not spell out any new ones; in any case, Iraq allowed UN and International Atomic Energy Agency (IAEA) inspectors to return.

The inspections, however, found little. Was this because there was nothing to find? The administration thought not. Secretary of State Colin Powell told the Security Council in early February that, "instead of cooperating actively with the inspectors to ensure the success of their mission, Saddam Hussein and his regime are busy doing all they possibly can to ensure that inspectors succeed in finding absolutely nothing." While not necessarily disagreeing with this assessment, the members of the Security Council largely supported waiting for more evidence from continued inspections. President Bush did not. "The Iraqi regime has used diplomacy as a ploy to gain time and advantage," he told the nation on March 17, giving Saddam and his family forty-eight hours to step down. The UN itself, he argued, "has not lived up to its responsibilities, so we will rise to ours. . . . The security of the world requires disarming Saddam Hussein now." Two nights later, the war began.[15]

Some members of Congress who were unhappy with the president's planning for and conduct of the war would later claim that their votes were meant to internationalize the war through the UN. But the resolution plainly made the president's discretion independent of UN deliberations: if he felt that diplomacy would no longer "adequately protect the national security of the United States" against Iraq, he was simply to tell Congress so within forty-eight hours of the start of hostilities. The decision was up to him. Indeed, as with the September 14 resolution, some lawmakers seemed to suggest that it always had been—that the administration had been right in the first place to claim it didn't need congressional approval. Sen. John Kerry (D-MA), running for the Democratic Party's presidential nomination, fended off criticism of his "yes" vote by claiming it was irrelevant. "We did not give the president any authority that the president of the United States didn't have," he said in February 2004.[16] Certainly by the time war came in March, Congress was irrelevant, by its own choice. Its October debate was five months past.

As noted in chapter 1, some members did express concern that the October resolution was a blank check reminiscent of the 1964 Gulf of Tonkin grant of authority in Vietnam. It was later, though, that additional parallels to the Tonkin debate came into clearer focus. Developments since the fall of Baghdad in April 2003 suggested that—as forty years before—the case for immediate action was far fuzzier than in the picture painted by the administration. This threatened to open a new "credibility gap."

As it was, the case for war was presented in bold, certain strokes. The administration expressed no doubt that Iraq possessed forbidden arms. In the fall of 2002 the president and his staff gave a series of addresses about what Vice President Cheney called "irrefutable evidence" of an Iraqi nuclear program. That October the president told the public that "we do [know]" that Iraq "has dangerous weapons today."[17] British information about the impending strength of Iraq's nuclear program was repeated as fact by the president in his 2003 State of the Union address.[18] A new Pentagon intelligence analysis unit, the Policy Counterterrorism Evaluation Group, told White House staffers that there was (in the vice president's words) "overwhelming evidence" of ties between Iraq and al Qaeda. Powell's presentation to the UN in February 2003 stated, "When we confront a regime that harbors ambitions for regional domination, hides weapons of mass destruction and provides haven and active support for terrorists, we are not confronting the past, we are confronting the present." The president's assistant for national security, Condoleezza Rice, entitled a January 2003 op-ed piece "Why We Know Iraq Is Lying," and most observers generally accepted her view. For many in the public, those "known" Iraqi lies mattered a great deal: more than half of Americans surveyed in the spring of 2003 believed that Saddam Hussein had been "personally involved" in September 11. Six in ten believed that Iraq was a threat that required quick action and that could not be contained.[19]

CIA director George Tenet reportedly told the president that the case against Iraq was a "slam dunk." The preamble to the Iraqi force resolution had been accordingly certain about the threat Hussein posed, and hostile scrutiny of the administration's claims accordingly sparse. Iraq "remains in material and unacceptable breach of its international obligations," Congress declared, by "continuing to possess and develop a significant chemical and biological weapons capability, actively seeking a nuclear weapons capability, and supporting and harboring terrorist organizations." Three other clauses linked the use of force against Iraq to the war on terrorism and, at least by implication, to some Iraqi role in the September 11 attacks, expressing among other things legislative determination to "continue to take all appropriate actions against international terrorists and terrorist organizations, including those" responsible for September 11.

Of course, as noted earlier, the vast majority of members of Congress didn't bother to read the National Intelligence Estimate (NIE), the executive summary of which elided away much of the nuance contained in the full document. However, had they done so, they might have been only marginally more informed. In July 2004 the Senate Intelligence Committee concluded that the "major key judgments" of the full NIE were "either overstated, or were not supported by, the underlying intelligence reporting. . . . The Intelligence Community did not accurately or adequately explain to policymakers the uncertainties behind the judgments in the [NIE]." The analysis was hampered by a lack of timely hard evidence from reliable informants. Worse, CIA's surety ignored the fact that its conclusions were projected from past estimates that were themselves speculative. "Analysts interpreted ambiguous data as indicative of the active and expanded WMD [weapons of mass destruction] effort they expected to see," the committee complained. "Mechanisms . . . of alternative or competitive analysis were not utilized." The upshot was "a hypothesis in search of evidence."[20]

As a result Tenet's "slam dunk" would clang loudly off the rim. The British claim regarding Iraq's search for uranium had been debunked by a CIA analyst in advance of the president's speech. Many others within the administration knew that the aluminum tubes touted as "irrefutable evidence" that Iraq was implementing its atomic ambitions were most likely unusable for that purpose. The Defense Department's intelligence unit, it seemed, had been specially constructed to go around the CIA (Tenet knew nothing of its White House briefing) and to provide information that was more favorable to the administration's case for war; Powell's speech was girded by similarly unreliable sources, some of whom had evidently fabricated data.

In October 2003 U.S. inspector David Kay reported that his survey teams had found no evidence to date that Iraq had possessed weapons of mass destruction before the war and in January 2004 chastised the intelligence community for promulgating what he now saw as a false belief in those weapons' existence: "we were almost all wrong, and I certainly include myself." The inspectors' final report released in September 2004 repeated this conclusion: Saddam wanted weapons, but he didn't have them. The administration itself would later repudiate the notion that there were direct links between Iraq and September 11; as the 9/11 Commission reported, NSC staff analysis as early as the week after the attacks found no compelling signs of Iraq–al Qaeda cooperation. The commission's more exhaustive work could also find "no credible evidence" of such ties. Instead, Iraq became home to a significant number of al Qaeda–linked terrorists only after the American occupation created both a governing vacuum and an excuse for those seeking to vent their hatred.²¹

Before the "slam dunk," the CIA had been a clear organizational winner, post–September 11. While unhappy with the failure to detect the plots, officials mainly expressed frustration that the post–Church Committee checks on the CIA's behavior had made the agency risk-averse and less willing to do the hard (and sometimes sordid) work needed to obtain accurate intelligence. "Post-Church," summed up Harvard's Michael Ignatieff, "we may have betrayed a fatal preference for clean hands in a dark world of terror in which only dirty hands can get the job done." Recruiting human sources had taken a backseat to using remote surveillance, to the point where the CIA had only one thousand overseas operatives—fewer officers than the FBI has in New York City alone. Before the Iraq war, it had a grand total of four sources reporting from within that country.²²

Money poured into the CIA as it quickly expanded recruitment and brought retired officers back to work. Agency operatives played a heroic role in the Afghan campaign and as early as February 2002 had set up operations in northern Iraq.

However, the failure to find weapons of mass destruction in Iraq, along with the lengthy investigations into the September 11 attacks, put the CIA on the organizational defensive. George Tenet resigned in July 2004, and Florida congressman Porter Goss took his place. The 9/11 Commission went further, calling for the creation of a National Counterterrorism Center (NCTC) and a powerful national intelligence director to manage and coordinate the sprawling sweep of foreign, defense, and homeland intelligence efforts. In August, seeking to forestall legislative efforts to implement those recommendations, President Bush issued executive orders creating an NCTC under the CIA director's purview and broadening the director's power over the portion of the foreign intelligence budget not linked to tactical military operations. The orders did not give the director complete budgetary authority or control over hiring and firing across all the intelligence agencies, as the commission report urged. Just prior to the 2004 election, the House and Senate passed very different versions of intelligence reorganization (in the Senate's case, based closely on the commission's recommendations) but were unable to hash out a bill until the public outcry of the 9/11 victims' families pressured the president to urge a compromise. The final statute codified the extant NCTC and created a new director of national intelligence (DNI) separate from CIA. How the DNI's powers would work in practice was not immediately clear. The position was tasked with drawing up government-wide intelligence budgets but had limited authority to transfer funds between programs and lacked day-to-day control over how monies were spent. Intelligence budgets would remain classified, scuttling Senate plans to create a new Appropriations subcommittee to review intelligence funding.

More generally, Congress failed to fundamentally restructure its intelligence oversight capacity, though the Senate did remove term limits on Intelligence Committee service. At the same time, the administration successfully pressed to preserve the Pentagon's autonomy in the new setup. Reports suggested that the Defense Department was using that freedom to greatly expand its own intelligence operations, which it claimed were subject to fewer legal restraints and less congressional oversight than the CIA's covert missions. Pentagon lawyers argued that "traditional . . . military activities" and their "routine support," exempt from the operations requiring timely legislative notification, might include a vast range of clandestine ventures, given an indefinite, global war on terror.[23]

EXECUTIVE POWER & HUMAN RIGHTS

Meanwhile, the intelligence community's already-renewed freedom of covert action brought renewed charges of excess. In Iraq, for example, the goal of identifying and eliminating the anti-American insurgency's leadership raised the specter of the Vietnam-era "Phoenix Program." The CIA pushed to rehabilitate cooperative allies of Saddam Hussein, briefly installing as the new intelligence head a man who had commanded units involved in the slaughter of Kurd and Shiite civilians under Saddam.[24] A permissive set of rules governing interrogation was approved by the president, allowing the CIA to set up secret detention centers abroad; for high-level terror suspects, reportedly, the order allowed treatment on the edge (or over the edge) of torture—for example, techniques like "water boarding," where a bound prisoner is held underwater to the brink of drowning. Other detainees were sent to third countries with few constraints on outright torture or kept as unofficial "ghosts" in army facilities. A series of memos from the CIA's general counsel and from the Justice Department's Office of Legal Counsel (OLC) claimed for the agency wide custodial and interrogation powers that in some cases overrode the Geneva Conventions governing the treatment of prisoners and civilians during wartime and occupation. OLC argued that, "to facilitate interrogation," formal charges should not be brought against potential suspects, as this would trigger Geneva protections preventing detainees from being moved to other countries. The need to obtain reliable information on terrorist plans was clear. But allowing secret, unconstrained behavior had obvious risks: in the spring of 2004, investigations found at least five cases where detainees died in CIA custody.[25] However, these issues were hardly the agency's exclusive province. Indeed, at the same time the army was pursuing more than thirty criminal investigations linked to the deaths of prisoners.[26]

It is worth taking a step backward, for these issues arose from a broader prior dilemma for the intelligence community and the armed services as a whole. Namely, how should the United States classify, treat, and physically house suspected terrorist operatives captured abroad? Were those detained in Afghanistan, for example, prisoners of war, as under the traditional rules of military engagement? If so, detainees would have certain rights to humane treatment under the 1949 Geneva Conventions, to which the United States is a signatory. Among them would be the right to communicate with the outside world and the right not to talk to their captors. That clearly posed a dilemma. If a given prisoner had information about fellow members of worldwide terror cells and the plots they had in motion, how could authorities not try to obtain it? And how could that prisoner then be allowed to alert those confederates to change their plans?

It would have been possible, presumably, to hold formal hearings to determine whether individual detainees should, in fact, be classified as prisoners of war or not. Indeed, U.S. military regulations prescribed just that, as did later court decisions. Non-Iraqis seized in that country during the U.S. occupation and believed to be members of terrorist organizations were also evaluated on a case-by-case basis.

However, the administration did not originally choose this course. In Afghanistan, the White House rejected the hearings process as unwieldy and unnecessary, arriving instead at a blanket definition of prisoners captured there as "unlawful enemy combatants." Since such combatants were not fighting on behalf of an established state or in uniform, the administration reasoned, they were not covered by the laws of war. Precedents to this effect went back to the Revolutionary War capture and hanging of the British spy Major John André but focused largely on the 1942 Supreme Court decision in *Ex parte Quirin,* which classified German saboteurs who entered the country in civilian dress as "unlawful combatants" or "enemy belligerents." Some of those captured were retained in Afghanistan; some 650 others were housed at a newly built facility at the naval base at Guantánamo Bay, Cuba.[27]

A January 2002 memo from White House counsel Alberto Gonzales reminded the president that, "as you have said, the war against terrorism is a new kind of war. . . . In my judgment, this new paradigm renders obsolete Geneva's strict limitations on questioning of enemy prisoners and renders quaint some of its [other] provisions." Gonzales's analysis built on extensive research within OLC, the office charged with (in Gonzales's term) "definitive" interpretation of such questions. OLC held that a "transnational terrorist organization," since not a nation-state, was not party to the Geneva Convention and that exempting al Qaeda prisoners from Geneva protections would, in turn, exempt U.S. soldiers from prosecution under the War Crimes Act.

On February 7 the president declared that "pursuant to my authority as Commander in Chief and Chief Executive of the United States . . . I . . . determine that none of the provisions of Geneva apply to our conflict with al Qaeda in Afghanistan or elsewhere throughout the world." He added that "our values as a Nation . . . call for us to treat detainees humanely" and "consistent with the principles of Geneva." In practice, in Secretary of Defense Rumsfeld's translation, those detained in Afghanistan would be treated in "a manner that is *reasonably* consis-

tent" with the conventions—"for the most part." What the other parts
might mandate was not then disclosed. However, with Rumsfeld's
approval, previous army regulations constraining interrogation methods
were superseded; at Guantánamo Bay the use of tactics such as sleep
deprivation and lengthy placement of prisoners in "stress positions" or in
hoods was sanctioned. Further, according to the reporter Seymour
Hersh, Rumsfeld had already approved a highly secret program aimed at
carrying out "instant interrogations—using force if necessary" around
the world. As one intelligence official told Hersh, the rules were to
"grab whom you must, do what you want." That might include sexual
humiliation, thought to be particularly effective in shaming Arab subjects to cooperate, and the use of attack dogs.[28] These techniques were
widely transferred to other military facilities in Afghanistan and Iraq,
beyond the program's original intent and often in tragically embellished
form. The most notorious example was at the Abu Ghraib prison outside Baghdad, where photographs and even videotape showed the repel-
lant juxtaposition of graphic, often sexual, torture and grinning U.S. soldiers. General Antonio Taguba's investigation of Abu Ghraib found
"numerous incidents of sadistic, blatant, and wanton criminal abuses"
inflicted on detainees—and this in a place where the Geneva Conventions *were* generally supposed to apply.[29]

The link between executive power and human rights was made
explicit in internal administration deliberations. Most notable was the
Justice Department's ruling in August 2002 on the applicability of the
Convention against Torture, as implemented by American law, to
ongoing interrogations. In a memo to the White House, OLC head Jay
S. Bybee concluded that the term *torture* could be applied only to acts
sufficient to cause, for example, "organ failure . . . or even death," and
then only if inflicting such pain (and not, say, gaining information) was
the "precise objective" of the interrogator.[30] However—even in such a
case—the law did not apply to questioning stemming from "the President's constitutional power to conduct a military campaign." Since, "as
Commander in Chief, the President has the constitutional authority to
order interrogations of enemy combatants to gain intelligence information"—since, indeed, this is a "core function of the Commander in
Chief"—Congress could not make laws that encroached on the exercise
of that authority. A later memo constructed by a working group of

Defense Department attorneys came to the same conclusion: "in order to respect the President's inherent constitutional authority to manage a military campaign, 18 U.S.C. § 2340A (the prohibition against torture) as well as any other potentially applicable statute must be construed as inapplicable to interrogations undertaken pursuant to his Commander-in-Chief authority." In this sense, at least, the president was above the law. While administration officials later argued this analysis was unnecessary or even irrelevant—since the president did not intend to order torture—they did not, tellingly, argue it was wrong.[31]

TRIBUNALS & TRIBULATIONS

"Unlawful enemy combatants" were to be brought to trial, if at all, not through the regular court system but through a system of military tribunals established through a military order issued by President Bush on November 13, 2001. The order stated that individuals bound over for the tribunals had no right to "seek any remedy" in state or federal court. Though American citizens would later be designated as "enemy combatants," as discussed later, the tribunal system was targeted at noncitizens who were determined by the president to (a) be a present or former member of al Qaeda, (b) be "engaged in, aided or abetted, or conspired to commit acts of international terrorism or acts in preparation thereof" that would have "adverse effects" on the "United States, its citizens, national security, foreign policy, or economy," or (c) have "knowingly harbored" someone who had.

While individuals detained under this order were to be "treated humanely," the interrogation rules noted previously were deemed by administration lawyers to meet that condition. Rules for the tribunals were to be set via Defense Department regulation, providing for a "full and fair trial," though the order added that "it is not practicable to apply . . . the principles of law and rules of evidence generally recognized in the trial of criminal cases in the United States." White House counsel Gonzales argued that "everyone tried before a military commission will know the charges against him, be represented by qualified counsel and be allowed to present a defense." After sharp criticism, the regulations issued by the Pentagon in March 2002 required that trials be presumed open rather than closed and that capital punishment be imposed only upon unanimous, secret ballot vote of the tribunal members. Notably, though, the original order provided that the record of any trial—including "any conviction or sentence"—was to be sent on to the president "for review and final decision." The regulations provided for intermediary review, but the president could still presumably overturn a tribunal decision not to impose the death penalty or even its decision to acquit a given suspect. There was no appeal outside the military chain of command, and the top of that chain seemingly had little doubt of the proper outcome, at least early on. The president called the detainees "killers," and Rumsfeld elaborated: they were, he said, "the most dangerous, best-trained, vicious killers on the face of the earth." The military lawyers assigned to serve as defense counsel were sharply critical as the process moved forward; one commented, in light of the evidentiary standards and review process involved, that the system "is not set up to provide even the appearance of a fair trial." The truth of this critique could not be immediately evaluated. The first "combatants" were not designated for trial by a tribunal until February 2004, more than two years after their capture. Others, the Defense Department said, could be held indefinitely—even if acquitted at trial or after serving a sentence meted out by a tribunal. By the fall of that year, some 150 detainees had been released or transferred to custody in their home countries, but only 4 had moved through even preliminary trial proceedings. In November a district court judge muddied the waters further by holding that proceedings under the military order were illegal unless preceded by "a competent tribunal's" determination that detainees were not, in fact, prisoners of war.[32]

The preventive detention of those seeking to do the United States harm, especially of those fanatically devoted to that cause, has obvious appeal. Still, even if good or necessary policy, the power of the president to issue such an order without delegated authority from Congress was far from self-evident. The wording of the 2001 order, including direct presidential review, tracked Franklin Roosevelt's similar proclamation in 1942 concerning the *Quirin* saboteurs. Yet Roosevelt's order, though issued during a declared war, was itself criticized at the time for stacking the deck against the defendants and was subsequently altered when a second set of Nazi saboteurs was captured in late 1944. Further, the 1942 order was drafted retrospectively to apply to a specific case, not prospectively to the entire population of people not American citizens—comprising more than 20 million persons within the United States itself.[33]

As justification, the Bush administration drew on the commander-in-chief power, on the president's own declaration of a national emergency, on the September 14 resolution authorizing military force, and on the Uniform Code of Military Justice (UCMJ). Since the order applied to noncitizens on American soil as well as those captured abroad, it had implications for the right of habeas corpus: was the president unilaterally suspending it, as Lincoln had done during the Civil War? The order also brushed up against the Sixth Amendment's guarantee of a jury trial (which applies on the face of it to "all criminal prosecutions") by redefining actions previously handled by criminal courts as violations of the "laws of war." This is most clear in the order's invocation of the UCMJ, which authorizes military tribunals only in the "laws of war" context—as opposed to under the "law of nations," which the September 11 attacks did clearly violate.[34]

Certainly Congress could have suspended habeas corpus, as it did during the Civil War and Reconstruction. It could have declared war—since not doing so might be read (in this case probably incorrectly) as an intentional limitation on the president's authority. And certainly it had authority to authorize tribunals—after all, Article I, Section 8, of the Constitution vests the power to "define and punish . . . offenses against the Law of Nations" directly in Congress. However, legislators did none of these things. Congress was not asked to act, except to appropriate funds, which it did; nor did it bestir itself to act, which must itself be considered a deliberate choice, especially since lawmakers did not even voice much complaint about the president's own chosen actions. To the contrary, most lawmakers felt that criticism would, in the words of Sen. Jeff Sessions (R-AL), "have the tendency to erode unity in the country and undermine respect for our leadership in a time of war" and that "aggressive oversight," in the words of Sen. Orrin Hatch (R-UT), would be "counterproductive." The risk that tribunal powers would be inappropriately expanded, most felt, was not consonant with the risk of additional terrorist attacks.[35]

The judicial response was more complicated, though in any case far from swift. The tribunal order's attempt to rule out the opportunity for judicial review was soon challenged: even in the *Quirin* case, the

Supreme Court had rejected Roosevelt's effort to dismiss the German saboteurs' ability to ask the court to at least review their case. Attorneys representing Guantánamo Bay prisoners soon asked federal courts to do the same.

In so doing another question arose: were those prisoners subject to the jurisdiction of American courts in the first place, since they could be said to be held on foreign soil? In its briefs to the Supreme Court, the administration said no: since Cuba retained "ultimate sovereignty" over the base, Guantánamo Bay was "outside the sovereign territory of the United States" and thus, as one of the lawyers later put it, "the legal equivalent of outer space."[36] The prisoners' counsel noted that the Guantánamo Bay naval base could hardly be said to be under Cuban control. Indeed, they pointed out, the U.S. Endangered Species Act specifically referenced the base as American territory, so as to protect the Cuban iguana. The iguanas thus had rights superior to the detainees.

Lower courts sided with the administration. The D.C. Circuit Court of Appeals, for example, held that "no court in this country has jurisdiction" since the detainees "are now abroad" and thus did not fall under constitutional protections. Justice Kennedy's concurring opinion for the Supreme Court's June 2004 reversal of the D.C. circuit court decision, however, pointed out that "this lease is no ordinary lease." The Court majority noted that an American citizen charged with an offense at Guantánamo Bay would certainly have habeas corpus rights, and "there is little reason to think Congress intended the geographical coverage of the statute to vary depending on the detainee's citizenship." The decision did not go to the merits of the case but only established judicial jurisdiction over detainees' challenges to custody (indeed, dissenters claimed it established such wide jurisdiction over cases abroad as to be untenable). However, the Court's warning that the "case of military necessity" was made "weaker" by the base population's "indefinite detention without trial or other proceeding" did prompt the Defense Department to begin moving ahead with the long-stalled tribunal process. Such procedures, it was hoped, would serve as sufficient due process to satisfy the courts in future cases, though subsequent lower court decisions like the one noted previously clouded that hope, at least temporarily.[37]

Further, in response to the related *Hamdi* case, discussed later in this chapter, the Pentagon also ordered the creation of a Combatant Status Review Tribunal. This board was to hold hearings for each of the 594 detainees at Guantánamo Bay, so as to determine their status as legitimate prisoners of war, enemy combatants, or innocent bystanders. Of the first 104 decisions, 103 detainees were affirmed as enemy combatants and one was released.[38]

BUDGETING FOR WAR: THE OVERSIGHT DEFICIT

In April 2003 the head of the U.S. Agency for International Development assured taxpayers in a televised interview that the costs of occupying and rebuilding Iraq would be relatively minimal. "The American part of this will be $1.7 billion," he said. "We have no plans for any further-on funding for this." After all, as Deputy Defense Secretary Paul Wolfowitz told Congress around the same time, Iraq "can really finance its own reconstruction, and relatively soon." In earlier testimony, Wolfowitz had denounced estimates that suggested reconstruction would cost over $60 billion. But by early September 2003 the administration had requested $20 billion in reconstruction aid as part of an $87 billion request supporting operations in Iraq and Afghanistan. A January 2004 CBO report suggested that anywhere from $55 to $100 billion was a plausible estimate in the near term.[39]

The projected costs of the war itself were likewise opaque. White House policy was to refuse to make an estimate—"fundamentally, we have no idea what is needed," Wolfowitz told the House Budget Committee. He added, just three weeks before the war, "I am reluctant to try to predict anything about what the cost of a possible conflict in Iraq would be. . . . But some of the higher-end predictions that we have been hearing recently . . . are wildly off the mark." That dig was aimed at General Eric Shinseki, the U.S. Army chief of staff, who had told Congress that "several hundred thousand soldiers" would be needed to win the war and to administer the occupation. Shinseki was soon retired; White House economic adviser Larry Lindsey had already been fired for his prediction that the war would cost between $100 and $200 billion (a figure in line with other outside estimates, such as that of economist and former Reagan aide William Nordhaus). Part of the problem was that the Office of the Secretary of Defense, albeit not the whole of the Defense Department, felt that resistance in Iraq would be minimal since Iraqis would greet American troops as "liberators." A large occupation force would not be required if, as presumed, Iraqis would be throwing flowers rather than rocket-propelled grenades at U.S. servicemen.[40]

The Lindsey estimate proved prescient: by late 2004 more than $125 billion had been spent and a new $80 billion appropriations request was being readied for 2005.[41] Still, Congress did not push much past the administration's original assumptions. Its dilemma was real: having allowed the president wide discretion in conducting the war, it had little leeway to rein in those choices. The administration, through occupation administrator L. Paul Bremer, insisted that none of the first supplemental appropriations request for $87 billion was optional. It was, he said, "a carefully considered, integrated request" and "urgent" for "the safety of our troops." The president threatened to veto the package if any of the bill was turned into a loan. House leader DeLay, having earlier framed March 2003 tax votes as a matter of presidential patriotism, called the October 2003 vote on the supplemental budget a "second war resolution." It passed 303–125 and 87–12 in the House and Senate, respectively.

Likewise, as the regular budget that year rolled around, Sen. John Warner (R-VA), chair of the Armed Services Committee, would state matter-of-factly, "We have an obligation to live up to the president's budget request." If the war in Iraq was part of the war on terror—and after a year of occupation, even if it was not—losing was not an option. Further, holding up appropriations might deny American soldiers the tools they needed. (Indeed, stories relating that military families were sending privately obtained body armor, boots, global positioning system units, and the like—and that the army was short of armored vehicles and other basics for troop safety— made lawmakers eager to spend more, not less.)[42]

With funding in hand, the administration used it without much reference to legislative intent or oversight, a pattern that went back to the $40 billion Emergency Response Fund created immediately after September 11. The president had been given much of that amount to spend on assisting victims of the attacks and to strengthen the American security position. Few strings were attached; as the Office of Management and

Budget (OMB) put it, "the president asked and Congress provided unprecedented flexibility for funds to wage the war on terrorism." However, the administration was supposed to provide a plan for how the funds were to be used and to provide quarterly reports on their disposition. Those reports were fitful and ended in May 2003. Further, in the summer of 2002 some of this antiterror funding—and other older appropriations as well—was utilized in the Persian Gulf, apparently as preparation for the war with Iraq, long before that war was publicly decided upon. The *Washington Post*'s Bob Woodward put the prewar spending figure at $700 million (the Pentagon countered with an estimate of $178 million). According to Woodward, a top White House official defended the diversion of funds from Afghanistan to Iraq by saying that the White House didn't want "to disturb the karma of Congress." Woodward's conclusion: "Congress got had."[43]

As the $87 billion supplemental moved through the legislative process, Congress and its karma sought to avoid a repeat performance by attaching reporting requirements to those funds. An inspector general's post was added to the Coalition Provisional Authority (CPA) administering the occupation; the inspector general was to issue regular public reports on spending and (as discussed later) contracting. However, the president was given special authority to quash portions of those reports, even those to Congress. No information could be disclosed if it was "specifically required by Executive order to be protected from disclosure, in the interest of national defense . . . or in the conduct of foreign affairs"; and the president could waive, "for national security reasons," the inclusion of "any element" in the quarterly reports the law demanded. In a signing statement, President Bush additionally made clear that he intended the inspector general to "refrain" from audits into intelligence or counterintelligence, ongoing criminal investigations, or "sensitive operation plans." Those topics were left undefined but could in principle wall off much of the CPA's work.[44]

Complicating accounting, and accountability, was the trend toward using civilian contracting for tasks that were once purely military. Contractors made up some 10 percent of American personnel in Iraq by the spring of 2004, performing functions ranging from construction to translation to food service to tank repair. Contractors even served as security details for CPA officials and as prison interrogators. As this suggests, the gathering and analysis of intelligence data were in many cases effectively privatized. This was not always inappropriate, given the shortage of military linguists and the availability of private sector expertise. But neither was it always clear who was responsible for what, as military and civilian personnel carried out the same tasks (if at radically different rates of pay).[45]

Nor were clear procedures for competitive contracting announced. Even before the war started, the firm of Kellogg Brown & Root (KBR) received a no-bid contract worth as much as $7 billion over five years. Originally this was announced as a way to efficiently repair Iraqi oil fields likely to be damaged in the war; later, however, it was made public that the contract also included future operation of, and distribution to market from, those oil fields. This raised eyebrows, both for the size of the contract and because of Vice President Cheney's close ties to KBR's parent company, Halliburton.[46] In October the top contracting official for the Army Corps of Engineers charged that Halliburton officials had been allowed to join internal Defense Department discussions of the KBR contract before its terms were settled.

Pentagon audits of bills for gasoline and food services later led to charges from House Budget Committee Democrats that "Halliburton has routinely and systematically overcharged the U.S. government." As bad publicity mounted, the $7 billion KBR contract was shortened to one year and then opened to competition. As or more troubling were charges of more overt corruption; in January 2004, for instance, the *Wall Street Journal* reported that two Halliburton employees had received $6 million in kickbacks from a Kuwaiti company in exchange for extending it a lucrative subcontract. There was no way to know whether it was the event itself or the reporting of it that was aberrant, since the administration was hesitant to release what Rep. Henry Waxman (D-CA) called "basic information" on the "scope and status" of contractors and bidding. Still, various bills filed to require competitive bidding languished in committee. When the administration's $87 billion supplemental budget request came before Congress, Rep. Jim Kolbe (R-AZ) and others insisted on including such a provision, along with the inspector general's office noted previously. But as passed, the open bidding requirement could still be waived if the head of the CPA and the executive agency awarding the contract both agreed, though the reasons for the waiver had to be published.[47]

The fuzzy status of the CPA itself made oversight yet more difficult. The CPA, which vanished from government upon the reassumption of nominal sovereignty by the Iraqi government in June 2004, had come into being sometime in the spring of 2003, replacing an earlier Office of Reconstruction and Humanitarian Assistance. Bremer, CPA's head, reported to the Defense Department. Yet the CPA had no basis in statute or even executive order; the Congressional Research Service (CRS) was left to guess it had been created by a secret National Security Presidential Directive. Another possibility was that it was "an amorphous international organization" established pursuant to a UN Security Council resolution. As a result, CRS fretted, "it is unclear whether CPA is a federal agency" and thus to what rules it might be subject: "the lack of an authoritative and unambiguous statement about how this organization was established, by whom, and under what authority leaves open many questions, particularly in the areas of oversight and accountability." Indeed, in 2003 the army denied that the Congress's General Accounting Office (GAO) had the right to audit CPA spending or contracting decisions, since the "CPA is a multinational coalition" and the "GAO does not have jurisdiction over this process." CPA issued regulations, but not subject to the Administrative Procedure Act (thus not published in the *Federal Register* or open to public comment). No clear chain of command could be identified.[48] All that seemed clear was that the president was meant to be in charge.

UNILATERAL AUTHORITY & EXECUTIVE PRIVILEGE

War and spending powers, then, were expanded both by presidential fiat and by congressional delegation. Prosecution of the war on terrorism on the domestic front followed a similar pattern. The president used his extant powers aggressively. Most publicized were his broad claims of inherent authority to designate even American citizens as enemy combatants and thus not subject to the regular legal process. He also used tools like the International Emergency Economic Powers Act (IEEPA), seizing private assets his administration designated as linked to terrorism.

However, the president's administrative arsenal also received additional reinforcement via legislative action. In the wake of lax airport security on September 11, for example, that function was federalized in a new Transportation Security Administration. As noted earlier, by the fall of 2004 serious discussions were under way aimed at creating a director of national intelligence in order to consolidate some fifteen extant agencies that had failed to cooperate or to share intelligence information with each other.

That proposal built on another large-scale effort at coordination. In September 2001 President Bush had used an executive order to create the OHS, seeking to superintend hundreds of scattered executive branch functions applicable to the purpose. Later, acknowledging that the OHS had insufficient clout over the offices it ostensibly channeled, the president proposed the creation of an enormous new Department of Homeland Security (DHS). Congress agreed (indeed, the proposal had originally been congressional), and the reorganization was signed into law in late November 2002. DHS combined 170,000 employees from twenty-two agencies into a $37 billion organization. The president demanded, and received, sweeping new powers over this new bureaucracy, including flexibility over pay levels and work assignments and the authority to revamp hiring and firing procedures. The legislation also included language mandating that the department keep the information it received from private industry secret, even from state and local government; leakers could be criminally prosecuted. The broad exemption was meant to protect from public view any vulnerabilities in "critical infrastructure." However, by providing that such communications could not be released without the permission of the entity submitting them, the provision opened the door for industry to use DHS as a hiding place for damning reports on, say, the dumping of hazardous wastes. To prevent this, Congress and the GAO were specifically granted access to such information. However, in a detailed signing statement, President Bush effectively revoked that exemption. "The executive branch does not construe this provision," Bush wrote,

> to impose any independent or affirmative requirement to share such information with the Congress or the Comptroller General and shall

construe it in any event in a manner consistent with the constitutional authorities of the President to supervise the unitary executive branch and to withhold information the disclosure of which could impair foreign relations, the national security, the deliberative processes of the Executive, or the performance of the Executive's constitutional duties.

Parallel limiting language was repeated in other sections dealing with potential oversight of the president's use of his new civil service authority, in the requirement that DHS send budget information directly to Congress, and in some twenty other sections of the law.[49]

Executive privilege was not invoked formally with regards to matters linked to September 11. But the doctrine hit the headlines in the spring of 2004 when the 9/11 Commission requested that national security adviser Rice testify under oath on the intelligence available to the president before the attacks. Originally the president resisted, arguing that Rice's appearance would harm presidents' ability to receive candid advice about sensitive issues. This rationale gained little traction with the public, in part because Rice had already spoken widely to the media on similar topics while seeking to rebut charges that Bush had been inattentive to terrorism for the first eight months of his term. Ultimately, Bush allowed Rice to testify. He argued that only the "truly unique and extraordinary circumstances" of September 11 justified his decision, going so far as to extract assurances from the House and Senate Republican leadership that her appearance "does not set, and should not be cited as, a precedent for future requests" for any White House official to testify before a legislative body.[50]

The administration had more success with less salient measures heightening government secrecy. For instance, Chief of Staff Card directed in March 2002 that agencies restrict access to what he called "sensitive but unclassified" information that might provide information on weapons of mass destruction or, more generally, "related to America's homeland security." According to the conservative Heritage Foundation, agencies responded by removing thousands of previously public documents from the possibility of FOIA disclosure. In other cases the administration charged huge sums for document searches conducted under FOIA, presenting a bill for nearly $375,000 to a public interest group seeking information on immigrants detained by the Justice Department after September 11.[51]

Not surprisingly, law enforcement powers received a major boost after the September 11 attacks. The FBI was told that its first job was now terrorism prevention, and the Justice Department worked aggressively to give the bureau and other entities additional resources. One front was administrative. In October 2001, for example, the department published rules crimping attorney-client privilege—to be implemented immediately, without public comment. The new regulations allowed prison authorities to monitor phone conversations and mail between prisoners and their lawyers if the attorney general had any suspicion that those communications might "further or facilitate" acts of terrorism. Originally, the prisoner had to be told that the government was listening in. Later, however, a statutory change rescinded the need for such notice.

Shortly after September 11, Attorney General John Ashcroft announced that he would allow the Justice Department's guidelines governing investigative behavior to be waived in "extraordinary cases" where this would "prevent and investigate terrorism." In May 2002, expressing "disappoint[ment]" that authority had not been used more frequently, he announced a broad revision of the guidelines. The new language gave FBI field offices more discretion to open counterterrorism investigations and rescinded some of the remaining Ford-era restrictions on domestic surveillance by the bureau. In some cases, this merely allowed agents to enter areas, real and virtual, open to the public. But it also meant agents were now allowed to monitor religious or political groups at will, independent of a formal investigation or probable cause that individuals in the group had committed or were plotting a crime.[52]

A number of administrative actions were aimed at noncitizens. The Justice Department used its power over immigration matters to locate and hold over five thousand resident aliens in preventive detention. Some were held as "material witnesses," meaning that they were deemed to have information pertinent to a crime and might flee unless detained, though no charges were filed against them; others were charged with violating the terms of their visas or other laws (from speeding to assault). Deportation hearings were accelerated, and the department ordered that more than six hundred hearings deemed of "special interest" be completely closed to the public, including to family members of the accused. The hearings themselves were not to appear on the public docket, and even the names of those detained were kept secret, leading to angry accusations drawing parallels to the Argentinian *desaparecidos* of the 1970s. Lower court orders to open the hearings were largely overturned, and in May 2003 the Supreme Court let stand a ruling by the Third Circuit Court of Appeals, which had upheld the government's ability to close the hearings.[53]

Governmental efforts to collect information about the behavior of noncitizens and citizens alike expanded dramatically. The creation and "mining" of vast, centralized databases of financial, communications, travel, and medical records were at the heart of the ominously named Total [later, "Terrorism"] Information Awareness program (TIA) housed within a research branch of the Pentagon. A parallel project hoped to develop biometric identification technology that could pick out individuals from a distance or within large crowds. The characterization of these projects as "computer dragnets" inimical to privacy rights forced their curtailment in late 2003.

THE PATRIOT ACT

Related projects continued, however, diffused across various agencies involved in foreign intelligence.[54] The administration also asked for legislative approval for a wide-ranging relaxation of limitations on Justice's surveillance and detention powers. The bluntly named Patriot Act created a host of new federal crimes and enhanced penalties for others, defining "domestic terrorism" and outlawing terrorist attacks on mass transportation facilities, harboring terrorists, or providing them with "material support" (including "expert advice"). It provided new charges associated with crimes ranging from the use of biological weapons to fraudulent charitable fund-raising. Terrorism was defined as a racketeering activity under the Racketeer Influenced and Corrupt Organizations (RICO) statutes, expanding prosecutorial tools. New money-laundering provisions made it easier for the treasury secretary to get access to bank records and to seize the assets of any person or entity taking part, or planning to take part, in terrorist activities; portions of the World War I–era Trading with the Enemy Act allowing the president to confiscate (not just freeze) foreign property in response to foreign aggression were resurrected.

A number of provisions dealt with immigration and resident aliens. Building on the 1996 antiterror law discussed in chapter 6, the Patriot Act expanded the definition of "engaging in terrorist activity" so that any alien soliciting money or membership for a certified terrorist organization or "espousing" terrorist activity could be deemed inadmissible to—and thus deportable from—the United States. Spouses or children of an inadmissible alien were likewise deemed inadmissible. More broadly, aliens suspected on "reasonable grounds" of terrorism could now be detained by the Justice Department for up to seven days without charge. (The administration's original request was for unlimited detention, without judicial review. The military order discussed previously may have served as another way to achieve that goal.)

The Patriot Act extended government surveillance powers as well. Some of the changes simply caught statutes up to the digital age—for example, by more readily permitting "roving" taps on suspects using multiple or portable phone lines and by allowing voice-mail messages to be seized pursuant to a warrant. Others added terrorist activities to the list of offenses where federal law specifically allows domestic wiretapping after obtaining a warrant. Federal power to trace the identities of incoming and outgoing calls (a sort of hidden, two-way caller ID) was expanded and extended to e-mail and to the addresses of Web sites that a computer user had visited. The government's ability to delay notifying the target of a warrant of that warrant's execution was also broadened to so-called sneak and peek searches, where officers are authorized to conduct a search but not to remove tangible evidence (though they can take pictures or download computer files) without leaving notice of their presence. Such notification could be delayed if a prosecutor could claim that notice was "jeopardizing an investigation or unduly delaying a trial."

Additional sections broadened the information available to the FBI through National Security Letters (NSLs), which themselves could now be issued by bureau field offices instead of Washington. The enhanced NSLs required telephone or e-mail logs, bank records, credit reports, and a wide array of financial records (including those from casinos, pawn shops, and used-car dealerships) to be turned over to the FBI if the bureau felt they were "relevant" to an ongoing intelligence investigation. In late September 2004 a district court judge held that the language was too broad and that NSLs amounted to a warrant by other means, without judicial review. The government appealed the ruling.[55]

NSLs could not be used in criminal investigations in any case. However, other portions of the Patriot Act aimed to breach the Foreign Intelligence Surveillance Act (FISA) "wall" between counterintelligence and criminal cases. In later testimony, Attorney General Ashcroft would blame "the wall"—and specifically its purported reinforcement by the Clinton administration—for much of the FBI's difficulty in uncovering the September 11 plot. However, Ashcroft's own office had endorsed the Clinton-era interpretation of FISA in August 2001. A more telling critique was of bureaucratic culture: neither FBI nor CIA had much interest in sharing information. A report issued by Sen. Richard Shelby (R-AL) suggested, indeed, that invocation of the "wall" as a legal question was often simply a tool "for maintaining the independence that the FBI views as its birthright."[56]

That said, the statutory wall *had* at times been used as a barrier to legitimate investigations. There was good reason for this, given past abuses. But there were also potential trade-offs, made clear by the pre-9/11 investigative failures (for example, domestic law enforcement's failure to realize that several of the hijackers being tracked by the CIA had entered the United States). FISA had been amended in 1994 to allow physical searches as well as electronic surveillance and in 1998 to expand the FBI's ability to tap lines in terrorism investigations. But the Patriot Act went much further. The duration of FISA orders was extended, in the case of physical searches doubled to ninety days. Most critically, it allowed FISA surveillance if foreign intelligence information gathering was a "significant purpose," as opposed to the only, or primary, purpose, of the investigation; thus under the new law criminal investigation itself, and not foreign intelligence, could be the main reason for the surveillance.[57] It made FISA warrants easier to obtain—the FBI now had to show only that the request was part of an investigation relevant to a foreign intelligence operation rather than show it was linked to any particular individual's actions—and empowered the FBI to require production of "tangible things," such as business records and even library lending receipts. Further, domestic law enforcement officials were empowered to share information discovered through grand jury investigations with other federal authorities, from immigration to intelligence.

After the first-ever ruling from the FISA Court of Review upheld the new rules in late 2002, the number of applications for FISA warrants rose above seventeen hundred in 2003 (from about twelve hundred in 2002). Only three were rejected.[58]

The Patriot Act attracted much obloquy, ranging from the thoughtful to the hysterical. Some worried about FISA procedures being used to evade Fourth Amendment protections against unreasonable searches. Others were concerned about the treatment of aliens and immigrants. Others feared that the label of "domestic terrorist" could be used to prosecute anyone from abortion clinic picketers to antiglobalization protesters.[59]

One common criticism was the lack of deliberation accorded the act in Congress. The administration demanded immediate action: "we're at war," the president reminded lawmakers. "And in order to win the war, we must make sure that the law enforcement men and women have got the tools necessary, within the Constitution, to defeat the enemy."[60] The Patriot Act draft received no hearings or committee consideration in the Senate, going directly to the floor—where it was slotted for consideration under a unanimous consent order in the Senate that prohibited amendments or even discussion. Sen. Russ Feingold (D-WI) objected; nonetheless, after just four hours of debate, the bill passed unamended by a vote of 96 to 1. On the House side, the normally polarized Judiciary Committee (whose members ranged from Bob Barr [R-GA] on the far right to Barney Frank [D-MA] on the far left) rewrote the administration's draft to provide increased protections for civil liberties. However, at the behest of the White House, the new version passed unanimously in committee vanished from consideration: the rule adopted for the bill's consideration on the House floor provided that the Judiciary Committee's bill be replaced with language much closer to the administration's own proposal. The rule closed off all other amendments and allowed just one hour for debate. No advance analysis was provided of the 187 pages of new text. While this maneuver prompted recrimination—the rule prevailed only on a near perfect party-line vote,

214–208—many members feared the political impact of a "no" vote on the bill itself, and it passed overwhelmingly.[61]

It should be noted that in conference committee the bill regained some of the checks that civil libertarians had urged. One shift, for instance, curtailed Justice's proposal to detain immigrants indefinitely. Others raised the bar somewhat for various warrants and searches. Most significant was a sunset provision for many (though not all) of the changes in the surveillance regime; they were to expire on January 1, 2006, unless extended.

After the conference report was passed by huge majorities, President Bush signed the act into law on October 26, 2001. In doing so, the president emphasized that "This government will enforce this law with all the urgency of a nation at war."[62] Little oversight was expected—or accepted—in this process. Attorney General Ashcroft told critics of the law that raising "phantoms of lost liberty" was "giv[ing] ammunition to America's enemies and pause to America's friends." His message, he said, was "this: your tactics only aid terrorists." The Senate Judiciary Committee sent twenty-seven letters to the Justice Department on the implementation of the Patriot Act and other laws—all went unanswered. When its House counterpart asked for information on how often various Patriot Act provisions had been used, the Justice Department refused to give any details for months. Only a threatened subpoena from House Judiciary Committee chair F. James Sensenbrenner (R-WI) elicited answers. When conservative senator Larry Craig (R-ID) urged mild revisions to the Patriot Act in 2003, Ashcroft attacked the bill before it even reached committee, arguing there was no point to discussing something that would "undermine our ongoing campaign" against terrorism. Senate Judiciary Committee chair Hatch evidently agreed; no hearings were held until September 2004, in conjunction with efforts to repeal the bill's sunset provisions.[63] At that time, Deputy Attorney General James Comey defended the law that, he argued, "has changed our world and has made us immeasurably safer," especially by breaking down the FISA wall.[64]

There were, nonetheless, signs that law enforcement had not always used its new discretion appropriately. In 2003, the Justice Department's inspector general reported that authorities had made scant effort to discriminate between valid terror suspects and other individuals. More than seven hundred aliens were arrested in the months after September 11. Many were jailed for months, often without access to attorneys or formal charges against them. And some—notably in the Metropolitan Detention Center in Brooklyn, New York—were physically abused, verbally harassed, and repeatedly strip searched, mistreatment all caught on videotape. None were ever charged as terrorists. In 2004, after the Madrid train bombings, the FBI secretly surveilled and very publicly detained an Oregon lawyer whose fingerprint was claimed to be a "100 percent" match to one found in Spain. But the print had been wrongly identified. That summer the FBI was accused of harassing antiwar activists planning to demonstrate at the Democratic National Convention in Boston. Others charged that the bureau had abused its ability to detain material witnesses without filing charges. More generally, Patriot Act powers surfaced in mundane cases ranging from drug enforcement to political corruption, even as the administration at once emphasized the act's utility in fighting terrorists but downplayed the frequency with which its most controversial provisions were used.[65]

To be sure, the pressures on law enforcement immediately after September 11 were immense. But the lingering effects on civil liberties demanded debate that did not occur. In any case, said the attorney general, "We make no apologies." In his 2004 State of the Union address, President Bush asked Congress to make the existing provisions of the Patriot Act permanent and to add new ones. He elaborated in a speech on April 19 (Patriots' Day): the act, he said, was "essential law. . . . We can't return to the days of false hope." This meant giving the Justice Department the power to issue administrative subpoenas to obtain time-sensitive records without judicial review, banning bail for terror suspects, and making additional terror-related crimes eligible for capital punishment. Other proposed changes, not mentioned by the president in his speech, would make it easier to keep classified information from criminal defendants and would expand FBI's FISA surveillance over "lone-wolf" noncitizens suspected of terrorist activities but without affiliation with an international group. In the fall of 2004 the House leadership included key provisions of the president's proposal in their version of the intelligence community restructuring bill and added tough language allowing DHS to detain indefinitely foreigners charged with terrorist ties and expanding the government's capacity to deport aliens without judicial review. The final version included the "lone wolf" provision and new restrictions on bail for terror suspects, while increasing the penalties for harboring illegal aliens and making it illegal to attend terrorist-run training camps. It also refined—and expanded—the criteria that defined "material support" to terrorist operatives, in response to a court ruling that had found those criteria overly vague.

While contentious—the Patriot Act provisions of the House bill helped stall the broader intelligence restructuring in conference committee—the 2004 enactments were tame compared to other portions of the proposed Domestic Security Enhancement Act of 2003, immediately dubbed "Patriot II." Prepared secretly in the Justice Department until leaked in February (on the eve of the Iraq war), Patriot II would have provided for greatly expanded wiretapping in criminal—not intelligence—investigations of U.S. citizens as well as of aliens. Access to consumer credit reports was also to be eased by allowing federal investigators merely to certify that the information therein would be used "in connection with their duties to enforce federal law"—not to investigate any particular crime.

FISA was to be amended again too. The attorney general's power to bar or remove aliens would be expanded anew; and FOIA would be amended to exempt information about aliens detained during terror investigations. FISA surveillance could be in place for seventy-two hours before a warrant was obtained—or in some situations, under new "presidential authorization exceptions," for up to a year. Even the attorney general, currently permitted to authorize FISA orders without court permission for fifteen days during periods of declared war, would receive enhanced power to do so any time Congress authorized the use of military force or during times of national emergency.

Most dramatic, perhaps, especially given the actions and claims concerning aliens, was the provision providing that an American could "voluntarily" lose citizenship by "serving in a hostile terrorist organization" as designated by the administration. Providing material support—attending a rally? buying a raffle ticket?— to such a group, even without knowledge of their status, could result in the president's stripping one's citizenship.[66] It was a breathtaking proposal, and it was not enacted.

Nonetheless, the Patriot Act's sunset clause guaranteed that the debate over Patriot II, and more broadly the proper balance between security

and civil liberties, would be renewed in 2005. There seemed little likelihood that the act would be allowed to expire.

CITIZEN COMBATANTS?

Those debates would be shaped by the president's unprecedented claim to
unilateral power over the rights not just of aliens but of American citizens.
Specifically, President Bush claimed the authority to remove defendants
from the judicial process by designating them as terrorist "enemy combatants" parallel to the aliens discussed previously in the war powers section. Such people, he said, did not have to be charged with a specific
crime or represented by an attorney. And they could be held indefinitely
without trial. In this view of presidential power, judicial review of a given
suspect's case was not necessary—nor indeed permissible.

Bush's claims were challenged by two individuals presenting different
sets of facts. One, Yaser Hamdi, was a Saudi national born in Louisiana.
He was captured on the Afghan battlefield and originally detained at
Guantánamo Bay. When identified as a U.S. citizen, he was transferred
to a military brig for interrogation and remained there for two and a half
years without being criminally charged. This was legal, the administration argued, under the president's powers as commander in chief, which
were "at their height" in this case: Hamdi was "a classic battlefield
detainee," and "the Executive's determination that an individual is an
enemy combatant is a quintessentially military judgment." Further,
recall the September 14 resolution: had not Congress allowed the president the use of "all necessary and appropriate force against those . . . persons" the president determined to be connected with the September 11
attacks? And had not legislators asserted, in the same statute, that "the
President has authority under the Constitution to take action to deter
and prevent acts of international terrorism against the United States"? As
a result, any judicial review was unwarranted. "The court may not second-guess the military's enemy combatant determination, and therefore
no evidentiary proceedings concerning such determination are necessary," the administration told the Fourth Circuit Court of Appeals.
"Going beyond that determination would require the courts to enter an
area in which they have no competence, much less institutional exper-

tise, and intrude upon the Constitutional prerogative of the Commander in Chief." At most, the administration later said, judges could decide whether there was any factual basis for the determination that Hamdi was an enemy combatant. But judges could not question the merits of that determination. Thus so long as something like the one-and-a-half-page "Mobbs Declaration" provided by Pentagon aide Michael Mobbs existed, judges would have to accept the president's decision.

A district court rejected this argument, saying the Mobbs Declaration was "insufficient" and that it "leads to more questions than it answers." After all (quoting now from the declaration itself), it merely affirmed that Hamdi had been "determined by the U.S. military . . . to meet the criteria for enemy combatants." But the Fourth Circuit Court overturned that judgment, averring that while judicial deference was "not unlimited" judges should nonetheless be "highly deferential": since it was undisputed that Hamdi was "captured in a zone of active combat operations abroad, further judicial inquiry is unwarranted when the government has responded to the petition by setting forth factual assertions which would establish a legally valid basis for the detention." Actually testing those assertions went beyond the court's jurisdiction: Hamdi was "not entitled to challenge" them.[67]

Clearly the circumstances of Hamdi's capture featured prominently in the administration's argument and the circuit court's decision. But the president's claim was not limited to the foreign battlefield. New York native José Padilla was arrested in Chicago on May 8, 2002, as he arrived at O'Hare International Airport from Pakistan. He was detained as a material witness to a conspiracy to use a radiological (i.e., "dirty") bomb against American targets. It later emerged that the dirty bomb plot had probably been discarded and that Padilla hoped instead to blow up apartments by exploding gas ovens. Presumably he could have been criminally charged in connection with either set of plans. However, when a court required that he be either charged or released, Padilla was instead designated an enemy combatant by order of the president and transferred to military custody. "The authority of the commander-in-chief to engage and defeat the enemy encompasses the capture and detention of enemy combatants wherever found, including within the nation's borders," the administration argued. There need not be any rules for determining who was an enemy combatant and who would be a regular criminal, Solicitor General Theodore Olson noted; instead, "there will be judgments and instincts and evaluations and implementations that have to be made by the executive that are probably going to be different from day to day, depending on the circumstances."[68]

A legal standard that changed "from day to day" clearly had ramifications for the Fifth and Fourteenth Amendments' notions of due process and equal protection of law. Padilla argued that any crimes he had committed could be adequately managed by civilian courts. After all, in *Ex parte Milligan* after the Civil War, the Supreme Court had held that even wartime did not justify evasion of a functioning court system (see chapter 2). Further, he argued, the administration's actions violated the 1971 Non-Detention Act's provision that no person may be detained "except pursuant to an act of Congress" (see chapter 4).

The administration responded that, as "a belligerent associated with the enemy" who had returned to the country in order to harm it, Padilla was properly subject not to U.S. law but to the laws of war: the appropriate case was not *Milligan* but *Quirin,* the Nazi saboteur case discussed earlier. Thus the president's inherent authorities more than sufficed: "The President's exercise of that core Article II power [i.e., the commander-in-chief power] is not conditioned on any action by Congress." As for the 1971 statute, the administration argued that it did not apply to wartime—and that even if it did, the September 14 Authorization for Use of Military Force (AUMF) was sufficient warrant for the president's orders. "Nothing in the terms of Congress's Authorization suggests a limitation to a foreign battlefield," the Justice Department noted, pointing out that the resolution had after all been passed in response to acts on domestic soil. "Is Padilla just the same as somebody you catch in Afghanistan?" Deputy Solicitor General Paul Clement was asked in oral argument; "he is just the same," Clement replied. As with *Hamdi,* the courts were to stay out of the way. "The fact that executive discretion in a war situation can be abused," Clement noted, "is not a good and sufficient reason for judicial micromanagement and overseeing of that authority."

In late 2002 a district court ruled in favor of the administration on all points but one—American enemy combatants were possible, and any judicial review did indeed owe the executive great deference, but a detainee was to be allowed to consult an attorney to help him challenge the evidence presented by the government.

The administration balked and appealed, arguing that Padilla's lawyer might be used, even unwittingly, to carry messages to other terrorists. However, the Second Circuit Court of Appeals rejected not just this claim but the president's more basic assertion. It ruled in December 2003 that "the President lacks inherent constitutional authority as Commander-in-Chief to detain American citizens on American soil outside a zone of combat." Going back to the 1952 *Youngstown* case, the court decided that the Non-Detention Act explicitly denied presidents the power to detain American citizens on American soil; to overcome this, the detention power would have had to be "clearly and unmistakably indicated," and the September 14 authorization failed this test. The president could simply not act alone on his own say-so. The court concluded,

> we are as keenly aware as anyone of the threat al Qaeda poses to our country and of the responsibilities the President and law enforcement officials bear for protecting the nation. But presidential authority does not exist in a vacuum, and this case involves not whether those responsibilities should be aggressively pursued, but whether the President is obligated, in the circumstances presented here, to share them with Congress.

The short answer was "yes."[69]

The Supreme Court heard the *Padilla* and *Hamdi* cases on the same day in April 2004. By a 5–4 vote, the justices set Padilla's case aside on technical grounds since he had not filed his petition in the correct federal court: it should have been done in South Carolina rather than in New York. The dissenters fiercely protested that the "exceptional" nature of the case overrode the legal fine print: "at stake in this case is nothing less than the essence of a free society," argued Justice John Paul Stevens. "Even more important than the methods of selecting the people's rulers and their successors is the character of the constraints imposed on the Executive by the rule of law."[70]

The court chose instead to use Hamdi's case to flesh out Stevens's claim. It largely agreed with him. All told, some eight justices agreed that

the administration had overstepped its constitutional bounds. As Justice
Antonin Scalia wrote (joined by Stevens), "the very core of liberty
secured by our Anglo-Saxon system of separated powers has been freedom from indefinite imprisonment at the will of the Executive." The
president, Scalia felt, had suspended habeas corpus, which was a power
reserved to the Congress. Since Congress had not done so, Hamdi
needed to be either charged or released.

The sound bite commonly drawn from the plurality opinion written
by Justice Sandra Day O'Connor was along similar lines. "A state of war
is not a blank check for the President when it comes to the rights of the
Nation's citizens," the Court declared. "Whatever power the United
States Constitution envisions for the Executive in its exchanges with
other nations or with enemy organizations in times of conflict, it most
assuredly envisions a role for all three branches when individual liberties
are at stake."

As a result, the president's claims that judges had no role in examining the combatant cases, and that the presence of *any* evidence in the
record painting a suspect as an enemy combatant must be deferred to as
sufficient evidence, were set aside. Such suspects were owed due
process—at the least, the accused needed to be told of the evidence
against him and a fair hearing to rebut it.

Nonetheless, Scalia's opinion was not a concurrence but a dissent.
The lead opinion held that, while Congress had not suspended the
habeas writ, the September 14 Authorization for Use of Military Force
(AUMF) did constitute legislative delegation to the president sufficient
to name enemy combatants: "Congress has in fact authorized Hamdi's
detention, through the AUMF." The 1971 Non-Detention Act did not
apply (a contention that sparked a different dissenting opinion), because
taking prisoners was deemed so central to armed conflict that "it is of no
moment that the AUMF does not use specific language of detention."
The Court therefore did not need to discuss whether the president's
commander-in-chief power extended to detaining Hamdi and others: so
long as they were among those covered by the AUMF, Congress had
done the extending. The issue was whether they *were* covered, and the
Court held that the president had not bothered to prove that point.[71]

Nor did the administration try to do so, in this case at least. Hamdi—
having been declared so dangerous to national security that he could not
be allowed access to counsel—was released from prison without charge

in October 2004 and returned to his family in Saudi Arabia. The decision, then, was a win for him (and perhaps for Padilla, whose habeas petition was refiled in the appropriate district, while the government pondered bringing criminal charges against him). But whether it was a long-term loss for the president was less certain. "Our opinion only finds legislative authority to detain under the AUMF once it is sufficiently clear that the individual is, in fact, an enemy combatant," wrote the four justices led by O'Connor, but the Court left the definition of sufficient clarity itself rather hazy. The justices declined to state whether citizens detained beyond the Afghan battlefield might apply; nor was adequate due process specified beyond the "core elements" noted previously. A full-blown judicial proceeding was not, it seemed, required: "enemy combatant proceedings may be tailored to alleviate their uncommon potential to burden the Executive at a time of ongoing military conflict." The status review hearings noted earlier in this chapter were the military's first effort to "tailor" such proceedings without involving the courts. The process did not provide the detainees with lawyers or with the chance to review the evidence against them. And in subsequent cases, despite the Court ruling, the administration continued to strenuously resist detainees' efforts to obtain counsel and hearings before federal judges.[72]

The unsettled situation recollected a section of Justice Souter's opinion in the *Hamdi* case appealing to legislators for judgment. "In a government of separated powers," he wrote, "deciding finally on what is a reasonable degree of guaranteed liberty whether in peace or war (or some condition in between) is not well entrusted to the Executive Branch." After all, the president has a job to do: "the [executive's] responsibility for security will naturally amplify the claim that security legitimately raises." There was therefore the "need for an assessment by Congress before citizens are subject to lockup, and likewise the need for a clearly expressed congressional resolution of the competing claims."

No resolution, however, was forthcoming.

ETHICS: THE POLITICS OF TRUST

The September 11 attacks made Americans reevaluate, for a time, their attitudes toward government. In July 2001 a little more than a quarter of respondents said they trusted the federal government to do the right thing most or all of the time. But in October 2001, 57 percent said so. In July, 50 percent of those polled said their feelings toward the government were at least "somewhat" favorable—in October that figure brushed 80 percent.

But by May 2002 both figures had dropped back down—to 40 and 60 percent, respectively, and by late 2003 just 27 percent answered "most of the time" to the question of how often they trusted government to do the right thing.[73] The quick return of these figures to "normal" post-Watergate levels reflected many things, of course, but among them was surely the fact that even in the wake of tragedy government itself acted distressingly "normal" in many ways. To be sure, the most pressing ethical questions of the immediate post–September 11 period were less of outright criminality than of credibility. The United States, political leaders frequently declared, was on a "war footing." As detailed earlier, in a variety of areas the Bush administration utilized that footing to extend executive claims to secrecy and control over information. And it made broad statements—about the costs and rationales for the Iraq war, about broader budget outcomes, about the nature of foreign detainees—without allowing independent verification of the evidence used to support them.

Indeed, it was largely efforts to prevent the spread of information that most rebounded against the administration and even resulted in illegality. One such case, ironically, involved a statute protecting secrecy—violated when the identity of a CIA agent was revealed to the press, despite federal law protecting undercover intelligence operatives from disclosure. The agent's husband, former ambassador Joseph Wilson, had revealed a 2002 report discrediting the president's 2003 State of the Union claim concerning supposed Iraqi efforts to import uranium from Africa. With the expiration of the Independent Counsel Act in 1999, the Justice Department regained control of investigations into allegations of executive misbehavior. But Attorney General Ashcroft's close ties to the White House staff most likely responsible for the leak led to familiar accusations of conflicting interests. Ashcroft ultimately recused himself from the case, though resisting calls to name an outside counsel; his deputy appointed a U.S. attorney from Chicago to direct the investigation.[74]

A second case was not about defense but drugs—namely, a new Medicare prescription drug program. As noted in chapter 5, extraordinary arm-twisting had led to GOP approval of a $400 billion entitlement expansion. But lawmakers soon discovered that the program, when implemented, would cost at least a third more than that, a fact that might have doomed passage among conservatives already uneasy at the hefty price tag. The higher figure had been circulating within the administration for some time—a June 2003 memo by Medicare's chief actuary put the cost at $550 billion or more. However, this information was not shared with Congress until after the bill was safely in law. The actuary claimed his job had been threatened if he released cost data. If true, that sort of disciplinary action violated statutes protecting the rights of federal employees to communicate with Congress, for just such reasons of oversight.[75]

The abuses later revealed by the Abu Ghraib photos and an array of subsequent investigations were down the chain of executive command (though not always far down). They were hardly instituted by White House fiat. But they highlighted what can arise when doors are closed. And the administration tried in myriad ways to keep them tightly shut. Some of those efforts were symbolic, if poignant, such as the ban on photographs of the flag-draped coffins returning from Iraq. Others were substantive. Even the blue-ribbon 9/11 Commission was created over the president's objections and received only grudging, delayed cooperation from the White House, whether the issue was access to preattack intelligence briefs, the extension of the commission's reporting deadline, or testimony from national security adviser Rice.[76]

All this dented the president's reputation for candor. The administration's "fetish for secrecy," as columnist Robert Novak termed it, did not welcome the checks that prevent abuse of trust. Another, earlier assessment concluded by saying Bush had not learned "the lessons of Watergate" and that "secrecy is the way of dictatorships, not democracies." This could perhaps have been dismissed as a partisan screed—except that the author was Nixon counsel John W. Dean.[77]

CONCLUSIONS: AMBITION RISING?

The horror of the September 11 attacks accelerated the demise of the resurgence regime. The attacks made executive authority seem both more necessary and more legitimate. President Bush's standing to lead soared, and he seized the role—and the reins. Congress followed along, endorsing administration initiatives in war, spending, and law enforcement with few legislative questions asked and little executive information volunteered.

The impressive Republican gains in the 2002 midterm elections—solidifying control of the House and returning the Senate to GOP hands, after extensive personal campaigning by the president in key races—seemed to confirm the wisdom of this strategy. Members noted with some trepidation the fate of Sen. Max Cleland (D-GA), defeated for reelection at least in part because of his opposition to the administration's homeland security reorganization proposal. It is worth noting in this context that such deference was actively encouraged. And if the patriotism of a quadriplegic Vietnam War veteran could be questioned successfully, who might be next? House Majority Leader DeLay called opponents of Bush's policy "hand-wringers and appeasers"; Speaker Dennis Hastert (R-IL) suggested that critics of the Iraq war "may not undermine the president as he leads us into war, and they may not give comfort to our adversaries—but they come mighty close." In his successful challenge to Senate Minority Leader Tom Daschle in 2004, former representative John Thune (R-SD) said Daschle's critiques of the president "embolden the enemy." Advertisements in battleground states sought to paint candidates opposing the president's post-9/11 policy as endorsing the Taliban's attacks on human rights.[78]

But this sort of loyalty test was largely gratuitous. Even under divided government in 2002, President Bush was successful on nearly 90 percent of the roll call votes on which he took a position—a figure higher than President Clinton's success rate under unified Democratic government in 1993 and 1994. Democratic senators supported Bush at rates of 71 percent in 2001 and 67 percent in 2002; Republican senators' support for Clinton was never above 46 percent during the period 1998–2000, and even that was up from 1995–96. "On major legislation, Congress has so reliably bowed to Bush's demands that he has yet to veto a bill in his three years in the White House," one summary of the 2003 legislative session pointed out (nor did he veto one in 2004, when his fourth year success on roll call votes was the highest in a generation). Despite the billions of dollars at stake in Iraq contracting, in the end Senate Minority Leader Daschle correctly noted "the lack of any expressed concern in the Congress. There has been virtually no oversight in either the House or the Senate." As late as March 2004, the House of Representatives adopted by a vote of 327–93 a post hoc resolution stressing the need for the Iraq war. Even at home, Congress showed little inclination to keep tabs on crucial aspects of policy implementation; in late 2004 a task force headed by retired senator Warren Rudman (R-NH) scolded Rudman's former colleagues for having "done almost nothing" to ensure that homeland security programs were given effective oversight.[79]

Overshadowing the president's legislative agenda, of course, were his unilateral claims of power—which also received general deference from Congress and the courts. Still, as the 2004 campaign heated up, the frozen ambition of the other branches of government seemed to have thawed as well. Bush's opponent, Sen. John Kerry, fiercely criticized many of the administration's claims and policies, touting his own military service and challenging President Bush's leadership even on national security issues. The Supreme Court's *Hamdi* decision served notice of judicial concern regarding executive overreach and of judges' willingness to step into the fray.

Congress also began to grow more restive. Legislative enthusiasm for early renewal or expansion of the Patriot Act seemed decidedly muted, especially in the Senate, and legislators pondered legal protections for federal whistle-blowers facing administration retaliation. The graphic photographs of humiliation and torture inflicted by American servicemen on imprisoned Iraqis shocked Congress and the nation, as did the kidnappings and grotesque beheadings of foreign civilians by terror cells. As insurgent attacks were mounted by the thousands, U.S. troops continued to die not only in Iraq but in an Afghanistan still rife with warlords and patriarchs. And the list of post–September 11 attacks continued to grow with deadly al Qaeda train bombings in Madrid that drove Spanish troops out of the allied coalition in Iraq.[80]

None of this pointed to a "mission accomplished," as the president had declared in May 2003. Public trust, as already noted, showed signs of ebbing. The president's approval ratings plunged below 50 percent for the first time in his term and hovered there through Election Day. From early in the Iraq conflict, references to Vietnam had been freely extended, if not always appropriately drawn. As the administration continued to describe the situation in Iraq as "a remarkable success story," and as weapons of mass destruction failed to appear, the credibility gap, at least, of the Johnson-Nixon years returned to the fore. The return of covert operations and the abuses they can hide merely elaborated the Vietnam metaphor, complete with revelations of wrongdoing exposed by Seymour Hersh. High-ranking Defense Department officials "created the conditions that allowed transgressions to take place," one Pentagon consultant observed. "And now we're going to end up with another Church Commission. . . . Congress is going to get to the bottom of this."[81]

In these circumstances the administration's ongoing budget requests served as intermittent outlets for legislative frustration. Defense Department personnel testifying on behalf of an additional $25 billion for Iraq were assailed for the request's lack of specificity, for the imprecision of prior spending estimates, and for the ongoing interrogation scandal. "This is a blank check," said Sen. John McCain (R-AZ), and it seemed that blank checks were less fashionable than before. News that some $3.4 billion originally appropriated for reconstruction needed to be spent on shoring up Iraqi security attracted further criticism: Senator Hagel called the request "an acknowledgment that we are in deep trouble." Sen. Richard Lugar (R-IN), chair of the Senate Foreign Relations Committee, scored the administration's prewar claims, saying that "the nonsense of that is apparent. The lack of planning is apparent."[82]

In some ways the galvanizing effect of elections, court decisions, and legislative hearings came as no surprise. Political contexts had changed; the world had changed; but the Constitution, and the hold it gave each branch on each of the others, had not changed.

Yet how deep the overall impact of this reaction would be was far from obvious. Even as some senators began to voice their doubts, others suggested that "collective hand-wringing" over such issues was merely "a distraction from fighting and winning the war."[83] President Bush was narrowly reelected in November. The result was quickly interpreted as an endorsement of the president's vision of a forceful and unapologetic chief executive. Indeed, even had Kerry won the presidency, fundamental change in its workings seemed unlikely, given his campaign commitments to an aggressive foreign policy and the bitterly divided government he would have faced.

Thus, what did seem clear by Election Day 2004 was that the resurgence regime no longer bound, or even consistently guided, legislative-executive interaction. The question was, What would replace it? This is the grist for the concluding chapter, which assesses the path of power traced in this volume, moving from "what" to "why." There are reasons to expect presidents to remain aggressive in their claims to power and Congress to remain more deferential than not to presidential claims. In the American system of government, strong executive leadership is at once unacceptable and unavoidable: it is to this fundamental tension we now turn.

VIII. "PRACTICAL ADVANTAGES & GRAVE DANGERS"

Imperial Presidency or Invisible Congress?

Having traced the broad sweep of presidential power across American history, with particular attention to its vicissitudes after Vietnam and Watergate, it is time to evaluate it. In so doing we revisit the motivating question of this book. Is there a "new imperial presidency"? That is, has the governmental balance of power shifted back to the president to an extent comparable to the Vietnam/Watergate era?

The short answer is "yes." As previous chapters have detailed, the 1970s resurgence regime has eroded and presidential power has expanded. These developments have come in concert but are not completely reciprocal. That is, not everything that weakens Congress strengthens the president; other actors, or none, may gain instead, for American governance is not a zero-sum game. Still, presidents have regained freedom of unilateral action in a variety of areas, from executive privilege to war powers to covert operations to campaign spending. There are meaningful parallels between the justificatory language of the Nixon administration and that of our most recent presidents: each stressed the notion of "inherent" presidential power, the broad sweep of the constitutional "rights" of the office. This development would have endured even had President Bush failed of reelection in 2004. The default position between presidents and Congress has moved toward the presidential end of the interbranch spectrum—and irreversibly so.

As with most interesting questions, though, the short answer is rarely the full story. The best response might instead be "it depends." Read as simple sequence, the events detailed in this book present a set of linear trends: the rise of presidential power to the 1960s, the overstretch of the presidency past "Savior" to "Satan," the resurgence of other political actors through the 1970s, and the countersurge of presidential initiative starting in the 1980s and accelerating into overdrive after September 11, 2001. That is certainly accurate, as generalizations go. Nonetheless, this concluding chapter is the appropriate place to introduce complicating variations on this theme. In part, we must ask whether it overstates the case: has the presidency as an office become so inherently powerful? Precedents matter—and accrete—and future presidents will rely upon what is established now as the "normal" balance of presidential-congressional power. But despite the consistent and often successful efforts of presidents over more than two centuries to expand their institutional resources past the sparse grants of Article II, they ultimately remain subject to its constraints and part of a set of potential checks and counterbalances. The modern presidency has many potent tools and a global reach, surely unforeseen by the architects of the Constitution. Yet the framework they designed remains. Presidential power, in a real sense, is the residual left over after subtracting out the power of other actors in the system.[1]

As such, the power of the president, however great, remains conditional. President Carter's speechwriters, planning for his trip to Atlantic City, prepared jokes on the theme that all Washington gamblers know the "odds are with the House." Less jocularly, before the full sweep of Watergate was known, Kennedy aide Ted Sorensen commented that "Congress already has enormous power, if it only had the guts to use it."[2] This observation remains decidedly relevant to the current revival of presidential unilateralism.

If so, the presidency is contingently, not inherently, imperial. Such was suggested at the start of the book and strongly confirmed by the events traced in the text. Indeed, as frequently noted in this volume, Congress was and is the first branch of government: the constitutional structure gives Congress the whip hand. This means that when the presidency expands, it is because Congress has chosen to stay that hand. And this allows us to frame the crucial question a different way: When does Congress choose not to push back against presidential prerogative? When does legislative ambition fail to counteract presidential ambition? Is it a question of "guts," as Sorensen charged, or something else? And should we worry about it?

These are hard questions. The answer even to the last is not as obvious as it seems. For while the very word *imperial* in this context has a sharply negative connotation, if this is a simple matter of vocabulary we need to rethink our lexicon, lest we avoid the real issue at hand: the demands that motivate the history of the presidency in the modern era and the tension framed by those demands. On the one hand, after all, how can one provide direction to an enormous nation, with an enormous national executive establishment, with enormous public expectations—and still hope to limit the authority necessary to meet those needs? A nation cannot meet crises, or even the day-to-day needs of governing, with 535 chief executives or commanders in chief. The problems of administration that arose during the Articles of Confederation period in a much smaller country, with a much smaller Congress, in what seemed a much larger world, were sufficient to drive the framers to submerge their fear of monarchy and to empower a single person as president. These days the flutter of a butterfly's wing in Wellington shifts the climate of Washington; a globalized, polarized world seems to call out for endowing leadership sufficient to match its powers to the tasks at hand.

On the other hand, presidential "leadership" is not by definition virtuous, if it does violence to constitutional tenets. To accede to presidential hagiography—and thus executive dominance—is extraordinarily problematic for a republican form of government. The words of Patrick Henry noted earlier echo over the years: "If your American chief be a man of ambition, and abilities, how easy is it for him to render himself absolute? . . ." We want men, and women, of ambition and abilities to serve as our presidents. But to pledge that their preferences should without need of persuasion become policy, that they should as a matter of course substitute command for coalition building, is to cede something of the soul of self-governance.

The ultimate aim must therefore be, as Schlesinger himself remarked in *The Imperial Presidency,* to "devise means of reconciling a strong and purposeful Presidency with equally strong and purposeful forms of democratic control." We need a strong president, he argued, but a strong president *"within the Constitution."*[3] Supreme Court Justice Robert Jackson perhaps put the dilemma best: "comprehensive and undefined presidential powers," he wrote in 1952, "hold both practical advantages and grave dangers for the country."[4] The remainder of this chapter will consider aspects of each in turn before turning to a final evaluation of presidential power in a separated system.

PRACTICAL ADVANTAGES

More than 4 million civilian and military employees work in the federal executive branch, across fifteen cabinet-level departments and more than one hundred agencies. The federal budget is more than $2 trillion annually (as much as the 1960 through 1974 budgets combined). American interests, both corporate and strategic, reach into every corner of the globe: there are McDonald's restaurants from Brasilia to Beijing and over two hundred thousand American troops stationed in twelve dozen countries—a figure that does not include the additional deployments of the Iraq war.

Thus the United States, since the New Deal at least, has had a heavy-laden ship of state, unlikely to steer in any direction at all without a single hand at the tiller. Times of crisis, as at present, make delegation of power to the president even more tempting for good reasons of efficiency and effectiveness. As Richard Nixon would argue long after leaving the White House, "the alternative to strong Presidential government is government by Congress, which is no government at all."[5]

His basic reasoning is suggested by the framers' first debates: that, as Hamilton foresaw in *Federalist* No. 70, the structural advantages of the executive—unity, decision, dispatch—are well suited to overcoming fragmentation in other parts of the government. Where fast, unified action is necessary, the president is the only actor in our political system who can provide it.

That fragmentation is most obvious at the other end of Pennsylvania Avenue. Despite common grammatical usage, including in this book, Congress is not an "it" but a "they." That is, Congress is not singular but plural and a fractious plural at that. The geographic basis of House representation—the "territorial imperative"—means that no two House members share identical interests.[6] The distinctive constituencies and terms of the House and Senate generate few overlapping sympathies across the chambers. Sequential majorities and supermajorities are required for action, but only a small minority for inaction. This became even more true after the application of reforms in the 1970s designed to apply the openness and decentralization aimed at the executive branch to Congress itself. The reforms enhanced the power of subcommittees and gave party rank-and-file more power to override seniority in selecting committee chairs. What nineteenth-century observers like Woodrow Wilson condemned as "committee government" often atomized further into "subcommittee government" instead. As a result, one scholar noted, members of Congress can make laws "only with sweat patience, and a remarkable skill in the handling of creaking machinery." But stopping laws is a feat "they perform daily, with ease and infinite variety."[7]

Thus even an alert and aggressive Congress has endemic weaknesses.[8] Its large size and relative lack of hierarchy hamper quick decision making. The specialized jurisdictions inherent in the committee system, so necessary for dividing labor, also divide issues and make their comprehensive consideration across functional lines nearly impossible. (Nor do House members' two-year terms give much incentive for long-term planning.) For similar reasons Congress has difficulty in planning and agenda setting. The ready acceptance of the idea of a presidential legislative program after World War II was partly a question of legislative convenience, a way to weed through innumerable proposals and provide a focus for limited floor time. Finally, with so many members, each seeking press attention, Congress also finds it hard to keep a secret. As President George H. W. Bush's counsel, Boyden Gray, put it, "any time you notify Congress, it's like putting an ad in the *Washington Post.* Notification is tantamount to declaration."[9]

In short, Congress has the problems inherent to any body of individuals that must take collective action. The decisions that are rational for a single member—especially those aimed at gaining particular benefits for his or her district—are not always good decisions for the body as a whole.[10] James Madison wrote as early as 1791 that whenever a question of "general. . . advantage to the Union was before the House . . . [members] commonly resorted to local views." Then, as now, coalition building had to overcome decentralized inertia, with the result that governing often comes down to, in the words of LBJ budget official Charles Schultze, "a lot of boodle being handed out in large numbers of small boodle."[11]

Worse, fragmentation is not limited to the legislative branch. After all, Congress created most of the executive branch as well—and in its own image. The "politics of bureaucratic structure" result in a bureaucracy far different than what organization theorists would draw up on a blank page, one rarely aligned along functional lines or with clear lines of executive authority. Legislative majorities hope to institutionalize their own interests in government agencies and to structurally insulate those preferences against future majorities seeking to meddle. They hope to gain access to the bureaucratic decision-making process and to influence it whenever desirable. They hope to gain points with constituents for fixing the errors agencies make, perhaps to the point of structuring agencies that cannot help but make errors. If nothing else, the historical pattern of executive branch development has spurred a particular array of legislative committees—and organized special interests linked to both.[12]

As the size and scope of the national government grew, its organizational inefficiencies became more obvious and more meaningful. This in turn focused increased attention on the need for direction and coordination—for a chief executive who could actually manage the executive branch. The areas of homeland security and intelligence analysis are only the most recent cases where failures of communication or analysis within the bureaucracy have magnified the need for those qualities.

Globalization in some ways highlights the continuing limits of the presidency's authority: its incumbent is not, after all, president of the world. Yet the practical advantages of presidential leadership vis-à-vis the legislature, at least, are further magnified in an era where rapid transportation, instantaneous communication, and huge flows of trade have changed the context of governance in ways that play to presidential strengths. Both opportunities and threats arise quickly and demand immediate response. Their resolution requires a broad national view, not territorialism; resident expertise, not the give-and-take of log-rolling compromise. Further, if, as Richard Neustadt suggested, the cold war's omnipresent fear of nuclear war made the president for a time the "final arbiter" in the balance of power, the rise of rogue states and nonstate actors with access to similar weaponry ups the ante again. In this one sense at least the "modern presidency" described earlier may have given way to a "postmodern" one.[13] As the Bush administration argued to the

Supreme Court on behalf of the president's power to designate enemy combatants,

> The court of appeals' attempt to cabin the Commander-in-Chief authority to the conduct of combat operations on a traditional battlefield is particularly ill-considered in the context of the current conflict. . . . The September 11 attacks not only struck targets on United States soil; they also were launched from inside the Nation's borders. The "full power to repel and defeat the enemy" thus necessarily embraces determining what measures to take against enemy combatants found within the United States. As the September 11 attacks make manifestly clear, moreover, al Qaeda eschews conventional battlefield combat, yet inflicts damage that, if anything, is more devastating.[14]

The line between arguing that the president is constitutionally weak and arguing that he therefore *ought* to be institutionally feeble is a thin one. We may fear a strong presidency, but other, external dangers pose their own real threat to liberty as well.

GRAVE DANGERS

Yet neither should that latter fact lead us to entirely discount the former fear. The temptation is to shift the burden of action from the Congress to the president: Dick Cheney, while still a member of Congress in the 1980s, wrote that "if Congress does not have the will to support or oppose the president definitively, the nation should not be paralyzed by Congress's indecision." Certainly, as noted earlier, Congress is much better at stopping things than at running them. Still, compare Cheney's formulation with that of George Washington. "The Constitution vests the power of declaring war in Congress," Washington wrote in 1793; "therefore, no offensive expedition of importance can be undertaken until after they shall have deliberated upon the subject, and authorized such a measure."[15]

Should congressional "indecision"—a state that itself likely reflects a lack of national consensus around the president's proposal—be enough to hand unilateral authority to the executive? Where does the burden of proof lie? True, the world has changed dramatically since Washington's time. But a quick review of the perils the first president faced—with foreign empires all about, no armed forces to speak of, an enormous debt burden, and an untried system of government—makes one wonder whether that is sufficient rationale for setting aside his position.

Indeed, the need for checks on power is timeless. The dangers of unilateral authority are immense, because once those claims are accepted they logically admit no limits. Abraham Lincoln, as a member of Congress, took a rather different view from Representative Cheney. Representative Lincoln felt that President James Polk's argument for beginning the Mexican War was deceptive and worried that presidential power, once freed from constraint, could not be reined in:

> Let me first state what I understand to be your position. It is, that if it shall become *necessary, to repel invasion,* the President may, without violation of the Constitution, cross the line, and *invade* the territory of another country; and that whether such *necessity* exists in any given case, the President is to be the *sole* judge. . . .

> Allow the president to invade a neighboring nation, whenever he shall deem it necessary to repel an invasion, and you allow him to do so, whenever he may choose to say he deems it necessary for such purpose—and you allow him to make war at pleasure. Study to see if you can fix any limit to his power in this respect, after you have given him so much as you propose. If, today, he should choose to say he thinks it necessary to invade Canada, to prevent the British from invading us, how could you stop him? . . . Your view destroys the whole matter [of constitutional restraint on presidents] and places our president where kings have always stood.[16]

Nor has the progression of power to which Lincoln alluded been wholly theoretical—not least, perhaps, in Lincoln's own tenure as president. Recall (from chapter 2) the arguments he made during the Civil War, in suspending individuals' rights to habeas corpus, spending unappropriated funds, or expanding the army. Well, one might reply, but that was a national crisis if ever there was one. But consider then the case made in district court by the Truman administration defending the seizure of the steel mills in 1952. "So," asked a district court judge,

> you contend the Executive has unlimited power in time of an emergency?
>
> *Mr. Baldridge* (assistant Attorney General): He has the power to take such action as is necessary to meet the emergency.
>
> *Judge Pine:* If the emergency is great, it is unlimited, is it?
>
> *Baldridge:* I suppose if you carry it to its logical conclusion, that is true.
> . . .
>
> *Pine:* And the Executive determines the emergencies and the Courts cannot even review whether it is an emergency.
>
> *Baldrige:* That is correct.

The judge pressed: did the Constitution really limit the powers of Congress and limit the powers of the judiciary, "but it did not limit the powers of the executive"? Baldridge replied, "That is the way we read Article II of the Constitution." However, he pointed out, there were two limits on presidential power: "one is the ballot box, and the other is impeachment."[17]

A parallel argument reemerged in 1974 when the Supreme Court heard the *U.S. v. Nixon* case. As recounted in chapter 3, Attorney General Richard Kleindienst had already asserted a very broad definition of executive privilege: the judgment as to what information could be released, he told Congress, "is made by the President of the United States and only by the President of the United States." Sen. Lawton Chiles (D-FL) asked, "You think the Founding Fathers designed this document just to put absolute judgment in one man . . . to determine whether he thought something was in the public interest or not?" Kleindienst replied:

> Unlike the President, the Congress has a remedy because if the Congress feels the President is exercising this power as a monarch or tyrant you have an impeachment proceeding. . . . Leaving aside the normal remedy of impeachment, which I do not think will be used but once

every three hundred years, it is our political process which determines the ultimate result. . . . If [political actors] abuse their powers they lose elections, and they do not come back.

Later, the president's attorneys argued that Nixon's claims were "based squarely on the Constitution," since executive privilege was wholly a matter of presidential discretion, "inherent in the executive power." If a president misused that discretion, he could be punished—but only by the political process. Since Nixon was in his second term and could not run for reelection, only one option remained. "The President is not above the law," Nixon attorney James St. Clair told the Court during oral arguments. But, "as the president, the law can be applied to him in only one way, and that is impeachment."[18]

In both cases, presidents claimed that inherent power vested in them by the Constitution allowed them to act in important ways without check by Congress or court. The relevance to more recent claims, especially in the enemy combatant cases discussed in chapter 7, is clear. The cases are not entirely equivalent, of course. After September 11 Congress gave the president a potential claim to authority not present in 1952 or 1974, with its large, vague, grant of power authorizing presidential action against anyone he decided was responsible for the September 11 attacks. Nor do the enemy combatant arguments explicitly mention impeachment or even reelection. However, by inference those are the only responses not ruled out, since neither courts nor Congress is deemed necessary or welcome actors in the process. Even if one somehow reads the September 14 resolution as granting permission to suspend civilian courts, the administration claimed it didn't need such a legislative authorization to pursue its detention policies.

For example, recall the administration's argument in the *Rumsfeld v. Padilla* case. The president claimed that he could, on the basis of "some evidence," remove someone from the court system and hold them without charge or trial. Deputy Solicitor General Paul Clement was subsequently asked during oral arguments before the Supreme Court to state the limits of this argument. For example, if the circuit court had correctly held that the September 14 resolution was insufficient authorization for such power, did the president still have the authority to detain and deny trials to American citizens? Yes, Clement replied. Given the emergency created on September 11, "I think he would certainly today, which is to say September 12th [2001] or April 28th [2003]." And, in fact, "I would say the President had that authority on September 10th." In that case, he was asked, could you shoot an enemy combatant, or torture him? Well, no, said Clement, "that violates our own conception of what's a war crime." Still, a justice pressed, what if it were an executive command, what if torture were necessary to garner intelligence? "Some systems do that to get information."

"Well," replied Clement, "our executive doesn't."

"What's constraining? That's the point. Is it just up to the good will of the executive?"

"You have to recognize that in situations where there is a war—where the Government is on a war footing—that you have to trust the executive to make the kind of quintessential military judgments that are involved in things like that."[19]

The result comes back to what Schlesinger decried in the 1970s as a "plebiscitary presidency," where presidents claim broad discretion to act, constrained only by quadrennial referendum on their decisions—a problematic model in the world of term-limited incumbents and four presidential elections running where the winner has received less than 51 percent of the popular vote. In the meantime, voters must trust that the president was acting in their interests. "Our executive doesn't," the administration claimed, but at the same time the Justice Department had ruled a ban on torture was unconstitutional if it interfered with the president's running of a war. "Our executive doesn't," the administration claimed; but Abu Ghraib suggested our executive branch, at least, could.[20]

The point is too important to be a punch line. The broader argument must accept that executive discretion is, in fact, increasingly important. The amount of information pouring into government is immense, and the public and even legislators will normally be privy to only a small fraction of it. Preemptive or preventive warfare, by its nature, enhances the executive. Its successful prosecution requires extensive intelligence gathering, the discretionary ability to adjust troops and resources, and, for preemption, the element of surprise.[21] Not so long ago, such an approach was virtually ruled out: the early government template for the cold war, NSC-68, stated in 1950, "It goes without saying that the idea of 'preventive' war—in the sense of a military attack not provoked by a military attack upon us or our allies—is generally unacceptable to Americans." The idea of a first strike to wipe out the Soviet missiles being assembled on Cuba in 1962 was rejected by President Kennedy in part because of arguments (most vehemently from his brother Robert) that the United States was not that kind of country: "it's a Pearl Harbor thing."[22] But in late 2002, preventive action was affirmatively ruled in. There seemed little movement in Congress to question that doctrine or the expansion of executive authority it implied.

Yet these developments make the "grave dangers" of which Justice Jackson warned even more salient. A "war footing" against an obvious enemy on a defined battlefield is one thing; even there, as Justice William O. Douglas once pointed out (in an affirming, not cautionary, manner), "the war power does not necessarily end with the cessation of hostilities." But what about when, as now, there is no clear point when hostilities cease, no clear boundary to the battlefield, no clear set of combatants? Justice Jackson concurred with Douglas's ruling but added that the "war power" was too often "undefined and undefinable," prone to be claimed by governments urging "hasty decision to forestall some emergency." He urged that, "particularly when the war power is invoked to do things to the liberties of people . . . that only indirectly affect conduct of the war and do not relate to the management of the war itself, the constitutional basis should be scrutinized with care."[23]

Even if Congress must overcome structural handicaps, then, it has little excuse not to "scrutinize with care" the workings of the executive branch. Presidential authority is not the flip side of congressional authority: the relationship is not a zero-sum game. There is a clear normative difference between a presidential assertion of power that stands because of congressional inertia and a power delegated to the president after full and free debate. Edward Corwin pointed out long ago that "the principle of departmental autonomy does not necessarily spell departmental conflict. . . . mutual consultation and collaboration are quite as logical deductions from it." Justice Antonin Scalia's dissent in *Hamdi* reminds us that "The Founders warned us about the risk, and equipped us with a Constitution designed to deal with it." And Chief Justice William Rehnquist put the question in a manner relevant to today's debates: "it may fairly be asked by those whose civil liberty is curtailed," he wrote, "whether they are any better off because Congress as well as the Executive has approved the measure. As a practical matter, the answer may be no, but from the point of view of governmental authority under the Constitution, it is clear that the President may do many things in carrying out a congressional directive that he may not be able to do on his own."[24] The individual might not be better off, in practical terms, but both practically and morally the nation is better off.

One could envision a powerful president and a powerful Congress both, where the empowerment of the president was thoughtful rather than reflexive. The framers anticipated that civil liberties might have to be limited from time to time—that the right of habeas corpus, for example, might be suspended. Some means of preventive detention might have to be enacted. The balance between liberty and security remains in constant play, each side weighted by events and (as Justice Jackson put it) "a little practical wisdom"; as was oft-remarked after September 11, "the Constitution . . . is not a suicide pact."[25]

But the calibration of the scales was always meant to be conducted through deliberation, not by dictate. Rather than simply agreeing to "trust the executive," as repeated administrations urged, lawmakers were expected to involve themselves with determining the rule of law. To be sure, in an era of rapidly developing threats and technologies, presidents might need to be granted discretion over the utility and use of force. But Harry Truman's comments after Congress passed the Formosa Resolution, handing President Eisenhower authority to do what he would to defend Taiwan, are instructive. He didn't necessarily want to criticize the policy, "but, he said, he did want to criticize one aspect of the situation: that the Senate had not adequately debated the subject. Had there been such a debate he would have felt no anxiety at all over the ultimate decision, whatever it might have been." He added, "I have got tired a long time ago of some mealy-mouthed Senators who kiss Ike on both cheeks."[26]

The irascible former president could not resist this last shot (mainly aimed at then Senate majority leader Lyndon Johnson), but he was right that the American system contemplated little in the way of interbranch affection. Cooperation, surely—but not deference without debate. "Exercise of [Congress's] own power is the constitutional answer to the imperial presidency," Anthony Lewis observed in 1976. And while this is certainly less efficient than allowing presidents to do what they will, the branches are separated not to oil the wheels of governance but to allow for a little sand in the joints. "The purpose was not to avoid friction," Justice Louis Brandeis wrote, "but, by means of the inevitable friction incident to the distribution of the governmental powers among three departments, to save the people from autocracy." Speaker of the House Newt Gingrich later put the point more succinctly: "the price of freedom," he said, "is frustration."[27]

The first branch's job is not to manage policy implementation on a day-to-day basis. Nor is it always to pass a new law: the resurgence regime bears witness to the inadequacy of creating a statutory framework in the absence of political will reinforcing its component parts. But Congress has a critical task nonetheless. Its job is to use debate and deliberation to distill priorities and to set clear standards; to oversee and judge the decisions and actions of others by those standards; to expose both the bad and good efforts of government to public scrutiny; and to revisit its earlier debate in the light of later events. All this is Congress's job; and debate, judgment, and oversight are delegated to other actors in the system at our potential peril. How can it be induced to do that job?

GETTING CONGRESS TO DO ITS JOB

As noted at the outset, it is no surprise that the Bush administration—or in fact any administration—has tried to push the boundaries of its authority. The framers of the Constitution expected as much. It is not a question of personality but position: one need assign no bad motive to a president to predict that he will prefer to have more power—and for Congress to have less. Sen. Evan Bayh (D-IN), noting presidential efforts to avoid the "irritant" of legislative oversight, asked rhetorically, "Do you think they want more oversight? I don't ascribe sinister motives. This administration has shown that they like to act unilaterally wherever possible."[28] The comments were about George W. Bush, but they would not be out of place describing his predecessors—or successors. There is no reason to think that a President Kerry taking the oath of office on January 20, 2005, would have renounced presidential power. Indeed, Kerry, in voting to give the administration the authority to use force in Iraq, maintained during the 2004 campaign that he would have cast the same vote even after knowing the facts on the ground in Iraq: after all, he said, "I believe it's the right authority for a president to have." In casting the vote itself, Kerry noted that Congress was "affirming the President's right and responsibility to keep the American people safe."[29] And when divided government returns to the scene, as it would have under a Kerry presidency, the assertion of unilateral authority will be more tempting still. Future presidents facing legislative stalemate will devise strategies to evade congressional checks, their administrative claims bolstered both by the precedents of the war on terror and the wide-ranging internal legal holdings of the Bush administration counsel determining what presidents can and can't do.

The critical question, then, is straightforward: why has Congress been so acquiescent? The fact is that we have had an invisible Congress as much as an imperial president. Much of the expansion in presidential power has not been taken but given; as James Sundquist points out, "one of the striking facts of the modern presidency is the extent to which it was built through congressional initiative."[30] In short, while the framers expected that "ambition would counteract ambition," that other actors would rise to the occasion when presidential power overflowed its bounds, frequently in recent years this expectation has not been met. Why not?

I suggest that the answer is simply that the costs of such ambition have outweighed the benefits. Despite endless jokes at their expense, politicians are not stupid. To the contrary, they are quick to adjust to the institutional constraints, the rules of the game, within which they must operate. In recent times the game has changed in ways that dampen the incentives for legislative assertiveness vis-à-vis the president's claims to authority.

One dimension of the change surely stems from previous discussion: during periods of uncertainty or danger a strong presidency is genuinely seen as a positive good. Recent congressional debate is laced with references to the need for forceful, unified leadership in troubled times. "Success in time of war requires cohesion and unity," noted Rep. Tom Lantos (D-CA). "If you study the sweep of history in the United States and the history of the Presidency," Sen. Richard Durbin (D-IL) orated, "you understand that at times of crisis the President has an opportunity to rally the American people, to summon them to a higher calling and a greater commitment than they might otherwise reach. Time and again, each President faced with a national challenge has tried his best to do just that."[31]

But another and less laudable aspect of legislative lassitude is the siren call of blame avoidance. For the interbranch relationship to work, as Schlesinger wrote three decades ago, Congress "must *want* to know— and accept the risk that knowledge means an acceptance of responsibility."[32] But Congress has not always wanted knowledge and still less risk. Capitol Hill often claims to want a substantive part in key decisions; Sen. Arthur Vandenberg's famous assertion that "[we want to be] on the policy takeoffs, instead of merely on the crash landings" has become a mantra for legislators shut out of the action. But in practice legislators suspect they will get little electoral credit for the hard work required for deliberation and oversight and plenty of blame if they miscalculate— which will happen often enough, the real world being what it is. In the 1970s members of Congress assumed that acting assertively to stem presidential power and the erosion of public trust would have electoral benefits. In an age of terrorism, where one failure has high costs, it is an easy call to do too much delegation rather than too little. If things go well, members can take credit for having empowered the president; if things go badly, they can blame him. As Rep. Ron Paul (R-TX) suggested, "Congress would rather give up its most important authorized power to the President and the UN than risk losing an election if the war goes badly." Lyndon Johnson's rejoinder to Vandenberg's sentiment, then, is worth remembering. "I said early in my Presidency that if I wanted Congress with me on the landing of Vietnam, I'd have to have them with me on the take off," Johnson recalled. "And I did just that. But I failed to reckon with one thing: the parachute. I got them on the takeoff, but a lot of them bailed out before the end of the flight."[33]

As discussed earlier, grounding legislative representation in geographic dispersion guarantees that legislators will look to their district interests before they consider the national interest.[34] Collective action problems are inherent in any group but are especially virulent when individual incentives are bound to conflict (given district differences) and have no clear mechanism for reconciliation. Over time, Congress has tried various methods to coordinate itself, from strong party leadership to the oligarchical rule of committee barons and back again.

But if the problem is long-standing, it has been exacerbated by more recent political changes. The Watergate era coincided with major shifts in the electoral landscape, most notably the party reforms that followed the disastrous 1968 Democratic National Convention in Chicago. The subsequent rise of direct primaries as the main mechanism for selecting presidential nominees eviscerated the role of party elites in the campaign process and empowered the media in their stead. Candidate-centered, instead of party-centered, elections created organizations loyal not to a single platform but to individual political entrepreneurs.[35] This development had an impact on assumptions about presidential behavior: "the more popular the mode of selection," the political scientist James Ceaser has commented, "the more likely it becomes that a president will invoke the informal title of representative of the people's will along with—or perhaps in place of—the Constitutional powers of the office."[36] For candidates rising to the presidency through the primary, the traditional claim to be a "steward of the people" has become more tempting—and more convincing, even to members of Congress. It is interesting to note that, as the parties within Congress itself have polarized, one result has been to make real the long-chimerical dream of liberal political scientists for responsible party government. That is, the parties are, at last, unified around a substantive platform, enhancing the power of the president as party leader and agenda setter. Woodrow Wilson would presumably be pleased.

This is exacerbated by another effect of candidate-centered elections on the legislature, which has been to further undercut the sense of collective responsibility necessary for institutional maintenance. Richard Fenno put it most famously, perhaps, when he wrote that members often "run *for* Congress by running *against* Congress," attacking the institution as a way of bolstering their own indispensability. But the result is that "the institution bleeds from 435 separate cuts."[37] The collective institutional incentives—as simple as pride—that the framers thought would govern behavior have been replaced in some measure by personal incentives. Rapid turnover in the 1970s, exemplified by the large class of "Watergate babies" elected in 1974, brought to Congress a

new cohort of members good at self-promotion in the new media game
and reliant largely on their own campaign skills rather than party organizations. With less owed to party leaders, and with the Vietnam War and
Watergate as their formative political experiences, they had the incentives and ability to challenge legislative leaders as well as the president.[38]
Yet having pushed through internal reforms giving individual legislators
more power to be effective policy entrepreneurs, this cohort also walled
off their electoral fates from those policy decisions. They used new staff
resources to build up district offices that focused on constituent correspondence and assistance, more than doubling the percentage and at least
tripling the raw numbers of staff members stationed in the home district.
The number of days spent in session in Washington dropped dramatically from the 1970s to the 1990s and early 2000s.[39]

After all, issues were divisive, but constituent service was not: "they
can get reelected on their newsletter," complained House Speaker Tip
O'Neill (D-MA). Members mastered the "permanent campaign," constantly attentive to local concerns and at once solicitous and wary of the
exploding number of single-issue interest groups. Voters and groups
remember costs imposed longer and with more venom than the gratitude with which they remember benefits accrued—thus, so did their
legislators. Staying "one step ahead of the blame" was a crucial strategy
for members of Congress who sought to avoid association with tough
national choices (such as deficit reduction, entitlement reform, and
defense procurement) that necessarily had winners and losers. Insulation
was a better electoral bet than assertion. In any case divided government,
a rarity in American politics before the 1950s but a near fixture from
1969 into the start of the twenty-first century, made it hard for voters to
sort out where responsibility should really be assigned. A constant blare
of advertising, abetted by the collapsing campaign finance regime, aimed
to shift that task from hard to impossible.[40]

It worked. By the early 1990s, all else being equal, incumbents
received an additional twelve percentage points of the vote simply by
virtue of their status—up from a mere two points in the first half of the
twentieth century. Meanwhile the number of marginal districts, where
either party could win depending on national electoral trends, declined
precipitously. As the 2004 elections approached, analysts predicted there
would be fewer than 40 competitive House races out of 435. In the end

only 8 seats were decided by a difference of five percentage points or less.[41]

The trend away from competition was reinforced by repeated redistrictings that served to further dampen the choices offered voters. Partisan gerrymandering—that is, the drawing of legislative districts to make them safe for one party or another—accelerated after 1990 and 2000 as new technology brought new knowledge of census block demographics and new ease in manipulating them. In 2004 the Supreme Court upheld Pennsylvania's district map, even though a statewide Democratic majority of four hundred thousand registered voters had been effectively compressed into just six of nineteen districts. After the 2000 census the Texas legislature (with prodding from the U.S. House GOP leadership) decided to redistrict not once but twice, so as to take advantage of a new Republican majority in the State House and wipe out Democratic incumbents. Justices ordered a review of the case by lower courts but declined to become immediately involved.[42]

Such strategies generally have known no party label, and the Court may have done well to steer clear, but the implications for representation were ominous: even though a clear plurality of the public (42 percent) described themselves as moderate on election eve 2004, a finding basically unchanged for three decades, ideological polarization in Congress reached its highest postwar level by 2002. While in earlier eras, northeastern Republicans and southern Democrats overlapped in the middle of the ideological spectrum, by the 1990s these species of partisans were largely extinct. Members clustered instead to the far left and far right.[43]

What Richard Neustadt presciently termed a "snarly sort of politics" ensued. There was, for legislators, no incentive to find a middle ground, to debate the merits of issues at all—since ideology had dictated the proper answer. Such behavior was rational, if one's district was homogenous and the most likely challenge was from a primary opponent. Voters who might argue the point had been defined out of the district. The small governing majorities of the post-Watergate era only hardened the divisions. As already discussed, assertive presidents leading unified government improved their standing as a result—"an indolent majority," John Stuart Mill observed long ago, "like an indolent individual, belongs to the person who takes most pains with it." Likewise in divided government: since a majority of Congress was unlikely to be able to coalesce against their exertions, presidents were simultaneously empowered to be more aggressive in pursuing unilateral action.[44]

Congressional deference to presidential power thus made increasing sense as the post-Watergate era advanced into the twenty-first century. It was not merely a question of the body's own inherent limits. Rather, its members' own efforts and wider developments in political time changed the costs and benefits of legislative action. The good news for the interinstitutional balance of power returns to the point made at the outset of this chapter: that Congress retains the ability to act, and react, to presidential claims of authority and to check presidential ambition. Legislators have the power of the purse; the power of lawmaking initiative and statutory specificity; the power to oversee and expose; and even the power, if need be, to remove executive officials from office. The bad news is that there is little reason to think that, on their own, those legislators will have much incentive to replicate their past resurgence.

THE IMPERIAL ELECTORATE

Still, Congress is not always on its own. Any legislative resurgence will likely herald another one, long overdue: the resurgence of the imperial electorate. This is the silver lining on the flip side of the insulating curtain described earlier: Congress is extraordinarily responsive to public demands. Public pressures recalibrate congressional incentives. Thus, Congress will want to act when the American people tell it to do so. When the general interest becomes salient to constituents, it overwhelms special interests.[45]

It is true that the realm of legislative-executive relations has rarely attained this status. As Sen. Orrin Hatch asked in late 2001, "do any members of this committee really believe that in this time of crisis, the American people, those who live outside the capital beltway, really care whether the president, the secretary of defense, or the attorney general took the time to pick up the telephone and call us, prior to implementing these emergency measures?"[46] Turnout in the 2002 congressional elections barely topped one-third of the voting age population; in 2004, even as record numbers went to the polls, more than four in ten voters did not bother to bestir themselves. Congress is as responsive to ambivalent apathy as it is to directed calls for action.

But that does not change the burden on the public to provide the latter. There is a temptation to rely on extrapolitical mechanisms to save us from ourselves—perhaps, for example, to rely on the judicial system to play the primary checking role. To be sure, the courts, in pursuing their own empowerment, have resisted some of the more pronounced claims of presidential authority over the years. They take their role—to say what the law is—seriously enough. Still, court constraints can only be reactive. Judges do not, or should not, set policy priorities looking forward. They may reflect political consensus, but they rarely build it. Indeed, folk wisdom suggests that they do little more than "follow th' illiction returns."[47] As we have seen, the courts over time have repeatedly allowed Congress's precedential deference to become presidential power.

Thus, as Justice Potter Stewart observed in the Pentagon Papers case, "The only effective restraint upon executive policy and power . . . may lie in an enlightened citizenry—in an informed and critical public opinion which alone can protect the values of a democratic government."[48] Much rests on the hope that the American people *will* care, that they will seek out the information they need to hold elected officials in all branches of government responsible for the results of their leadership. Trust in the *legitimacy* of government—that it is "a government of laws, not men"—is critical. But blind trust in any particular government leads to complacency. Accountability depends as much on the electorate's healthy skepticism as it does on healthy discourse between its branches of government. Ronald Reagan's arms control aphorism—"trust, but verify"—is thus not bad advice for American voters. To verify, though, voters must take charge of their own government; they must inquire, probe, care—and vote.

Such a development would be a stiff challenge in the best of circumstances, given the American belief in nonparticipation as a God-given right. The difficulty is exacerbated, though, by the very explosion of data resources that should make government more accountable. President Bill Clinton liked to say that, "if there's enough time and enough information, the American people nearly always get it right."[49] But the

Internet and the rise of cable and satellite television have both compressed time and expanded information in ways that make "getting it right" ever more onerous. The twenty-four-hour news cycle makes reflection a luxury. Further, the broadcast news of the past is now "narrowcast."[50] Viewers can readily avoid public affairs entirely through devotion to channels filled twenty-four hours by golf or romance; the civic-minded may seek validation of their extant political preconceptions from a source geared toward reinforcing them. Studies during the 2004 election showed that voters choosing divergent media outlets—say, Fox News versus National Public Radio—came away with very different views of the world, even "separate realities" as regarded the war in Iraq and al Qaeda involvement in the September 11 attacks.[51] Abraham Lincoln reputedly said, "If given the truth, [the people] can be depended on to meet any national crisis. The great point is to bring them the real facts." But sorting out "real" facts from false ones has become a full-time job. Rumor flies over the Internet at the same rate as truth, and often faster.

Clouding the picture further is the submergence of honest debate in the "snarl" noted previously. Special interest politics demands constant mobilization—which requires in turn the constant stoking of outrage, the equating, at top volume, of policy disagreement with personal perfidy. Both ends play against the middle. However substantively important the "moral issues" of recent election seasons might be, as amplified by scaremongers on the left or right they distract from the very real issues of power and governance that require public attention.

More ominously still, presidents and their allies have been quick to doubt the motives, honor, and patriotism of anyone doubting the wisdom of presidential leadership. Such charges arose during the 1998–99 impeachment imbroglio, when those who opposed the president were lumped into a "vast right-wing conspiracy" out to bring him down. The president's defenders painted his critics as vitriolic partisans on a vendetta, sowing personal destruction in order to reap political gain.[52] But such rhetoric took a more chilling tone after September 11. President Bush's own caution to the world community that "you are either with us or you are against us" was taken by his domestic advocates as license to draw up an enemies list of sorts: Attorney General John Ashcroft's comment that to question administration decisions was to "aid terrorists" has already been noted. House Majority Leader Tom DeLay, raising the rhetorical bar still higher, suggested, after the capture of Saddam Hussein, not that several Democrats' comments were inaccurate or unfair, which they were, but instead that they were "hateful, moronic," and, ironically, "beyond the pale." Later, he attacked a Democratic congressman who had criticized postwar planning in Iraq: "in a calculated and craven political stunt, the national Democrat Party declared its surrender in the war on terror," DeLay declared. The president himself pushed the point home during the relentlessly negative 2004 campaign. At a New Hampshire campaign stop in September, for example, President Bush responded to acerbic attacks on his Iraq policies by telling his audience about

> some of the lessons that I have learned and the country must learn about the world we live in today. Our world changed, obviously, on September the 11th, 2001. We were confronted with an enemy that has no conscience, period. . . . They stand for exactly the opposite we stand for. . . . We believe in freedom of speech. They say, if you speak wrong, you're in trouble.

But having said this, the president suggested that actually utilizing such freedoms was dangerously disloyal. Any criticism of his administration, after all, sent "mixed signals" that demoralized the Iraqi people, coalition allies, and U.S. troops and encouraged terrorists to doubt American resolve.[53]

The unfortunate implication of such rhetoric is that policy decisions, and the public trust, won't withstand the give-and-take of criticism. When debating the House resolution of March 2004 reaffirming the Iraq war (albeit now in terms of human rights rather than weapons of mass destruction), Rep. Henry Hyde (R-IL) told Democrats to "put your bruised feelings aside and support it. If we want to go into bruised feelings . . . [t]hose kinds of ideas are not conducive to getting together and embracing each other in the unity that must prevail if we are to win." In some ways the argument hearkens back to the era of "scientific administration," when scholars urged that politicians find the single correct, rational policy to achieve public ends and then keep out of the way of its administration. But even in that model goals were to be set by the messy processes of democracy.[54] And democracy, as a wise political scientist once noted, "is a political system for people who are not too sure that they are right."[55] Presidents, however much they might disclaim the possibility of error, are not infallible.

To encourage open debate is to acknowledge that it will sometimes be caustic, obnoxious, and "beyond the pale." Unfair criticism ought to be rebutted, with eloquence—and with evidence. But if the accusations that various actors are "politicizing" issues of state, and that they are thus somehow unpatriotic, are successful in silencing criticism, the polity has lost much more than it has gained. It is a sad day for a nation built on argument when the public gets the message that it should be intolerant of politics, afraid of honest discussion and the negotiated outcome of a marketplace of ideas. The American system of checks and balances depends on politics and politicizing, on the robust debate—and, critically, its role in consensus building—stressed previously. Persuading the public that they need not get excited about politics is hardly a remedy; people need to be energized, not turned away. Thus urging top-down government in the name of calm and unity, in the end, may well undermine its stated purpose. If there have been vehemently unjust attacks on presidents—and there have been many[56]—that is a risk worth running. For to do otherwise runs a much greater risk: that presidents, already necessarily possessed of more concentrated power than the framers ever imagined, utilize that power in an atmosphere of subdued deference. In this sense, accusations that opposing views constitute treason are the embodiment of their own charge.

Sen. Robert Taft (R-OH), known as "Mr. Republican," was asked in 1951 whether arguing about foreign policy gave aid and comfort to enemy. Well, Taft said, "I think that the value of such aid and comfort is grossly exaggerated. The only thing that can give real aid and comfort to the enemy is the adoption of a policy which plays into their hands." As Taft himself knew, the best way to prevent adoption of such policy is to give it a full airing. Readers picking up a newspaper on the sixtieth anniversary of Pearl Harbor could read the Ashcroft comments that free speech aided America's enemies; but Taft, within two weeks of the actual event in 1941, staked a strong claim to open debate: "As a matter of general principle," he stated, "I believe there can be no doubt that criticism in time of war is essential to the maintenance of any kind of democratic government."[57] An invisible Congress would lead to an imperial presidency. An invisible electorate is the best bet for empowering both.

Taft's principle, in war or peace, becomes all the more important given the actual and potential scope of presidential authority. Their perennial complaints about legislative interference and activist judges notwithstanding, presidents have done a good job of counteracting their constitutional weaknesses. They have strategically utilized their formal powers; they have constructed a supportive staff apparatus; they have used their "bully pulpit" to preach their preferences; they have pushed unilaterally into the interstices of the Constitution, aided by the expansion of the American state and its role in the world. As one eminent political scientist put it, "an office the Framers left largely unfinished was completed by those who held it."[58]

Yet this is not quite right. Though the office has received a lot of renovation, both by those who have held it and those who have beheld it, it cannot be said to be complete. It is a project, a story, that continues. And with that in mind, the American people must overcome the obstacles discussed here to make their case for America's ideals. For to write a happy ending—to ensure that presidential power does not become presidential government—is the task of all those concerned with the American experiment in democracy.

NOTES

PREFACE

1. John Lewis Gaddis, *Strategies of Containment* (New York: Oxford University Press, 1982), vii; the terms themselves, he notes, come from J. H. Hexter.

2. Arthur M. Schlesinger Jr., *The Imperial Presidency* (Boston: Houghton, Mifflin, 1973), x.

3. Dissent to *Rumsfeld v. Padilla,* 03–1027 (June 28, 2004).

CHAPTER 1

1. See, e.g., Karen DeYoung and Colum Lynch, "Bush Lobbies for Deal on Iraq," *Washington Post* (March 12, 2003), A1; on that date alone the *Post* ran twenty-four stories with the word *Iraq* in the lead paragraph.

2. *Congressional Record,* February 12, 2003, S2268–70.

3. Ryan quoted in Juliet Eilperin, "On War, Congress Gets Earful: Divided Electorate Vents to Lawmakers," *Washington Post* (March 19, 2003), A14; Blunt quoted in Carl Hulse and David Firestone, "On the Hill, Budget Business as Usual," *New York Times* (March 23, 2003), A19.

4. Department of Justice Brief, *John Doe I, et al., v. George W. Bush, et al.,* U.S Court of Appeals, 1st Circuit No. 03–1266 (2003).

5. Wilson quoted in John Hart Ely, *War and Responsibility: Constitutional Lessons of Vietnam and Its Aftermath* (Princeton: Princeton University Press, 1993), 3. For an opposing view, see John C. Yoo, "War and the Constitutional Text," *University of Chicago Law Review* 69 (fall 2002): 1639–84.

6. *Congressional Record,* March 11, 2003, H1721; David E. Rosenbaum, "Votes in 2 Chambers Back Bush Tax Cuts," *New York Times* (March 22, 2003), A8; Alan Fram, "On Budget, Republicans Say Wartime Is No Time for Dissent," *Boston Globe* (March 21, 2003), A2.

7. Sheryl Gay Stolberg, "An Order of Fries, Please, but Do Hold the French," *New York Times* (March 12, 2003), A1.

8. The votes were 296–133 in the House and 77–23 in the Senate. For more discussion of the resolution, see chapter 7.

9. The resolution (H.J. Res. 114) was signed by President Bush on October 16, 2002, and became Public Law 107–243. "For Gephardt, Risks and a Crucial Role," *Washington Post* (October 3, 2002), A1; Alison Mitchell, "Lawmakers Begin Push to Give Bush Authority on Iraq," *New York Times* (October 4, 2002), A1.

10. Dana Priest, "Congressional Oversight of Intelligence Criticized," *Washington Post* (April 27, 2004), A1; *Congressional Record,* October 10, 2003, S10233.

11. *Congressional Record* (October 9, 2003), S10154.

12. Schlesinger, *Imperial Presidency,* 377.

13. James T. Patterson writes, "The war . . . accelerated the rise of an imperial presidency and contributed powerfully—thanks to Nixon's quest for control—to the constitutional crisis of Watergate." *Grand Expectations: The United States, 1945–74* (New York: Oxford University Press, 1996), 769.

14. Stanley I. Kutler, *The Wars of Watergate* (New York: Knopf, 1990).

15. Transcript of June 23, 1972, Oval Office conversation between Nixon and Haldeman, Nixon Presidential Materials Project, National Archives and Records Administration.

16. Michael Schudson, *Watergate in American Memory: How We Remember, Forget, and Reconstruct the Past* (New York: Basic Books, 1992), 20–27; James Madison, *Federalist* No. 51, in Clinton Rossiter, ed., *The Federalist Papers* (New York: Mentor, 1961), 321–22.

17. James Sundquist, *The Decline and Resurgence of Congress* (Washington, DC: Brookings Institution, 1982); Melvin Small, *The Presidency of Richard Nixon* (Lawrence: University Press of Kansas, 1998), 310.

18. In an interview with *Time* magazine (November 10, 1980), Ford warned, "We have not an imperial presidency but an imperiled presidency. Under today's rules . . . the presidency does not operate effectively. . . . That is harmful to our overall national interests" (30).

19. "The President's News Conference, April 18," *Public Papers of the Presidents, 1995,* 547.

20. R. W. Apple Jr., "Testing of a President," *New York Times* (December 12, 1998), A1.

21. On executive orders see Phillip J. Cooper, *By Order of the President* (Lawrence: University Press of Kansas, 2002), and the discussion in chapters 4 and 5.

22. *Public Papers of the Presidents, 1995,* September 25, 1475.

23. The General Accounting Office was renamed the Government Accountability Office in July 2004.

24. "Authorization for Use of Military Force," Public Law 107–40 (September 14, 2001).

25. Neil A. Lewis and Eric Schmitt, "Detainees Facing Years in Cuba Brig," *International Herald Tribune* (February 14, 2004), 1; Department of Justice, Office of Legal Counsel, memorandum for Alberto R. Gonzales, Counsel to the President, "Standards of Conduct for Interrogation under U.S.C. §§ 2340–2340A," August 1, 2002, 34ff. Additional discussion of these topics may be found in chapter 7.

26. This title is in capital letters because it is formed by a rather strained acronym: "Uniting and Strengthening America by Providing Appropriate Tools Required to Intercept and Obstruct Terrorism." I will refer to the law simply as the Patriot Act.

27. See Public Law 107–56 (October 26, 2001); President's Military Order of November 13, 2001; Government's Brief and Motion, August 27, 2002, *Jose Padilla v. George Bush, Donald Rumsfeld, et al.,* U.S. Dist. Court, Southern Dist. of New York—Case No. 02–4445. Again, see chapter 7 for elaboration of this argument.

28. Adam Nagourney, "Shift of Power to White House Reshapes Political Landscape," *New York Times* (December 22, 2002), A1.

29. Lyndon Johnson Library oral history (AC 82–19) of Kenneth O'Donnell, who was a staffer to both Kennedy and Johnson; transcript of presidential press conference, Office of the White House Press Secretary, November 4, 2004.

30. Donald R. Wolfensberger, "The Return of the Imperial Presidency?" *Wilson Quarterly* (spring 2002): 36–41; Arthur M. Schlesinger Jr., "The Imperial Presidency Redux," in Schlesinger, *War and the American Presidency* (New York: W. W. Norton, 2004), 45–67.

31. Nixon quoted in conversations of July 1, 1972, and May 11, 1973, in Stanley I. Kutler, *Abuse of Power: The New Nixon Tapes* (New York: Free Press, 1997), 92, 453; Victor Lasky, *It Didn't Start with Watergate* (New York: Dial Press, 1977).

32. Quoted in Thomas E. Cronin, "'Everybody Believes in Democracy Until He Gets to the White House . . .': An Examination of White House–Departmental Relations," *Law and Contemporary Problems* 35, no. 3 (1970): 573–625.

33. This Jackson quotation and the subsequent statement are from his concurring opinion to *Youngstown Sheet and Tube Co. v. Sawyer,* 343 U.S. 579 (1952).

34. Schudson, *Watergate in American Memory,* chap. 1; Dalia Sussman, "Watergate: Some Sorta Scandal, Right?" *ABC News* (June 17, 2002), reports the results of an ABC News poll conducted June 7–9, 2002, by TNS Intersearch; Suzanne Garment, *Scandal: The Culture of Mistrust in American Politics,* paperback ed. (New York: Anchor, 1992), 41.

35. Quoted in Robert Dallek, *An Unfinished Life: John F. Kennedy, 1917–1963* (Boston: Little, Brown, 2003), 132.

CHAPTER 2

1. Whether the president should be a "she" was not, of course, discussed at the time; in talking about the presidency I will defer to historical fact and use the masculine pronoun to describe the office's occupants. But "he" should be read as "he, someday she."

2. Randolph is quoted in Jack N. Rakove, *Original Meanings: Politics and Ideas in the Making of the Constitution* (New York: Knopf, 1996), 257. For a detailed description of the Constitutional Convention as it led to the drafting of Article II, see, among many sources, Rakove, *Original Meanings,* chap. 9, and Forrest McDonald, *The American Presidency: An Intellectual History* (Lawrence: University Press of Kansas, 1994), chap. 7.

3. Cato, often identified as Gov. George Clinton of New York, Letter V of November 22, 1787, in Ralph Ketcham, ed., *The Anti-Federalist Papers and the Constitutional Convention Debates* (New York: Mentor, 1986), 317f.

4. Madison, *Federalist* No. 48 and No. 51, in Rossiter, ed., *Federalist Papers.*

5. Baldwin quoted in McDonald, *American Presidency,* 177.

6. Henry, speech of June 7, 1788, in Ketcham, *Anti-Federalist Papers,* 213–14; Cato, Letter V, in Ketcham, *Anti-Federalist Papers,* 317–21; Hamilton, *Federalist* Nos. 69, 70, 77, and Madison, *Federalist* No. 51, in Rossiter, ed., *Federalist Papers.*

7. North Carolina and Rhode Island ratified the Constitution in November 1789 and May 1790, respectively.

8. Edward S. Corwin, *The President: Office and Powers,* 5th rev. ed., with Randall W. Bland, Theodore Hinson, and Jack W. Peltason (New York: New York University Press, 1984), 3.

9. The Twenty-second Amendment creates presidents who are "lame ducks" for the whole of their second terms. The Twentieth Amendment moved the presidential inauguration from March to January 20 and provides that Congress shall normally come into session on January 3. This means that Congress is already lying in wait when the president takes office at the start of his term; previously, Congress usually returned to session in the fall, giving new presidents useful breathing room. Other amendments affecting the president are the Twelfth Amendment, providing for separate ballots for president and vice president as a response to the Electoral College tie of 1800, and the Twenty-fifth Amendment, providing for an acting president in the event of presidential disability short of death and for filling vice presidential vacancies. Thus nearly 220 years after its writing, the text of Article II remains largely the same.

10. H. L. Mencken, *Notes on Democracy* (New York: Alfred A. Knopf, 1926), 185; Erwin C. Hargrove and Michael Nelson, *Presidents, Politics, and Policy* (New York: Alfred A. Knopf, 1984), 45–46.

11. John Hart, *The Presidential Branch,* 2d ed. (Chatham, NJ: Chatham House, 1995); he credits Nelson Polsby with the phrase.

12. "The Pacificus-Helvidius Letters," in Michael Nelson, ed., *The Evolving Presidency,* 2d ed. (Washington, DC: CQ Press, 2004), 39–47 (emphases in original). For more detail on the proclamation, see Stanley Elkins and Eric McKitrick, *The Age of Federalism: The Early American Republic, 1788–1800* (New York: Oxford University Press, 1993), 336–65.

13. John Locke, *Second Treatise of Government,* ed. C. B. Macpherson (Indianapolis: Hackett, 1980 [1690]), 84; see §§159–160 generally.

14. Theodore Roosevelt, *An Autobiography* (New York: Da Capo Press, 1985 [1913]), 372; William Howard Taft, *Our Chief Magistrate and His Powers* (1916), quoted in the extremely useful Christopher H. Pyle and Richard M. Pious, eds., *The President, Congress, and the Constitution: Power and Legitimacy in American Politics* (New York: Free Press, 1984), 70–71.

15. David Gray Adler and Michael A. Genovese, "Introduction," in Adler and Genovese, eds., *The Presidency and the Law: The Clinton Legacy* (Lawrence: University Press of Kansas, 2002), xxii, xxiii, xxv; see also Supreme Court Justice James McReynolds's dissent in *Myers v. United States* (1926).

16. Cleveland called the "take care" clause an "impressive and conclusive additional requirement. . . . This I conceive to be equivalent to a grant of all the power necessary to the performance of his duty in the faithful execution of the laws." See his *The Independence of the Executive* (Princeton: Princeton University Press, 1913), 14–15.

17. Jefferson to John V. Colvin, September 10, 1810, reprinted in Pyle and Pious, *President, Congress,* 62; Roosevelt, *Autobiography,* 371; Buchanan quoted in Richard Pious, *The American Presidency* (New York: Basic Books, 1979), 48.

18. Hamilton, *Federalist* No. 70 (and see Jay, *Federalist* No. 64), in Rossiter, ed., *Federalist Papers;* "Pacificus," no. 1.

19. Pyle and Pious, *President, Congress,* 78. More generally, see Pious, *American Presidency,* 55–60; Phillip Shaw Paludan, *The Presidency of Abraham Lincoln* (Lawrence: University Press of Kansas, 1994), 71.

20. Lincoln, Message to Congress, July 4, 1861; Lincoln to Albert G. Hodges, April 4, 1864, reprinted in Pyle and Pious, *President, Congress,* 65 (emphases in originals).

21. Schlesinger, *Imperial Presidency,* 64.

22. Quoted in Wilfred E. Binkley, *President and Congress,* 3d rev. ed. (New York: Vintage, 1962), 185.

23. *Ex parte Milligan,* 71 U.S. (4 Wall.) 2 (1866).

24. William H. Rehnquist, *All the Laws but One: Civil Liberties in Wartime* (New York: Alfred A. Knopf, 1998), 221.

25. Binkley, *President and Congress,* chaps. 8–9; Cleveland message to the Senate, quoted in Cleveland, *Independence of the Executive,* 69.

26. *In re Neagle*, 135 U.S. 1 (1890) (emphasis in original); *In re Debs,* 158 U.S. 564 (1895). More broadly, see Peter M. Shane and Harold H. Bruff, *Separation of Powers Law* (Durham, NC: Carolina Academic Press, 1996).

27. *U.S. v. Midwest Oil Co.,* 236 U.S. 459 (1915).

28. Sidney M. Milkis and Michael Nelson, *The American Presidency: Origins and Development, 1776–2002,* 4th ed. (Washington, DC: CQ Press, 2003), 119–21. Whig presidents were exceptions; William Henry Harrison, in his brief term, argued that the notion that presidents better understood "the wants and wishes of the people than their representatives" was "preposterous." See Milkis and Nelson, *American Presidency,* 132.

29. Arthur Schlesinger argues this was not the intent in any case. See Arthur M. Schlesinger Jr., "How to Democratize American Democracy," in Schlesinger, *War and the American Presidency,* 85–86.

30. James W. Ceaser, *Presidential Selection: Theory and Development* (Princeton: Princeton University Press, 1979), 74.

31. James Bryce, *The American Commonwealth,* vol. 1 (New York: Macmillan, 1888), 100. See also Milkis and Nelson, *American Presidency,* 129; Ceaser, *Presidential Selection,* chap. 3.

32. Ceaser, *Presidential Selection,* 170 and, more generally, chap. 4, esp. 197–212; see also Jeffrey K. Tulis, *The Rhetorical Presidency* (Princeton: Princeton University Press, 1987).

33. Tulis, *Rhetorical Presidency,* 17–20, 128; see also Samuel Kernell, *Going Public: New Strategies of Presidential Leadership,* 3d ed. (Washington, DC: CQ Press, 1997).

34. James Sterling Young, *The Washington Community, 1800–1828* (New York: Columbia University Press, 1966), 165.

35. James L. Sundquist, *The Decline and Resurgence of Congress* (Washington, DC: Brookings Institution, 1981), 130–31.

36. Note that Washington did veto one bill he thought was bad policy; it would have reduced the size of the army. See Milkis and Nelson, *American Presidency,* 93n34.

37. Leonard White, *The Federalists* (New York: Macmillan, 1948), 370.

38. Milkis and Nelson, *American Presidency,* 137.

39. Employment statistics are from Harold W. Stanley and Richard G. Niemi, *Vital Statistics on American Politics, 1999–2000* (Washington, DC: CQ Press, 1999), table 8–8.

40. See Louis Fisher, *Constitutional Conflicts between Congress and the President,* 4th rev. ed. (Lawrence: University Press of Kansas, 1997), 88–89; David M. Kennedy, *Over Here: The First World War and American Society* (New York: Oxford University Press, 1980); Harold Relyea, of the Congressional Research Service, "National Emergencies in the United States," statement before the House Judiciary Committee, Subcommittee on the Constitution, February 28, 2002, 9–10.

41. Sometimes, controversially, the authority to issue one is claimed to derive simply from the executive power.

42. Kenneth R. Mayer, *With the Stroke of a Pen: Executive Orders and Presidential Power* (Princeton: Princeton University Press, 2001), 66–67, 75; see also Phillip J. Cooper, *By Order of the President: The Use and Abuse of Executive Direct Action* (Lawrence: University Press of Kansas, 2002), 4–8.

43. Madison quoted in David Gray Adler, "Clinton, the Constitution, and the War Power," in Adler and Genovese, eds., *Presidency and the Law,* 22; Corwin, *President: Office and Powers,* 262.

44. See Pyle and Pious, *President, Congress,* chap. 5; Lincoln is quoted on p. 322; see also Schlesinger, *Imperial Presidency,* 63. For a longer review through the lens of Vietnam, see Jacob K. Javits, with Don Kellerman, *Who Makes War: The President Versus Congress* (New York: William Morrow, 1973).

45. Roosevelt, *Autobiography,* 568.

46. From his 1908 book, *Constitutional Government in the United States,* quoted in Binkley, *President and Congress,* 215.

47. Richard E. Neustadt, *Presidential Power: The Politics of Leadership* (New York: Wiley, 1960), 5.

48. Fred I. Greenstein, "Toward a Modern Presidency," in Fred I. Greenstein, ed., *Leadership in the Modern Presidency* (Cambridge, MA: Harvard University Press, 1988), 3; William E. Leuchtenburg, *In the Shadow of FDR: From Harry Truman to Ronald Reagan* (Ithaca: Cornell University Press, 1983). As Leuchtenburg put it elsewhere, "By almost all accounts, the presidency as we know it today begins with Franklin Delano Roosevelt." See Leuchtenburg, "Franklin D. Roosevelt: The First Modern President," in Greenstein, *Leadership,* 7.

49. Greenstein, "Modern Presidency," 4.

50. Quoted in James MacGregor Burns, *Roosevelt: The Lion and the Fox* (New York: Harvest, 1956), 151.

51. Kernell, *Going Public,* 75, 79.

52. Sorensen quoted in Kernell, *Going Public,* 86.

53. See Martha Joynt Kumar, "The Office of the Press Secretary," in Martha Joynt Kumar and Terry Sullivan, eds., *The White House World* (College Station: Texas A&M University Press, 2003), 236.

54. For a detailed discussion of the history of the Brownlow Committee, see Matthew J. Dickinson, *Bitter Harvest: FDR, Presidential Power, and the Growth of the Presidential Branch* (New York: Cambridge University Press, 1997), chap. 3; a useful short history of the EOP is John Burke, "The Institutional Presidency," in Michael Nelson, ed., *The Presidency and the Political System,* 7th ed. (Washington, DC: CQ Press, 2003). Staffing figures are from Lyn Ragsdale, ed., *Vital Statistics on the Presidency,* rev. ed. (Washington, DC: CQ Press, 1998), table 6–1.

55. Milkis and Nelson, *American Presidency,* 294ff; Hart, *Presidential Branch;*

Stanley L. Falk, "The National Security Council under Truman, Eisenhower, and Kennedy," *Political Science Quarterly* 79 (1964): 403–34; Andrew Rudalevige, *Managing the President's Program: Presidential Leadership and Legislative Policy Formulation* (Princeton: Princeton University Press, 2002), chap. 3; Bradley Patterson, *The White House Staff* (Washington, DC: Brookings Institution, 2000); Paul Schott Stevens, "The National Security Council: Past and Prologue," *Strategic Review* 17 (1989): 58.

56. Schlesinger, *Imperial Presidency*, 156–59; Mark J. Rozell, "The Clinton Legacy: An Old (or New) Understanding of Executive Privilege?" in Adler and Genovese, eds., *Presidency and the Law,* 63. While the phrase "executive privilege" was new, presidents dating back to George Washington had grappled with the issue of sharing information with Congress and the judiciary; see chapter 3 for more detail.

57. Clinton Rossiter, *The American Presidency* (New York: Harcourt, Brace, and World, 1956), 104; Aaron Wildavsky, "Salvation by Staff," in Wildavsky, ed., *The Presidency* (Boston: Little, Brown, 1969); Peter W. Sperlich, "Bargaining and Overload: An Essay on Presidential Power," in Wildavsky, ed., *The Presidency,* 188; contemporary textbook authors like Joseph Kallenbach and Louis Koenig took a similar stance. Note that Wildavsky proposed strict ground rules for staff behavior: in this sense he believed in salvation by staff but not through faith alone.

58. Sundquist, *Decline and Resurgence,* 133–37.

59. House committee chair's admonishment to Eisenhower and Kennedy's statement quoted in Rudalevige, *Managing the President's Program,* 45, 2.

60. Rudalevige, *Managing the President's Program,* chap. 4.

61. Sundquist, *Decline and Resurgence,* 202. Note too that, as the number of laws grew, so did opportunities for the president to act under old statutes (recall that the banks were closed in 1933 under a World War I law).

62. See, e.g., Fisher, *Constitutional Conflicts.*

63. *Panama Refining Co. v. Ryan,* 293 U.S. 388 (1935); *Schechter Poultry Corp. v. U.S.,* 295 U.S. 495 (1935); *U.S. v. Curtiss-Wright Export Corp. et al.,* 299 U.S. 304 (1936); Mayer, *With the Stroke of a Pen,* 70–74.

64. Quoted in Leuchtenburg, "First Modern President," 36.

65. Robert H. Jackson, "Acquisition of Naval and Air Bases in Exchange for Over-Age Destroyers," 39 *Op. Attorney General* 484, August 27, 1940.

66. Barton J. Bernstein, "The Road to Watergate and Beyond: The Growth and Abuse of Executive Authority Since 1940," *Law and Contemporary Problems* 40 (spring 1976): 76–77; Schlesinger, *Imperial Presidency,* 114; Pious, *American Presidency,* 54ff.

67. Truman quoted in Kernell, *Going Public,* 25; Bernstein, "The Road to Watergate," 81.

68. It is interesting to note that Richard Nixon, then a senator, voted against allowing Truman the authority to move troops without congressional

approval. See Dean Acheson, *Present at the Creation: My Years in the State Department* (New York: W. W. Norton, 1969), 415; Bernstein, "The Road to Watergate," 79n105; Schlesinger, *Imperial Presidency,* 135–40.

69. NSC-68 quoted in Gaddis, *Strategies of Containment,* 91; the entire document is now available from various sources, including the Federation of American Scientists Web site, http://www.fas.org/irp/offdocs/nsc-hst/nsc-68.htm (accessed April 22, 2004).

70. A chillingly banal 1942 note in the Roosevelt Library, from FDR to his aide Edwin Watson, reads in its entirety (I have suppressed the victim's name): "Secretly, will you get Edgar Hoover to look into the opinions of W———? I want to know if he is heart and soul with the Government or otherwise." Memo of December 19, 1942, President's Secretary's File, Box 133, Folder *Executive Office of the President: Rowe, James H.,* Franklin D. Roosevelt Library.

71. See *Nardone v. U.S,* 302 U.S. 379 (1937); Bernstein, "Road to Watergate," 64; Robert H. Jackson, *That Man: An Insider's Portrait of Franklin D. Roosevelt* (New York: Oxford University Press, 2003), 68–73.

72. Athan Theoharis, *Spying on Americans: Political Surveillance from Hoover to the Huston Plan* (Philadelphia: Temple University Press, 1978); Nicholas M. Horrock, "238 Break-Ins Committed by FBI over 26 Years," *New York Times* (September 26, 1975), 1; William C. Banks and M. E. Bowman, "Executive Authority for National Security Surveillance," *American University Law Review* 50 (October 2000): 1–130.

73. Neustadt, *Presidential Power,* 3. Or, as the presidency scholar Louis W. Koenig put it in a 1965 article title, "More Power to the President (Not Less)," *New York Times Magazine* (January 3, 1965).

74. Paul H. Appleby to D. C. Stone, no title, memo of August 9, 1944. Record Group 51 (Office of Management and Budget), Entry 9B, folder *B1–7, Relations with Members of Congress and Congressional Committees,* National Archives and Records Administration, College Park, Maryland.

75. Charles Beard, *President Roosevelt and the Coming of the War, 1941* (New Haven: Yale University Press, 1948); Bernstein, "The Road to Watergate and Beyond," 78; survey is cited in Thomas E. Cronin, "A Resurgent Congress and the Imperial Presidency," *Political Science Quarterly* 95 (summer 1980): 210.

76. Rossiter, *American Presidency,* 14, 151, and chap. 1 generally; Rossiter, letter to *Herald Tribune* (New York), May 29, 1953 (quoted in Schlesinger, *Imperial Presidency,* 152). The contemporary view of Eisenhower has been amended dramatically by the opening of Eisenhower's papers and especially by Fred Greenstein's book *The Hidden-Hand Presidency: Eisenhower as Leader* (New York: Basic Books, 1982); Greenstein's research is reflected in Neustadt's 1990 revisions to *Presidential Power.*

77. Neustadt, *Presidential Power,* 167, 184–85; testimony before Senate Government Operations Committee, 1963, quoted in Schlesinger, *Imperial Presidency,* 166.

78. James MacGregor Burns, *The Deadlock of Democracy* (Englewood Cliffs, NJ: Prentice-Hall, 1963); James MacGregor Burns, *Presidential Government: The Crucible of Leadership,* paperback ed. (Boston: Houghton Mifflin, 1973 [1965]), 330, 346–47.

79. Hargrove and Nelson, *Presidents, Politics, and Policy,* 4; Corwin, *President: Office and Powers,* 354. As Pyle and Pious put it, in *President, Congress,* 49, some suggest that "all assertions of presidential power that end well are, *ipso facto,* legitimate."

80. George C. Herring, *America's Longest War: The United States and Vietnam, 1950–1975,* 2d ed. (New York: Alfred A. Knopf, 1986), 135–41; for public opinion data see Lawrence R. Jacobs and Robert Y. Shapiro, "Lyndon Johnson, Vietnam, and Public Opinion," *Presidential Studies Quarterly* 29 (September 1999): 608.

CHAPTER 3

1. Schlesinger, *Imperial Presidency,* x, 252.

2. Cranston quoted in Leuchtenburg, "Franklin D. Roosevelt," 35; Marcus Cunliffe, "A Defective Institution?" *Commentary* (February 1968): 28; George Reedy, *The Twilight of the Presidency,* paperback ed. (New York: Mentor, 1970), 27; Hargrove and Nelson, *Presidents, Politics, and Policy,* 4–5.

3. Robert Dallek, *Flawed Giant: Lyndon Johnson and His Times, 1961–1973* (New York: Oxford University Press, 1998); Michael A. Genovese, *The Watergate Crisis* (Westport, CT: Greenwood, 1999); Kutler, *Wars of Watergate;* Keith W. Olson, *Watergate: The Presidential Scandal That Shook America* (Lawrence: University Press of Kansas, 2003).

4. Stephen E. Ambrose, *Nixon: Volume III, Ruin and Recovery, 1973–1990* (New York: Touchstone, 1992), 61.

5. See the bibliographic essays in James T. Patterson, *Grand Expectations: The United States, 1945–1974* (New York: Oxford University Press, 1996), and Melvin Small, *The Presidency of Richard M. Nixon* (Lawrence: University of Kansas Press, 1999).

6. Hugh Sidey, *A Very Personal Presidency* (New York: Scribners, 1968), 98.

7. Hart, *Presidential Branch;* John Burke and Fred Greenstein, with Larry Berman and Richard Immerman, *How Presidents View Reality: Decisions on Vietnam, 1954 and 1965* (New York: Russell Sage, 1989); Irving Janis, *Groupthink: Psychological Studies of Policy Decisions and Fiascoes,* 2d ed. (Boston: Houghton Mifflin, 1982).

8. John H. Kessel, *The Domestic Presidency: Decision-Making in the White House* (North Scituate, MA: Duxbury Press, 1975), 18; Karen M. Hult and Charles E. Walcott, *Empowering the White House: Governance under Nixon, Ford, and Carter* (Lawrence: University Press of Kansas, 2003), 166.

9. White House and EOP staff figures are from Hart, *Presidential Branch,* table 4.2; Ragsdale, *Vital Statistics on the Presidency,* tables 6.1–6.3; on the Nixon chief of staff operation, see Hult and Walcott, *Empowering the White House,* 19–20.

10. Frederick C. Thayer, "Presidential Policy Processes and 'New Administration': A Search for Revised Paradigms," *Public Administration Review* 31 (1971): 555.

11. David Archer, quoted in Kessel, *Domestic Presidency,* 81; John Ehrlichman to Cap Weinberger, no title, June 26, 1972, White House Subject Files, folder *[CF] FG 6–16: Office of Management and Budget, 1971–74,* Nixon Presidential Materials Staff, College Park, Maryland. More generally, see Andrew Rudalevige, "The 'M' in OMB: The Office of Management and Budget and Presidential Management of the Executive Branch, 1939–2003," paper presented at the 2003 annual meeting of the American Political Science Association, Philadelphia, August 2003.

12. Jacobs and Shapiro, "Lyndon Johnson, Vietnam," 592–616; Lawrence R. Jacobs and Robert Y. Shapiro, "The Rise of Presidential Polling: The Nixon White House in Historical Perspective," *Public Opinion Quarterly* 59 (summer 1995): 163–95.

13. Stephen Hess, *Organizing the Presidency,* 2d ed. (Washington, DC: Brookings Institution, 1988 [1976]), 6; Ehrlichman quoted in Harold Seidman and Robert Gilmour, *Politics, Position, and Power,* 4th ed. (New York: Oxford University Press, 1986), 82.

14. Richard P. Nathan, *The Plot That Failed: Nixon and the Administrative Presidency* (New York: John Wiley & Sons, 1975).

15. *Adams v. Richardson,* 480 F.2d 1159 (1973); "Statement on Signing the Military Appropriations Authorization Bill," November 17, 1971, *Public Papers of the Presidents, 1971; Local 2677 v. Phillips,* 358 F. Supp. 60 (1973).

16. J. Anthony Lukas, *Nightmare: The Underside of the Nixon Years* (New York: Penguin, 1988), 19–21.

17. Lukas, *Nightmare,* 22; Kutler, *Wars of Watergate,* 104–8.

18. Dean memo quoted in Kutler, *Wars of Watergate,* 104.

19. Transcript from Kutler, ed., *Abuse of Power,* 149–50.

20. Lukas, *Nightmare,* 12–13; and see Kutler, *Wars of Watergate,* 77f.

21. Small, *Presidency of Richard M. Nixon,* 86.

22. Athan Theoharis, *Spying on Americans: Political Surveillance from Hoover to the Huston Plan* (Philadelphia: Temple University Press, 1978), 149; see also James Kirkpatrick Davis, *Spying on America: The FBI's Domestic Counterintelligence Program* (Westport, CT: Praeger, 1992).

23. Reprinted in Ward Churchill and Jim Vander Wal, *The COINTELPRO Papers: Documents from the FBI's Secret Wars against Domestic Dissent* (Boston: South End Press, 1990), 125, 213–16; Small, *Presidency of Richard M. Nixon,* 158f.

24. Theoharis, *Spying on Americans,* 121ff.

25. David Wise, *The American Police State* (New York: Random House, 1976), 183–96; see also Theoharis, *Spying on Americans;* Lukas, *Nightmare,* 36–39; Nelson Rockefeller et al., *Report to the President by the Commission on CIA Activities within the United States* (hereafter Rockefeller Commission Report), June 6, 1975, (Washington, DC: U.S. Government Printing Office), on-line at http://history_matters.com/archive/church/rockcomm/contents.htm (chapter 11); John M. Crewdson, "CIA Men Opened Three Senators' Mail and Note to Nixon: Panel Says Aides Inspected Correspondence of U.S. Citizens for Twenty Years," *New York Times* (September 25, 1975), 1.

26. Small, *Presidency of Richard Nixon,* 157f; Attorney General John Mitchell quoted in Schlesinger, *Imperial Presidency,* 257; conversation in Kutler, *Abuse of Power,* 515.

27. Mitchell in Sidney E. Zion, "Fight Over Wiretaps," *New York Times* (June 22, 1969), E16. Testimony of John D. Ehrlichman, July 24, 1973, in Gerald Gold, ed., *The Watergate Hearings: Break-in and Cover-up* (New York: Bantam Books, 1973), 511.

28. Schlesinger, *Imperial Presidency,* 258f. The Commission on Campus Unrest was chaired by Republicans William Scranton and W. Matthew Byrne.

29. Quoted in Lukas, *Nightmare,* 31.

30. Kutler, *Wars of Watergate,* 99, with Krogh's memo quoted on 97–98; Tom Wicker, *One of Us: Richard Nixon and the American Dream* (New York: Random House, 1991), 628–29.

31. Lukas, *Nightmare,* 30–37; Richard Reeves, *President Nixon: Alone In the White House* (New York: Simon & Schuster, 2001), 235–36.

32. Lukas, *Nightmare,* 15, 17.

33. Wicker, *One of Us,* 626–28; Wise, *American Police State;* Lukas, *Nightmare,* 47–62.

34. Kutler, *Wars of Watergate,* 112.

35. Quoted in Lukas, *Nightmare,* 70.

36. Kutler, *Abuse of Power,* 10.

37. Kutler, *Abuse of Power,* 6.

38. Kutler, *Wars of Watergate,* 109; Lukas, *Nightmare,* 71; Kutler, *Abuse of Power,* 16.

39. Lukas, *Nightmare,* 91.

40. Lukas, *Nightmare,* 94, 104; Fred Emery, *Watergate: The Corruption of American Politics and the Fall of Richard Nixon,* paperback ed. (New York: Touchstone, 1995), 60–62; John Ehrlichman, *Witness to Power: The Nixon Years* (New York: Simon and Schuster, 1982), 399–407; Richard M. Nixon, *RN: The Memoirs of Richard Nixon,* paperback ed. (New York: Touchstone, 1990), 514.

41. George Lardner Jr. and Walter Pincus, "Watergate Burglars Broke into Chilean Embassy as Cover, Tapes Show," *Washington Post* (February 26, 1999),

A9. The United States helped overthrow Allende in 1973; see the discussion of this in the section on war powers in this chapter.

42. Lukas, *Nightmare*, 94. On Brookings, see Kutler, *Abuse of Power*, 3, 6, 8, 10, 13, 17.

43. The rise of secrecy in terms of governmental classification of documents is an important related topic, though it goes beyond the scope of this chapter. In March 1973 Nixon proposed a revision of the federal criminal code to expand official secrecy such that disclosure of anything classified as secret would be a crime, even if the classification was inaccurate; it also would have made it a crime to publish said information and, in fact, to fail to turn it over to the government immediately. See Schlesinger, *Imperial Presidency*, 340ff; more broadly, see Daniel Patrick Moynihan, *Secrecy* (New Haven: Yale University Press, 1998).

44. Rozell, "Clinton Legacy," 62; Nixon, "Statement on Executive Privilege, March 12," and "Statement about the Watergate Investigations, August 15," both in *Public Papers of the Presidents, 1973*, 185, 701.

45. In one 1968 case, the Defense Department refused to give information pertaining to the 1964 Gulf of Tonkin incident to the Senate Foreign Relations Committee; Senate Judiciary Committee requests that various staff testify about the controversial nomination of Abe Fortas to become the Supreme Court's chief justice were also rejected. Pierson is quoted in Mark J. Rozell, *Executive Privilege: Presidential Power, Secrecy, and Accountability*, 2d rev. ed. (Lawrence: University Press of Kansas, 2002), 41–42.

46. Nixon, "Statement on Executive Privilege"; Schlesinger, *Imperial Presidency*, 251; Rozell, *Executive Privilege*, 62ff.

47. Hearings before the Senate Subcommittee on Intergovernmental Relations, "Executive Privilege, Secrecy in Government, Freedom of Information," 93d Congress, 1st session, April 10, 1973, vol. 1, 20, 45, 51.

48. Dallek, *Flawed Giant*, 147–51; Herring, *America's Longest War*, 119–22. McNamara's comment, from NSC minutes, is on p. 121.

49. 88th Congress, H. J. Res 1145 (Public Law 88–408).

50. Louis Fisher, *Presidential War Power* (Lawrence: University Press of Kansas, 1995), 116.

51. Johnson quoted in Dallek, *Flawed Giant*, 153; McNamara quoted in Fisher, *Presidential War Power*, 117; Adair quoted in Herring, *Longest War*, 122.

52. See Fisher, *Presidential War Power*, 117; Johnson quoted in Dallek, *Flawed Giant*, 155. Dallek (155) argues that "the bulk of recent evidence suggests [the attack] did" occur; Fisher is far less sure.

53. Javits, with Kellerman, *Who Makes War*, 259.

54. Leonard C. Meeker, "The Legality of U.S. Participation in the Defense of Vietnam," *U.S. Department of State Bulletin*, March 28, 1966, 483f; Schlesinger, *Imperial Presidency*, 184.

55. Pyle and Pious, *President, Congress,* 340.

56. Dallek, *Flawed Giant,* 262–68; Pyle and Pious, *President, Congress,* 317–18; James Sundquist, *Decline and Resurgence,* 123–24, 239–40.

57. Herring, *Longest War,* chap. 6; Fisher, *Presidential War Power,* 119–20.

58. Quoted in Roger Morris, *An Uncertain Greatness: Henry Kissinger and American Foreign Policy* (New York: Harper & Row, 1977), 4.

59. Schlesinger, *Imperial Presidency,* 198.

60. Larry Berman, *No Peace, No Honor: Nixon, Kissinger, and Betrayal in Vietnam* (New York: Free Press, 2001), 104. The reference is to longtime Nixon spiritual adviser and well-known evangelist Rev. Billy Graham.

61. Herring, *Longest War,* 225; Berman, *No Peace,* 50–51.

62. *Public Papers of the Presidents, 1970,* 405–9.

63. Herring, *Longest War,* 234–39; Seymour M. Hersh, *The Price of Power: Kissinger in the Nixon White House* (New York: Summit Books, 1983), chap. 16; Sundquist, *Decline and Resurgence,* 251.

64. Francis D. Wormuth, "The Nixon Theory of the War Power: A Critique," *California Law Review* 60 (May 1972): 623–703; Sundquist, *Decline and Resurgence,* 249; Pyle and Pious, *President, Congress,* 337–38. Cases cited by Rehnquist included the *Prize Cases* and *Durand v. Hollins.*

65. Herring, *Longest War,* 248, 252–54.

66. Sundquist, *Decline and Resurgence,* 255–56; Kirsten Lundberg, "Congressional Oversight and Presidential Prerogative: The 1991 Intelligence Authorization Act," Case C14–01–1605.0, Kennedy School of Government Case Program, Harvard University, 2001.

67. John Prados, *Presidents' Secret Wars,* rev. ed. (Chicago: Ivan R. Dee, 1996), 308–10 and chap. 13 generally. Hersh, in *Price of Power* (81), puts the number killed at over forty thousand, though Herring, *Longest War* (232), thinks even twenty thousand is too high.

68. Hersh, *Price of Power,* chaps. 14–15; Prados, *Secret Wars,* 300–303 and chap. 14 generally. Helms is quoted on p. 275.

69. Hersh, *Price of Power,* 259.

70. Gregory F. Treverton, *Covert Action: The Limits of Intervention in the Postwar World* (New York: Basic Books, 1987), 98–107; Hersh, *Price of Power,* 258–96; Prados, *Secret Wars,* 317–21.

71. Prados, *Secret Wars,* 322–24; Hersh, *Price of Power,* 187.

72. Berman, *No Peace,* 238.

73. Allen Schick, *Congress and Money: Budgeting, Spending, and Taxing* (Washington, DC: Urban Institute Press, 1980), 17.

74. Harold Laswell, *Politics: Who Gets What, Where, and How* (New York: Meridian Books, 1958 [1936]).

75. Madison, *Federalist* No. 58, in Rossiter, ed., *Federalist Papers,* 359.

76. Edwin L. Dale Jr., "Washington Report: Why U.S. Budget Figures Miss the Mark," *New York Times* (June 15, 1975), F4; more generally see Allen

Schick, with Felix LoStracco, *The Federal Budget: Politics, Policy, Process* (Washington, DC: Brookings Institution, 2000), chap. 1.

77. James P. Pfiffner, *The President, Budget, and Congress: Impoundment and the 1974 Budget Act* (Boulder, CO: Westview, 1979), chap. 2; Schick, *Federal Budget*, 14; Sundquist, *Decline and Resurgence*, 200.

78. "Annual Budget Message to the Congress, Fiscal Year 1967," January 24, *Public Papers of the Presidents, 1966*, 48, 68. Note that a fiscal year differs from a calendar year. "Fiscal Year 1967," for example, meant the twelve months ending on June 30, 1967, thus the year beginning on July 1, 1966. In 1975 the start of the fiscal year was shifted to October 1. Thus, fiscal year (or FY) 2006 is the year starting October 1, 2005, and ending September 30, 2006.

79. Pfiffner, *The President, the Budget, and Congress*, 41.

80. See the Revenue and Expenditure Control Act of 1968 (Public Law 90–364); Schick, *Congress and Money*, 35–37.

81. Quoted in Louis Fisher, *Congressional Abdication on War and Spending* (College Station: Texas A&M Press, 2000), 117. A "balanced full employment budget" was meant to be balanced if the nation reached full employment. The nation did not, and the budget was not. See Allen J. Matusow, *Nixon's Economy: Booms, Busts, Dollars, and Votes* (Lawrence: University Press of Kansas, 1998), 91, 164, 205–6.

82. Roy Ash to Nixon, "Establishment of Departmental Objectives," April 4, 1973; "Congress and the Budget Battle," September 11, 1973; "Battle of the Budget—Phase II," May 8, 1973. All in White House Central Files: Staff Member and Office Files: Roy Ash, Box 7, *Ash Memos to the President, February 1973 to December 1973*, Nixon Presidential Materials Staff.

83. Fisher, *Abdication*, 118; this section is drawn largely from Fisher, *Abdication*, 115–20, and Pfiffner, *President, Budget, and Congress*, 41–44.

84. Weinberger quoted in Fisher, *Abdication*, 116 (emphasis added). Sneed and Nixon quoted in Schlesinger, *Imperial Presidency*, 239; see also Sundquist, *Decline and Resurgence*, 208. Sneed also argued that "the warrant of historic practice" added a constitutional gloss to Nixon's actions, parallel to the 1915 *Midwest Oil* case discussed in chapter 2. See Pfiffner, *President, Budget, and Congress*, 66. It is interesting to note that then assistant attorney general William Rehnquist argued strongly in 1969 *against* the president's ability to impound, at least in domestic spending.

85. Nixon quoted in Schick, *Congress and Money*, 43; Humphrey quoted in *Congressional Record*, February 20, 1973, S2873; *Local 2677 v. Phillips*, 358 F. Supp. 60 (1973).

86. Quoted in Sundquist, *Decline and Resurgence*, 86–87.

87. For greater detail on Nixon's economic policies, see Matusow, *Nixon's Economy*, chaps. 6–7; and Small, *Presidency of Richard Nixon*, 208–14.

88. Small, *Presidency of Richard Nixon*, 212; Sundquist, *Decline and Resurgence*, 212; Fisher, *Abdication*, 119.

89. Nixon was speaking to interviewer David Frost in 1977. He was honest enough to continue, "And, I guess, if I'd been in their position, I'd have done the same thing." Quoted in Ambrose, *Nixon: Volume III,* 510.

90. Gallup Polls of May 26–29 and June 16–19, 1972; Olson, *Watergate,* chap. 2; Theodore H. White, *The Making of the President 1972* (New York: Atheneum, 1973).

91. Colson was evidently angered that some of his staff had taken the previous weekend off. See Stephen E. Ambrose, *Nixon: Volume II, The Triumph of a Politician, 1962–1972* (New York: Simon & Schuster, 1989), 605. Mitchell quoted in Olson, *Watergate,* 176.

92. Olson, *Watergate,* 30ff; Small, *Presidency of Richard Nixon,* 254f.

93. Kutler, *Abuse of Power,* 67–69; Emery, *Watergate,* 205.

94. Kutler, *Abuse of Power,* 252–54; Gerald Gold, ed., *The White House Transcripts: Submission of Recorded Presidential Conversations to the Committee on the Judiciary of the House of Representatives by President Richard Nixon* (New York: Bantam, 1973), 155.

95. Herbert Kalmbach, testimony of July 16, 1973, in Gold, *Watergate Hearings,* 447–48.

96. Kutler, *Abuse of Power,* 112–13; more generally see the Watergate cites already presented and Anthony Corrado, *Paying for Presidents: Public Financing in National Elections* (New York: Twentieth Century Fund Press, 1993), 4–5. The 1971 law was the original Federal Election Campaign Act, which replaced the 1925 version of the Federal Corrupt Practices Act.

97. Herbert E. Alexander, *Financing Politics: Money, Elections, and Political Reform* (Washington, DC: CQ Press, 1976), 112–18; Olson, *Watergate.*

98. Small, *Presidency of Richard Nixon,* 264–66.

99. Alexander, *Financing Politics,* 119–20.

100. Colson memo reprinted as Exhibit 121 in "Testimony of Witnesses," Book III, *Hearings before the House Committee on the Judiciary pursuant to H. Res 803,* 93d Congress, 2d Session, July 12–17, 1974, 483–87; see also Lukas, *Nightmare,* 182ff. A transcript of the Nixon-Kleindienst conversation of April 19, 1971, is available from the Nixon Presidential Materials Staff or on-line at http://www.washingtonpost.com/wp-srv/nation/specials/watergate/watergatefront.htm (accessed October 13, 2004).

101. Kutler, *Abuse of Power,* 116.

102. A fourth article regarding the bombing of Cambodia, and a fifth, charging income tax evasion, were defeated.

103. Phillip Trimble, "The President's Foreign Affairs Power," *American Journal of International Law* 83 (October 1989): 752.

104. Gary Orren, "Fall from Grace: The Public's Loss of Faith in Government," in Joseph S. Nye Jr., Philip D. Zelikow, and David C. King, eds., *Why People Don't Trust Government* (Cambridge, MA: Harvard University Press, 1997), 81.

105. Schlesinger, *Imperial Presidency,* 275.

106. Ambrose, *Nixon,* Vol. III, 508.

CHAPTER 4

1. Stephen Krasner, "Structural Causes and Regime Consequences," in Krasner, ed., *International Regimes* (Ithaca: Cornell University Press, 1983), 2.

2. *Congressional Record,* April 18, 1973, 13190. For an array of similar quotes see Sundquist, *Decline and Resurgence,* chap. 1.

3. Sundquist, *Decline and Resurgence,* 1, 7. See also Cronin, "Resurgent Congress," 209–37.

4. Press conference quoted in John Hershey, *Aspects of the Presidency: Truman and Ford in Office* (New Haven: Ticknor & Fields, 1980), 141; Gerald R. Ford, *A Time to Heal* (New York: Harper & Row, 1979), 132; more broadly, see Shirley Anne Warshaw, *Powersharing: White House-Cabinet Relations in the Modern Presidency* (Albany: State University of New York Press, 1996), 94 and chap. 4 generally; Hult and Walcott, *Empowering the White House,* 31–35.

5. Carter quoted in Warshaw, *Powersharing,* 101; Jordan quoted in Dom Bonafede, "Carter White House Staff Is Heavy on Functions, Light on Frills," *National Journal* (February 12, 1977); see also Hult and Walcott, *Empowering the White House,* 38.

6. Warshaw, *Powersharing,* 108; Hult and Walcott, *Empowering the White House,* 166; Bonafede, "Carter White House Staff."

7. It was, perhaps, Nixon's needs that were the problem. On Nixon's staffing, and the similarity of Ford and Carter to the Nixon model, see Hult and Walcott, *Empowering the White House.*

8. David Halberstam, *The Best and the Brightest* (New York: Fawcett Crest, 1973), 556; John M. Orman, *Presidential Secrecy and Deception: Beyond the Power to Persuade* (Westport, CT: Greenwood Press, 1980), 107–8.

9. *U.S. v. Nixon,* 418 U.S. 683 (1974); see the full documentation from the case in Leon Friedman, ed., *United States v. Nixon: The Complete Case* (New York: Chelsea House, 1974).

10. Rozell, *Executive Privilege,* 72, 75, 90, and chap. 4 generally; George Lardner Jr., "Secrecy System Pronounced Sound," *Washington Post* (December 9, 1988), A25.

11. Public Law 93–579; Herbert N. Foerstel, *Freedom of Information and the Right to Know: The Origins and Applications of the Freedom of Information Act* (Westport, CT: Greenwood, 1999), 65–67.

12. Johnson, "Statement by the President upon Signing S. 1160," Office of the White House Press Secretary, July 4, 1966, available at http://www.gwu.edu/~nsarchiv/nsa/foia/FOIARelease66.pdf (accessed April 2, 2004); *Environmental Protection Agency v. Mink,* 410 U.S. 73 (1973); Sen.

Edmund Muskie's comments in the *Congressional Record,* October 17, 1974, S36083–84; Foerstel, *Freedom of Information,* chap. 2.

13. Public Law 93–502; Edward Levi, "Attorney General's Memorandum on the 1974 Amendments to the Freedom of Information Act," February 1975, available at http://www.usdoj.gov/foia/74agmemo.htm (accessed April 2, 2004); Foerstel, *Freedom of Information,* 49.

14. See *Nixon v. Administrator of General Services,* 433 US 425 (1977). However, Nixon and then his estate continued to press for compensation, a case that lasted nearly a quarter century and was not settled until 2000, when the government agreed to pay the Nixon estate $18 million. The estate had sought approximately $200 million, including interest.

15. 5 USC 552b. There are ten categories of exception that mainly parallel FOIA, including meetings that discuss classified information, banking reports, litigation or law enforcement investigations, or sensitive personal information.

16. Public Law 92–463; Jay S. Bybee, "Advising the President: Separation of Powers and the Federal Advisory Committee Act," *Yale Law Journal* 104 (October 1994): 51–128. Note that groups advising the CIA or Federal Reserve are normally exempt and that meetings may be closed using the same criteria as the Sunshine Act.

17. See the review in *U.S. v. Duggan,* 743 F.2d 59 (2d Cir. 1984).

18. *United States v. United States District Court (Keith),* 407 U.S. 297 (1972).

19. In June 1974 Kissinger threatened to resign if he was not cleared of misleading the Senate about his role in the wiretaps during his confirmation hearings; the resulting hearings placed the lion's share of the blame on President Nixon, who was in no position to resist that conclusion. U.S. Senate, Committee on Foreign Relations, *Dr. Kissinger's Role in Wiretapping,* hearings of September 1973 through July 1974, 93d Congress, 2d session (Washington, DC: U.S. Government Printing Office, 1974).

20. Quoted in Lukas, *Nightmare,* 541.

21. Levi guidelines quoted in Athan G. Theoharis, "FBI Surveillance: Past and Present," *Cornell Law Review* 69 (April 1984): 889.

22. "No agency . . . shall request or otherwise encourage, directly or indirectly, any person, organization, or government agency to undertake activities forbidden by this Order or by applicable law." Executive Order 12036 (January 24, 1978); Geoffrey R. Stone, "The Reagan Amendment, the First Amendment, and FBI Domestic Security Investigations," in Richard O. Curry, ed., *Freedom at Risk* (Philadelphia: Temple University Press, 1988), 277.

23. Theoharis, "FBI Surveillance," 889–90.

24. FISA is Public Law 95–511, codified at 50 U.S.C. §§ 1801–1862; *In re: Sealed Case 02–001,* U.S. Foreign Intelligence Surveillance Court of Review (November 18, 2002), 3–5, 8ff. Sen. Birch Bayh (D-IN) quoted in George Lardner Jr., "Carter Signs Bill Limiting Foreign Intelligence Surveillance," *Washington Post* (October 26, 1978), A2.

25. Senate Special Committee on the Termination of the National Emergency, 1973, quoted in Cooper, *By Order of the President*, 39–40; Cronin, "Resurgent Congress," 213.

26. Harold C. Relyea, "National Emergency Powers," Report 98–505-GOV, Congressional Research Service, June 28, 2001. After the *Chadha* decision invalidated the legislative veto, a joint resolution was substituted for the concurrent resolution.

27. Sundquist, *Decline and Resurgence*, 332; Paul C. Light, *Monitoring Government: Inspectors General and the Search for Accountability* (Washington, DC: Brookings Institution, 1993). See also the testimony of comptroller David M. Walker presented in *Inspectors General: Enhancing Federal Accountability*, GAO Report 04–117T (October 8, 2003). The main Inspector General Act is Public Law 95–452; however, the first inspector general was appointed in the Department of Health and Human Services in 1976 to investigate allegations of Medicaid fraud. Another was included in the newly created Energy Department in 1977.

28. A bill requiring sunset provisions for all government programs was popular enough to pass the Senate in 1978 with eighty-seven votes, though it failed to win House approval. See Allen Schick, *Congress and Money*, 171–72; Sundquist, *Decline and Resurgence*, 329–30; *CQ Almanac, 1978,* 850.

29. Sundquist, *Decline and Resurgence*, 344–45; Barbara Hinkson Craig, *The Legislative Veto: Congressional Control of Regulation* (Boulder, CO: Westview, 1983), 18–20.

30. Craig, *Legislative Veto*, 19–26; Sundquist, *Decline and Resurgence*, 354.

31. Sundquist, *Decline and Resurgence*, 332.

32. Schlesinger, *Imperial Presidency*, 330.

33. S. Report 129, 91st Congress, 1st session, quoted in Fisher, *Abdication*, 58–61, and Sundquist, *Decline and Resurgence*, 246.

34. Fulbright quoted in Sundquist, *Decline and Resurgence*, 256.

35. Fisher, *Presidential War Power*, 128–33; Sundquist, *Decline and Resurgence*, 254–60, quoting the joint statement of Reps. Clement Zablocki (D-WI) and Thomas Morgan (D-PA); *Public Papers of the Presidents, 1973,* 893–95. Concurrent resolutions are voted on by both chambers but not presented to the president. Thus they are not "law" in the way that joint resolutions, which are signed by the president, are.

36. *Congressional Record,* October 10, 1973, 33550; see also the debate of November 7, 1973.

37. War Powers Resolution (Public Law 93–148), sections 2–5, 8; Kissinger quote (though it is hard to believe he meant it) in John T. Rourke, *Congress and the Presidency in U.S. Foreign Policymaking* (Boulder, CO: Westview, 1983), 286; Javits in *Congressional Record,* November 7, 1973, 36187.

38. Kathryn S. Olmsted, *Challenging the Secret Government: The Post-Watergate Investigations of the CIA and FBI* (Chapel Hill: University of North Carolina

Press, 1996), 46; see also Kirsten Lundberg, "Congressional Oversight"; Pyle and Pious, *President, Congress,* 384; Gregory F. Treverton, "Intelligence: Welcome to the American Government," in Thomas E. Mann, ed., *A Question of Balance: The President, the Congress, and Foreign Policy* (Washington, DC: Brookings Institution, 1990), 76.

39. Seymour Hersh, "Huge CIA Operation Reported in U.S. against Antiwar Forces, Other Dissidents in Nixon Years," *New York Times* (22 December 1974), 1.

40. The Rockefeller Commission's official name was the Commission on CIA Activities within the United States. It was created by Executive Order 11828 on January 4, 1975. The quoted sentences are from p. 10 of the full report, which can be found on-line at http://history-matters.com/archive/church/rockcomm/contents.htm (accessed April 28, 2004). See also Olmsted, *Challenging the Secret Government,* 83–84.

41. The Church Committee was named for Sen. Frank Church (D-ID); its official name was the Select Committee to Study Governmental Operations with Respect to Intelligence Activities. The Pike Committee was formally the House Select Intelligence Committee.

42. Quoted in Olmsted, *Challenging the Secret Government,* 88, 96.

43. Rockefeller Commission Report, 149.

44. Executive Order 11905 (Ford); Executive Order 12036 (Carter); Gates, *From the Shadows,* 135–40, 142; Charles R. Babcock, "Spy Agency Infighting Hurt U.S., Turner Says," *Washington Post* (May 13, 1985), A3.

45. Robert M. Gates, *From the Shadows* (New York: Touchstone, 1997), 60–61; Public Law 96–450; see also Fisher, *Presidential War Power,* 174; Loch K. Johnson, *The Making of International Agreements: Congress Confronts the Executive* (New York: New York University Press, 1984), 137; Treverton, "Intelligence," 77–80.

46. Johnson, *Making of International Agreements,* 136; Frank J. Smist Jr., *Congress Oversees the United States Intelligence Community, 1947–1989* (Knoxville: University of Tennessee Press, 1990), chap. 5.

47. Fisher, *Presidential War Power,* 173–76. The Clark Amendment was named for Sen. Dick Clark (D-IA).

48. Johnson, *Making of International Agreements,* 59, table 17. Other figures are from Ragsdale, *Vital Statistics on the Presidency,* tables 7–1, 7–2.

49. See Public Law 92–403 (1 U.S. Code 112b), amended by Public Law 95–426.

50. Johnson, *Making of International Agreements,* 138–44.

51. *Public Papers of the Presidents, 1976,* 1481–85.

52. Sundquist, *Decline and Resurgence,* 206.

53. For a detailed discussion of these questions, see James P. Pfiffner, *The President, the Budget, and Congress* (Boulder, CO: Westview, 1979), chap. 5.

54. But he assured Nixon: "As a matter of principle, however, your con-

tinued efforts to use all available options to control spending, and to fight in the courts those which are initially foreclosed, will enable you to retain your firm anti-inflationary posture before the public and Congress." Roy Ash to Nixon, "Impact on Litigation on Battle of the Budget," June 27, 1973, White House Central Files: Staff Member and Office Files: Roy Ash, Box 7, *Ash Memos to the President, February 1973 to December 1973*, Nixon Presidential Materials Staff.

55. Russell Train was the administrator of the EPA.

56. Pfiffner, *President, Budget, and Congress,* 100ff; *Train v. City of New York,* 420 U.S. 35 (1975). The Court overturned the EPA's failure to follow the formula for allotting money to the states on the grounds that any discretion the administration might have would come at a later stage of the process, when actual funds were expended. But the justices suggested that discretion was dubious even then.

57. Fisher, *Abdication,* 119.

58. Sundquist, *Decline and Resurgence,* 214; rescission data in Schick, *Congress and Money,* 401ff, esp. table 32.

59. Schick, *Congress and Money,* 22.

60. Public Law 93–250.

61. Sundquist, *Decline and Resurgence,* 221, 228–29, 231; Joel Havemann, *Congress and the Budget* (Bloomington: University of Indiana Press, 1976), 195f.

62. G. Calvin Mackenzie, "The State of the Presidential Appointments Process," in Mackenzie, ed., *Innocent until Nominated: The Breakdown of the Presidential Appointments Process* (Washington, DC: Brookings Institution, 2001), 10.

63. Quoted in Steven M. Gillon, *"That's Not What We Meant to Do": Reform and Its Unintended Consequences in Twentieth-Century America* (New York: W. W. Norton, 2000), 203.

64. Corrado, *Paying for Presidents,* 1.

65. For a cogent discussion of the 1974 FECA amendments, see Frank J. Sorauf, *Inside Campaign Finance: Myths and Realities* (New Haven: Yale University Press, 1992), 7–10; and see the Federal Election Commission publication "Public Financing of Presidential Elections." Each candidate's primary spending could not exceed $10 million (in 1974 dollars). The spending caps were linked to inflation—but donation caps were not.

66. See Gillon, *"That's Not What We Meant to Do,"* 204–9.

67. Public Law 95–521; Carter, "Remarks on Signing S. 555 Into Law," October 26, *Public Papers of the Presidents, 1978,* 1854–56.

68. *CQ Almanac, 1975* (Washington, DC: CQ Press, 1976), 519–20; *CQ Almanac, 1978* (Washington, DC: CQ Press, 1979), 835–50.

69. The "special prosecutor" became the "independent counsel" in the 1982 revisions (Public Law 97–409).

70. 28 CFR §0.37; Katy J. Harriger, *The Special Prosecutor in American Politics,* 2d rev. ed. (Lawrence: University Press of Kansas, 2000), 44. Because of these regulations, the Supreme Court later held in *U.S. v. Nixon,* the office was

sufficiently removed from the president to move the tapes dispute out of the realm of "intrabranch" argument.

71. See *Hearings on S.2803 and S. 2978 Before the Subcommittee on Separation of Powers of the Senate Committee on the Judiciary,* 93d Congress, 2d Session (1974).

72. The Justice Department led by John Mitchell and Richard Kleindienst and the FBI under L. Patrick Gray had certainly not covered themselves in investigative glory. Roosevelt, Truman, Eisenhower, Kennedy, and Nixon all appointed their party's national chairman or their campaign manager as attorney general; Bobby Kennedy, of course, had the added benefit of consanguinity.

73. Quoted in Harriger, *Special Prosecutor,* 85. Overall, Harriger concludes, "the executive branch's influence on this issue was minimal. Its views, as a rule, were suspect because its opposition was predictable" (69).

74. As this suggests, the attorney general was given little leeway in determining whether a charge against an executive official was warranted. The 1982 amendments increased the attorney general's discretion somewhat (so as to examine the specificity and credibility of the evidence), but the 1987 reauthorization tightened it again (so that the attorney general could weigh *only* that specificity and credibility).

75. Quotes from 28 U.S.C. §§592–94. See Jack Maskell, *Independent Counsel Provisions: An Overview of the Operation of the Law,* Congressional Research Service Report 98–283A (March 20, 1998); Joseph S. Hall, Nicholas Pullen, and Kandace Rayos, "Independent Counsel Investigations," *American Criminal Law Review* 36 (summer 1999): 809–33.

76. Harriger, *Special Prosecutor,* 234–35.

77. Robert J. Spitzer, "The Independent Counsel and the Post-Clinton Presidency," in Adler and Genovese, eds., *Presidency and the Law,* 89–94; "The Independent Counsel Act: From Watergate to Whitewater and Beyond," Symposium, *Georgetown Law Journal* 86 (July 1998).

78. Senate committee report quoted in Maskell, *Independent Counsel Provisions,* 7. Writing for the Court, Chief Justice William Rehnquist argued that the ICA did not violate the separation of powers principle. Because the counsel was an "inferior officer," the Court held, Congress had the power to have the position appointed by someone other than the president and even outside the executive branch. That the president could not control the prosecutorial powers of the counsel or fire her was also upheld, as Rehnquist compared the position to a regulatory commissioner—many of whom are appointed for fixed terms and can only be removed for cause. See *Morrison v. Olson,* 487 U.S. 654 (1988).

79. *Morrison v. Olson,* 487 U.S. 654 (1988), 705, 711, 713f.

80. Garment, *Scandal,* 83.

81. G. Calvin Mackenzie, with Michael Hafken, *Scandal Proof: Do Ethics Laws Make Government Ethical?* (Washington, DC: Brookings Institution, 2002), 83.

82. Gerhard Casper, "The Constitutional Organization of the Government," *William and Mary Law Review* 26 (winter 1985): 187–88.

83. Dom Bonafede, Daniel Rapoport, and Joel Havemann, "The President versus Congress: The Score since Watergate," *National Journal* (May 29, 1976), 738.

84. Gordon S. Jones and John A. Marini, eds., *The Imperial Congress: Crisis in the Separation of Powers* (New York: Pharos Books, 1988), 1.

CHAPTER 5

1. Richard M. Nixon, *In the Arena,* paperback ed. (New York: Pocket Books, 1991), 238; Thomas M. Franck, ed., *The Tethered Presidency: Congressional Restraints on Executive Power* (New York: New York University Press, 1981); Marvin Stone, "Presidency: Imperial or Imperiled?" *U.S. News and World Report* (January 15, 1979), 88; Harold M. Barger, *The Impossible Presidency* (Reading, MA: Addison-Wesley, 1984).

2. Michael Lind, "The Out-of-Control Presidency," *New Republic* (August 14, 1995), 18, 23. For an early treatment of the Reagan presidency's importance, see Ryan J. Barilleaux, *The Post-Modern Presidency: The Office after Ronald Reagan* (Westport, CT: Praeger, 1988).

3. Francine Kiefer, "Clinton Perfects the Art of Go-Alone Governing," *Christian Science Monitor* (July 24, 1998), 3; see also David Gray Adler, "Clinton in Context," in Adler and Genovese, eds., *Presidency and the Law.*

4. Mayer, *With the Stroke of a Pen,* 24. A good example is the International Emergency Economic Powers Act, described in chapter 4 and discussed further in chapter 6.

5. Pfiffner, *President, Budget, and Congress,* 132; Fisher, *Abdication,* 125; Schick, *Congress and Money,* 254.

6. Reagan, with just under 51 percent of the popular vote, won forty-four states and 91 percent of the Electoral College in 1980; this was due in part to the presence of third-party candidate John Anderson in the race. On the economic program, see Reagan's January 20 inaugural address and his February 18 "Address Before a Joint Session of the Congress on the Program for Economic Recovery," *Public Papers of the Presidents, 1981;* William E. Pemberton, *Exit with Honor: The Life and Presidency of Ronald Reagan* (Armonk, NY: M. E. Sharpe, 1998); Kernell, *Going Public,* 149 and more generally chap. 5.

7. Hedrick Smith, *The Power Game: How Washington Works,* paperback ed. (New York: Ballantine, 1988), 460–63; David A. Stockman, *The Triumph of Politics: Why the Reagan Revolution Failed* (New York: Harper & Row, 1986), 200; Kernell, *Going Public,* 148; Pemberton, *Exit with Honor,* 103.

8. See Office of Management and Budget, *Budget of the United States Government, Fiscal Year 2005: Historical Tables* (Washington, DC: U.S. Government

Printing Office, 2004), table 7.1; Office of Management and Budget, *Citizens' Guide to the Federal Budget, Fiscal Year 2000* (Washington, DC: Government Printing Office, 1999), table 2–2.

9. Aaron Wildavsky, *The New Politics of the Budgetary Process* (Glenview, IL: Scott, Foresman, 1988), 205; Gallup Organization, "Short Questions Q.24," *Gallup Poll Monthly* 355 (April 1995): 29; *Congressional Record,* February 2, 1995, H1089.

10. Included here are the Tax Equity and Fiscal Responsibility Act (TEFRA) of 1982, the Deficit Reduction Act of 1984, the Consolidated Omnibus Reconciliation Act of 1985, the Tax Reform Act of 1986, and the Omnibus Reconciliation Act of 1987.

11. Gramm-Rudman-Hollings, which also changed the date of the budget resolution to April 15, was officially the Balanced Budget and Emergency Deficit Control Act of 1985 (Public Law 99-177); Fisher, *Abdication,* 130–34; see also Irene S. Rubin, *Balancing the Federal Budget* (Chatham, NJ: Chatham House, 2003), 37–40.

12. Fisher, *Abdication,* 131.

13. See *Bowsher v. Synar,* 478 U.S. 714 (1986).

14. Waxman in *Congressional Record,* December 11, 1985, 36075; CBO staffer Phil Joyce quoted in Rubin, *Balancing the Budget,* 53; see also Fisher, *Abdication,* 136.

15. These quotes are, respectively, Rep. Peter Blute (R-MA) in *Congressional Record,* February 2, 1995, H1092, and Rep. William Martini (R-NJ) before the House Government Reform and Oversight Committee, January 12, 1995.

16. Cohen in *Congressional Record,* March 22, 1995, S4308; Michel in Fisher, *Abdication,* 144.

17. Specter in *Congressional Record,* November 9, 1993, S15382.

18. Presidential deferrals of spending, which had gone into effect until overturned by the action of one chamber of Congress, had been eliminated in 1983 when the *Chadha* decision, discussed in chapter 6, negated this sort of legislative veto. The phrase "bill-ettes" is from Sen. Robert Byrd (D-WV); see, among other places, *Congressional Record,* March 21, 1995, S4227. For more on the various approaches and for extensive detail on the eventual structure of the bill, see Andrew Rudalevige, "In Whose Interest? Deficit Politics and the Item Veto," paper presented at the 1997 annual meeting of the American Political Science Association, Washington, DC.

19. *Clinton v. City of New York,* 524 U.S. 417 (1998); Nixon, *In the Arena,* 237; Fisher, *Abdication,* 151.

20. Jonathan Weisman, "The Tax-Cut Pendulum and the Pit," *Washington Post* (October 8, 2004), A1; see also the figures at the Treasury Department's Bureau of the Public Debt Web site, http://www.publicdebt.treas.gov. The amount used here is the "net interest" figure used by the Office of Management and Budget.

21. Congress's 2004 attempt to pass transportation reauthorization bogged down in conference committee after the House passed a $275 billion bill and the Senate one that cost $318 billion. The bills contained some three thousand earmarks, most famously the two "bridges to nowhere" (nearly literally) pushed by Rep. Don Young (R-AK) and totaling $325 million. Figures from Congressional Budget Office, *The Budget and Economic Outlook: An Update, September 2004* (Washington, DC: CBO, 2004); Office of Management and Budget, *Budget of the United States Government, Fiscal Year 2006* (Washington, DC: U.S. Government Printing Office, 2005), table S-1; Brian Friel, "Defending Pork," *National Journal* (May 8, 2004): 1404–9; Edmund L. Andrews, "Trim Deficit? Only If Bush Uses Magic," *New York Times* (February 7, 2005), C1. See also David Baumann, "Why Government by CR Matters," *National Journal* (November 1, 2003); Alexis Simendinger, David Baumann, Carl M. Cannon, and John Maggs, "Sky High," *National Journal* (February 7, 2004).

22. President's News Conference, November 4, 2004, Office of the White House Press Secretary. The president went on, "I think it would help the executive branch work with the legislative branch to make sure that we're able to maintain budget discipline." An item veto was included in the president's budget proposals in fiscal years 2003, 2004, 2005, and 2006 and regained special salience after the 2004 election. See Louis Fisher, *A Presidential Item Veto,* Report RS21991, Congressional Research Service (December 2, 2004). Gallup poll data reported in Simendinger et al., "Sky High," 375.

23. Richard Oppel Jr., "Bush Plans for Tax Cuts Barely Avert House Setback," *New York Times* (March 31, 2004), A18; Jim VandeHei, "Bush Enacts Fourth Tax Cut," *Washington Post* (October 5, 2004), A8; Edmund L. Andrews, "How Tax Bill Gave Business More and More," *New York Times* (October 13, 2004), A1. For a good sample of the promises made during the presidential campaign, see the transcripts of the three debates between John F. Kerry and George W. Bush in September and October 2004.

24. Quoted in Ron Suskind, *The Price of Loyalty: George W. Bush, the White House, and the Education of Paul O'Neill* (New York: Simon & Schuster, 2004), 291.

25. Andrew Taylor and John Cranford, "Omnibus-Wielding Majority Finds Power in the Package," *CQ Weekly* (November 20, 2004), 2724; "Missed Deadlines," *National Journal* (January 10, 2004), 101; Sheryl Gay Stolberg, "In Congress, Growing Doubts on Spending Process," *New York Times* (November 24, 2004), A19; Andrew Taylor, "Correcting Resolution on Tax Return Language Ties up Last Loose End," *CQ Weekly* (December 11, 2004), 2930.

26. Baumann, "Why Government by CR Matters," 3345; Elizabeth Drew, *Showdown: The Struggle between the Gingrich Congress and the Clinton White House,* paperback ed. (New York: Touchstone, 1997).

27. David Baumann, "The Breakdown of the Budget Process," *National Journal* (January 10, 2004), 96–97.

28. Andrew Taylor, "GOP Gropes for Way Out of Appropriations Morass," *CQ Weekly* (September 4, 1999), 2043; Specter quoted in Victoria Allred, "Versatility with the Veto," *CQ Weekly* (January 20, 2001), 176.

29. Barbara Sinclair, "Context, Strategy, and Chance: George W. Bush and the 107th Congress," in Colin Campbell and Bert A. Rockman, eds., *The George W. Bush Presidency: Appraisals and Prospects* (Washington, DC: CQ Press, 2004); Janet Hook, "$328-Billion Spending Bill Caps House Year," *Los Angeles Times* (December 9, 2003), A18; Dan Morgan, "House Passes $328 Billion Spending Bill," *Washington Post* (December 9, 2003), A1; "Omnibus Negotiations Center on Policy Riders, Debt Limit," *CQ Today Midday Update* (November 10, 2004); Stolberg, "Growing Doubts"; Bush in "President's News Conference," December 20, 2004, Office of the White House Press Secretary.

30. Dan L. Crippen, "Observations on the Current State of the Federal Budget Process," address at the fall symposium of the American Association for Budget and Program Analysis, November 22, 2002. Available at CBO Web site, http://www.cbo.gov (accessed October 14, 2004).

31. *Deconstructing Distrust,* Pew Research Center for the People and the Press, released March 10, 1998, available on-line at http://people-press.org/reports/print.php3?PageID=593 (accessed April 28, 2004), Q3, Q6, Q19 (which presents parallel National Election Studies data covering 1958–96); G. Calvin Mackenzie and Judith M. Labiner, "Opportunity Lost: The Rise and Fall of Trust and Confidence in Government after September 11," report for the Center for Public Service, Brookings Institution, May 30, 2002, table 1.

32. Garment, *Scandal,* 2.

33. For a broader description of developments, see Mackenzie, with Hafken, *Scandal Proof,* especially table 4–2.

34. Reagan statement from "The President's News Conference," June 18, *Public Papers of the President, 1985,* 779. For a succinct discussion and useful bibliography of Iran-contra, see Dickinson, *Bitter Harvest,* chap. 1. The scandal is also addressed in chapter 6.

35. Lawrence E. Walsh, *Final Report of the Independent Counsel for Iran/contra Matters, Volume I: Investigations and Prosecutions* (Washington, DC: United States Court of Appeals, District of Columbia Circuit), August 4, 1993, 561.

36. For Dole, see Douglas Jehl, "Republicans Honor Weinberger," *New York Times* (February 19, 1993), A18; James C. Roberts, "CPAC over Thirty Years: Conservatives Have Come a Long Way," *Human Events Online* (February 3, 2003), 16, available at http://www.humaneventsonline.com/article.php?id=272 (accessed May 24, 2004); Walter Pincus, "Bush Pardons Weinberger in Iran-Contra Affair," *Washington Post* (December 25, 1992), A1. Meese is quoted in Richard L. Berke, "The Iran-Contra Report: Report Is Dividing the Parties Again," *New York Times* (January 19, 1994), A9; Jeffrey Toobin, *A Vast Conspiracy* (New York: Touchstone, 2000), 70.

37. See the materials covered by document *353149CU/LE,* a memo from Bush counsel C. Boyden Gray to Phillip D. Brady, the staff secretary, entitled "Enrolled Bill Memo and Veto Message re S. 323" and dated September 23, 1992. The quoted memo is dated September 10, 1992, and written by W. Lee Rawls, assistant attorney general for the Justice Department's Office of Legislative Affairs. In the end, the Senate did not take up the renewal bill. WHORM Subject File General, Series LE, George H. W. Bush Presidential Library, College Station, Texas.

38. George Stephanopoulos, *All Too Human: A Political Education* (Boston: Little, Brown, 1999); Toobin, *Vast Conspiracy,* 66; Louis Fisher, "The Independent Counsel Statute," in Mark J. Rozell and Clyde Wilcox, eds., *The Clinton Scandal and the Future of American Government* (Washington, DC: Georgetown University Press, 2000).

39. Quoted in Toobin, *Vast Conspiracy,* 67.

40. For a broad narrative overview, see Michael Isikoff, *Uncovering Clinton* (New York: Crown, 1999); Peter Baker, *The Breach: Inside the Impeachment and Trial of William Jefferson Clinton* (New York: Scribner, 2000); Kenneth W. Starr, *The Starr Report: The Findings of Independent Counsel Kenneth W. Starr on President Clinton and the Lewinsky Affair* (New York: PublicAffairs, 1998).

41. Fisher, "The Independent Counsel Statute," 67–68; Spitzer, "Independent Counsel," 98–99.

42. Olson quoted in Hall, Pullen, and Rayos, "Independent Counsel Investigations," 827; General Accounting Office, *Financial Audit: Independent and Special Counsel Expenditures for the Six Months Ended March 31, 2004,* GAO-04–1014 (September 30, 2004). This GAO audit shows $871,204 in expenditures on the Cisneros case, on top of more than $800,000 spent in the previous six months ending September 30, 2003 (see GAO-04–525).

43. Acting Assistant Attorney General Dennis K. Burke to George W. Gekas, Chairman, Subcommittee on Commercial and Administrative Law, House Judiciary Committee, letter of April 13, 1999, reprinted at http://www.brook.edu/dybdocroot/gs/ic/Burke/01.htm (accessed February 5, 2004).

44. Corrado quoted in Ruth Marcus and Charles Babcock, "The System Cracks under the Weight of Cash," *Washington Post* (February 9, 1997), A1; Zell Miller, "A Sorry Way to Win," *Washington Post* (February 25, 2001), B7.

45. *Buckley v. Valeo,* 424 U.S. 1 (1976).

46. Gillon, *"That's Not What We Meant to Do,"* 214–15.

47. David B. Magleby, ed., *Outside Money: Soft Money and Issue Advocacy in the 1998 Congressional Elections* (Lanham, MD: Rowman & Littlefield, 2000), chaps. 3–4.

48. Gillon, *"That's Not What We Meant to Do,"* 222–23; Sorauf, *Inside Campaign Finance,* 148.

49. Victoria Farrar-Myers, "In the Wake of 1996: Clinton's Legacy for

Presidential Campaign Finance," in Adler and Genovese, eds., *Presidency and the Law;* Gillon, *"That's Not What We Meant to Do,"* 227.

50. Marcus and Babcock, "The System Cracks"; see also Jane Mayer, "Inside the Money Machine," *New Yorker* (February 3, 1997): 33–34; Gillon, *"That's Not What We Meant to Do,"* 226; Dick Morris, *Behind the Oval Office: Winning the Presidency in the Nineties* (New York: Random House, 1997), 150–53.

51. Quoted in Corrado, *Paying for Presidents,* 10; spending figures for 1996–2004 are from the Center for Responsive Politics, available at http://www.opensecrets.org (accessed October 14, 2004).

52. *McConnell, et al. v. Federal Election Commission,* 02–1674 (2003).

53. One estimate tallied spending by 527 groups at $386 million during the 2004 campaign: see "'04 Elections Expected to Cost Nearly $4 Billion," Center for Responsive Politics, October 21, 2004. RNC chair Ed Gillespie quoted in Glen Justice, "F.E.C. Declines to Curb Independent Fund-Raisers," *New York Times* (May 14, 2004), A16; Eliza N. Carney, Peter H. Stone, and James A. Barnes, "New Rules of the Game," *National Journal* (December 19, 2003). Note that a federal district court judge ruled in September 2004 that the FEC's regulations were "deficient" and would need to be rewritten, but her decision was immediately appealed and in any case did not affect the 2004 election. See Glen Justice, "Judge, Clarifying Decision, Says Spending Rules Stand," *New York Times* (October 20, 2004), A22.

54. Michael Slackman, "G.O.P. Convention Cost $154 Million," *New York Times* (October 14, 2004), A1; Anthony Corrado, "Financing the 2000 Elections," in Gerald M. Pomper, ed., *The Election of 2000* (Chatham, NJ: Chatham House, 2001), 95.

CHAPTER 6

1. Edwin Meese, III, *With Reagan: The Inside Story* (Washington, DC: Regnery, 1992), 322.

2. Terry M. Moe, "The Politicized Presidency," in John Chubb and Paul E. Peterson, eds., *New Directions in American Politics* (Washington, DC: Brookings Institution, 1985), 235; Barilleaux, *Post-Modern Presidency.* But see Richard Rose, *The Postmodern President: The White House Meets the World* (Chatham, NJ: Chatham House, 1988), who argues that the president's inability to manage the global community that so drastically affects the outcomes of the policies he pursues makes him "postmodern" in the sense of that word in other academic disciplines: fragmented and searching for meaning and "truth."

3. Recess appointments allow presidents to temporarily fill vacancies that occur when the Senate is not in session, an important power when slow travel and a lighter schedule meant long absences of Congress from Washington. These days, given year-round congressional sessions, its exercise is somewhat

self-conscious. See Louis Fisher, *Recess Appointments of Federal Judges,* Report RL31112, Congressional Research Service, September 5, 2001; Pete Earley, "Reagan Names Interim Board for Legal Services Corp.: Recess Appointments Bypass Senate," *Washington Post* (November 24, 1984), A1; Myron Struck, "Reagan's Recess Hirings Elicit Resentment," *Washington Post* (July 11, 1984), A17; Henry B. Hogue, *Recess Appointments: Frequently Asked Questions,* Report RS21308, Congressional Research Service, September 10, 2002, 2.

4. See John Anthony Maltese, "The Presidency and the Judiciary," in Nelson, ed., *Presidency and the Political System,* 510–11; David A. Yalof, *Pursuit of Justices: Presidential Politics and the Selection of Supreme Court Nominees* (Chicago: University of Chicago Press, 1999), chap. 6.

5. Richard P. Nathan, *The Administrative Presidency* (New York: Macmillan, 1983), 75; on "responsive competence," see Moe, "Politicized Presidency"; Stephanopoulos, *All Too Human,* 210; Suskind, *Price of Loyalty,* 48–49 (emphasis in original); Rudalevige, "The 'M' in OMB."

6. Paul C. Light, *Thickening Government* (Washington, DC: Brookings Institution, 1995), 190–92 (these figures are for executive branch positions classified at levels EL-1 through EL-5); Thomas J. Weko, *The Politicizing Presidency: The White House Personnel Office, 1948–1994* (Lawrence: University Press of Kansas, 1994); Mackenzie, "The State of the Presidential Appointments Process," and James P. Pfiffner, "Presidential Appointments: Recruiting Executive Branch Leaders," both in Mackenzie, ed., *Innocent until Nominated,* 37, 56–57.

7. Karen M. Hult, "The Bush White House in Comparative Perspective," in Fred I. Greenstein, ed., *The George W. Bush Presidency: An Early Assessment* (Baltimore: Johns Hopkins University Press, 2003), 69.

8. Fisher, *Recess Appointments;* Neil A. Lewis, "Bypassing Senate for Second Time, Bush Seats Judge," *New York Times* (February 21, 2004), A1, quoting Sen. Charles Schumer (D-NY); Sheryl Gay Stolberg, "Democrats Issue Threat to Block Court Nominees," *New York Times* (March 27, 2004), A1; Neil A. Lewis, "Deal Ends Impasse Over Judicial Nominees," *New York Times* (May 19, 2004), A17.

9. On Carter, see Warshaw, *Powersharing,* chap. 5; more generally, see Hult and Walcott, *Empowering the White House.*

10. Barilleaux, *Post-Modern Presidency,* 17–21.

11. See Dickinson, *Bitter Harvest,* figure 1.2.

12. John Hart, "President Clinton and the Politics of Symbolism: Cutting the White House Staff," *Political Science Quarterly* 110 (autumn 1995): 385–403.

13. Emanuel quoted in Alexis Simendinger, "The Paper Wars," *National Journal* (July 25, 1998), 1737; Mayer, *With the Stroke of a Pen,* 79–87; Cooper, *By Order of the President,* 232 and chap. 2 generally. See also William G. Howell, *Power without Persuasion: The Politics of Direct Presidential Action* (Princeton: Princeton University Press, 2003), 83–85.

14. Harold Hongju Koh, *The National Security Constitution: Sharing Power after the Iran-Contra Affair* (New Haven: Yale University Press, 1990), 46–48; Relyea, "National Emergency Powers."

15. Cooper (*By Order of the President*, 70) suggests that they "hide in plain sight." For an extended discussion of the "first mover" advantage orders grant, see Howell, *Power without Persuasion.*

16. Cornelius M. Kerwin, *Rulemaking: How Government Agencies Write Law and Make Policy*, 3d ed. (Washington, DC: CQ Press, 2003).

17. W. Andrew Jack, "Note: Executive Orders 12,291 and 12,498: Usurpation of Legislative Power or Blueprint for Legislative Reform?" *George Washington University Law Review* 54 (May 1986): 521. See also the texts of those executive orders and, more generally, Mayer, *With the Stroke of a Pen*, 125–34. For a recent appraisal, see Cindy Skrzycki, "Tiny OIRA Still Exercises Its Real Influence Invisibly," *Washington Post* (November 11, 2003), E1.

18. In February 2004 more than sixty scientists, including twenty Nobel Prize winners, signed a letter charging that the administration had disbanded advisory committees, salted other committees with unqualified members, and "censored reports by others when their scientific conclusions conflicted with administration policies," especially in regard to a draft EPA report on global warming. See James Glanz, "At the Center of the Storm over Bush and Science," *New York Times* (March 30, 2004), D1; Tom Hamburger and Alan C. Miller, "Mercury Emission Rule Geared to Benefit Industry, Staffers Say," *Los Angeles Times* (March 16, 2004), A1; Andrew C. Revkin, "Bush vs. the Laureates: How Science Became a Partisan Issue," *New York Times* (October 19, 2004), F1; more broadly, see Alexis Simendinger, "How Bush Flexes His Executive Muscles," *National Journal* (January 26, 2002), 233.

19. Cooper, *By Order of the President*, 90–91, 94–96, 101, 105.

20. See Cooper, *By Order of the President*, 144. For example, Reagan called them National Security Decision Directives, George H. W. Bush called them National Security Directives, Clinton called them Presidential Decision Directives, and George W. Bush called them National Security Presidential Directives.

21. Cooper, *By Order of the President*, 165, 194–95, and chap. 6 generally.

22. "Statement on Signing the Departments of Commerce, Justice, and State, the Judiciary, and Related Agencies Appropriations Act, 2002," November 28, *Public Papers of the Presidents, 2001*, 1459; Cooper, *By Order of the President*, chap. 7, esp. 204–5.

23. Examples are largely from Cooper, *By Order of the President*, chap. 7; for George H. W. Bush, see also Charles Tiefer, *The Semi-Sovereign Presidency* (Boulder, CO: Westview, 1994); for George W. Bush, see *Public Papers of the Presidents, 2001*, May 24, 575, and December 28, 1554. In 1988 Reagan refused to enforce an extension of the requirement that certain departmental budget

requests be included in the White House budget (as noted in chapter 3, these requirements arose to constrain the Nixon administration).

24. *Ameron, Inc., et al., v. U.S. Army Corps of Engineers, et al.*, 787 F.2d 875 (3d Cir. 1986); on the difficulty of overturning signing statements, see Cooper, *By Order of the President*, 222; 18 Opinions of the Office of Legal Counsel 199 (November 2, 1994), available at http://www.usdoj.gov/olc/nonexcut.htm (accessed February 8, 2005), which also contains examples of Supreme Court decisions that ignored the chance to rule signing statements out of order, from *Myers v. U.S.* in 1926 to *Freytag v. Commissioner* in 1991.

25. *INS v. Chadha*, 462 U.S. 919 (1983); Fisher, *Constitutional Conflicts*, 155.

26. Jessica Korn, *The Power of Separation: American Constitutionalism and the Myth of the Legislative Veto* (Princeton, NJ: Princeton University Press, 1996); Joel D. Aberbach, "What's Happened to the Watchful Eye?" *Congress and the Presidency* 29 (spring 2002), table 1; David Naither, "Congress as Watchdog: Asleep on the Job?" *CQ Weekly* (May 22, 2004), 1190. On the wave of stalled reauthorization bills, see Alex Wayne and Bill Swindell, "Capitol Hill Gridlock Leaves Programs in Limbo," *CQ Weekly* (December 4, 2004), 2834.

27. K. Daniel Glover, "'In the Belly of the Beast,'" *National Journal* (November 1, 2003), 3350–52; Light, *Monitoring Government*, 212ff. and chap. 8.

28. Stone, "Reagan Amendment," 278–79; Banks and Bowman, "Executive Authority"; *Alliance to End Repression v. City of Chicago*, 742 F.2d 1007 (7th Cir. 1984).

29. Senate Select Committee on Intelligence, *Inquiry into the FBI Investigation of the Committee in Solidarity with the People of El Salvador (CISPES)*, Senate Hearing 100–151, 100th Cong. (1988); William Greider, *Who Will Tell the People? The Betrayal of American Democracy* (New York: Simon and Schuster, 1992), 366; Ross Gelbspan, *Break-ins, Death Threats, and the FBI: The Covert War against the Central America Movement* (Boston: South End Press, 1991), esp. chaps. 11, 16. The Capitol bombing, it should be noted, was quickly linked to a small splinter group from the May 19 Communist Organization (138).

30. Banks and Bowman, "Executive Authority"; David Cole, *Enemy Aliens* (New York: New Press, 2003), 185–86.

31. Gates, *From the Shadows*, 191ff.; John M. Oseth, *Regulating U.S. Intelligence Operations* (Lexington: University Press of Kentucky, 1985), 148ff.

32. Oseth, *Regulating U.S. Intelligence Operations*, 153–59; Executive Order 12333.

33. Gelbspan, *Break-ins, Death Threats, and the FBI*, 14–15.

34. Executive Orders 12036, 12333; Koh, *National Security Constitution*, 59, 257n114.

35. "According to the accompanying interpretive memorandum prepared by the Justice Department, the FBI may authorize a full investigation if there are

statements threatening or advocating the use of violence, and an apparent ability to carry out the violence in a way that would violate federal law." The tools allowed during preliminary investigations were also expanded. Banks and Bowman, "Executive Authority," 108.

36. Public Law 104–132; Public Law 104–208; *CQ Almanac, 1996* (Washington, DC: CQ Press, 1997), section 5, 18ff.; Banks and Bowman, "Executive Authority," 109–11.

37. *U.S. v. Nixon,* 418 U.S. 683 (1974); Rozell, *Executive Privilege,* 96–99; Fisher, *Constitutional Conflicts,* 187–88.

38. Rozell, *Executive Privilege,* 106–7.

39. "News Conference with Prime Minister Romano Prodi of Italy," May 6, *Public Papers of the Presidents, 1998,* 700. Clinton replied that he could not comment on an ongoing proceeding but insisted that "the facts are quite different in this case."

40. *In re Sealed Case,* 121 F. 3d 729 (D.C. Cir. 1998). The specific definition of privilege covered "communications authored or solicited and received by those members of an immediate White House adviser's staff who have broad and significant responsibility for investigating and formulating the advice to be given the President on the particular matter to which the communications relate."

41. Quoted in Ellen Nakashima and Dan Eggen, "White House Seeks to Restore Its Privileges," *Washington Post* (September 10, 2001), A2.

42. "Memorandum for the Attorney General," December 12, *Public Papers of the Presidents, 2001,* 1509–10. While this memo is dated after September 11, it was the result of a lengthy back-and-forth with Congress—the original hearing on the matter had been scheduled for September 13.

43. Executive Order 13233 (Bush); Executive Order 12667 (Reagan). An earlier attempt by the Reagan Justice Department to provide former presidents with absolute privilege over their records, as an aspect of regulatory cost-benefit analysis, was overturned by the circuit court in 1988; see *Public Citizen v. Burke,* 843 F. 2d 1473 D.C. Cir. (1988), and Bruce P. Montgomery, "Nixon's Ghost Haunts the Presidential Records Act: The Reagan and George W. Bush Administration," *Presidential Studies Quarterly* 32 (December 2002): 796–99.

44. Montgomery, "Nixon's Ghost," 801–7.

45. Quoted in Rozell, *Executive Privilege,* 98.

46. Edwin Meese, III, "Attorney General's Memorandum on the 1986 Amendments to the Freedom of Information Act," December 1987, available at http://www.usdoj.gov/04foia/86agmemo.htm (accessed April 2, 2004); Public Law 99–570; Foerstel, *Freedom of Information,* 51–57; Diana M. T. K. Autin, "The Reagan Administration and the Freedom of Information Act," in Curry, ed., *Freedom at Risk,* 69–72.

47. See Foerstel, *Freedom of Information,* 59.

48. The Clinton executive order was Executive Order 12958; some 900

million pages were declassified from FY95 to FY01. This process continued under the main Bush order (Executive Order 13292), though agencies were given three more years to review documents that would otherwise have been declassified in 2003. Classification figures from the government's Information Security Oversight Office, reported in Jack Nelson, "U.S. Government Secrecy and the Current Crackdown on Leaks," Working Paper 2003–1, Joan Shorenstein Center on the Press, Politics, and Public Policy, Kennedy School of Government, Harvard University, 10; Executive Order 13292, March 25, 2003. The orders granting HHS, EPA, and the Agriculture Department the right to classify documents were issued on December 10, 2001; May 6, 2002; and September 26, 2002, respectively; they may be found in the *Federal Register*.

49. Thomas Blanton, director of the private National Security Archive, quoted in Dana Milbank and Mike Allen, "Release of Documents is Delayed," *Washington Post* (March 26, 2003), A15. More broadly—and for similar reaction by legislators of both parties—see Alison Mitchell, "Cheney Rejects Broader Access to Terror Brief," *New York Times* (May 20, 2002), A1; Alexis Simendinger, "The Power of One," *National Journal* (January 26, 2002); Kirk Victor, "Congress in Eclipse," *National Journal* (April 5, 2003), 1069–70.

50. *Walker v. Cheney,* Civil Action 02–0340, U.S. District Court for the District of Columbia (December 9, 2002), 17 (the roster of task force members is on pp. 5–6); "GAO Press Statement on *Walker v. Cheney,*" February 7, 2003, available on-line at http://www.house.gov/reform/min/pdfs/pdf_inves/pdf _energy_cheney_gao_no_appeal_state.pdf (accessed April 24, 2004); Dana Milbank, "GAO Ends Fight with Cheney Over Files," *Washington Post* (February 8, 2003), A4; Peter Brand and Alexander Bolton, "GOP Threats Halted GAO Cheney Suit," *The Hill* (February 19, 2003).

51. Theodore B. Olson et al., Brief for the Petitioners, *Cheney v. U.S. District Court for the District of Columbia,* U.S. Supreme Court Case 03–475, April 2004.

52. Judicial Watch brief quoted in Linda Greenhouse, "Administration Says a 'Zone of Autonomy' Justifies Its Secrecy on Energy Task Force," *New York Times* (April 24, 2004), I16; *Cheney v. U.S. District Court for the District of Columbia,* No. 03–475 (decided June 24, 2004). The appeals court subsequently dismissed the suit in May 2005.

53. Foerstel, *Freedom of Information,* 71; *Taylor v. Dept. of the Army,* 684 F.2d 99 (D.C. Circuit 1982).

54. Louis Fisher and David Gray Adler, "The War Powers Resolution: Time to Say Goodbye," *Political Science Quarterly* 113 (spring 1998): 1.

55. Adler's article, in homage to Francis Wormuth, is entitled "The Clinton Theory of the War Power," *Presidential Studies Quarterly* 30 (March 2000): 155.

56. Arguably, recent deployments in Colombia and the Philippines providing hundreds of military advisers to those countries' governments could be

included, to the extent those troops become involved (even unintentionally) in combat operations there. However, Congress has approved those deployments, though not U.S. participation in direct combat. See, e.g., Juan Forero, "Congress Approves Doubling U.S. Troops in Colombia to 800," *New York Times* (October 11, 2004), A9; Glen Martin, "Battling Rebels in Philippines: U.S. Playing Critical Role in Campaign against Muslim Insurgents," *San Francisco Chronicle* (July 6, 2003), A1.

57. See Sundquist, *Decline and Resurgence,* 258–59; Ely, *War and Responsibility,* 117; *Congressional Record,* October 10, 1973, 33555ff.

58. See Clinton's letter of June 29, 1993, to the congressional leadership (three days after the attack).

59. Quoted in Fisher and Adler, "Time to Say Goodbye," 5.

60. U.S. Department of Justice Office of Legal Counsel, letter of September 27, 1994, quoted in Fisher and Adler, "Time to Say Goodbye," 11n36; Clinton in *Public Papers of the President, 1994,* 1419.

61. Quoted in Fisher, *Abdication,* 164; see also Tiefer, *Semi-Sovereign Presidency,* 125–28; Eileen Burgin, "Rethinking the Role of the War Powers Resolution: Congress and the Persian Gulf War," *Journal of Legislation* 21 (1995): 28ff. The Justice Department's position was echoed by Clinton secretary of state Madeleine Albright in 1998, when she argued that "we are talking about using military force [against Iraq], but we are not talking about war. This is an important distinction." See Adler, "Clinton Theory," 162.

62. Cheney's and Bush's quotes are in Fisher, *Presidential War Power,* 149–51; see also Ely, *War and Responsibility,* 3.

63. Fisher and Adler, "Time to Say Goodbye," 11. Only Ford, in 1975, has invoked Section 4(a)(1), and his report was moot, since it came after military action was completed.

64. Fisher, *Presidential War Power,* 140–41; Peter Huchthausen, *America's Splendid Little Wars: A Short History of U.S. Military Engagements, 1975–2000* (New York: Viking, 2003), chap. 4.

65. Fisher, *Presidential War Power,* 194–97. For a parallel argument, see Ely, *War and Responsibility,* 119–20.

66. See Richard F. Grimmett, *War Powers Resolution: Presidential Compliance,* Congressional Research Service report IB81050, March 24, 2003, 13; on treaty obligations, see the WPR, Sec. 8 (a)(2) and 8(b).

67. Hostilities began on March 24 and ended on June 21, 1999. It should be noted, though, that President Clinton did not request or announce a thirty-day extension to the sixty-day window as provided for in the WPR. Further, air war was certainly meant to be included in the WPR, given the example of Cambodia unfolding before its drafters. Note that in 2002 George W. Bush asked for authorization for war with Iraq; this is discussed in chapter 7.

68. See Barry M. Blechman, *The Politics of National Security* (New York: Oxford University Press, 1990), 186; see also Huchthausen, *Splendid Little Wars.*

69. Burgin, "Rethinking the Role of the War Powers Resolution," 23–24, 40–42.

70. The Senate vote was 52–47; the House tally was 250–183. The quoted resolutions are H. Con. Res. 32 and H. Res. 95 of 1991.

71. Grimmett, *War Powers Resolution,* 4–5.

72. *Campbell v. Clinton,* 52 F. Supp. 2d (D.D.C. 1994); more generally, see Ronald J. Sievert, "Campbell v. Clinton and the Continuing Effort to Reassert Congress' Predominant Constitutional Authority to Commence, or Prevent, War," *Dickinson Law Review* 105 (winter 2001): 157–79. The Powell quote, from *Goldwater v. Carter,* is on p. 167.

73. Gingrich quoted in Fisher, *Abdication,* 111; Dole quoted in Bob Woodward, *The Choice* (New York: Simon & Schuster, 1996), 332; Gilman in Barry Schweid, "U.S. Troops Stay in Bosnia, House Rejects Test of War Powers Act," *Chicago Sun-Times* (March 19, 1998), 37.

74. King in Timothy Burger, "Near-Total Support from Congress," *New York Daily News* (August 21, 1998), 6; Thompson in Jack Torry, "Congress Approves Attacks by U.S.," *Pittsburgh Post-Gazette* (August 21, 1998), A15.

75. R. W. Apple Jr., "House to Debate Impeachment Today as US Continues Air Assault on Iraq," *New York Times* (December 18, 1998), A1; Francis X. Clines, "In Capitol, One Crisis Too Many," *New York Times* (December 17, 1998), A29.

76. Johnson, *Making of International Agreements,* 136.

77. Leslie Gelb, "Overseeing of CIA by Congress Has Produced Decade of Support," *New York Times* (July 7, 1986), A1; Olmsted, *Challenging the Secret Government,* 63, 181; *The 9/11 Commission Report: Final Report of the National Commission on Terrorist Attacks Upon the United States* (New York: W. W. Norton, 2004), 105–6.

78. Olmsted, *Challenging the Secret Government,* 177; *CQ Almanac, 1986,* 70; Theodore Draper, *A Very Thin Line: The Iran-Contra Affairs* (New York: Touchstone, 1991), 586; Koh, *National Security Constitution.*

79. Kenneth E. Sharpe, "U.S. Policy toward Central America: The Post-Vietnam Formula under Siege," in Nora Hamilton et al., eds., *Crisis in Central America: Regional Dynamics and U.S. Policy in the 1980s* (Boulder, CO: Westview, 1988), 21–24.

80. Draper, *Very Thin Line,* 18–24.

81. Draper, *Very Thin Line,* chap. 17.

82. Indeed, even when military aid resumed in 1986 after Nicaraguan president Daniel Ortega's ill-considered visit to Moscow, and a presidential finding brought the CIA back into the operation, the agency was instructed not to inform the oversight committees. See Treverton, *Covert Action,* 4.

83. Draper, *Very Thin Line,* 343–46.

84. See Koh, *National Security Constitution,* who argues that the system has not been reformed even in the scandal's wake. Louis Fisher has commented that

"efforts to understand the full dimensions [of the scandal] . . . were regularly thwarted by the strategy of destroying or withholding information, denying classified documents, and issuing presidential pardons. . . . There is hardly a shadow of political accountability." "Constitutional Violence," in Adler and Genovese, eds., *Presidency and the Law,* 198.

85. Quoted in Lundberg, "Congressional Oversight," 27.

86. *9/11 Commission Report,* 104–7; Martin Kady II and Helen Fessenden, "Conference without Compromise Threatens Intelligence Rewrite," *CQ Weekly* (October 16, 2004), 2455.

87. *Dames & Moore v. Regan* 452 U.S. 654 (1981); Loch Johnson, *Making of International Agreements,* 125–33 (quote is on p. 133); Kiki Caruson, "International Agreement-making and the Executive-Legislative Relationship," *Presidency Research Group Report 25* (fall 2002): 21–28.

88. See Pyle and Pious, *President, Congress;* see also David Gray Adler, "Termination of the ABM Treaty and the Political Question Doctrine," *Presidential Studies Quarterly* 34 (March 2004): 156–66. Case references are *Goldwater v. Carter,* 444 U.S. 996 (1979); *Kucinich v. Bush,* 236 F. Supp. 2d 1 (D.D.C. 2002).

89. Quoted in Rourke, *Congress and the Presidency,* 289–90; for the Clinton years, see James Lindsay, "Deference and Defiance: The Shifting Rhythms of Executive-Legislative Relations in Foreign Policy," *Presidential Studies Quarterly* 33 (September 2003): esp. 534–37.

90. Byrd in *Congressional Record,* December 13, 2001, S13120.

91. William J. Bennett, *The Death of Outrage: Bill Clinton and the Assault on American Ideals* (New York: Free Press, 1998); Nelson, *Presidency and the Political System;* David T. Canon and Kenneth R. Mayer, "Everything You Thought You Knew about Impeachment Is Wrong," in Leonard V. Kaplan and Beverly I. Moran, eds., *Aftermath: The Clinton Impeachment and the Presidency in the Age of Political Spectacle* (New York: New York University Press, 2001), 47.

CHAPTER 7

1. See, e.g., Frank Bruni, "Bush Cites News Article to Renew Attack on Gore's Fund-Raising," *New York Times* (September 15, 2000), A31; Cheney quoted from NBC News broadcast interview of January 27, 2003, in Tom Curry, "Executive Privilege Again at Issue," MSNBC.com, February 1, 2003, available at http://www.msnbc.com/news/695487.asp?cp1=1 (accessed May 1, 2004); Adam Clymer, "Judge Says Cheney Needn't Give Energy Records to Agency," *New York Times* (December 10, 2002), A1; Card quoted in Alexis Simendinger, "Power Plays," *National Journal* (April 17, 2004), 1168. Bush quoted in *Weekly Compilation of Presidential Documents* 38 (March 13, 2002), 411.

2. Nagourney, "Shift of Power to White House," A1; Victor, "Congress in Eclipse," 1066–70; Obey quoted in Lisa Caruso, "You've Got to Know

When to Hold 'Em," *National Journal* (July 12, 2003), 2258; Hagel quoted in David E. Rosenbaum, "In the Fulbright Mold, without the Power," *New York Times* (May 3, 2004), A16.

3. Sources differ as to the exact times of impact, within a minute or two; see, e.g., House Permanent Select Committee on Intelligence and Senate Select Committee on Intelligence, *Report of the Joint Inquiry into the Terrorist Attacks of September 11, 2001,* Senate Report 107-351/House Report 107-792, December 2002, 141–43, from which the death toll (as of December 2002) is calculated.

4. See Proclamation 7463, "Proclamation of National Emergency by Reason of Certain Terrorist Attacks"; text of Bush address from *CQ Almanac, 2001* (Washington, DC: CQ Press, 2002); Waters quoted in Carolyn Lochhead and Carla Marinucci, "'Freedom and Fear Are at War': Message to Americans, Warning to Taliban," *San Francisco Chronicle* (September 21, 2001), A1.

5. *Congressional Record,* September 14, 2001, H5682, S9416–18; Nancy Kassop, "The War Power and Its Limits," *Presidential Studies Quarterly* 33 (September 2003), 513–14; John Lancaster and Helen Dewar, "Congress Clears Use of Force, $40 Billion in Emergency Aid," *Washington Post* (September 15, 2001), A4.

6. Eric Schmitt, "New Power to Down Jets Is Last Resort, Rumsfeld Says," *New York Times* (September 28, 2001), B7.

7. "President Delivers State of the Union Address," January 29, 2002, Office of the White House Press Secretary; Kassop, "War Power and Its Limits"; *National Security Strategy of the United States of America,* September 17, 2002, available at http://www.whitehouse.gov/nsc/nss.html (accessed May 4, 2004), especially part V. Note that additional details on the policy, some classified, were released in December 2002; the classified version evidently discussed the use of preemptive nuclear strikes to halt the transfer of weapons of mass destruction. See Mike Allen and Barton Gellman, "Preemptive Strikes Part of U.S. Strategic Doctrine," *Washington Post* (December 11, 2002), A1.

8. Public Law 105–338.

9. Suskind, *Price of Loyalty,* 70–76; Glenn Kessler, "U.S. Decision on Iraq Has Puzzling Past," *Washington Post* (January 12, 2003), A1; Bob Woodward, *Plan of Attack* (New York: Simon & Schuster, 2004); John Donnelly, "Cheney States Case for Action on Iraq," *Boston Globe* (August 27, 2002), A1.

10. Mike Allen and Juliet Eilperin, "Bush Aides Say Iraq War Needs No Hill Vote," *Washington Post* (August 26, 2002), A1.

11. Rumsfeld to Jim Lehrer, PBS *Newshour,* September 18, 2002; he also said at a July 30 news conference, "Are there al-Qaeda in Iraq? Yes." This remark quoted in Allen and Eilperin, "Bush Aides." For similar claims see, for example, Todd S. Purdum, "The U.S. Case against Iraq: Counting Up the Reasons," *New York Times* (October 1, 2002), A5. Princeton's Anne-Marie Slaughter quoted in Neil A. Lewis with David E. Sanger, "Bush May Request Congress's Backing on Iraq, Aides Say," *New York Times* (August 29, 2002), A1.

12. DeLay quoted in Alison Mitchell and Carl Hulse, "Congress Authorizes Bush to Use Force Against Iraq," *New York Times* (October 11, 2002), A1; Daschle quoted in Anne E. Kornblut and Susan Milligan, "President Seeking Free Hand on Iraq," *Boston Globe* (September 20, 2002), A1.

13. Quoted in Susan Milligan, "Bush Insists on Plan to Use Force without UN Backing," *Boston Globe* (October 2, 2002), A16.

14. Public Law 107–243; Bush quoted in Ron Suskind, "Without a Doubt," *New York Times Magazine* (October 17, 2004).

15. United Nations Security Council Resolution 1441, November 8, 2002; "U.S. Secretary of State Addresses the U.N. Security Council," February 3, 2003, transcript from the Office of the White House Press Secretary, available at http://www.whitehouse.gov/news/releases/2003/02/20030205–1.html (accessed May 10, 2004); "Remarks to the Nation: President Says Saddam Hussein Must Leave Iraq Within 48 Hours," March 17, 2003, transcript from the Office of the White House Press Secretary, available at http://www.whitehouse.gov/news/releases/2003/03/20030317–7.html (accessed May 10, 2004).

16. Kerry in debate of Democratic candidates at the University of Southern California, February 25, 2004; see also Jodi Wilgoren, "Kerry Says His Vote on Iraq Would Be the Same Today," *New York Times* (August 10, 2004), A18.

17. David Barstow, William J. Broad, and Jeff Gerth, "How the White House Embraced Disputed Arms Intelligence," *New York Times* (October 3, 2004), A1; see also Dana Priest, "Inquiry Faults Intelligence on Iraq," *Washington Post* (October 24, 2003), A1; Richard W. Stevenson, "Remember 'Weapons of Mass Destruction'?" *New York Times* (December 18, 2003).

18. "The British government has learned that Saddam Hussein recently sought significant quantities of uranium from Africa," President Bush told Congress on January 28, 2003.

19. Woodward, *Plan of Attack,* 249; Greg Miller, "Cheney Is Adamant on Iraq 'Evidence,'" *Los Angeles Times* (January 23, 2004); James Fallows, "Blind into Baghdad," *Atlantic* 293 (January–February 2004): 52–77; Condoleezza Rice, "Why We Know Iraq Is Lying," *New York Times* (January 23, 2003); poll data from April 11–13, 2003, and March 23–24, 2003, reported in the trend data for the *New York Times*/CBS News Poll, April 23–27, 2004, reported in the *Times* on April 29.

In a March 2004 appearance on NBC's *Meet the Press,* Defense Secretary Rumsfeld would claim the administration had never referred to the Iraqi threat as *immediate* or *imminent.* But this was not so. See James P. Pfiffner's dispassionate treatment of the matter in "Did President Bush Mislead the Country in His Arguments for War with Iraq?" *Presidential Studies Quarterly* 34 (March 2004): 25–46.

20. *Report on the U.S. Intelligence Community's Prewar Intelligence Assessments on Iraq* (hereafter *Senate Intelligence Report*), Select Committee on Intelligence, United States Senate, July 7, 2004, 14, 16, 19, 21, 22.

21. *Senate Intelligence Report,* 239–57; Barstow, Broad, and Gerth, "How the White House Embraced Disputed Arms Intelligence"; Kay's October 2, 2003, statement before the House Permanent Select Committee on Intelligence, the House Appropriations Committee Subcommittee on Defense, and the Senate Select Committee on Intelligence; and Greg Miller, "Insider Faults CIA on Iraq Analysis," *Los Angeles Times* (January 31, 2004), A1; Dana Priest, "Inquiry Faults Intelligence on Iraq," *Washington Post* (October 24, 2003), A1; Charles Duelfer, *Comprehensive Report of the Special Advisor to the Director of Central Intelligence on Iraq's Weapons of Mass Destruction,* Central Intelligence Agency, September 30, 2004; Woodward, *Plan of Attack,* 434–42; Jonathan Landay, "Iraqi Defector, Source on WMD Claims, Was Cited as Unreliable," *Philadelphia Inquirer* (May 18, 2004), A1; *9/11 Commission Report,* 66, 334; 9/11 Commission Staff Statement No. 15, 5, available at http://www.9-11commission.gov/staff_statements/staff_statement_15.pdf (accessed October 18, 2004).

22. Michael Ignatieff, "Lesser Evils: What It Will Cost Us to Succeed in the War on Terror," *New York Times Magazine* (May 2, 2004), 49–50; Douglas Jehl, "Caution and Years of Budget Cuts Are Seen to Weaken C.I.A.," *New York Times* (May 11, 2004), A1; Woodward, *Plan of Attack,* 107.

23. *9/11 Commission Report,* 403–16; Executive Orders 13354 and 13355; Douglas Jehl and David E. Sanger, "Bush Signs Order Bolstering CIA Director's Power," *New York Times* (August 27, 2004), A1; Walter Pincus, "CIA Chief's Power a Hurdle in Intelligence Reform," *Washington Post* (October 17, 2004), A13; Andrew Taylor, "In 'Farce,' Senators Pick Apart Oversight Restructuring Plan," *CQ Weekly* (October 9, 2004), 2390; "Recommended, and Actual, Intelligence Reorganization," *CQ Weekly* (December 11, 2004), 2942; Walter Pincus, "National Intelligence Director Proves to Be Difficult Post to Fill: Uncertainties over Role, Authority, Are Blamed for Delays," *Washington Post* (January 31, 2005), A4. For discussion of U.S. Code, Titles 10 and 50, and Department of Defense interpretations of them, see Barton Gellman, "Secret Unit Expands Rumsfeld's Domain: New Espionage Branch Delving into CIA Territory," *Washington Post* (January 23, 2005), A1; see also Seymour M. Hersh, "The Coming Wars: What the Pentagon Can Now Do in Secret," *New Yorker* (January 24–31, 2005).

24. Seymour M. Hersh, "Moving Targets: Will the Counter-Insurgency Plan in Iraq Repeat the Mistakes of Vietnam?" *New Yorker* (December 15, 2003); Hersh, "Coming Wars"; Jim Hoagland, "Bremer's Legacy," *Washington Post* (May 6, 2004), A35.

25. James Risen, David Johnston, and Neil A. Lewis, "Harsh C.I.A. Methods Cited in Top Qaeda Interrogations," *New York Times* (May 13, 2004): A1; Bob Drogin, "Abuse Brings Deaths of Captives into Focus," *Los Angeles Times* (May 16, 2004), A1; Dana Priest, "Memo Lets CIA Take Detainees out of Iraq: Practice Is Called Serious Breach of Geneva Conventions," *Washington Post* (October 24, 2004), A1; Douglas Jehl, "U.S. Action Bars Right of Some Cap-

tured in Iraq," *New York Times* (October 26, 2004), A1; Jack Goldsmith, Office of Legal Counsel, "Re: Permissibility of Relocating Certain 'Protected Persons' from Occupied Iraq," draft memo of March 19, 2004, to Alberto Gonzales, White House Counsel. A similar but even broader conclusion was reached by OLC in October 2003; see Jehl, "U.S. Action."

26. Bradley Graham, "Number of Army Probes of Detainee Deaths Rises to 33," *Washington Post* (May 22, 2004), A17; more broadly see James P. Pfiffner, "Torture as Public Policy," unpublished manuscript, George Mason University School of Public Policy, 5; and Karen J. Greenberg and Joshua L. Dratel, eds., *The Torture Papers* (New York: Cambridge University Press, 2005).

27. *Ex parte Quirin,* 317 U.S. 1 (1942); Louis Fisher, "Military Tribunals: A Sorry History," *Presidential Studies Quarterly* 33 (September 2003): 491.

28. Gonzales memo of January 25, 2002, entitled "Decision re Application of the Geneva Convention on Prisoners of War to the Conflict with Al Qaeda and the Taliban," quoted in John Barry, Michael Hirsh, and Michael Isikoff, "The Roots of Torture," *Newsweek* (May 24, 2004), 30–31; Rumsfeld quoted in Katharine Q. Seelye, "First 'Unlawful Combatants' Seized in Afghanistan Arrive at U.S. Base in Cuba," *New York Times* (January 12, 2002), A7 (emphasis added); Seymour Hersh, "The Gray Zone: How a Secret Pentagon Program Came to Abu Ghraib," *New Yorker* (May 24, 2004); John Hendren, "Officials Say Rumsfeld OK'd Harsh Interrogation Methods," *Los Angeles Times* (May 21, 2004), A1. The full texts of the Gonzales and OLC memos, and many others besides, were later made public and are collected on-line in various places, including the FindLaw.com Web site, and in Greenberg and Dratel, eds., *Torture Papers.*

29. Antonio Taguba, *Article 15–6 Investigation of the 800th Military Police Brigade,* U.S. Army (February 26, 2003); this is one of several official reckonings, with others in progress. Journalistic treatments include Seymour M. Hersh, "Torture at Abu Ghraib," *New Yorker* (May 10, 2004), and *Chain of Command: The Road from 9/11 to Abu Ghraib* (New York: HarperCollins, 2004); Barry, Hirsh, and Isikoff, "Roots of Torture"; Douglas Jehl and Eric Schmitt, "Afghan Policies on Questioning Taken to Iraq," *New York Times* (May 21, 2004), A1; Douglas Jehl, Steven Lee Myers, and Eric Schmitt, "Abuse of Captives More Widespread, Says Army Survey," *New York Times* (May 26, 2004), A1; Neil A. Lewis, "Broad Use of Harsh Tactics Is Described at Cuba Base," *New York Times* (October 17, 2004), A1; Jehl, "U.S. Action."

30. More precisely, torture referred to acts that inflicted pain "equivalent in intensity to the pain accompanying serious physical injury, such as organ failure, impairment of bodily function, or even death." But inflicting such pain was not illegal unless done with "the specific intent to inflict severe pain"—"even if the defendant knows that severe pain will result from his actions, if causing such harm is not his objective, he lacks the requisite specific intent." See Bybee to

Gonzales, "Re: Standards of Conduct for Interrogation under 18 U.S.C. §§2340–2340A," Office of Legal Counsel, U.S. Department of Justice, August 1, 2002, 1–6, esp. 3.

31. Bybee, "Standards of Conduct," 31–39; Working Group Report on Detainee Interrogations in the Global War on Terrorism: Assessment of Legal, Historical, Policy, and Operational Considerations, U.S. Department of Defense, April 4, 2003, 21 and Section III generally. More generally, see Pfiffner, "Torture as Public Policy," 12–14. Pfiffner points out that Article I, Section 8, of the Constitution gives Congress power "to make rules for the government and regulation of the land and naval forces." The later administration position may be found in the written responses of Alberto Gonzales to Sen. Joseph Biden and other members of the Senate Judiciary Committee during confirmation hearings on his elevation to attorney general, January 2005.

32. President's Military Order of November 13, 2001, esp. Sections 1–4, 7, as printed in the *Federal Register* 66, 57833ff; Alberto Gonzales, "Martial Justice, Full and Fair," *New York Times* (November 30, 2001); Joseph Lelyveld, "'The Least Worst Place': Life in Guantánamo," in Richard C. Leone and Greg Anrig Jr., *The War on Our Freedoms: Civil Liberties in an Age of Terrorism* (New York: PublicAffairs, 2003); Neil A. Lewis and Eric Schmitt, "Cuba Detentions May Last Years," *New York Times* (February 13, 2004), A1; Neil A. Lewis, "Justice Memos Explained How to Skip Prisoner Rights," *New York Times* (May 21, 2004), A12; Tim Golden, "After Terror, a Secret Rewriting of Terror Law," *New York Times* (October 24, 2004), A1; Tim Golden, "Administration Officials Split over Stalled Military Tribunals," *New York Times* (October 25, 2004), A1.

Bush quoted in Lelyveld, "Least Worst Place," 104; Rumsfeld quoted in Wayne Washington, "Rumsfeld Defends Detainee Conditions," *Boston Globe* (January 28, 2002), A1; Marine Major Michael Mori, quoted in Neil A. Lewis, "Military Defenders for Detainees Put Tribunals on Trial," *New York Times* (May 4, 2004), A1. Mori gave the example of motions (for the admission of evidence, e.g.), which are not decided by the panel of judges but by the officer who approved the charges against the defendant in the first place. See also the arguments of defense counsels Lt. Commander Charles Swift in Jess Bravin, "As War Tribunal Opens, Legality Is Challenged," *Wall Street Journal* (August 25, 2004), B1, and Lt. Colonel Sharon Shaffer in Jess Bravin, "U.S. Tribunal's Hearings Befuddle Attorneys, War-Crimes Suspects," *Wall Street Journal* (August 30, 2004), A2. The case in question was *Hamdan v. Rumsfeld,* Civil Action No. 04–1519, United States District Court for the District of Columbia (November 8, 2004); the decision is under appeal as of this writing.

33. See Fisher, "Military Tribunals," 491–95, 503–4. According to the Census Bureau, there were 20.6 million noncitizens among the 286 million U.S. population in 2003.

34. For a more detailed approach to this question, see Jennifer Elsea, "Presidential Authority to Detain 'Enemy Combatants,'" *Presidential Studies Quarterly* 33 (September 2003): 585; Kassop, "War Powers," 517–20.

35. Sessions and Hatch quoted in Robin Toner, "Senators Spar Carefully in Hearing on Security," *New York Times* (December 7, 2001); Relyea, "Presidential Authority," 596–97.

36. See the cases of *Rasul v. Bush* (03–334) and *Al Odah v. U.S.* (03–343), administration brief, 15–17; Barry, Hirsh, and Isikoff, "Roots of Torture"; petitioners' brief in *Odah,* 22–23; *Al Odah v. U.S.* (02–5251), U.S. Court of Appeals, D.C. Circuit (March 11, 2003).

37. *Rasul v. Bush* was decided June 28, 2004. Justices Scalia, Rehnquist, and Thomas dissented. The tribunal system itself was challenged in federal district court in late October 2004, resulting in the *Hamdan v. Rumsfeld* district court decision noted here and in note 32, this chapter. Later decisions at the district court level favored both the government and detainees in turn; appeals seeking resolution from the circuit court of appeals were pending as of this writing. See Carol D. Leonnig, "Judge Rules Detainee Tribunals Illegal," *Washington Post* (February 1, 2005), A1.

38. "Combatant Status Review Tribunal Order Issued," U.S. Department of Defense News Release No. 651–04, July 7, 2004; Toni Locy, "Tribunal Orders Release of Guantánamo Detainee," *USA Today* (September 8, 2004); Neil A. Lewis, "Guantánamo Prisoners Getting Their Day, but Hardly in Court," *New York Times* (November 8, 2004), A1.

39. Dana Milbank and Robin Wright, "Off the Mark on Cost of War, Reception by Iraqis," *Washington Post* (March 19, 2004): A1; *Paying for Iraq's Reconstruction,* Congressional Budget Office, January 23, 2004.

40. Milbank and Wright, "Off the Mark on Cost of War"; Fallows, "Blind into Baghdad."

41. Jonathan Weisman and Thomas E. Ricks, "Increase in War Funding Sought," *Washington Post* (October 26, 2004), A1; Public Law 109-13.

42. Bremer quoted in Kirk Victor, "Escalating Hostilities," *National Journal* (October 4, 2003), 3021; Warner quoted in Richard A. Oppel Jr., "In Rebuff to Bush, Senate Raises Bar for Tax Cuts," *New York Times* (March 11, 2004), A20; John Diamond, "Buying Own Gear Is Common for Troops," *USA Today* (June 25, 2003). The supplemental budget became Public Law 108–106 on November 6, 2003.

43. For details of the Emergency Response Fund, see the *Congressional Record,* September 14, 2001, S9413; Woodward, *Bush at War,* 137; Dan Moran, "Democrats Question Use of 9/11 Emergency Fund," *Washington Post* (April 27, 2004), A19; Woodward interview with Matt Lauer on NBC's *Today,* April 19, 2004.

44. Public Law 108–106, §3001 et seq.; Bush, "Statement on Signing the Emergency Supplemental Appropriations Act for Defense and for the Recon-

struction of Iraq and Afghanistan, 2004," *Weekly Compilation of Presidential Documents* 39 (November 6, 2003): 1549.

45. Ariana Eunjung Cha and Renae Merle, "Line Increasingly Blurred Between Soldiers and Civilian Contractors," *Washington Post* (May 13, 2004), A1; David Barstow, "Security Companies: Shadow Soldiers in Iraq," *New York Times* (April 19, 2004), A1; Dan Baum, "Nation Builders for Hire," *New York Times Magazine* (June 22, 2003), 32.

46. Cheney served as Halliburton's CEO before becoming vice president in 2001.

47. Erik Eckholm, "Top Army Official Calls for a Halliburton Inquiry," *New York Times* (October 25, 2004); Letter of May 6, 2003, Rep. Henry A. Waxman to U.S. Army Corps of Engineers; Letter of November 6, 2003, Waxman to U.S. AID; memo of March 10, 2004, Waxman to Democratic Members of House Government Reform Committee entitled "New Information about Halliburton Contracts," all available at http://www.house.gov/reform/min/ (accessed May 14, 2004); Victor, "Escalating Hostilities," 3021; Public Law 108–106, §§2202-03.

48. Jackie Spinner and Ariana Eunjung Cha, "U.S. Decisions on Iraq Spending Made in Private," *Washington Post* (December 27, 2003), A1; L. Elaine Halchin, *The CPA: Origins, Characteristics, and Institutional Authorities,* Report RL32370, Congressional Research Service, April 29, 2004.

49. Public Law 107–296; Gail Russell Chaddock, "Federal Work Culture Set for Makeover," *Christian Science Monitor* (December 11, 2002), 2; Christopher H. Schmitt and Edward T. Pound, "The Power of the Fine Print," *U.S. News & World Report* 135 (December 22, 2003): 27, referring to Section 214(a)(1)(D)(ii); "Statement by the President," Office of the White House Press Secretary, November 25, 2002, available at http://www.whitehouse.gov/ news/releases/2002/11/20021125–10.html (accessed May 14, 2004).

50. Philip Shenon and Elisabeth Bumiller, "Bush Allows Rice to Testify on 9/11 in a Public Session," *New York Times* (March 31, 2004), A1; "Excerpts from White House Letter on Rice's Testimony," *New York Times* (March 31, 2004), A14. The charges against Bush had been raised in testimony and a book by former NSC counterterrorism aide Richard A. Clarke.

51. Card memo and guidance of March 19, 2002, Justice Department Web site, available at http://www.usdoj.gov/oip/foiapost/2002foiapost10.htm (accessed May 13, 2004); the Heritage Foundation's Mark Tapscott's "Growing Secrets Increase Concern: Loopholes Abound to Hide Information," *Harrisburg Patriot-News* (November 24, 2002), F1; Dana Milbank, "Under Bush, Expanding Secrecy," *Washington Post* (December 23, 2003): A19; Christopher H. Schmitt and Edward T. Pound, "Keeping Secrets," *U.S. News & World Report* 135 (December 22, 2003): 18–29; "Washington in Brief," *Washington Post* (February 1, 2005), A4.

52. Karen Branch-Brioso, "Ashcroft's New Powers Anger Civil Libertari-

ans, Defense Lawyers," *St. Louis Post-Dispatch* (November 11, 2001), B1; "Remarks of Attorney General John Ashcroft: Attorney General Guidelines," May 30, 2002, U.S. Department of Justice; Bill Miller, "Ashcroft: Old Rules Aided Terrorists; FBI Agents Get Freer Hand," *Washington Post* (May 31, 2002), A13.

53. David Cole, *Enemy Aliens: Double Standards and Constitutional Freedoms in the War on Terrorism* (New York: New Press, 2003), 25; Adam Liptak, Neil A. Lewis, and Benjamin Weiser, "After Sept. 11, a Legal Battle over Limits of Civil Liberty," *New York Times* (August 4, 2002), A1; Lyle Denniston, "Justices Won't Review Secret Deportation Hearings," *Boston Globe* (May 28, 2003), A3. Note that the 6th Circuit Court of Appeals ruled for opening hearings, warning ominously that "democracies die behind closed doors." That ruling was not appealed, meaning that hearings would stay open in the four states of the 6th Circuit Court of Appeals and closed elsewhere. The FOIA charges noted in note 51 were in relation to these detention cases.

54. For information on TIA and other data collection efforts, see Ann Davis, "Data Collection Is Up Sharply Following 9/11," *Wall Street Journal* (May 22, 2003), B1; Michael Sniffen, "High-Tech Spying Program Closed," *Chicago Tribune* (September 25, 2003), 11; "Washington in Brief," *Washington Post* (September 26, 2003), A14; and the documents collected by the Electronic Privacy Information Center at http://www.epic.org/privacy/profiling/tia (accessed April 17, 2005). TIA director John M. Poindexter defends the program in "Finding the Face of Terror in Data," *New York Times* (September 10, 2003), A25.

55. Public Law 107–56; Charles Doyle, "Section by Section Analysis of the USA PATRIOT Act," CRS RL31200, Congressional Research Service, December 10, 2001; Kathleen M. Sullivan, "Under a Watchful Eye," in Leone and Anrig, eds., *War on Our Freedoms;* Harry F. Tepker, "The USA PATRIOT Act," *Extensions* (fall 2002): 9–13; Bob Barr, "Testimony Submitted to the Senate Judiciary Committee Concerning the USA PATRIOT Act, the SAFE Act, and Related Matters," September 22, 2004, available at http://judiciary. senate.gov (accessed October 25, 2004); Keith Perine, "Judge Puts Civil Liberties Ahead of Patriot Act Provision," *CQ Weekly* (October 2, 2004), 2305. The case is *John Doe and ACLU v. Ashcroft, et al.,* expected to be heard by the Second Circuit Court of Appeals in 2005.

56. Shelby report in Cam Simpson, "Murky 'Wall' a Scapegoat for 9/11 Failures," *Chicago Tribune* (April 15, 2004), 24; Stuart Taylor Jr., "9/11: Save Some Blame for Courts that Created the 'Wall,'" *National Journal* (April 17, 2004); see also the response to Ashcroft by former Justice Department official Jamie S. Gorelick, his main target, in "The Truth about 'the Wall,'" *Washington Post* (April 18, 2004), B7. See also the *9/11 Commission Report,* 78–80.

57. The original Justice Department draft would have required merely that it be "a" purpose.

58. Eric Lichtblau, "Secret Warrant Requests Increased in 2003," *New York Times* (May 3, 2004), A18.

59. For a discussion on the "thoughtful" end of the spectrum, see the essays in Leone and Anrig, eds., *War on Our Freedoms;* Cole, *Enemy Aliens.* The on-line magazine *Slate* also produced a substantive four-part series entitled "Should You Be Scared of the Patriot Act?" available at http://slate.msn.com/id/2087984/ (accessed May 20, 2004).

60. "President: FBI Needs Tools to Track Down Terrorists," remarks at FBI Headquarters, Office of the White House Press Secretary, September 25, 2001.

61. The vote on engrossment was 337–79. See *Congressional Record,* October 12, 2001, H6712-26, 6739–58.

62. *CQ Almanac, 2001* (Washington, DC: CQ Press, 2002), 1–10; Tepker, "PATRIOT Act," 10. For a detailed but rather self-promoting list of changes to administration proposals, see the section-by-section analysis of the Patriot Act produced by Sen. Patrick Leahy (D-VT) and available at http://leahy.senate.gov/press/200110/102401a.html (accessed May 19, 2004). The vote on the conference committee report was 98–1 in the Senate (only Feingold dissented) and 357–66 in the House.

63. Neil A. Lewis, "Ashcroft Defends Antiterror Plan and Says Criticism May Aid Foes," *New York Times* (December 7, 2001), A1; Adam Clymer, "Justice Dept. Balks at Effort to Study Antiterror Powers," *New York Times* (August 15, 2002), A14; Dan Eggen, "Ashcroft Assailed on Policy Review," *Washington Post* (August 21, 2002), A2; Dan Eggen, "White House Intensifies Efforts to Safeguard Patriot Act," *Washington Post* (January 30, 2004), A2; John Ashcroft to Sen. Orrin Hatch, letter of January 28, 2004. While Justice was unable to respond to congressional inquiry, Attorney General Ashcroft did manage to squeeze in a multicity speaking tour in 2003, promoting the Patriot Act to hand-picked law enforcement audiences, and the Justice Department also launched an extensive Web site, http://www.lifeandliberty.gov, to combat what it claimed were inaccuracies in critics' accounts of the act.

64. James B. Comey, Deputy Attorney General, "A Review of Counter-Terrorism Legislation and Proposals," statement to the U.S. Senate Committee on the Judiciary, September 22, 2004, available at http://judiciary.senate.gov (accessed October 25, 2004).

65. Eric Lichtblau, "Ashcroft Seeks More Power to Pursue Terror Suspects," *New York Times* (June 6, 2003); Michael Isikoff, "Brooklyn's Version of Abu Ghraib?" *Newsweek* (May 24, 2004), 5; *The September 11 Detainees: A Review of the Treatment of Aliens Held on Immigration Charges in Connection with the Investigation of the September 11 Attacks,* Office of the Inspector General, U.S. Department of Justice, June 2003; Office of the Inspector General, U.S. Department of Justice, *Supplemental Report on September 11 Detainees' Allegations of Abuse at the*

Metropolitan Detention Center in Brooklyn, New York, December 2003; *Report to Congress on Implementation of Section 1001 of the USA PATRIOT Act,* Office of the Inspector General, U.S. Department of Justice, July 2003; Sarah Kershaw and Eric Lichtblau, "Spain Had Doubts before U.S. Held Lawyer in Madrid Blasts," *New York Times* (May 26, 2004), A1; Eric Lichtblau, "Inquiry into FBI Questioning Is Sought," *New York Times* (August 18, 2004), A16; Adam Liptak, "For Post-9/11 Material Witness, It Is a Terror of a Different Kind," *New York Times* (August 19, 2004), A1; J. M. Kalil and Steve Tetreault, "Patriot Act: Law's Use Causing Concerns," *Las Vegas Review-Journal* (November 5, 2003); U.S. Department of Justice, *Report from the Field: The USA PATRIOT Act at Work* (July 13, 2004), available at http://www.lifeandliberty.gov/docs/071304 _report_from_the_field.pdf (accessed October 25, 2004).

66. Ashcroft quoted in Lichtblau, "Ashcroft Seeks More Power"; "President Bush Calls for Renewing the USA PATRIOT Act," Hershey, Pennsylvania, Office of the White House Press Secretary, April 19, 2004; Alexander Bolton, "Presidential Push Fails to Quell GOP Fear of Patriot Act," *Hill* (May 12, 2004); Anita Ramasastry, "Patriot II: The Sequel," Findlaw.com (February 17, 2003); Martin Kady II and Helen Fessenden, "Conference without Compromise Threatens Intelligence Rewrite," *CQ Weekly* (October 16, 2004), 2455; Dan Eggen, "Measure Expands Police Powers: Intelligence Bill Includes Disputed Anti-Terror Moves," *Washington Post* (December 10, 2004), A1.

67. Theodore Olson et al., "Brief for the Respondents in Opposition," *Hamdi v. Rumsfeld* (U.S. Supreme Court, 03–6696); Paul J. McNulty et al., "Brief for Respondents-Appellants," *Hamdi v. Rumsfeld* (4th Circuit Court of Appeals, June 19, 2002); *Hamdi v. Rumsfeld,* 296 F.3d 278 (4th Circuit, 2002); "Declaration of Michael H. Mobbs, Special Advisor to the Under Secretary of Defense for Policy," July 24, 2002; Elsea, "Presidential Authority to Detain," 584–85, 591.

68. Olson quoted in Charles Lane, "In Terror War, 2nd Track for Suspects," *Washington Post* (December 1, 2002), A1; more broadly, see Elsea, "Presidential Authority to Detain," 591–94; Anthony Lewis, "Security and Liberty: Preserving the Values of Freedom," in Leone and Anrig, eds., *War on Our Freedoms,* 52–58; Richard B. Schmitt, "Government Says Padilla Plotted High-Rise Attacks," *Los Angeles Times* (June 2, 2004), A1.

69. Linda Greenhouse, "Detention Cases before Supreme Court Will Test Limits of Presidential Power," *New York Times* (April 18, 2004), I19; administration briefs submitted at various levels regarding *Padilla v. Rumsfeld* and *Rumsfeld v. Padilla;* 2d Circuit opinion in *Padilla v. Rumsfeld* (December 18, 2003). The transcript of the oral arguments before the Supreme Court may be found on the Court's Web site, http://www.supremecourtus.gov/oral_arguments/ argument_transcripts/03–1027.pdf (accessed May 10, 2004). The Non-Detention Act is Public Law 92–128, codified at 18 USC 4001 (a);

as noted in chapter 4, it was passed to repeal the Emergency Detention Act of 1950.

70. *Hamdi v. Rumsfeld,* 03–6696, and *Rumsfeld v. Padilla,* 03–1027, both decided June 28, 2004.

71. The four justices were joined by two others (Breyer and Ginsburg) for the portion of the opinion setting aside the circuit court opinion and requiring due process for suspected combatants. But Breyer and Ginsburg dissented from the notion that the AUMF provided sufficient permission to hold Hamdi in light of the Non-Detention Act, especially given what was known about his involvement in the Afghanistan hostilities. They found it unlikely that the AUMF was intended to allow indefinite detentions given that even the Patriot Act allowed detaining noncitizens for only seven days without charge. As noted, Justices Scalia and Stevens also would have released Hamdi immediately. Thus, only Justice Thomas held both that the AUMF gave the president sufficient power and that the combatant proceedings to date were acceptable. Thomas wrote that "this detention falls squarely with the Federal Government's war powers, and we lack the expertise and capacity to second-guess that decision."

72. Neil A. Lewis, "Disagreement over Detainees' Legal Rights Simmers," *New York Times* (November 1, 2004), A15; Lewis, "Guantánamo Prisoners Getting Their Day"; Dan Eggen, "Two Indicted on Charges Related to Terrorism," *Washington Post* (September 17, 2004), A3. On the government's original official position on Hamdi, see the "Declaration of Donald D. Woolfolk," submitted June 13, 2002, as part of the administration's court filings. Woolfolk testified that "permitting such access to detainee Hamdi may create substantial harm to U.S. national security interests."

73. July 2001, October 2001, and May 2002 figures are from Mackenzie and Labiner, "Opportunity Lost," tables 1–2; October 2003 figures are from *Newsweek* poll of October 9–10, reported briefly in Howard Fineman and Karen Breslau, "Arnold's Earthquake," *Newsweek* (October 20, 2003): 26–31, and in more detail in *Newsweek*'s press release: "*Newsweek* Poll: California Recall Election Reaction," PR Newswire, October 11, 2003.

74. The statute is the 1982 Intelligence Identities Protection Act. See, e.g., Eric Lichtblau, "Special Counsel Is Named to Head Inquiry on C.I.A. Leak," *New York Times* (December 31, 2003), A1.

75. This issue erupted again in early 2005 when a new administration estimate put the ten-year net cost of the prescription drug program not at $550 billion but at over $720 billion. A spokesman said the discrepancy stemmed from shifting the ten years measured to those when the drug program was actually operating. Sheryl Gay Stolberg and Robert Pear, "Mysterious Fax Adds to Intrigue over the Medicare Bill's Cost," *New York Times* (March 18, 2004); Robert Pear, "Agency Sees Withholding of Medicare Data from Congress as

Illegal," *New York Times* (May 4, 2004), A17; Robert Pear, "Inquiry Proposes Penalties for Hiding Medicare Data," *New York Times* (September 8, 2004), A16; Ceci Connolly and Mike Allen, "Medicare Drug Benefit May Cost More Than Reported: New Estimate Dwarfs Bush's Original Price Tag," *Washington Post* (February 9, 2005), A1.

76. Alexis Simendinger, "The Papers, Please," *National Journal* (November 1, 2003), 3354; David E. Sanger, "When Goals Meet Reality," *New York Times* (March 31, 2004), A1; Eric Schmitt, "Defense Leaders Faulted by Panel in Prison Abuse," *New York Times* (August 24, 2004), A1; Douglas Jehl and Eric Schmitt, "Army's Report Faults General in Prison Abuse," *New York Times* (August 26, 2004), A1.

77. Robert Novak, "Iraq Reconstruction Held Up by D.C. Infighting," *Chicago Sun Times* (February 26, 2004), 43; John W. Dean, "More Than Just His Location Remains Undisclosed: Why Dick Cheney's Secrecy Scheme for Pre-9/11 Information Makes No Sense," FindLaw.com, available at http://writ.news.findlaw.com/dean/20020524.html (accessed April 24, 2004). Dean would go on to elaborate his claim, arguing that the Bush administration's assertions of secrecy were, in the words of his book, *Worse than Watergate* (Boston: Little, Brown, 2004). See also Jim Rutenberg, "White House Keeps a Grip on Its News," *New York Times* (October 14, 2002), C1.

78. Anne Kornblut and Wayne Washington, "GOP Rebukes Daschle for War Plan Criticism," *Boston Globe* (March 19, 2003), A1; Dana Milbank, "Tying Kerry to Terror Tests Rhetorical Limits," *Washington Post* (September 24, 2004), A1.

79. Presidential support scores from *CQ Almanacs* for relevant years, 1994–2002; Joseph J. Schatz, "With a Deft and Light Touch, Bush Finds a Way to Win," *CQ Weekly* (December 11, 2004), 2900. Hook, "$328-Billion Spending Bill," A18; Morgan, "House Passes $328 Billion Spending Bill," A1; Daschle comments in *Congressional Record,* January 23, 2004, S207. The House Resolution was H.Res. 557, adopted March 17, 2004. The Rudman report is cited in "Rudman-Foley Task Force Scolds Congress on Homeland Security Oversight," *CQ Today Midday Update* (December 10, 2004).

80. A partial list of attacks by al Qaeda or other Islamic terrorist groups includes an April 2002 bombing of a Tunisian synagogue, killing 21; an October 2002 bombing of nightclubs in Bali, killing 202; a November 2002 bombing of a Kenyan resort hotel, killing 13; May 2003 bombings of residential compounds in Saudi Arabia, killing 34, and of Jewish targets in Casablanca, Morocco, killing 20; the August 2003 bombing of UN headquarters in Baghdad, killing 24; the November 2003 bombings of synagogues, a bank, and the British consulate in Instanbul, Turkey, killing nearly 60; the March 2004 bombings of Shiite shrines in Baghdad and Karbala, Iraq, killing 185; the September 2004 seizure of a school in Beslan, Russia, killing some 328, many of them children; and the October 2004 execution-style slayings of 49 Iraqi army recruits. This list excludes killings in Israel, Palestine, and Chechnya, among others. A

report detailing one month's worth of insurgent attacks in Iraq is detailed in James Glanz and Thom Shanker, "Iraq Study Sees Rebels' Attacks as Widespread," *New York Times* (September 29, 2004), A1.

81. Pentagon consultant quoted in Hersh, "The Gray Zone"; David E. Rosenbaum, "Uncertainty Reigns as Nov. 2 Nears," *New York Times* (October 31, 2004), IV2.

82. Eric Schmitt, "Senators Assail Request for Aid for Afghan and Iraq Budgets," *New York Times* (May 14, 2004), A1; Tyler Marshall, "The Conflict in Iraq: Unease Shadows Bush's Optimism," *Los Angeles Times* (September 17, 2004), A1.

83. Sen. John Cornyn (R-TX) quoted in Carl Hulse and Christopher Marquis, "G.O.P. Split Over Inquiry on Prisoner Abuse," *New York Times* (May 19, 2004), A12.

CHAPTER 8

1. Thanks to William Howell and Jon Pevehouse for suggesting this formulation.

2. Carter in Rudalevige, *Managing the President's Program,* 134; Sorensen in Charles Roberts, ed., *Has the President Too Much Power?* (New York: Harper's Magazine Press, 1974), 27.

3. Schlesinger, *Imperial Presidency,* x (emphasis in original).

4. Jackson, concurring opinion to *Youngstown Sheet and Tube Co. v. Sawyer,* 343 U.S. 579 (1952).

5. Nixon, *In the Arena,* 238.

6. Kenneth A. Shepsle, "The Changing Textbook Congress," in John Chubb and Paul Peterson, eds., *Can the Government Govern?* (Washington, DC: Brookings Institution, 1989).

7. Robert Bendiner, *Obstacle Course on Capitol Hill* (New York: McGraw-Hill, 1964), 15.

8. Much of this section is drawn from James Sundquist's comprehensive discussion of these weaknesses in *The Decline and Resurgence of Congress,* esp. chaps. 7 and 14, and from Kenneth R. Mayer and David T. Canon, *The Dysfunctional Congress? The Individual Roots of an Institutional Dilemma* (Boulder, CO: Westview, 1999).

9. Quoted in Lundberg, "Congressional Oversight," 24.

10. Morris P. Fiorina wrote that "district interests are special interests, whose sum is *not* the national interest." See *Congress: Keystone of the Washington Establishment,* 2d ed. (New Haven: Yale University Press, 1989), 127, and, more generally, Mayer and Canon, *Dysfunctional Congress?*

11. Madison in Mayer and Canon, *Dysfunctional Congress?* 48; Schultze in Rudalevige, *Managing the President's Program,* 127.

12. Terry Moe, "The Politics of Bureaucratic Structure," in Chubb and Peterson, eds., *Can the Government Govern?;* Fiorina, *Congress: Keystone.*

13. Neustadt, *Presidential Power,* 317. For extended treatments of rather dif-

ferent uses of the term *postmodern,* see Rose, *Postmodern President,* and Barilleaux, *Post-Modern Presidency.* As noted in chapter 6, my conclusion is closer to Barilleaux's, though owing much to Rose's discussion of global pressures on American policy.

14. Theodore B. Olson et al., "Brief for the Petitioner," *Rumsfeld v. Padilla* (03–1027), 37.

15. Cheney, "Congressional Overreaching in Foreign Policy," in Robert A. Goldwin and Robert A. Licht, eds., *Foreign Policy and the Constitution* (Washington, DC: American Enterprise Institute, 1990), 120; Washington quoted in Stuart Taylor Jr., "An Invasion of Iraq Requires the Approval of Congress," *National Journal* (August 31, 2002), 2434.

16. Letter to William Herndon, quoted in Pyle and Pious, *President, Congress,* 298–99 (emphasis in original).

17. See the transcript in H. L. Pohlman, *Constitutional Debate in Action: Governmental Powers* (New York: HarperCollins, 1995), 182–83 and chap. 4 generally.

18. For Kleindienst's testimony, see Pohlman, *Constitutional Debate in Action,* 232–34; for *U.S. v. Nixon,* see Leon Friedman, ed., *United States v. Nixon: The Complete Case* (New York: Chelsea House, 1974), 480, 574, 596.

19. From the transcript of the oral arguments before the U.S. Supreme Court in *Rumsfeld v. Padilla,* April 28, 2004, available from the Court's Web site, http://www.supremecourtus.gov.

20. Even after the administration backed away from the original OLC August 2002 definition of torture in 2004 in hopes of easing White House Counsel Gonzales's appointment as attorney general, it did not retreat from its broader claims of presidential prerogative in this area. In June 2004 and again in his confirmation hearings Gonzales argued that the claims were unnecessary, even "irrelevant" because the president did not intend to authorize torture, but not that they were wrong. In any case, he argued that the CIA was not bound by the president's directive in 2002 to treat detainees at Guantánamo Bay humanely. And the administration successfully fought efforts to include a legislative ban on "extreme interrogation measures" in the intelligence reform act. R. Jeffrey Smith and Dan Eggen, "Justice Department Memo Redefines 'Torture,'" *Washington Post* (December 31, 2004), A9; Eric Lichtblau, "Gonzales Says Humane Policy Order on Detainees Doesn't Bind C.I.A.," *New York Times* (January 19, 2005), A17; Douglas Jehl and David Johnston, "White House Fought New Curbs on Interrogations, Officials Say," *New York Times* (January 13, 2005), A1; written responses of Alberto Gonzales to questions posed by members of the Senate Judiciary Committee, January 2005.

21. Preemption and prevention are not, of course, the same thing. Preemption supposes imminence: a "direct, immediate, specific threat," such as an invading force massed on one's border. As such, it has had far more legitimacy over time. See Schlesinger, *War and the American Presidency,* 23–24.

22. NSC-68 is discussed in chapter 2. Robert Kennedy, from the transcript of a meeting held on October 22, 1962, in Ernest R. May and Philip D. Zelikow, eds., *The Kennedy Tapes: Inside the White House during the Cuban Missile Crisis* (Cambridge, MA: Harvard University Press, 1997), 234. Kennedy had earlier (October 18) argued, "We've fought for fifteen years with Russia to prevent a first strike against us. Now, in the interest of time, we do that to a small country? I think it's a hell of a burden to carry" (149). See also Schlesinger, *War and the American Presidency*, 22–23.

23. *Woods v. Cloyd W. Miller Co.,* 333 U.S. 138 (1948).

24. Corwin, *President: Office and Powers,* 218; Rehnquist, *All the Laws but One,* 219.

25. Justice Jackson, dissenting opinion to *Terminiello v. City of Chicago,* 337 U.S. 1 (1949); Justice Arthur Goldberg, in *Kennedy v. Mendoza-Martinez,* 372 U.S. 144 (1963), mirroring Jackson's language in *Terminiello.*

26. William S. White, "Daughter Chides Truman on Talk," *New York Times* (April 18, 1955), 12.

27. Brandeis, dissent to *Myers v. U.S.,* 272 U.S. 52 (1926); Anthony Lewis, "Farce or Tragedy," *New York Times* (February 2, 1976), 23; Gingrich quoted in Haynes Johnson and David S. Broder, *The System: The American Way of Politics at the Breaking Point,* paperback ed. (Boston: Little, Brown, 1997), xiv.

28. Quoted in Victor, "Escalating Hostilities," 3023.

29. Wilgoren, "Kerry Says His Vote," A18; *Congressional Record,* October 9, 2002, S10175.

30. Sundquist, *Decline and Resurgence,* 155.

31. *Congressional Record,* March 17, 2004, H1143; *Congressional Record,* October 2, 2003, S12330–31. Durbin went on: "In this situation, after 9/11, President Bush came to us and summoned the American people to be unified. . . . He summoned us to humility. . . . He also summoned us to courage and the courage that America has to display every day in confronting the war on terrorism."

32. Schlesinger, *Imperial Presidency,* 375.

33. Vandenberg in James Reston, "Bewildered Congress Faces World Leadership Decision," *New York Times* (March 14, 1947); Ron Paul, in "Congress Abdicates War Powers," *New American* (November 4, 2002), 5; LBJ in Ely, *War and Responsibility,* 53.

34. This is largely a matter of choice: the Constitution does not require that states be divided up into districts represented by only one member, only that a certain number of members represent a given state.

35. See, among many others, Nelson Polsby, *The Consequences of Party Reform* (New York: Oxford University Press, 1983); Thomas E. Patterson, *Out of Order* (New York: Vintage, 1994); Martin P. Wattenberg, *The Rise of Candidate-Centered Politics* (Cambridge, MA: Harvard University Press, 1992). Some scholars have argued that party elites have by now managed to adapt somewhat

to the primary process by manipulating funding and activist endorsements. See Marty Cohen, David Karol, Hans Noel, and John Zaller, *Beating Reform: The Resurgence of Parties in Presidential Nominations* (Chicago: University of Chicago Press, forthcoming.)

36. Ceaser, *Presidential Selection,* 16.

37. Richard F. Fenno Jr., *Home Style: House Members in Their Districts* (Boston: Little, Brown, 1978), 168 and chap. 7.

38. For a nice discussion of these trends, see Thomas E. Mann, "Making Foreign Policy: President and Congress," in Mann, ed., *Question of Balance,* 15.

39. Staff figures from Norman J. Ornstein, Thomas E. Mann, and Michael J. Malbin, eds., *Vital Statistics on Congress, 1999–2000* (Washington, DC: American Enterprise Institute, 2000), chap. 5. Days spent in session available from the calendar of the House of Representatives, compiled at http://thomas.loc.gov/home/ds/index.html (accessed January 17, 2005). The average number of House session days in the decade 1970–79 was 160; by 1990–99 this figure had fallen to 135, itself skewed upward by the very busy "Republican Revolution" session of 1995. For the post-9/11 sessions of 2002 and 2003, the House was in session just 126 and 138 days, respectively, and just 110 days in 2004.

40. O'Neill quoted in Morris P. Fiorina, "The Presidency and Congress: An Electoral Connection?" in Nelson, ed., *Presidency and the Political System,* 2d ed., 424; David Maraniss and Michael Weisskopf, *"Tell Newt to Shut Up!": How Reality Gagged the Gingrich Revolution* (New York: Touchstone, 1996), 179. See, generally, Norman J. Ornstein and Thomas E. Mann, eds., *The Permanent Campaign and Its Future* (Washington, DC: American Enterprise Institute, 2000).

41. For a good brief review of incumbency advantage, see Gary King, "Constituency Service and Incumbency Advantage," *British Journal of Political Science* 21 (January 1991): 119–28. For 2004, see, e.g., Charlie Cook, "2004 Competitive House Race Chart," *Cook Political Report,* May 14, 2004. Cook felt that only fourteen races, 3 percent of the total, could be considered "toss-ups." See http://www.cookpolitical.com (accessed May 26, 2004).

42. *Vieth v. Jubelirer,* No. 02–1580 (decided April 28, 2004). See also David G. Savage and Scott Gold, "Justices Order Review of Texas' Political Map," *Los Angeles Times* (October 19, 2004), A10.

43. See the *New York Times*/CBS News Poll, October 28–30, 2004; for 1972–2002 data see the National Election Studies Guide to Public Opinion and Electoral Behavior, available at http://www.umichap.edu/~nes/nesguide/ (accessed May 24, 2004); Keith T. Poole and Howard Rosenthal, *Congress: A Political-Economic History of Roll Call Voting* (New York: Oxford University Press, 2000) and on-line updates at http://voteview.uh.edu/default_recpol.htm (accessed May 24, 2004).

44. Neustadt, *Presidential Power,* 157; see also Hugh Heclo's masterful vari-

ation on the theme, "Presidential Power and Public Prestige: A 'Snarly Sort of Politics,'" paper presented at the *"Presidential Power* Revisited" Conference, Woodrow Wilson International Center for Scholars, Smithsonian Institute, June 1996. For the role of the size of legislative majorities, see Howell, *Power without Persuasion*. John Stuart Mill, *Considerations on Representative Government* (London: Parker, 1861), 251.

45. R. Douglas Arnold, *The Logic of Congressional Action* (New Haven: Yale University Press, 1990).

46. Hatch quoted in Lewis, "Ashcroft Defends Antiterror Plan."

47. The quote is Finley Peter Dunne's fictional Mr. Dooley; but see the more rigorous treatments in Forrest Maltzman, Lee Sigelman, and Paul J. Wahlbeck, "Supreme Court Justices Really Do Follow the Election Returns," *PS: Political Science and Politics* 37 (October 2004): 839–42, and the classic Robert A. Dahl, "Decision Making in a Democracy: The Supreme Court as a National Policy-Maker," *Journal of Public Law* 6 (1958): 279–95.

48. *N.Y. Times Co. v. United States*, 403 U.S. 713 (1971). Or as James Madison put the point back in 1822, "a people who mean to be their own Governors must arm themselves with the power which knowledge gives." Quoted in Schlesinger, *Imperial Presidency*, 333.

49. Clinton, July 5 interview, *Public Papers of the Presidents, 2000*, 2103.

50. Austin Ranney, "Broadcasting, Narrowcasting, and Politics," in Anthony King, ed., *The New American Political System* (Washington, DC: AEI Press, 1990).

51. For example, 75 percent of Bush voters believed that Iraq was closely linked to al Qaeda; more than 60 percent believed that clear evidence of that link had been found; and one in five believed that Iraq was directly involved in the September 11 attacks. Steven Kull et al., "The Separate Realities of Bush and Kerry Supporters," report on a survey conducted by the Program on International Policy Attitudes and Knowledge Networks, Inc., October 21, 2004.

52. The phrase "vast right-wing conspiracy" was coined by First Lady Hillary Rodham Clinton in early 1998. See, e.g., David Maraniss, "Clinton & Clinton: First Lady's Energy, Determination Bind a Power Partnership," *Washington Post* (February 1, 1998), A1. See more broadly Jim Carville, *And the Horse He Rode in On: The People Vs. Kenneth Starr* (New York: Simon & Schuster, 1998); Joe Conason and Gene Lyons, *The Hunting of the President: The Ten Year Campaign to Destroy Bill and Hillary Clinton* (New York: St. Martin's, 2000).

53. Bush remarks in "Bush Welcomes President Chirac to White House," November 6, 2001, Office of the White House Press Secretary, and in "President's Remarks at Ask President Bush Event in Derry, New Hampshire," September 20, 2004, Office of the White House Press Secretary; Ashcroft quoted in Lewis, "Ashcroft Defends Antiterror Plan"; Hastert quoted in Anne Kornblut and Wayne Washington, "GOP Rebukes Daschle for War Plan Criti-

cism," *Boston Globe* (March 19, 2003), A1; DeLay quoted in his office's press release of December 16, 2003 entitled "Dean Flew Over the Cuckoo's Nest," available at http://www.majorityleader.gov/news.asp?FormMode=Detail& ID=208 (accessed May 20, 2004), and in Mike Allen, "Bush Apologizes, Calls Abuse 'Stain' on Nation," *Washington Post* (May 7, 2004), A1. The congressman in question was Rep. John Murtha (D-PA).

54. Hyde in *Congressional Record,* March 17, 2004, H1143. There is an interesting parallel to the Supreme Court's decision to resolve the 2000 election by accepting the *Bush v. Gore* case, which took even the most political of events, elections, out of political hands. The public, the Court held, had to be saved from the unseemly spectacle of representatives fulfilling their constitutional duty to determine the winner in the presidential race; *Bush v. Gore,* 531 U.S. 98 (2000). Justice Breyer's dissent (p. 155) is on point: "The decision by both the Constitution's Framers and the 1886 Congress to minimize this Court's role in resolving close federal presidential elections is as wise as it is clear. However awkward or difficult it may be for Congress to resolve difficult electoral disputes, Congress, being a political body, expresses the people's will far more accurately than does an unelected Court. And the people's will is what elections are about."

55. E. E. Schattschneider, *Two Hundred Million Americans in Search of a Government* (New York: Holt, Rinehart, and Winston, 1969), 53. Justice Learned Hand noted something similar in a 1944 essay: "The Spirit of Liberty is the spirit which is not too sure that it is right; the spirit of liberty is the spirit which seeks to understand the minds of other men and women; the spirit of liberty is the spirit which weights their interests alongside its own without bias." See *The Spirit of Liberty: Papers and Addresses of Learned Hand,* 3d enlarged ed. (New York: Alfred A. Knopf, 1974), 190.

56. For recent examples from the war on terror, see Sen. Edward Kennedy's speech to the Senate of May 10, 2004, or Rep. Robert Wexler's (D-FL) House speech of March 17, 2004.

57. Taft quoted in Schlesinger, *Imperial Presidency,* 137, and from his speech to the Executive Club of Chicago, December 19, 1941, quoted among many other places in Michael Tomasky, "Dems' Fightin' Words," *American Prospect* 13 (August 26, 2002).

58. Robert Dahl, "Introduction," in John Hersey, *Aspects of the Presidency: Truman and Ford in Office* (New York: Ticknor & Fields, 1980), xi.

INDEX

Abu Ghraib prison, 228, 255, 271
Adair, Ross, 78
Adams, Brock, 130
Adams, John Quincy, 154
Adler, David Gray, 28, 192, 199
Administrative Procedure Act, 107, 237
Afghanistan: "Northern Alliance" of, 217; Soviet invasion of, 122, 124, 142; Taliban regime of, 214, 217, 256; treatment of detainees from, 226–29, 248, 250, 253; U.S. and, 11, 140, 150, 172, 192, 199, 217, 233, 235, 257
AFL-CIO, 121, 162
Agency for International Development, U.S., 233
Agenda-setting power, presidential, 8, 35, 40, 45–48, 172, 285. *See also* Communication, presidential; Presidency, as "tribune of the people"
Agnew, Spiro, 98
Agriculture, Department of, 96–97, 114, 189
Albert, Carl, 70, 90
Albright, Madeleine, 320n62
Aliens, treatment of. *See* Justice, Department of

Allende, Salvador, 74, 84, 120
Al Odah v. U.S., 328n36
Al Qaeda, 3, 11, 214, 227, 229, 251, 257, 267, 334n80; and links to Iraq, 219, 222–23, 224, 282
Ambrose, Stephen, 58
Anderson, Jack, 97
Anderson, John, 309n6
André, John, 227
Angola, 124
Anthrax, 214
Anti-Ballistic Missile (ABM) Treaty of 1972, 206, 208
Antiterrorism and Effective Death Penalty Act of 1996, 182, 242
Apple, R. W., 8, 200
Appleby, Paul, 54
Appointment power, 8, 24, 25, 36–37, 96, 168–70, 176; and power to remove appointees, 36–37; recess appointments, 168–70
Argentina, 202, 241
Armey, Richard, 1
Arms Export Control Act, 156
Arthur, Chester, 32
Articles of Confederation, 19–20, 263
Ash, Roy, 89, 90, 127, 130, 306n54
Ashcroft, John, 189, 240, 243, 245, 246, 254, 282–83, 331n63

Atomic Energy Act of 1954, 206
Authorization for Use of Military
    Force (September 14, 2001). *See*
    September 11, 2001, terrorist
    attacks of

Babbitt, Bruce, 159
Balanced Budget Amendment, 147
Baldridge, Holmes, 269
Baldwin, Abraham, 22
Bank of the United States, 36
Barr, Bob, 244
Barrett, David, 159
Bay of Pigs invasion, 44, 51, 73, 74,
    93, 203
Bayh, Birch, 304n24
Bayh, Evan, 274
Beard, Charles, 54
Beard, Dita, 97
Beecher, William, 71
Bin Laden, Osama, 214, 217
Bipartisan Campaign Finance
    Reform Act (BCRA) of 2002, 9,
    164–66
Black Panthers, 52, 65, 66
Blunt, Roy, 2
Blute, Peter, 310n15
Bob Roberts, 209
Boland, Edward, 202; and Boland
    Amendments, 202–3
Bork, Robert, 98
Bosch, Juan, 79
Bosnia, 192, 195, 199
Boxer Rebellion, 38
Brandeis, Louis, 274
Bremer, L. Paul, 234, 237
Breyer, Stephen, 340n54
Brookings Institution, 74
Brown, Ron, 158, 159
Brownlow Committee. *See* Presi-
    dent's Committee on Administra-
    tive Management
Bryce, Lord James, 34

Buchanan, James, 29, 30–31
Buckley v. Valeo, 139, 161–62
Budget and Accounting Act of 1921,
    46–47, 86
Budget Enforcement Act of 1990,
    146, 149
Budget process, 17, 36, 46, 85–91,
    115, 126–31, 141–55, 301n78; and
    continuing resolutions, 152–53;
    and emergency spending, 149; and
    PAYGO rules, 146–47, 149, 151.
    See also Budget and Accounting
    Act of 1921; Impoundment power;
    Line-item veto
Bundy, McGeorge, 44
Bureau of the Budget (BoB), 43, 46,
    61, 86. *See also* Office of Manage-
    ment and Budget
Burger, Warren, 183
Burns, James MacGregor, 55
Bush, George H. W., 144, 146,
    157–58, 163, 169, 205, 265;
    administrative strategy of, 174,
    176; and "axis of evil," 217; exec-
    utive privilege, 183–84; and intelli-
    gence oversight, 204; as vice presi-
    dent, 142, 157; and war powers,
    195, 197, 198
Bush, George W., 13, 15, 140, 172,
    178, 207, 230; and 2000 election,
    149, 164, 200; and 2004 election,
    xi, 164, 257–59, 261, 283, 311n23;
    and ABM treaty, 206–7; adminis-
    trative strategy of, 169–70, 174,
    176; appointments strategy of,
    169–70; approval ratings of, 215,
    257; attitude toward executive
    authority of, 191–92, 208, 211–12,
    237, 274; budget negotiations of,
    150–52, 154; call for tolerance by,
    214; economic policy of, 3,
    149–52; and executive privilege, 9,
    185–86, 191–92, 239; and military

order of November 13, 2001,
229–30, 242; and Patriot Act,
244–46; and policies after September 11 attacks, 214–59, 282–83;
President's Management Agenda
of, 169; and regulatory policy, 174;
and secrecy, 186–87, 189–92, 239,
254–55; speeches of, 214–15,
217–18, 220, 221, 246, 254; success
in Congress of, 256–57; vetoes
threatened by, 12, 154; and war
powers, 192, 216–22, 227–33,
248–53, 266–67, 270–71
Bush v. Gore, 340n54
Butterfield, Alexander, 98
Bybee, Jay S., 228
Byrd, Robert C., 2, 5, 208, 310n18

Cabinet, presidential, 61–62,
103, 136, 153, 168–69, 170;
fragmentation of, 266. *See also*
individual departments; Staff,
presidential
Califano, Joseph, 60
Cambodia, 5, 71, 77, 81, 114,
302n102, 320n67; invasion of, 5,
81–82, 84–85, 117; seizure of
Mayaguez, 193, 194
Campaign finance, 17, 131–33,
161–66, 261, 278; and 527 committees, 166; in 1972 election, 5, 9,
95–97, 164; in 1988 election, 163;
in 1996 election, 161, 163–64, 186;
in 2000 election, 9, 164; in 2004
election, 10, 164–65; and independent expenditures, 131–32,
162, 165–66; and ITT scandal, 97,
132, 166; and "milk money" scandal, 96–97; and "soft money,"
162–65
Campbell, Tom, 199
Campbell v. Clinton, 321n72
Canada, 183, 200, 268

Cannon, Howard, 133
Card, Andrew, 211, 212, 239
Cardozo, Benjamin N., 48
Carter, James E. ("Jimmy"), 7, 115,
141, 168, 173, 188, 262; and CIA,
122–23; and ethics in government,
133, 135; executive order on sur-
veillance of, 111–12, 180; and
executive privilege, 106, 183; staff
of, 103–4, 170; and treaty with
Taiwan, 206–7; and war powers,
193
Casey, William, 180, 201, 202
Case-Zablocki Act of 1972, 125–26,
205
Casper, Gerhard, 138
"Cato," 19, 22, 57
Caulfield, John, 70–71
Ceaser, James, 34, 277
Census, U.S., 149, 279
Central America. *See* Latin America
Central Intelligence Agency (CIA),
44, 50, 83–85, 110–12, 115,
120–24, 157, 176, 200–205, 243;
and FOIA, 188, 189; and Huston
Plan, 69; and Intelligence Identities
Protection Act, 254; and interrogation, post–September 11, 226–29,
336n20; and Iraq, 219, 222–24,
225–26; and National Counterterrorism Center, 224–25; and
Phoenix Project, 83, 225; and
"plumbers," 73–74, 120; and Project CHAOS, 66–68, 70, 106, 111,
121–23, 179; in Reagan administration, 180–81; and Watergate
investigation, 93–94, 98. *See also*
Covert operations
CHAOS, Project. *See* Central Intelligence Agency; Surveillance
Chapin, Dwight, 92
Chappaquiddick, Martha's Vineyard,
71, 73

Cheney, Richard B. ("Dick"), 9,
    152, 211, 212, 267–68; and 2001
    energy task force, 9, 189–91; as
    Ford staff chief, 103; and Iraq, 219,
    222, 236; as secretary of defense,
    195
Chile, 74, 84, 120, 126
Chiles, Lawton, 91, 269
China, People's Republic of, 50, 61,
    72, 80, 125, 151, 206
Church, Frank, 82, 121
Church Committee, 121–23, 201,
    210, 224, 258
Cisneros, Henry, 159, 160
Civil liberties, 73, 100, 109–13, 121,
    179–80, 226–33, 241–53, 272–73,
    295n70. See also Surveillance
Civil Rights Act of 1964, 63
Civil War, U.S., 30–32, 36, 38, 39,
    86, 213, 231, 250, 268
Clark, Richard, 125
Cleland, Max, 256
Clement, Paul, 250, 270–71
Cleveland, Grover, 29, 32, 36,
    291n16
Clinton, Hillary Rodham, 158, 184,
    339n52
Clinton, William J. ("Bill"), 8, 9,
    139, 146, 148, 171, 181–82, 186,
    199, 205, 207–8, 243, 281; admin-
    istrative strategies of, 172, 174,
    176; and executive privilege, 9,
    184–85; and health care plan of, 8,
    162; impeachment of, 136, 140,
    160, 200, 209; investigations into,
    158–60, 184, 282; and Kosovo,
    192, 196, 197, 198; and presidential
    memoranda, 174; recess appoint-
    ments by, 169–70; and secrecy,
    189; success in Congress of, 9, 140,
    153–54, 256; and war powers, 9,
    140, 192, 194–99
Clinton v. City of New York, 148–49

Coalition Provisional Authority
    (CPA), 235–37. See also Iraq, costs
    of reconstruction of
Cohen, William, 111, 147
Colby, William, 121
Cold war, 5, 139
Colombia, 319n56
Colson, Charles, 65, 73, 92, 93, 94,
    97
Comey, James, 245
Commander-in-chief power. See
    War powers
Commerce, Department of, 62
Commission on Domestic Unrest
    (Scranton Commission), 68
Committee to Re-elect the President
    (CRP), 74, 92–97. See also Elec-
    tions, of 1972
Communication, presidential, 35, 40,
    41–42, 45, 61–62, 142–43, 170. See
    also Bush, George W., speeches of
Comptroller general. See General
    Accounting Office
Congo, 83
Congress, U.S.: anthrax attacks on,
    214; constituent service by, 266,
    278; and delegation of power to
    president by, 37, 47–48, 113–14,
    128–29, 221, 280; fragmentation
    of, 13, 42, 53–55, 85–86, 129,
    204–5, 263, 264–65, 272, 276–77,
    280; general powers of, 12–15, 17,
    21–22, 24–26, 212, 261–64, 280;
    and implementation of War Pow-
    ers Resolution, 193–200 (see also
    War Powers Resolution of 1973);
    "invisibility" of, 15, 18, 139,
    207–8, 231, 253, 256, 261, 275–85;
    karma of, 235; and Korean War,
    50; oversight role of, 114–16, 120,
    123–24, 154–55, 177–78, 190–92,
    200–205, 225, 233–37, 238–39,
    245, 257–59, 280; and Patriot Act,

244–45; "power of the purse" of, 85–86, 117, 124, 126–31, 141–55, 202–3, 205, 233–35, 239, 255, 280; responsibilities of, 272–80; and "resurgence regime" post-Watergate, x, 8, 17–18, 101–38, 140, 155, 255, 258, 261–62; session length of, 278; session start date of, 290n9; staff of, 278. *See also* Elections

Congressional Budget Act (CBA) of 1974, 7, 10, 129–31, 138, 141, 143, 209, 211

Congressional Budget Office (CBO), 10, 129, 141, 145–46, 154, 172, 233

Congressional Research Service (CRS), 237

Constitution, U.S.: Amendments to, First, 112, 161–62, 165, 179, 283; Amendments to, Fourth, 30, 110, 112–13, 244; Amendments to, Fifth, 250; Amendments to, Sixth, 231; Amendments to, Twelfth, 290n9; Amendments to, Fourteenth, 250; Amendments to, Twentieth, 290n9; Amendments to, Twenty-Second, 290n9; design of, 16, 19–20, 24–26, 117, 147–49, 177, 212, 252, 253, 262, 269–70, 273–74, 275, 277, 284–85; and due process, 250, 252–53; "not a suicide pact," 273; ratification of, 2, 19, 22–24; right to counsel in, 250–51. *See also* Civil liberties; Congress; Presidency; Supreme Court

Constitutional Convention of 1787, 19–22, 53

"Contras." *See* Nicaragua; Iran-contra scandal

Coolidge, Calvin, 39, 41

Cooper, Charles, 203

Cooper-Church Amendment, 82

Corcoran, Tommy, 51

Cornyn, John, 335n83

Corps of Engineers, U.S. Army, 236

Corrado, Anthony, 161

Corwin, Edward, 25, 38, 55, 272

Council of Economic Advisers (CEA), 43, 44

Counterintelligence Program (COINTELPRO). See Federal Bureau of Investigation; Surveillance

Covert operations, 10, 83–85, 120–24, 157, 180–81, 200–205, 209, 224–25, 226, 261

Cox, Archibald, 98, 134–35

Craig, Larry, 245

Cranston, Alan, 58

Crippen, Dan, 154–55

Cuba, 39, 51, 79, 83, 124, 203, 232, 272. *See also* Guantánamo Bay

Curtiss-Wright case. See *U.S. v. Curtiss-Wright Export Co.*

Danes & Moore v. Regan, 205–6

Daschle, Tom, 220, 256, 257

Davis, David, 32

Dean, Howard, 164

Dean, John W., 64, 68, 93–95, 97, 255

Declaration of Independence, 19

Defense, Department of, 44, 61, 72, 74, 83, 84, 176, 178, 202, 225, 233–35, 258; and Combatant Status Review Tribunal, 233, 253; and contracting, 235–37, 256; and CPA, 237; and Office of the Secretary of Defense, 234; Policy Counterterrorism Evaluation Group within, 222, 223; and regulations for military tribunals, 229–33, 253; and TIA, 241

Defense Intelligence Agency (DIA),
69–70

Deferrals, budgetary, 128

Deficit, federal budget, 10, 87–89,
142–55

DeLay, Tom, 151, 220, 234, 256, 283

Dellinger, Walter, 194

Democratic National Committee
(DNC), 6, 64, 93, 96, 163, 246

Democratic Party, 34, 67, 92, 93,
163, 220, 277, 279, 283

Democratic-Republican Party, 26

Denmark, 49

Diem, Ngo Dinh, 73

Dillon, Douglas, 121

Director of National Intelligence
(DNI), 225, 238, 266

Divided government, 86, 171, 181,
256, 258, 275, 279–80

Dole, Robert, 157, 163, 199

Domestic Council, 61, 103–4, 171

Domestic Intelligence Guidelines. See
Federal Bureau of Investigation

Domestic Policy Staff. See Domestic
Council

Dominican Republic, 39, 79

Douglas, William O., 272

Duane, William, 37

Dukakis, Michael, 162, 163

Durbin, Richard, 275–76

Durenberger, David, 201

Dylan, Bob, 209

Eagleton, Thomas, 194

Economic Stabilization Act of 1970,
90–91

Ehrlichman, John, 61–64, 68, 70, 97,
102, 103, 105; and Domestic
Council, 61; and "plumbers,"
72–74, 94

Eisenhower, Dwight D., 41–42,
44–45, 46, 50–51, 54, 60, 86, 273,
295n76

Elections, 34, 269–71; of 1832, 34; of
1864, 31; of 1936, 48; of 1948, 46;
of 1960, 42; of 1968, 34, 67; of
1972, 88, 91–97, 131–32, 164; of
1976, 135; of 1980, 141; of 1988,
163; of 1992, 144, 163; of 1994,
148, 163; of 1996, 161, 163–64,
186; of 1998, 140, 160; of 2000,
149, 164; of 2002, 12, 256, 280; of
2004, 11, 17, 164–66, 257–59, 261,
280, 283, 311n23; candidate-centered, 277–78; gerrymandering of,
279, 337n34; incumbency advantage in, 278–79; and "permanent
campaign," 278–83; primary, 34,
277, 279; and salience of general
interest in, 280; vital role of,
280–85; and voter turnout in,
281–82

Electoral College, 22, 24, 25, 33–34,
290n9, 309n6

Electronic FOIA Act of 1996,
188–89

Ellsberg, Daniel, 67, 72–74, 93, 120

El Salvador, 181, 201–2

Emancipation Proclamation, 30, 38

Emanuel, Rahm, 171

Emergency Detention Act of 1950,
repeal of, 114, 250, 251, 332n69

Emergency powers, 113–14, 214

Employment, federal, 37, 44, 60, 238,
264, 285; and contracting, 169,
235–37, 256

Employment Act of 1946, 43, 91

Endangered Species Act, 232

Enemy combatants, 11, 12, 15, 212,
226–33, 248–53, 266–67, 270–71

Energy, Department of, 176, 188

Entitlement spending, 86, 88, 150.
See also Medicare program; Social
Security

Environmental Protection Agency,
169, 189, 316n18

Environmental Protection Agency v. Mink, 107
Ervin, Sam, 76, 91, 126, 128, 199
Espionage Act of 1917, 37
Espy, Mike, 159, 184, 185
Ethics, executive. *See* Campaign finance; Ethics in Government Act; Independent counsel; Trust in government
Ethics in Government Act (EGA), 7, 131, 133–37, 156
Ethiopia, 125
Executive agreements, 49, 124–26, 205–6
Executive Office of the President (EOP), 43, 46, 59–61, 63, 103–4, 170–71
Executive orders, 38, 45, 48, 171–75, 208. *See also* Executive power
Executive power, 9, 17, 24, 25, 26–33, 37, 40, 48–53, 63, 68, 127, 139, 167–92, 208, 227, 237–41, 247, 251, 255–57, 267–72. *See also* Executive agreements; Executive orders
Executive privilege, 9, 17, 44–45, 75–76, 104–6, 182–87, 191–92, 208, 239, 261, 270. *See also* Secrecy
Ex Parte Milligan, 32, 250
Ex Parte Quirin, 227, 230–32, 250

Federal Advisory Committee Act (FACA) of 1972, 109, 189–91
Federal Bureau of Investigation (FBI), 52–53, 64, 67, 98, 111–13, 179, 186, 224; and COINTEL-PRO, 52, 65–66, 69, 70, 106, 121–22, 179; and counterterrorism, 181–82, 240–48 (*see also* Patriot Act); and Huston Plan, 69–70, 72; and Watergate "smoking gun," 6, 93–94, 98

Federal Communications Commission (FCC), 109
Federal Corrupt Practices Act of 1925, 302n96
Federal Election Campaign Act (FECA) of 1971, 95, 131
Federal Election Campaign Act of 1974, 7, 9–10, 131–33, 161–66, 302n96
Federal Election Commission (FEC), 115, 132, 162, 164, 166
Federalist Papers, 6, 14, 20, 23, 26, 85, 105, 264, 275
Federalist Party, 26
Federal Register, 114, 174, 237
Federal Reserve, 62
Federal Trade Commission (FTC), 115
Federal Water Pollution Control Act, 90
Feingold, Russell, 9, 164, 216, 244
Fenno, Richard, 277
Fielding, Lewis, 73–74
Fisher, Louis, 124, 149, 192, 196, 199
Fiske, Robert, 159
Fleischer, Ari, 186
Food and Drug Administration (FDA), 174
Ford, Gerald R., 6, 101, 126, 135, 173, 205; and campaign finance reform, 133; and executive privilege, 106, 183; and *Mayaguez,* 193, 194; pardon of Richard Nixon, 116; and presidency as "imperiled," 7, 139, 288n18; and rescissions, 128; and Rockefeller Commission, 121–23; staff of, 103–4; vetoes of, 107, 116
Foreign Assistance Act of 1961, 206
Foreign Intelligence Surveillance Act (FISA) of 1978, 7, 112–13, 210, 246–47; and FISA "wall," 112–13, 243–44, 245

Foreign Intelligence Surveillance
Court (FISC), 112, 244
Formosa Resolution of 1955, 50, 77,
273. *See also* Taiwan
Fortas, Abe, 299n45
Foster, Vince, 159
France, 3, 26, 49, 50, 214
Frank, Barney, 244
Franklin, Benjamin, 20
Franks, Tommy, 1
"freedom fries," 3
Freedom of Information Act (FOIA),
107, 109, 188–89; 1974 amend-
ments to, 7, 107–8, 192; 1986
amendments to, 188; and changes
after September 11, 239–40; exec-
utive orders regarding, 189
Freeh, Louis, 181
Friedman, Stephen, 171
Fulbright, William, 117

Gaddis, John Lewis, x
Gardner, John, 131
Garfield, James A., 32
Garment, Suzanne, 155
Gates, Robert M., 123, 180
Gelb, Leslie, 201
General Accounting Office (GAO),
9, 115, 128, 134, 146, 190, 237,
239; and suit against the vice presi-
dent, 190. *See also* Government
Accountability Office
Geneva Conventions, 226–28
Genovese, Michael, 28
George III, King, 19, 23
Gephardt, Richard, 4
Germany, 49
"Ghost" detainees, 226
Gilman, Benjamin, 199
Gingrich, Newt, 163, 199, 274
Goldwater, Barry, 122, 201, 202, 207
Goldwater v. Carter, 321n72, 322n88
Gonzales, Alberto, 227, 229, 336n20

Gore, Al, 149
Gorelick, Jamie S., 330n56
Goss, Porter, 224
Government Accountability Office,
288n23
Government in the Sunshine Act of
1976, 109
Graham, Billy, 80
Gramm-Latta reconciliation bill, 143
Gramm-Rudman-Hollings Act,
145–46
Grant, Ulysses S., 31
Gray, Boyden, 265
Gray, L. Patrick, 94, 308n72
Great Depression, 40, 86
Great Society, 87; and War on
Poverty, 90
Greenland, 49
Greenstein, Fred I., 40, 45
Grenada, 10, 187, 192, 193
Guantánamo Bay, Cuba, 11, 15, 217,
227–28; cases brought by detainees
at, 231–33, 248–53
Guatemala, 51, 83
Gulf of Tonkin Resolution of 1964.
See Tonkin Gulf Resolution
Gulf War of 1990–91, 1, 192, 194,
195, 197–98, 218, 219. *See also* Iraq

Habeas corpus, writ of, 30, 231–32,
252, 268, 273
Hagel, Chuck, 212, 258
Haig, Al, 67–68, 71, 72, 103
Haiti, 39, 149, 184, 192, 195
Halberstam, David, 104
Haldeman, H. R., 6, 60, 63, 70, 72,
73, 93, 94, 95, 97, 102, 103, 105
Halliburton Co., 236
Halperin, Morton, 71–72
Hamdan v. Rumsfeld, 327n32, 328n37
Hamdi, Yaser, 248–49, 252–53
Hamdi v. Rumsfeld, 232, 249–53, 257,
272

Hamilton, Alexander, 14, 23, 26–28, 42, 264
Hamilton, Lee, 175
Hand, Learned, 340n55
Harding, Warren G., 41
Hargrove, Erwin, 55, 58
Harriger, Katy, 136
Harrison, William Henry, 292n28
Hastert, Dennis, 256
Hatch, Orrin, 231, 245, 280
Hayes, Rutherford B., 32
Health, Education, and Welfare, Department of, 44, 63, 115
Health and Human Services, Department of, 178, 189
Helms, Richard, 83, 84, 85
Helvidius-Pacificus letters, 27–30, 38
Henry, Patrick, 22, 263
Herman, Alexis, 159
Hersh, Seymour, 66, 121, 228, 258
Hess, Stephen, 62
Hexter, J. H., 287n1
Highway Act of 1958, Federal, 87
Hiss, Alger, 71
Hitler, Adolf, 49
Hoar, George, 31
Hollings, Ernest, 145
Homeland Security, Department of, 238–39, 246, 257, 266
Homeland Security, Office of (OHS), 214, 238
Honduras, 202
Hoover, Herbert, 40, 41, 43
Hoover, J. Edgar, 51, 69–70, 72
Hoover Commissions, 43
Hopkins, Harry, 51
Hormel, James, 169
Hughes, Charles Evans, 48
Hughes-Ryan Amendment of 1974, 7, 120–21, 123–24
Human rights, 11, 126, 201–2, 225–29, 256
Humphrey, Hubert H., 90, 92–93, 97

Hunt, E. Howard, 73–74, 93, 94, 97. *See also* "Plumbers"
Hussein, Saddam, 1, 8, 11, 156, 195, 218–19, 221, 225–26, 283
Huston, Tom, 68, 69
Huston Plan, 69–70, 82, 120, 179
Hyde, Henry, 216–17, 283

Iceland, 49
Ickes, Harold, 51
Ignatieff, Michael, 224
Impeachment, 22, 25, 76, 269–70, 280; of Bill Clinton, 136, 140, 160, 200, 209; proceedings against Richard Nixon, 6, 98–99, 209
"imperial presidency," ix, 4, 5–7, 12, 15, 16, 18, 55, 57–59, 137, 261–85
Impoundment Control Act of 1974, 7, 128, 129, 138, 141
Impoundment power, 47, 57–58, 63, 87–90, 126–28
Independent counsel, 7, 98, 105, 134–37, 140, 156–61
Independent Counsel Act (ICA), 134–37, 157–61; expiration of, 9, 136, 158, 160–61, 209, 254
Indochina, 50, 116. *See also* Vietnam War
In re Debs, 32
In re Neagle, 32
Inspector General Act of 1978, 114–15
Inspectors general, 114–15, 176, 178, 305n27; in CPA, 235–36; in Justice Department, 245–46
"Institutional presidency." *See* Staff, presidential
INS v. Chadha, 177–78, 196
Intelligence oversight, by Congress, 17
Intelligence Oversight Act of 1980, 7, 123–24, 157, 181, 200–201, 203–4; amendments of 1991, 204; debate after September 11, 224–25

Intelligence Oversight Board, 122,
180
Interest groups, 87, 190, 282
Interior, Department of, 183
Internal Revenue Service, 64–65, 98,
166
International Atomic Energy Agency
(IAEA), 220
International Emergency Economic
Powers Act (IEEPA) of 1977, 114,
172, 237–38
International Labor Organization,
126
International Monetary Fund, 153
Internet, 282
Internment, of Japanese Americans in
World War II, 52
Iran, 51, 83, 142, 156, 172, 175, 192,
200, 203, 205, 217
Iran-contra scandal, 8, 136, 139,
156–58, 175, 181, 183, 200–203
Iraq, 1, 84, 156, 192, 194, 195, 217,
224, 255, 257; costs of reconstruc-
tion of, 233–37, 254, 258; insur-
gency in, 257, 335n80; National
Intelligence Estimate regarding, 4,
223; and "no fly zones,"192,
219–20; resolution authorizing
force against, October 2003, 3–4,
11, 219–23, 274–75; U.S. war in,
11, 15, 150, 218–24, 233–35, 247,
254, 258, 264, 283. See also Gulf
War of 1990–91
Iraq Liberation Act of 1998, 218
Israel, 126
Italy, 50

Jackson, Andrew, 33–34, 36, 37, 42,
57
Jackson, Henry, 125
Jackson, Robert H., 13–15, 52, 53,
263–64, 272, 273
Jackson-Vanik Amendment, 126

Japan, 49
Javits, Jacob, 78, 119–20, 193, 208
Jaworski, Leon, 105, 134–35
Jefferson, Thomas, 26, 29, 35, 38; and
Barbary pirates, 29, 38; and
treaties, 207
John Doe and ACLU v. Ashcroft,
330n55
John Doe I v. Bush, 287n4
Johnson, Andrew, 31, 37
Johnson, Loch, 124, 206
Johnson, Lyndon B., 4, 5, 12, 17, 58,
122, 212, 258; and budgeting,
87–88, 265; and decision not to
seek reelection, 80; and executive
privilege, 75, 107, 299n45; and
"groupthink," 60; as senator, 273;
and surveillance, 66–67; and Vietnam War, 56, 58, 60, 72, 74,
76–80, 117, 276
Joint Chiefs of Staff (JCS), 74
Jones, Gordon S., 138
Jones, Paula, 160
Jordan, 51
Jordan, Hamilton, 103
Judiciary, 7, 138, 185, 187, 232,
248–49, 257, 269, 281; appointments to, 168, 169–70; and decisions after September 11, 241, 243,
248–53, 330n53; and executive
orders, 172; and "'illiction
returns,'" 281; and "political questions," 127, 192, 207. See also individual case names; Supreme Court
Justice, Department of, 11, 12, 53,
64, 92, 93, 96, 115, 179, 181, 186;
and aliens, 240–41, 244, 245–46,
247; Criminal Division of, 113,
131; and domestic surveillance
guidelines, 111–13, 179–80; and
FISA warrants, 112–13, 243–44;
and immigration, 242, 244, 246;
and independent counsel investiga-

tions, 134–36, 158, 160–61, 254; Intelligence Evaluation Committee of, 70; and ITT antitrust suit, 97; Office of Intelligence Policy and Review of, 113; Office of Legal Counsel (OLC) of, 177, 226, 227–29, 336n20; Public Integrity Section of, 131; and terrorism, 182, 240–42, 245–46. *See also* Federal Bureau of Investigation; Patriot Act

Kalmbach, Herbert, 70, 94, 95–96
Kay, David, 223–24
Keith case, 110, 112
Kellogg Brown & Root, 236
Kennedy, Anthony, 232
Kennedy, Edward M., 133, 340n56; and Nixon, 70–71, 73
Kennedy, John F., 13, 18, 42, 44, 46, 51, 52, 54, 57, 71, 72, 73, 99, 122; assassination of, 42, 122
Kennedy, Robert F., 52, 67, 272, 308n72
Kennedy v. Mendoza-Martinez, 337n25
Kernell, Samuel, 41
Kerry, John F., xi, 164, 221, 257, 258, 274–75, 311n23
Keynes, John Maynard, 15
King, Martin Luther, Jr., 52, 67
King, Peter, 199
Kirkland, Lane, 121
Kissinger, Henry, 61, 63, 71–72, 80, 82, 83, 84, 102, 111, 119, 125
Kleindienst, Richard, 76, 94, 97, 269–70, 308n72
Kolbe, Jim, 236
Korea, North, 71, 217
Korea, South, 80, 126
Korean War, 13, 50, 53
Kosovo, 10, 192, 196–98
Kroc, Ray, 95
Krogh, Egil ("Bud"), 69, 71, 73

Kucinich v. Bush, 322n88
Ku Klux Klan, 52
Kutler, Stanley I., 69
Kuwait, 1, 195, 219, 236

Laird, Melvin, 72
Lake, Anthony, 72
Lantos, Tom, 275
Laos, 51, 77, 83–84, 120
Lasky, Victor, 13
Latin America, 38, 49, 156, 201–3; protests over U.S. policy in, 180
Leahy, Patrick, 4
Lebanon, 192, 195, 197; and barracks bombing, 196, 197
Legal Services Corporation, 168
Legislative program, presidential, 24, 35–36, 45–47, 86–87, 176, 183, 265
Legislative vetoes, 115–16, 128, 177–78, 196–97. See also *INS v. Chadha*
Leuchtenburg, William, 40
Levi, Edward, 111, 112, 179
Levin, Carl, 135, 215–16
Lewinsky, Monica, 159–60, 184, 185, 199
Lewis, Anthony, 273
Libya, 172, 192, 194
Liddy, G. Gordon, 73–74, 92, 93, 94
Light, Paul, 169
Lincoln, Abraham, 30–32, 37, 39, 231, 268, 282
Lind, Michael, 139
Lindsey, Larry, 171, 233–34
Line-item veto, 47, 147–49, 176, 209, 311n22
Line-Item Veto Act of 1996, 10, 148–49
Lippmann, Walter, 54
Locke, John, 27, 49–50
Loeb, William, 93
Long, Gillis, 102

Louisiana Purchase, 29, 38
Lugar, Richard, 258
Lukas, J. Anthony, 74
Lundberg, Kristin, 83

Mackenzie, G. Calvin, 131
Madison, James, 6–7, 13, 20, 21, 23, 26–28, 36–37, 38, 85–86, 216, 265, 339n48
Magruder, Jeb, 92
Malek, Fred, 63, 130
Management and Budget, Office of. *See* Office of Management and Budget
Marini, John A., 138
Martini, William, 310n15
McCain, John, 9, 164, 258
McCain-Feingold Act. *See* Bipartisan Campaign Finance Reform Act of 2002
McConnell, Mitch, 164, 165
McConnell v. Federal Election Commission, 165–66
McCord, James, 93
McDougal, James, 158
McDougal, Susan, 158
McGovern, George, 64, 92
McInnis, Scott, 3
McKinley, William, 39
McNamara, Robert, 77, 78
Media, 41–42, 62, 156, 158, 187, 282, 285; leaks to, 71–73, 187–88, 265. *See also* Communication, presidential
Medicare program, 86, 150, 151, 163, 254–55
Meese, Edwin, 158, 167, 188
Memoranda, presidential, 174. *See also* Executive orders
Mencken, H. L., 26
Metropolitan Detention Center, 246
Mexican War, 38–39, 268

Mexico, 38; U.S. occupation of Veracruz, 39
Michel, Robert, 147
Middle East, 51, 77, 125, 156, 203, 218, 220. *See also* Iran; Iraq; Lebanon; Persian Gulf; Saudi Arabia
Midwest Oil case. See *U.S. v. Midwest Oil Co.*
Military tribunals, 12, 212, 229–33
Mill, John Stuart, 279
Miller, Zell, 161
Mills, Wilbur, 97
MINARET, Project. *See* National Security Agency
Mitchell, John, 67–68, 92–95, 105, 308n72
Mobbs, Michael, 249, and Mobbs Declaration, 249, 252
Moffett, Toby, 143
Mondale, Walter, 122
Morris, Robert, 20
Morrison v. Olson, 136–37, 160
Moynihan, Daniel Patrick, 201
Muskie, Edward, 72, 76, 92–93
Myers v. U.S., 37

Nathan, Richard, 168
National Archives and Records Administration (NARA), 186–87
National Commission on Terrorist Attacks upon the United States. *See* 9/11 Commission
National Counterterrorism Center (NCTC), 224–25
National debt, 86, 144, 150, 310n20
National Economic Council (NEC), 171
National Emergencies Act of 1974, 114, 138
National Security Agency (NSA), 69–70; and Project MINARET, 66, 70, 111

National Security Council (NSC), 43–44, 72, 74, 84, 111, 156–57, 168, 171, 175, 194, 203–4, 224; growth of staff under Kennedy, 44; growth of staff under Nixon, 61. *See also* Iran-contra scandal; NSC-68

National Security Presidential Directives, 174–75, 204, 237, 316n20. *See also* Executive orders

National Security Strategy of the United States, 218, 271–72

Nelson, Michael, 55, 58

Neustadt, Richard E., 40, 54, 266, 279

Neutrality Act of 1940, 49

New Deal, 38, 40, 45, 48, 58

Newton, Huey, 66

Nicaragua, 39, 157, 172, 175; Sandinista regime of, 156, 202–3, 321n82; Somoza regime of, 202

9/11 Commission, 191–92, 204–5, 224–25, 239, 255

Nixon, Richard M., 4–5, 6–7, 13, 17, 42, 53, 57, 58, 66, 95, 104, 137, 173, 258, 264; and "battles of the budget," 88–91, 126–28, 130, 149; "Berlin Wall" of, 63, 102; and covert operations, 83–85; "enemies list" of, 65, 159; and executive privilege, 75–76, 104–5, 182–83, 270, 299n43; and Pentagon Papers, 72–74; resignation of, 6, 8, 53, 99, 101; Responsiveness Program of, 63–65, 100, 179; as senator, 294n68; and surveillance, 67–73, 109–10, 112; and Vietnam, 58, 61, 63, 67, 71–72, 80–85, 116–17, 125; and wage and price controls, 90–91; and War Powers Resolution, 116–19, 193, 194; and Watergate hush money, 94–95; and White House tapes, 98–99, 105.

See also Elections, of 1972

Nixon v. Administrator of General Services, 108, 187

Nol, Lon, 83

Non-Detention Act of 1971. *See* Emergency Detention Act of 1950

Nordhaus, William, 233

North, Oliver, 157, 203

North Atlantic Treaty Organization (NATO), 50, 125, 196

Novak, Robert, 255

NSC-68, 51, 271–72

Nussbaum, Bernard, 159

Oath of office, presidential, 29, 31

Obey, David, 212

O'Brien, Lawrence F., 64, 92, 93

Occupational Safety and Health Administration (OSHA), 109

O'Connor, Sandra Day, 253

O'Donnell, Kenneth, 289n29

Office of Communications, White House, 42, 62

Office of Economic Opportunity, 90

Office of Government Ethics, 134

Office of Legal Counsel (Olc). *See* Justice, Department of

Office of Management and Budget (OMB), 61, 88–89, 91, 130, 142, 145, 169, 172, 234–35; and regulatory review, 172–74

Olmsted, Kathryn, 120

Olson, Ted, 160, 250. *See also Morrison v. Olson*

Omnibus Budget Reconciliation Act of 1993, 146, 149

O'Neill, Paul, 130, 168

O'Neill, Thomas P. ("Tip"), 130, 278

Operation Rolling Thunder, 79

Oppenheimer, J. Robert, 51–52

Ortega, Daniel, 321n82

Padilla, José, 249–51, 253. See also
　Rumsfeld v. Padilla
Pakistan, 249
Palmer Raids, 33, 37
Panama, 192
Panama Refining Co. v. Ryan, 48,
　294n63
Paperwork Reduction Act of 1979,
　173
Pardon power, 24–25, 116, 185
Patman, Wright, 90
Patriot Act, 11, 15, 182, 241–48, 257,
　289n26; legislative adoption of,
　244–45; potential sunset of, 245,
　247–48, 257
Patriot II, 247
Paul, Ron, 276
Pearl Harbor, 49–50, 51, 272, 284
Pearson, Drew, 51
Pentagon. *See* Defense, Department
　of
Pentagon Papers, 67, 72–73, 77, 281
Perot, H. Ross, 144
Persian Gulf, 192, 193, 200; base
　construction in, 235
Philippines, 80, 319n56
Pierson, DeVier, 75
Pike, Otis, 121
Pike Committee, 121–23
Pine, David A., 269
Pinochet, Augusto, 84
Pious, Richard, 30, 50, 291n14,
　296n79
"Plumbers," 66–67, 68, 71–74, 93,
　111
Poindexter, John, 157, 330n54
Political Action Committees (PACs),
　132–33, 162
Political parties (*see also* names of
　specific parties), 34, 132, 162–66,
　277, 279–80
Polk, James K., 36, 38–39, 75, 268
Polling, in White House, 61–62

Postal Service, U.S., 214
Powell, Colin, 1, 221, 222, 223
Powell, Lewis, 110, 199
Prerogative power, 27–30, 49–50
Presidency, U.S.: in the Constitu-
　tion, 24–30, 35–39, 285; general
　powers of (*see also* specific powers),
　8, 12, 15–16, 20, 53, 99, 208–10,
　255–56, 259–60, 261–74, 285; in
　the "modern presidency," 40–53;
　structure of, 29–30, 172, 264–67;
　as "tribune of the people," 29,
　33–35, 42, 53, 277, 285
"Presidential branch." *See* Staff, presi-
　dential
Presidential Materials and Preserva-
　tion Act (PMPA) of 1974, 7, 108
Presidential Records Act (PRA) of
　1978, 7, 9, 108–9, 186–87
President's Committee on Adminis-
　trative Management, 43, 59
Preventive war. *See* National Security
　Strategy of the United States;
　Secrecy; War powers
Privacy Act of 1974, 7, 106–7
Proclamations, presidential, 38. *See
　also* Executive orders
Progressive Party, 34
Project Gemstone, 92–94. *See also*
　Watergate scandal
Putin, Vladimir, 206
Pyle, Christopher, 30, 291n14,
　296n79

Qatar, 1
Quayle, Dan, 174

Racketeer Influenced and Corrupt
　Organization (RICO) statutes,
　241
Radio, 35, 40
Randolph, Edmund, 19, 21
Rasul v. Bush, 328nn36, 37

Reagan, Ronald, Presidential Library, 9, 108–9, 186–87

Reagan, Ronald W., 8, 121, 157, 167, 281; and 1981 budget legislation, 141–44; administrative strategies of, 167–68, 172–76; and arms sales to Iran, 156–57; and Central America, 157, 201–3; executive orders on surveillance, 179–81; and executive privilege, 182–83, 186; and line-item veto, 147–48; and secrecy, 187–88; use of executive authority by, 139, 167–68, 179, 186, 205; and war powers, 194, 195–96, 197

Reedy, George, 58

Regulatory review, by Congress, 115–16; by president, 8, 173–74, 316n18, 318n43

Rehnquist, William H., 32, 82, 178, 272–73, 301n84, 308n78

Reno, Janet, 159, 184

Republican National Committee (RNC), 97, 164, 166, 183

Republican Party, 200, 209, 239, 254, 256, 279

Rescissions, budgetary, 128, 148

Resolution Trust Corporation, 158

Rice, Condoleezza, 222, 239, 255

Richardson, Elliot, 97–98

Ridge, Tom, 214

Rockefeller Commission, 121–22

Rockefeller, Nelson, 103, 121

Roosevelt, Franklin D., 13, 38, 39–40, 41, 48–50, 51, 54, 57, 58, 87, 104; and banking crisis, 45; "brains trust" of, 43; and Brownlow Committee, 43; and "court packing," 46, 48; "fireside chats" of, 41; and German saboteurs, 230–32; "hundred days" of, 45–46; and lend-lease, 49; and wiretapping, 51–52, 295n70

Roosevelt, Theodore, 28, 29, 35, 39, 42, 45; and the "bully pulpit," 41, 285

Rose, Richard, 314n2

Rossiter, Clinton, 54

Rostenkowski, Dan, 142

Rove, Karl, 169

Rubin, Robert, 171

Ruckelshaus, William, 98

Rudman, Warren, 145–46, 257

Rumsfeld, Donald, as Ford staff chief, 103; and Iraq, 1, 219, 324n19; on treatment of terror suspects, 11, 227–28, 230

Rumsfeld v. Padilla, 249–53, 270–71, 289n27, 336n19

Ryan, Paul, 2

Ryan, Stephen, 178

Safire, William, 71

Saudi Arabia, 181, 203, 214, 248, 253

Scalia, Antonin, 137, 160, 252, 272

Schechter Poultry Corp. v. U.S., 48

Schick, Allen, 141

Schlesinger, Arthur M., Jr., ix–xi, 4–5, 12, 31, 50, 57–58, 79, 80, 99, 116, 263, 271, 276

Schlesinger, James, 121

Schorr, Daniel, 121

Schultze, Charles, 265

Scott, Hugh, 82

Sears, John, 71

Secrecy, 51, 58, 72, 80, 104, 106–9, 116, 125, 175, 182–92, 205, 225, 235–37, 238–40, 245, 254–55, 265, 271, 299n43. *See also* Covert operations; Executive privilege

Secret Service, U.S., 70

Securities and Exchange Commission (SEC), 109

Sedition Act of 1918, 37

Segretti, Donald, 92

Senior Executive Service (SES), 168

Sensenbrenner, F. James, 245
September 11, 2001, terrorist attacks
    of, ix, 8, 10, 14, 17, 140, 150,
    185–86, 200, 210, 211–13, 223,
    231, 262, 267, 283; and Authoriza-
    tion for Use of Military Force
    (AUMF), 10, 215–17, 248, 250–53,
    270–71; description of, 213–15;
    and Emergency Response Fund,
    234–35; and FISA, 113, 243–47;
    and Iraq, 217–24; and public trust
    in government, 253–54; treatment
    of detainees after, 226–33, 248–53,
    254, 258, 266–67
Sessions, Jeff, 231
Shelby, Richard, 243
Shinseki, Eric, 233
Shultz, George, 62, 64–65, 88
Signing statements, presidential, 63,
    175–77, 235, 238–39
Sihanouk, Prince, 81, 83
Slaughter, Anne–Marie, 323n11
Smith, William French, 179, 181,
    182–83
Sneed, Joseph, 89
Social Security program, 86, 88, 144,
    149, 150, 151
Solomon, Gerald, 144, 147, 200
Somalia, 192
Sorensen, Theodore, 42, 262
Souter, David, 253
Southeast Asia Treaty Organization
    (SEATO), 77
Soviet Union, 49, 61, 72, 73, 125,
    175, 337n22; and invasion of
    Afghanistan, 122, 124; and Jewish
    emigration, 126
Spain, 125, 246, 257
Special Division, U.S. Court of
    Appeals, 135, 159. See also Inde-
    pendent counsel
Special prosecutor. See Independent
    counsel

Specter, Arlen, 148, 153–54
Sperling, Gene, 171
St. Clair, James, 270
Staff, presidential, 26, 40, 42–45, 53,
    58, 59–63, 102–4, 168–71, 285;
    and White House Personnel
    Office, 169. See also Cabinet, pres-
    idential
Starr, Kenneth, 159–60
State, Department of, 61, 80, 83, 84,
    115, 126, 156, 182
State of the Union message, 24, 35
Steinbrenner, George, 96
Stephanopoulos, George, 168
Stevens, John Paul, xi, 251–52
Stevens, Ted, 148
"Steward of the people." See Presi-
    dency, U.S., as "tribune of the
    people"
Stewart, Potter, 281
Stockman, David, 142–43
Stone, Clement, 95
Strachan, Gordon, 92
Strategic Arms Limitation Treaty
    (SALT), 71, 73, 208
Strategic Defense Initiative, 175
Strauss, Robert, 211
Students for a Democratic Society
    (SDS), 66
Sudan, 140, 192, 199
Sundquist, James L., x, 86, 102, 116,
    130, 275
Supreme Court, U.S., 6, 9, 10,
    31–33, 37, 46, 47–48, 52, 72, 82,
    98, 105, 107, 108, 110–11, 127,
    133, 136–38, 139, 148, 161, 165,
    176, 177–78, 182–83, 187, 205,
    207, 227, 232, 241, 250, 257, 267,
    269–71, 279. See also specific cases
    and justices
Surveillance, 51–52, 65–74, 109–13,
    121, 179–82, 208, 241–48
Sutherland, George, 47

Taft, Robert, 284, 285
Taft, William Howard, 28, 33, 36, 39, 45
Taguba, Antonio, 228
Taiwan, 50, 203, 206–7
Taliban regime, 11, 214, 215, 256
Taney, Roger, 37
Television, presidential use of, 35, 41–42. *See also* Communication, presidential
Tenet, George, 222–23; resignation of, 224
Tenure of Office Act, 37
Terminiello v. City of Chicago, 337n25
Terror, global war on, 5, 212. *See also* Afghanistan; Al Qaeda; Iraq
Terrorism, 10–12, 185, 204, 210, 226, 239, 241, 246, 257, 266–67; attacks post–September 11, 334n80; embassy bombings, Africa (1998), 214; first World Trade Center attack (1993), 181; Madrid train bombings (2004), 246, 257; Oklahoma City bombing (1995), 181; Saudi base bombings (1996), 181; *U.S.S. Cole,* 214. *See also* September 11, 2001, terrorist attacks of
Tet Offensive, 79–80
Thailand, 80, 84, 120, 125
Thompson, Fred, 199
Thune, John, 256
Tonkin Gulf Resolution, 4, 8, 76–78, 80, 82, 116–17, 200, 221, 299n45
Torture, 226–29, 255, 257, 271, 336n20
Total Information Awareness (TIA) program, 241
Trade authority, "fast track," 207
Trade Representative, Office of the United States (USTR), 62
Trading with the Enemy Act of 1917, 37, 45, 242
Train v. City of New York, 127

Transportation Security Administration, 238
Travel Office, White House, 159, 184
Treasury, Department of the, 37, 62, 70, 157; and terrorism, 182, 241–42
Treaties, 24, 27, 124–26, 205–7; abrogation of, 206–7. *See also* Executive agreements
Truman, Harry S., 41, 46, 50, 52, 125, 269, 273
Trust in government, 18, 99, 131–37, 155–56, 221–24, 253–54, 258, 281–85
Tulis, Jeffrey, 35
Turner, Stansfield, 122
Tyler, John, 36

Ulasewicz, Anthony, 70
Uniform Code of Military Justice (UCMJ), 231
Unilateral executive authority. *See* Executive power
United Kingdom, 49, 214, 219, 268; and intelligence on Iraq, 222–23, 254
United Nations (UN), 1, 4, 77, 126, 194, 200, 219; Bush speech to, 220; and sanctions against Iraq, 218; and weapons inspections, 220–21
United Nations Educational, Scientific, and Cultural Organization (UNESCO), 126
United Nations Security Council, 195, 197, 217, 220–21, 222, 237
Unlawful enemy combatants. *See* Enemy combatants
Uruguay, 126
USA PATRIOT Act of 2001. *See* Patriot Act
USSR. *See* Soviet Union

U.S. v. Curtiss-Wright Export Co., 47, 184, 201
U.S. v. Midwest Oil Co., 33, 38, 301n84
U.S. v. Nixon, 6, 7, 98, 105, 182–83, 185, 191, 269–70

Vandenberg, Arthur, 276
Veto power, 8, 22, 24, 36, 46, 86, 116, 126–27, 140, 154, 204
Vice presidency, 187, 290n9
Vietnam War, 5, 8, 16–17, 51, 56, 59, 63, 76–83, 99, 104, 116–18, 125, 278; and comparisons to Iraq, 257–58; and domestic unrest, 67–69, 81, 109; and Pentagon Papers, 72–73
Vote, right to, 34

Wallace, George, 92
Walsh, Lawrence, 156–58
Walters, Johnnie, 64
Warner, John, 234
War Power Acts, 48
War powers, 2, 8, 17, 24, 25, 38–39, 49–51, 57, 77, 117, 119–20, 176, 192, 195, 196, 207, 215–16, 219, 227–29, 248–53, 261, 267–72. *See also* War Powers Resolution
War Powers Resolution (WPR) of 1973, 7, 10, 85, 120, 138, 139, 192–200, 207, 211; constitutionality of, 176, 193; experience with, 192–200, 209; passage of, 117–20; role after September 11 attacks, 215, 216–17, 220
Washington, George, 20, 24, 36, 267–68, 294n56; Neutrality Proclamation of, 26–28, 38
Watergate scandal, 5, 6–7, 8, 13, 16–17, 55, 58–59, 91–100, 104, 159, 184, 199, 209, 255; and "dirty tricks," 92–93; illicit surveillance in, 64–74, 92–94; role of money in, 94–97; and "Saturday Night Massacre," 98, 134–35; "smoking gun" in, 6, 93–94, 98; and "Watergate babies," 277–78
Waters, Maxine, 215
Watson, Edwin, 295n70
Waxman, Henry, 146, 236
Weapons of mass destruction (WMD), 15, 218, 220–24, 258, 323n7
Weinberger, Caspar, 61, 89, 91, 157
West Point, 218
Wexler, Robert, 340n56
Whig Party, 292n28
Whistleblower protection statutes, 255, 257
White, Byron, 127, 177
Whitewater scandal, 136, 158–60, 178, 184. *See also* Impeachment
Wildavsky, Aaron, 144, 294n57
Williams, Edward Bennett, 64
Wilson, James, 2, 19, 28–29
Wilson, Joseph, 254
Wilson, Woodrow, 34–36, 38, 39, 40, 41, 45, 265, 277
Wiretapping. *See* Surveillance
Wolfowitz, Paul, 233
Woodward, Bob, 235
World War I, 38
World War II, 5, 38, 40, 45, 48–50, 55, 91, 117, 125, 150, 171, 265
Wormuth, Francis, 82, 319n55
Wright, James, 143

Young, David, 71, 73. *See also* "Plumbers"
Young, Don, 311n21
Youngstown Sheet and Tube v. Sawyer, 13–15, 53, 251
Yugoslavia, 195, 196. *See also* Bosnia; Kosovo

If you have had a dream about
Diana, Princess of Wales, then please visit our
website and tell us about it.

www.webshack-cafe.com/dreaming of diana

✦

leading to nervous disorders in infancy, behavioural problems in childhood and anti-social conduct in adolescence, is undetectable except by the most delicate and refined of instruments, namely, the hands of the paediatric osteopath. It is a form of treatment that has a dramatically uplifting effect on the quality of life of patients with serious conditions.

Here at the OCC, the only centre of its kind in Europe, we offer a unique and pioneering approach to child health care. From the first 14 patients that entered our doors when the charity was launched in 1991, more than 20,000 children and pregnant women are treated every year. It is our aim to make treatment accessible to all, requesting only voluntary donations as can be afforded.

Diana was clearly dedicated to the health and welfare of children in the UK and around the globe, and we are committed to continuing the work she supported. It is vital that we expand and grow so that we can reach all children everywhere. Please support us.

Patricia Ferrall, Executive Director
Stuart Korth, Director of Osteopathy DO MRO

Osteopathic Centre for Children
19A Cavendish Square
London WIM 9AD

Charity Registration No 1003934

The Osteopathic Centre For Children and Diana, Princess of Wales

In March of 1997, Diana, Princess of Wales paid a private visit, at her own request and in secret, to the Osteopathic Centre For Children (OCC). She spent a great deal of time with us, talking with the children, their parents and the paediatric osteopaths at our small premises in Central London, She asked then if she could launch the Charity's *Sweet Pea Appeal* whose aim is to try and raise the £2 million needed to help secure permanent, fully adapted premises, with more full time osteopaths benefiting more mothers and their children. The OCC became one of Diana's favoured charities and she was due to launch our *Sweet Pea Appeal* on her return from Paris at the end of August 1997.

Osteopathy is a non-invasive health care systems that has shown itself to be effective in treating conditions including asthma, cerebral palsy, glue ear, colic and hyperactivity. For young babies and pregnant women, treatment is often preventive, based on the classical, holistic principle of finding and then maintaining health, and hospital visits provide support and treatment for premature newborns in intensive and special care neonatal units. Many childhood ailments are traced back directly to unresolved strains at birth. Such trauma, while

I know it sounds silly but I rang Kensington Palace because I wanted William and Harry to know that she was okay. I think she wanted to stay to help them through that dreadful week until the funeral but I believe she has definitely crossed that road now.

Ann Ambrose, 38
District Administrator
Hedge End, Southampton

walked over to try and cross the road but decided to turn back into the woods. I watched her as she went back through the woods to the dirt path which led to a tiny cottage which had two windows and a chimney. A fire was burning inside, the door was open and there was lots of laughter coming from inside. I imagined a big, oldish, mumsy lady baking cakes inside. Diana came out from the woods to try to cross the road only to turn back once again. She went back into the cottage and I just knew that she was safe and would be happy.

✦

THERE was a road and situated right across it was an exclusive health club. No traffic could get through. I was standing on the balcony looking down. There were some well-to-do people sitting around having drinks, but they weren't aware of me. Couples with wonderful figures were walking along the pavement down to a path wearing full aerobic gear. Suddenly I saw Diana almost gliding along the dirt path out of some woods towards the road. She was barefoot and wearing a long pinkish frilled gown. She wore no jewellery or make up and looked ten years younger. She was determined to get somewhere, and twice

I'm not sure Diana ever realised the extent of her own power, which she both used and abused. I believe she was a very complex person and underestimated by both the Royal Family and the media. The tragic lack of love in her life defined her, yet she was also a woman of the 90s. I did warm to her though and believe she has changed the course of history. The British people experienced the nearest thing to an emotional revolution after her death.

I was in Paris on the night of the crash. I went to the hospital and everyone waiting outside was very subdued. All kinds of people were there – Parisians and tourists, and soon the world's media turned up in their droves. I can only describe the atmosphere as one of great misery and shock, with people just bursting into tears.

Diana's body was brought out at 5pm that afternoon, and that was the only time I felt emotional. She was in a plain navy van with just the flag draped over it. Being used to seeing her in limos and Mercedes, I thought 'Can this really be Diana?' When she left, so did I.

My own mother died in a car crash several years ago. She was also a very maternal woman, and a healer. A nurse who always cared for others.

Rita Kyne, 35
Television News Producer
Dublin, Ireland

I WAS STANDING in the bedroom of my family home. It was night and I was looking onto the park opposite the house. There were two children beside me and we were watching a woman who had a luminescent quality about her gliding through the park. I wasn't an adult in the dream, but felt more like an older child to the others. I became aware this glowing shape was Diana. It reminded me of a photo of her in which she wore a short, spangly white jacket with a long white dress underneath, where she looked very feminine and glamorous. I said to the children, 'That's your mother' but they were frightened, and so was I. They said they didn't like looking at their mother like that now, and that they wanted to see her the way she was. I said, 'That's what everyone looks like when they're dead, that's the way my mother looked when she died'. They were reassured by this and I felt less frightened and surprisingly reassured too. There was a strong feeling of warmth and contentment. I saw their faces and realised they were her children, William and Harry.

I watched the movie *Excalibur* that night, so that may explain parts of the dream, but I had this dream before I knew that she was to be buried on the island at Althorp. The curious thing was that the boy kneeling at the shore wasn't William.

James Panozzi, 50
Financial Software Developer
Rhode Island, USA

THE GHOST OF Diana, while floating over a mist covered lake, carries a sword to a teenage boy who is kneeling at the shore. The rays of the sun are just starting to break through the morning mist. I am standing well behind the boy, terrified that they will see me. She looks up at me for a moment and smiles and I am filled with an incredible warmth, a peace, an indescribable calm. The boy looks up into her eyes as she hands him the sword. A sunbeam falls on her and she vanishes into the light.

On the day of the funeral, I was determined not to mope in front of the TV. I picked up an old red rose, which meant something to me and walked to my favourite part of Hampstead Heath. I sat down on a bench, closed my eyes and had a wee chat to Diana in my head. Enter men in white coats! Anyway, I kind of wished her well and when nobody was looking, laid the flower down.

I left the Heath, and the streets were absolutely deserted. I was passing a local launderette when I heard Elton John's voice blaring out. I stopped and saw two old biddies in a trance in front of a portable television set. It was obviously the funeral coverage, so I opened the door and asked if I could go in. One of them nodded, and looking back, I entered as though it were a sacred place. I watched the rest of the funeral with two complete strangers, in total silence, tears pouring down our faces. It was like something out of a scene from an Alan Bleasdale drama.

I'm not in favour of royal set-ups, but Diana had the guts to question archaic protocol and they needed someone to bring them into the twentieth century. I think she was very brave.

Deborah Tate, 32
Comics Editor
Gospel Oak, London

I WAS PLUMMETING from a high place. I was aware that I was holding hands with someone and realised that it was Diana. I was surprised that I felt protective of her and remember thinking: 'She's been through enough crap!' The choice was mine to make, either we stopped or we crashed to the bottom. We stopped, literally inches from the ground.

I woke up feeling disturbed, as the dream was extremely vivid. She wasn't important to me in real life but I had quite liked her. In the dream I had felt incredibly sorry for her, especially when she started to talk about her children, as this is what really did affect me. I thought it was particularly tragic that in her last months it seemed as if she had found happiness at last. She looked brilliant, and was starting to emerge as a strong, confident woman.

Jane Fairburn, 31
Journalist
Glasgow, Scotland

I WAS IN A stately home that turned out to be Althorp. There were a whole lot of people around waiting for her funeral to begin. We had about three hours to kill, so I went for a wander round the house and came across a door, which I went through. Diana was sitting in this room on her own, wearing a plain red dress, like one I remembered seeing her in shortly before she died. I felt surprised because it was her funeral that I was waiting for. I said, 'What are you doing here? It's your funeral', and remember being struck by the fact that she looked fine, and seemed to have no injuries whatsoever. She said 'They're going to give me an injection, and after a while I'll die – I have to'. She seemed calm to begin with, but then started to cry, saying that she didn't want to leave her children. I went over to hold her hand, and she said, 'I wish I'd got to know you earlier'.

I had always liked her very much and when we were younger my sister was really into her. She kept a scrapbook about her, and we both followed her life. I had always admired her, but I suppose you get a bit less attached to these sort of things as you get older. Around the time I had the dream, I read a story that when Diana was nineteen, she called one of her friends and said, 'I've been told I'm going to marry Charles'. It really bothered me.

Vicki Wood, 21
Stage Manager
Edinburgh, Scotland

✴

THE SETTING WAS Westminster Abbey. On the floor was a memorial for Diana, exactly like the one that is already there for Winston Churchill. Next to it was a framed picture of her surrounded by poppies. On one side were three bowls that looked as though they should have been collecting rain, but they were actually filling with blood that was dripping from the ceiling. I remember feeling concerned by this.

✴

I woke up that morning when my friend rang me to tell me the news. I felt there was some relevance in the dream and really needed to tell someone about it. I did write to Mr Al Fayed to tell him that his son was happy in the dream, and to Mrs Shand Kydd in the hope it would somehow offer them some comfort. I'm not a practising Christian, so I'm surprised that my dream seemed to have a religious significance. I don't really understand it.

Anne Pollock
Nurse, 38
Cumbernauld, nr Glasgow, Scotland

concerned. 'You've been standing like that for too long,' and I touched her. 'Your muscles will start to ache'. She kept staring forward totally focused on the crowd. We could almost have leaned across and touched them, but I didn't see their faces because I was still looking at Diana. The pier was higher than the raft and Diana was looking up at them. I repeated, 'Look you'll have to put your arms down,' but when I touched her and tried to prise them down, they were rigid. It was like a force that did not want to be moved. Her arms didn't feel normal, they were hard, unlike soft tissue.

✦

✦

I WAS ON A slow moving raft with Diana and Dodi. Diana was standing and Dodi was kneeling at her feet looking up at her adoringly. She looked young. They were both wearing swimming costumes. Diana was a lot of people standing on the pier in front of us. There were African men, women and children, dressed in bright colours, singing, clapping and cheering, almost like a gospel choir. She was standing with her arms outstretched, fingers pointing up to the sky. It was a very 'Christ-like' pose. I said, 'Your arms are going to be very tired'. She didn't answer, but I was very

I am an Alexander Technique teacher, and was having problems within my work, basically wondering whether it was the right direction for my life to be taking. Since her death and watching all the footage of her on TV, I realised how much she touched people physically, and suddenly became aware of how essential touch is. My job is entirely about physical contact and since having this dream I suddenly feel happier about my work. It has made me realise how important it is. I am far more centred, confident and sure of where I am going.

Jacqui Rigby, 48
Alexander Technique Teacher
Acton, London

SATURDAY 20 SEPTEMBER: I'm at home and my mother says 'Guess who's coming round? Princess Diana!' I say, 'Don't be ridiculous!' At that moment a car pulls up and Diana gets out. She comes to the door and we shake hands. She sits on the settee between me and my friend and we talk. She makes a joke and playfully pokes him in the ribs. We just sit there laughing.

✶

MONDAY 1 SEPTEMBER: I am Princess Diana aged 19 and I'm dressed in a yellow sweater and a black and white checked skirt. It's night. I'm flying up the Mall, just floating and laughing on my own. I keep making mistakes and can hear voices telling me how to fly; that I'm not doing it right. I laugh and ask why. 'Because that's the way it works' they say. It's not like they're criticising, they're encouraging. I don't care. I'm learning to fly.

SATURDAY 6 SEPTEMBER: (the day of the funeral): again I'm Diana, flying, laughing, along the Mall, and there are people everywhere lining the streets below me. I'm asking 'Who are all these people? What are they doing here?', and the voices are saying 'They're all here for you'. I fly down and see the flowers and the inscriptions and I know that they are for me. But I'm still happy, laughing.

$*$

SATURDAY/SUNDAY 30/31 AUGUST: (the day of Diana's death) I'm at home and the doorbell rings. There's a police Range Rover and three or four officers standing in the driveway. One says 'I'm sorry. There's been a terrible accident.' I know instantly that someone has died. My daughter, Sidony, is staying with friends and I'm terrified its her. But the moment the policeman opens his mouth to tell me who it is, I wake up.

SUNDAY 31 AUGUST: I am Diana on the night of the crash in a heap on the back seat of the car with blacked out windows. I know instinctively that everyone is dead and that I am dying. I slip in and out of consciousness. I'm not scared at all, quite comfortable in fact.

My husband and I had been to my step-daughter's wedding and had stayed in a guest house that night. When we woke up, I related the dream to my husband, but it wasn't until we were on our way to breakfast, that we were greeted with the news of her death. I instantly burst into tears and completely went to pieces.

I know someone who comes from the village where she was brought up who has always said how she was brought up to believe that she was not special, and to appreciate her privilege.

Many people misinterpreted her. I get so angry with my husband. He says that she wasn't clever, but I tell him that you don't need to be a scholar in order to communicate. I remember seeing a picture of Charles aged about four shaking hands with his parents on their return from a trip abroad, and can't help comparing that with the image of Diana scooping both her boys up in her arms.

Janet Hodges, 58
Retired Secretary,
Pershore, Worcestershire

W<small>E WERE WALKING</small> in Abbey Park — some small grounds around an Abbey near to our home. We saw a woman who I recognised as Princess Diana. We didn't say anything to her, but I knew that it was her. In the dream, several days passed, and we saw her in the park again. A day or so later, I went swimming with her in an indoor pool. On these occasions we spoke to her, and she seemed to be seeking our reassurance. She said things like, 'What have I done?' and my husband and I, in an attempt to make her feel better, were saying 'We are on your side', 'You've done nothing wrong' and 'It's not your fault'. I felt sorry for her. She seemed unhappy, as though she'd been let down.

I always thought that Diana would commit suicide because I saw her as such a tragic figure. I thought the last cause of death would be a car crash. Everyone thought she was paranoid, but I didn't – I thought she was misinterpreted and that everyone *was* against her. I believe she put on a front of being strong because she was constantly fighting the Royal Family. I know that she used the media, but why not? They used her. She was getting her own back, and there was nothing wrong in using the newspapers to do that.

Lisa Barsi, 27
Radio Presenter
Cardiff, South Wales

✦

I DREAMT THAT I was at the funeral and Diana was wrapped in white towels with chains around her neck and across her bodice. The coffin was open with just a sheet on the top. At the start of the day they were very protective of this sheet, but towards the end of the funeral the sheet was falling off, and you could see a very troubled look on Diana's face.

✦

When I had this dream, I was actually at the Frankfurt Book Fair offering a fabulous book about weddings. Of course, one of the weddings featured was that of Diana and Charles. The conception of the book had pre-dated the events in Paris but it was impossible to look at the photographs without becoming introspective. There are so many books about Diana, and there is a thin line between celebration and cashing in.

Like most of the population, I spent many nights dreaming of Diana. This was a way of coming to terms with what had occurred, but the shock of waking up to realise that she was in fact dead, became a dread-making daily recurrence. It was only after her death that I realised how much interest I had in her in life. It was as if you knew her even though you'd never met her.

Simon Trewin, 30
Literary Agent
Dulwich, London

I WAS AT THE Frankfurt Book Fair but the ceilings were carpeted and the floors had light fittings seemingly growing out of them. Tables and chairs miraculously stayed above my head anchored by some invisible force, with cups of coffee containing their gravity-defying scalding liquid. As I picked my way through this other world, I saw Diana upside down sitting on a bean bag. She was reading aloud from a wedding book to a crowd of on-lookers. I knew she was Diana but they seemed strangely unaware of the fact and went about their business without giving her much attention. I climbed up to her and asked how things were going, she looked up with tears in her eyes and said 'They seem to have forgotten me already'.

✴

It did feel like I was at some big event or function, and that Sting and his missus would be probably be there. I always feel peeved if I'm relegated to the back tables at events, and kind of desperate to be in with the 'in crowd'! I think there's been a real witchhunt of women in the press. I slag people off in my show all the time and then feel really terrible about it. I've said horrid things about the Spice Girls, but when I saw them being booed off stage, and Geri with a tear in her eye, it was awful. It's a bit of a cliche, but we have a problem being nice to each other. Diana was under enormous stress and suffered low self-esteem and loathing. As with many women; confidence is a veneer that cracks under pressure, and the media know that. I heard mixed reports about her from others. Some people said she was a conniving, manipulative cow and others said she was really wonderful. But hell, I'm like that too. I would have liked to have seen her married to a solid bloke with enough time to have a baby girl before she hit 40. Y'know, picking up the kids from school, but still shopping and lunching.

Jenny Eclair, 37
Comedienne
Camberwell, London

✦

I WAS GOING TO Diana's funeral and was worried that I was going to be late. I was early though — I always am. It was in some catacombs and we were all sat at school desks with names tattooed on the them, and old fashioned inkwells. All the desks were numbered, but my ticket wasn't a gold embossed job, more like a scrappy raffle ticket from Safeways. I was obviously too big for the desk and I kept thinking, this isn't a very good seat I've been given. It was like getting the crap seats at the back of the Odeon. I was worried because that there was no way the cortège would get through the narrow tunnel between all the desks. There were three old women in buttoned up coats eating their sandwiches. My desk was near the exit, and I could see sunlight out onto a park beyond, like something out of *Mary Poppins* or *Oliver!*

✦

As soon as I heard about her death I knew that the blonde girl in my dream was Diana. Although I never felt close to her, I always admired and respected her. However since her death and having had this dream, I have changed my outlook towards my own life. I got divorced eleven years ago and ever since, my children have been distant towards me as if I was forever doing something wrong. I was always worried about how I might offend them. However, I have learned that you can't go on blaming yourself for evermore amen. I always have people telling me how to live my life and so did Diana, but she wouldn't have it. I've found the strength to say 'That's their life, they do what they want', and have started to get on with mine. I always thought that she was a gutsy lady, and that she was strong but just lacked the confidence to surge forward.

Myrna Watts, 54
Bakery Shop Assistant
Stone, Staffordshire

✦

THE WEEK BEFORE Diana died I had a dream that I was talking to a blonde-haired girl who looked like a friend of my daughter's, who we have always teased due to her striking resemblance to Princess Diana. She was wearing a long white dress and was very tall, I remember having to look up to her to talk to her. On the Tuesday night before Diana's death, I had another dream involving this girl, although I couldn't think why. I was standing in front of two mirrors; one that had already shattered, and another that fogged over and then shattered as well. I turned to my right and the girl in the white dress was there again. She just looked at me and smiled.

✦

I was so happy when I woke up that I rushed to tell my husband all about it. Since my daughter Sylvia died a year ago my dreams often make me cry. It's not often that I wake up with a smile on my face. I only wish that I could dream about her in the same way that I dreamt about Diana. In my bedroom, I have cross of Jesus and a picture each of Diana and Sylvia. Every morning I thank Jesus for the new day, and each night I say 'Good night, God bless' to them. She was so handsome and pretty and good. I kept all the press cuttings about her. When she was alive, I thought that she might get married again; I think that in my dream I might even have been at her wedding.

I actually think that I have changed since the dream. It made me feel so happy and content, because I now feel that Diana is looking after me. She is helping me to get over my daughter's death. Although I am still grieving, I feel a little happier everyday. I think that Diana helped people when she was down here, and now is doing the same up there, where I believe that she and my daughter are pals.

Olive Perks, 74
Retired Charity Worker
Paignton, Devon

✦

I was with my sisters in a crowded room, at a banquet or wedding. Diana was there wearing a lovely dress, all silvery, with sequins and pearls, and a tiara on her head. She came up to me and said, 'I want you to be my usher.' I replied, 'What, someone to look after you?' and she said, 'Yes, I want *you* to be my usher.' I couldn't believe it. I said 'Me? But I haven't got a nice dress to wear like you have,' and she said that it didn't matter, she wanted to have me. I was so excited, I rushed to my sister and said 'Diana wants an usher and she's picked me.' My sister said, 'You! What has she picked you for? You haven't even got a nice dress.' I said 'She's buying me one.' I just couldn't believe that she'd picked me. I then remember looking around as if I was guarding Diana.

✦

I am a Cypriot, and came to this country as a refugee in 1968. Since then I have never been back to the north of Cyprus where I was born. I married an English woman, and now have my own family over here.

I couldn't see why I should dream about Diana, she wasn't anything to me. Then I remembered that I had seen her on the Greek news around the time of my dream. She had been on holiday there and the Greek people liked her very much. I stay in touch with my home country by watching the Greek satellite channel. Some of my dream reminded me of home; the big doors and the houses on the roadside were like ones in Cyprus.

Costas Sergious, 50
Photographic Service Manager
Clacton-on-Sea, Essex

I WAS STANDING ON a pavement by the side of a road. In the distance was a black limousine. A woman and two or three men dressed in black came out and started to walk towards me. When they got close, I realised that the woman was Diana. They passed me and carried on along the road which went up a hill, and went out of sight. The next minute I was in a room with two large doors which were wide open. Diana walked in, sat in a big armchair, rested one elbow on the arm of the chair and rested her head on her hand. Then she started crying. I walked over to her and said, 'Don't cry'.

The rest of the dream wasn't about Diana and felt like a nightmare. I woke up feeling very disturbed. I had a cup of coffee, and about an hour later turned on the radio and heard people talking about Diana in the past tense. Gradually it dawned on me that she was really dead. I worked it out that my dream had occurred after the crash but at just about the time of Diana's death. I don't think this was a 'personal' dream as such, but that it had something to do with 'energy' around the event which I cannot begin to understand. I had never dreamed of Diana before and although I liked her, she was not particularly important to me.

Pamela Safier, 55
Psychotherapist
Kensington, London

✦

MY DREAM WAS long and complicated and I can't remember all of it. It began however with the knowledge that Charles and Diana had been killed separately. I could see Diana in her coffin and I think she was wearing an emerald green dress like the one she was wearing the only time I ever saw her, driving out of Kensington Palace into Kensington High Street. I didn't know in the dream how she had died but it was clear that it had been a killing rather than death from natural causes.

✦

I had the dream about two weeks after she died. To be honest, she was someone who I would look at to see what she was wearing. I was on her side though, but over the last few years, the more we heard about her emotional problems, the more I felt she was a victim of her own creation. I have no insights into the dream whatsoever.

Maria Trewin, 26
English Teacher,
Poland

✦

THE WHOLE FAMILY were at Diana's funeral and we sat behind Princess Margaret and Fergie. In the middle of the sermon, Princess Margaret lit a cigarette and Fergie turned to mum and said, 'Have you been to the swimming pool lately? What do you think of the new swimming instructor?'

✦

I adored her. I would buy any magazine and newspaper that she was in, and bought both Andrew Morton's books, because I think that she wanted to have them written. In the early 80s, I used to copy her hairstyles and got a lot of clothes ideas from her. I was just so interested in her, particularly in her romances. I thought Dodi was lovely, a really nice guy and would have loved for them to get married. I think that she had finally found romance which is what she'd always been looking for. I have a feeling life will never be the same.

Francesca D'Alton, 53
Civil Servant
Westbourne Park, London

✦

THE SECOND DREAM happened several weeks later, and this time Diana and I were shopping. She was wearing a skiing outfit with goggles pushed back over her hair. We both ended up looking at ourselves in a full length mirror; my hair was short like hers. I felt as if I was her friend, and woke up thinking that she wasn't really dead.

✦

I was in the back of the car when my fiancé was killed. I was unhurt but suffered from amnesia for a week afterwards; I couldn't remember anything, not even who I was. I wasn't able to express my feelings at the time, but since Diana's death I think I've cried for both of us.

✳

THE FIRST DREAM recurred over four consecutive nights in the weeks following her funeral. Thirty-five years ago my fiancé was killed in a car crash, after skidding on some black ice and in my dream I see his car, which drives into a tunnel, veers to one side and then crashes. His face then changes and becomes that of Diana, which is unexpected.

✳

That was the first of a very long series of Princess Diana dreams in which she paired the Prince and I together. I have no delusions of a proposal from the Prince, however these dreams are just wonderful.

Sarah Winn, 15
Schoolgirl
Brisbane, Australia

I WAS WALKING down a crowded street and I guess I was standing in front of Princess Diana, although I didn't know it at the time. On my right there was a beautiful white horse and I moved in front of the horse to pat it and talk to it. After talking to the horse for a short while I looked up to see that Prince William was riding it and his mother, the Princess, was walking it through the street guiding him. I said I couldn't believe I was in the company of a Princess and the heir to the greatest empire in the world, and I was occupying myself talking to the horse. They both laughed. The next scene was in a magnificent church and the Prince came in, and without me realising sat next to me. I treated him as I would any boy my age and joked around. After the mass I was walking in a park with Diana and she was telling me that although the Prince turned down almost every romantic interest and would probably do the same to me, she said that deep down he did have an interest in me.

To me, Diana was the most important member of the Royal Family and the only one with real charisma. Her glamour was part of who she was and I remember the dream so clearly because the image of her in it was so different. I'm not a fashion victim at all, but I am interested in haute couture. She was only human, but I didn't like to see her problems displayed. I didn't want to believe that she manipulated the media, I just didn't want to think of her that way.

Eric Le Guennec, 27
Supply French Teacher
Highgate, London

DIANA WAS LAID out in a glass display case, much like Eva Peron was when she died. She had an unreal quality, a bit like a waxwork. In the dream, it was obvious she was highly regarded. She was on show and I have a vague memory of people queuing to look at her. I was shocked to find that she had been buried wearing an awful outfit with such a horrid hairstyle. I only had a view of her from the waist up, but she was dressed in a very 80s style 'big' dress, all lace and frills and shoulder pads. Her hair looked like she'd had a bad perm. I thought how weird it was to see Diana Spencer in that way when she was normally so beautiful and stylish. I remember feeling very disappointed.

I often saw pictures of Diana leaving the gym, keys in hand, making her way to her car. It was such a contrasting image to that of the 'princess', as though it was the one ordinary thing she could do. I had always felt quite ambivalent about her, but in the past couple of years, I think she had found an inner strength that came from a newly developed sense of independence. And she looked the business too.

Rita Frances, 38
Writer
Crouch End, London

ONE NIGHT SHORTLY after the funeral, I dreamt that I was watching the procession. I was aware of everyone else, but no-one seemed to be aware of me. I could see the cortège and all the crowds and I remember being surprised at how many people were there as I looked around to see if there was anyone that I knew. As I was scanning the crowd, something caught my eye and I glanced in time to see Diana slipping off down a side street. She was wearing her gym gear and as she left, gave a backward glance – like a last look before leaving.

I woke up that morning to hear that she was dead and decided to go to Mass with my boyfriend, even though I never usually go to church. I had just passed my finals, which was then a very important stage in my life. I actually got quite ill through worrying about them. So when Diana said that to me in my dream, I thought wow, she really does care, because she had noticed the significant details in my life.

In a way, I do feel that part of Diana 'belonged' to us, although 'People's Princess' is a horrible term. But I believe she enjoyed and felt privileged to have a special place in our hearts. I remember her talking to some gay guys at an AIDS hospice, and one of them made a joke about them both being queens which made her laugh. Can you imagine any other Royal reacting like that?

Joanne Hook, 25
IT Customer Services Rep
Kingston Upon Thames, Surrey

I DREAMT THAT Charles and Diana had had a new baby together, and were holding a christening. It was a huge celebration that the general public had been invited to. I remember there were many designer presents, mostly Versace, lined up on huge tables in expensive carrier bags and boxes. These presents were not for the baby, but for the public and we could all choose what we wanted. There was a bit of a scramble for the best presents and by the time I got there most of the good items had gone. I ended up with some perfume, I think, and I remember being annoyed about this. At the same time I had a vague feeling of guilt, that behaving like this wasn't quite right. Diana was mingling freely amongst the crowds and when she came to me, she was so sincere. She took my hand and said, 'I'm so glad that you passed your exams, I know how much they meant to you,' and I felt even more guilty about the selfish grabbing for the presents.

The television coverage undoubtedly had a pull, but I found it voyeuristic and distasteful and within a few days had stopped buying any papers as I found them so unbalanced. It stopped being about Diana. Of course there were sad and tragic elements, and people were genuinely sympathetic, but there were also stories of fights breaking out as people tried to get a look at the coffin.

Directly after Diana's death I was involved in producing a photographic memorial book about her life and spent two or three weeks dedicated to that. I was very ambivalent about her when she was alive and found her remote and privileged. I do read *Hello!* but never bought a copy to particularly read about her. I think she had a very ambiguous relationship with the press. I do think they were unfair to her, but they are equally unfair to others

Emma Walters, 31
Book Editor
Kennington, London

✳

AFTER THE FUNERAL, I started having the same dream every night for about a week. I was in a church or cathedral for Diana's funeral and it was full of ordinary people. They were all hysterical and desperate, scrabbling to get a view of the coffin. My feelings in each dream were always the same, I felt very uncomfortable and just didn't want to be there.

✳

I never liked the Princess of Wales. I thought that she was rather a silly girl and she irritated me. She always seemed determined to have centre stage – if the woman didn't want to be in the limelight, then why didn't she get out of it? The dream has affected me because it was just so odd.

Gabriella Irvine, 72
Retired Health Visitor
Liverpool

✦

I<small>T WAS ABOUT</small> eight o'clock in the morning, about a month after her funeral, and I was drifting in and out of sleep. As I was nearing waking, I had a short dream about Diana, a bit like a vision. She was just standing with two or three people around her, who were trying to get her to move. She refused to budge and kept saying, 'No, I won't go'. She seemed quite angry. And that was it. The image was very vivid and has stayed with me.

✦

I am quite a royalist and my whole family had always liked Diana. Although I thought she was really beautiful, I never bought any of the papers to read gossip about her, but would obviously hear about her on the radio and TV. I was very upset when she died, and was quite touched by how much my dream affected me; I really felt quite emotional when I woke up.

Rob Fowler, 25
Musician/Actor
Morton, Lincolnshire

I⟨T WAS AS⟩ if I was behind the lens of a video camera, which was replaying media images from Diana's life. Some of them were moving images, but there were no words. They began with her wedding, the picture of her in the see-through skirt, the first time in public with her kids, news stories of her bulimia, separating from Charles, her association with Will Carling, the photographs in the gym, the Versace funeral with Elton John, and finally the crashed car. After this I pulled away from behind the camera, and saw this last image on a small TV, followed by block capital letters saying 'PRINCESS DIANA IS DEAD'. I felt as if I was controlling what I was seeing, yet I wouldn't have purposely pulled out un-pleasant images — like the separation from Charles. In the dream I didn't know that she was dead until I saw the picture of the car crash.

I was on holiday in a remote farm house, but unfortunately was laid up with flu. I had the dream on the Friday before she died and although I was aware that she and Dodi were being pursued, I had been pretty cut off for a couple of weeks. I wasn't very conscious of it at the time, but I think I was angry at the media intrusion, just sick of it really.

Diana was completely opposite to me. I got married five weeks ago in a combat wedding dress in gun metal grey with repro bullet proofing, and the whole bridal party was wearing trainers and combat vests. Despite this, I am quite shy. It was a very large wedding and we were shellshocked by the level of attention focused on us – and this was from people we loved and wanted to be there. I thought of Diana then, and was awed by the amount of intrusion that she put up with. I can't contemplate what it must be like to be continually knocked for everything you do. I'm amazed that she held it together.

She was just an ordinary, shy kindergarten teacher, yet proved herself to be incredibly tenacious and feisty. She was doing it her own way.

Angela Harrison, 28
Illustrator
Finsbury Park, London

I WAS CROUCHED behind a car in the sub-basement level of an underground car park. Diana came down in a lift wearing a raincoat, with a minder who was shielding her with an umbrella. It was as though she was escaping and I was helping her to get away by being a decoy. She started a conversation, and I was flattered she was turning to me, an ordinary member of the public, for advice. I said, 'Whatever happens, lay low. You must look after your children.'

I was not a follower of Diana's like many other women I know. However, I started crying and I couldn't explain why. Everyone around me seemed to be mourning her death, particularly the women. They were grieving as though they had personally known Diana.

Like Diana, I fight for what I believe in, the dignity and rights of others, and also for self-expression. I felt very good about speaking eloquently, even though I was unprepared, but I believe it's also true of life: we are at our best when we speak from the heart.

Margarita B. Marin-Dale, 39
Lawyer and Writer
Washington DC, USA

I don't know what I am going to say, but guess I'll just have to wing it. I decide I will just have to speak from the heart, and see how it goes. I speak about God. It is a very long and involved speech. I speak about Princess Diana and how death reminds us how fragile life is; we embrace Diana because in her, we also see ourselves.

A few people get bored with my speech and step out into a room with some vending machines. I get angry on the podium. Loudly and firmly I speak into the microphone, 'What is more important: God or vending machines?' I finish my speech and I know it has gone well. I decide I will end with a song. I start singing *Love Will Keep Us Together* and the audience joins in clapping and singing, as does the choir.

✦

A VOICE SAYS TO me 'You are like Princess Diana', and a camera lens zooms in on a portrait of the Princess with her two sons, William and Harry.

I am outside now in an area with a beautiful lake. I see a young boy among the people in the lake and we recognize each other. He is surprised to see me. I am speaking but I can't remember most of our conversation. He asks, 'Why don't you read to me anymore?' I tell him, 'I love you, but please understand, I cannot go back.'

I am in a restaurant which has a podium above the floor. I look at a program and am alarmed to see that I am listed as a speaker and scheduled to speak first. I'm not even properly dressed, I am wearing shorts and tennis shoes!

I was actually burgled recently both at home and at my office and the sense of violation was very strong. I have my own business, so I feel people are relying on me. I'm responsible for members of my family, and I felt responsible for the children in the dream although they weren't mine. I just assumed it was down to me.

I wasn't particularly sympathetic to Diana in life and I don't understand why everyone was so mad about her. I think Charles was a romantic but he was made out to be the stupid one that talks to trees; he was the real victim. It was only because she was young, pretty and flirtatious that people naturally took her side. She cultivated her beauty and her power, initiating the interest in her and manipulating it for her own gain. Everything became a photo opportunity, 'The Diana Industry'.

Charlie Charalambous, 42
Computer Software Director
East Finchley, London

I WAS IN A house and partly involved with its security and was aware that it was vulnerable to a break-in. Diana was a guest or temporarily living there. We chatted and she flirted with me a little. There were lots of kids running around — not mine or Diana's — their parents weren't around. Someone was trying to get in and it became quite threatening, but the alarm system wasn't working. I began to look around to decide whether it was worth attempting to challenge them. Diana was relatively cool about the whole thing. I talked to her as I felt responsible for her safety, but as she was calm, I believed I could deal with the situation. It was clear that she trusted me to deal with it, almost as though she expected it to happen — she certainly wasn't surprised. In fact, her very presence seemed to initiate the situation, and that was the price. Yet I felt we were friends. But I remember thinking, 'why is it left up to me?' There should have been other people helping.

It seemed as if she somehow belonged to the past because I said 'I really liked you', not 'I really like you' and it made me feel sad. I am Basque and do not like the Spanish king and queen as I think they lead too frivolous a life. I am a great fan of the English way of life and their royalty, particularly Charles and the Queen, but I admit I was critical of Diana.

My husband liked her very much, and I suppose I did too – you couldn't help but feel sorry for her, and I did want her to be happy and married. I don't believe that she could ever have stayed out of the spotlight, and said so when she announced that she was retiring from public life. I did feel that she took too much credit for her charity work – there are many people out there doing good things who don't get any credit at all. We were on holiday in Spain when the news broke and no-one in the street seemed to be talking about it. That's why I was surprised when I came home and one of the ladies in the old peoples' home, who is 99, was so upset – 'Diana, Diana' she kept saying. I couldn't quite understand it.

Maria Diaz Arenas Strickland, 41
Carer
Milton Keynes

＊

ABOUT SIX MONTHS before Diana died, I dreamt I was standing by the side of a road, opposite a car park where two or three men were waiting by a big black car. Diana seemed to come out of nowhere, crossed the road, and rushed over to the car park. I called out to her and said, 'Diana, I really liked you', and she smiled and lifted her hand as if to wave, and then I woke up.

＊

I have had many sad dreams since suffering with postnatal depression and then when my father died. This dream made me feel happy and comforted, and I actually haven't had a bad one since.

I'm not a royalist, but I did think that she should have had her own life. My husband was always against the coverage in the press about the Royal Family and we never bought the papers to read about her, believing that she should be left alone. I didn't even know what Dodi looked like and I am proud of this.

Julie Buckley, 36
Housewife
Mansfield, Nr Nottingham

✦

I WENT TO ALTHORP and Earl Spencer was there and he invited me in through some fields. The ground was just covered with flowers and I was very worried about treading on them. I kept saying things like 'We can't stand on these'. He said, 'Come and have a look at her', and opened the coffin, but I never saw her body. All I saw was this glow, and it was the most beautiful thing I have ever seen. It made me feel so happy. Then I heard my husband calling me, saying 'Leave her now, you've had your time with her'. I wanted to leave and said, 'I've got to go now'. I remember going away in a car and waving to her brother, who was saying 'Come back soon'. It felt so wonderful, because he had actually invited me in to see her.

✦

I was not particularly a fan but I have been surprised at the strength of my own reaction. As I work in the media, I do feel a certain implication of my profession in her death, although the public were the ones who were hungry for the next pictures of her. The media were merely feeding this frenzy. She was someone you thought you knew, but didn't know. One story about her that really affected me was how she spent one Christmas day on her own watching *EastEnders*. I think it's a shame that we just can't see her any more. No other public figure will ever provoke such a response in people as she has done.

Marie-Louise Kerr, 29
Radio Presenter
Derry, Ireland

＊

In my first dream, Diana and I were sitting in what seemed like a TV control room, watching footage on the monitors, although what exactly they were showing I couldn't say. Diana was sitting next to me, and I felt close enough to her emotionally as well as physically to talk to her as a friend. I said, 'How are you?' in the knowledge that she had already died. 'You're supposed to be dead. I didn't know you, but I thought you got a rough ride from the Royal Family. They treated you badly.' I remember feeling aggrieved for her.

In my second dream two months later, I was on a ski lift with a friend, although I have never skied before. Diana went past us. I remember thinking, what is she doing? She's dead. If she's trying to get a new identity, she'll have to find one that doesn't look like her.

＊

That morning I woke up to the news of Diana's death. I knew instantly that my dream was about her, and it made absolute sense to me. I believe that when an event as huge as this happens, people pick it up as if it were on a particular radio wavelength.

I am a deeply religious and observant Jewish woman, and, if anything, I disapproved of Diana's behaviour from a moral standpoint. I suppose I thought of her as rather a sad and confused person. But I think of things in a spiritual and godly way, and believe that the profound reaction to her death means she must have been someone very special spiritually in the world, and that G–d thought of her that way.

Linda Lyons, 36
Housewife and mother
Hendon, London

✦

I DREAMT THAT A friend was critically ill in hospital outside the UK. I had to get through a tunnel to get to her and remember that during the whole dream, events prevented me from reaching her. I ran anxiously between ticket offices aware that I needed to get through the tunnel to get to her. There was always a reason why I couldn't get a ticket. Either they didn't sell tickets for that particular tunnel or there weren't any left, or I was at the wrong office. I had one more to try, knowing that it was my last chance of reaching her, at which point I woke up.

✦

I had this dream two years ago. Diana was almost the epitome of what every man secretly wants: an angel in high heels and stockings with great legs. I fully recognised that she used her feminine wiles to twist men round her little finger, but paradoxically, I would have gone along 100 per cent with her. I was quite happy to be hypnotised and intoxicated by her and seemed to lose all my natural cynicism as far as Diana was concerned. I felt she could be manipulative but I did like her as a person. I would find it impossible to get angry with her. I adored her. When she died, it felt like when I lost my mother, who, despite dying in her fifties, was still young, and it struck me how unfair it was.

Steve Charles, 36
Fashion Photographer
Tooting, London

big eyed 'coy but vulnerable' look as I begged her not to be reckless and to take care of herself. Somehow I could see that she wasn't listening and wouldn't take my advice. By this time my regiment had marched on miles ahead. I told her that I would have to go or I would never catch up with them. I then attempted to find my regiment's position but by then had lost them. There seemed to be hundreds of foreign soldiers. I remember panicking slightly until a platoon from Liverpool suddenly appeared. I said to them, 'Well, you're English, aren't you?' and one of them said, 'That's okay la', you can join us'. We continued marching for miles through countryside until I noticed we were marching down a giant concrete subway.

✦

MY DREAM WAS set in Balham, South London. England was at war and there had just been a thousand bomber raid over London. Streets and buildings had been reduced to bricks and rubble and I was an English allied soldier at the head of a column marching through the ruins. I broke ranks as we marched through Balham High Street. Somehow I knew Princess Diana and she knew me, but bizarrely she was working in a tiny newsagent's kiosk in Balham tube station. I remember feeling a tremendous sense of love, warmth and protectiveness towards her and pleaded with her to go straight down into the tube tunnel with the other Londoners when the next air raid siren sounded. She gave me that familiar

When I was younger, I used to be a real fan of Lady Di's. I was about six when she got married and still have the books and newspaper cuttings that I collected at the time. However, more recently I became bored hearing about her and the Royal Family, and actually chose not to read about them. I didn't even know how old William and Harry were before her death, and was surprised to discover how much William, in particular, looked like Diana, and how mature he was. I never knew how devoted she was to them.

I became embarrassed by my obsession with her during my childhood, but now wish I had looked upon her more kindly. It was a shame that someone who was doing such good work got caught up in all the trappings that being a member of the Royal Family brought with it. I felt that the point of a lot of her activities, however well meaning, became lost because of who she was. I'm surprised that I dreamt about her at all, and thought 'god, was I really that affected by her?'

Anna Parker, 21
Graduate
Cardiff, South Wales

I T WAS SEVERAL weeks after Diana's funeral. I dreamt I was there, although there was nothing to suggest that it was a funeral. It took place around a bandstand, which had a very old-fashioned English feel to it, floral and ceremonial, not grim at all. Surrounding the bandstand were tiers of seats. I was sitting next to William and Harry, looking after them, although I remember being most aware of William. I looked across to the seats opposite and there was Diana in a blue suit. I remember thinking, this is weird, how can she be here? She was looking over to me to check that I was looking after them and looked concerned but didn't say anything. I just knew that she was checking.

As a single woman, I did empathise with her and for all her failings she was so vulnerable. She tried to be perfect, but did daft things, like we all do. Whereas we normally hide our problems and insecurities, she had to play them out in public. I thought she was immensely strong as I've been strong in my life. What she went through would have broken most people and she got through it.

Diana somehow internalised herself in people and became an integral part of their lives. I live in the west of Ireland, and spirituality is part of everyday life. I believe that this is what the saints did, they had this third dimension, an instinctive and intuitive god-given power of non-verbal communication. Diana undoubtedly also possessed this gift — she had it within her whole being.

Maighread Wynn, 58
Artist
Sligo, Eire

✦

I WAS TALKING ABOUT trying to move back to my old house in England with my daughters. I fled from there twenty years ago with my disabled son to get away from an alcoholic husband. I often have dreams where I'm trying to go back there, particularly in times of stress. The dream shifts to inside the house, as dreams do. Diana is there as my friend and possibly a neighbour and we're talking about how I might live there again. She is very supportive and someone I know very well, like family.

✦

I definitely thought that she was a bit unhinged, but I respected the work she did for AIDS. The ridiculous thing is that it wouldn't have counted for anything if she hadn't have been famous. But I grudgingly felt that redeemed her. I don't think she was a bad person, but she was naive in the way she handled her life.

I wasn't surprised at the manner of her death – I thought her lifestyle was out of control. A road traffic accident is not extraordinary, it happens every day.

Fred Wallace, 25
Medical Student
Hackney, London

I'M A MEDICAL student at a London hospital and dreamt that I was in the ER. The atmosphere was very exciting but the actual ER was quiet that night. I was standing back watching my colleagues trying to revive Diana but I wasn't particularly surprised that it was her. There was a strong impression that experienced doctors were in control – busy but not panicked. And yet although I was still a student and an observer, it didn't look good at all and there was a definite sense that this was a hopeless case.

I am a mother, and a grandmother, and I thought, what a terrible waste. How do you tell two children who are expecting to see their mother the next day that she is dead? I was really shattered. I couldn't believe someone so young should die in such a horrible way — in fact I felt quite angry. It seemed over the last year she'd got over many of her problems, and had pulled her life together. I loved to watch her on television — she had beauty, glamour and yet still had so much warmth. I always said she brought sunshine to that family. Two months after her death, when I see her picture in a paper or on television, I can't believe she's gone — she still seems so alive.

Souad Shamia, 59
Housewife and Grandmother
Harrow, Middlesex

✦

I WAS SITTING IN what felt like a community centre with Diana. We were discussing how to make sure that her children were safe from any harm. As we were both mothers, we talked about the protection of all children. I felt I knew her and didn't feel I was talking to a princess, but to a close friend — a warm person. She looked very smart and beautiful and was wearing a skirt-suit as she often did.

✦

I thought that the press made fun of Diana, and I went along with this. I couldn't see what she was trying to do, or how she could achieve anything. Our family own a souvenir shop and we stock Diana photos and T-shirts. It's not fair, but many people have made money out of her death; it's a natural thing to happen. It wasn't until she died that I realised how much publicity she gave to causes like the landmine situation in Angola.

I recently read an article about how she was trying to raise her sons differently and I respected her for this. I have a younger brother and sister whom I very much father, and I am also trying to raise them in my own way.

Aron Malhotra, 24
Self-employed
Wembley, Middlesex

I WAS PLAYING with two kids, they felt like William and Harry; it was as though I was related to them in some way. A woman came along and told me that whatever I was to do, it was for the children. I was asked to look upon these two children as if they were my brothers. I turned to look at her and it was Diana.

✦

I was very surprised to have dreamt about Diana as I never any held great sympathy for her. It felt very strange at the time. Although I kept abreast of the news, I was only vaguely aware of what she doing and not well read about her. I do remember the *Mirror* pictures of her and Dodi on the boat because they were everywhere. I'm not really interested in the royals. I suppose I felt sorry for her if anything. It seemed that the slightest association of anyone who was a member of the media made us all culpable. Many people I spoke to after her death even gave me a hard time, but I don't think that's fair – maybe society as a whole was to blame because everyone consumed her. She could sell anything: papers, books, even charities. She was the ultimate price tag.

Tori Hywel-Davies, 27
Features writer, city listings magazine
Toxteth, Liverpool

✦

DIANA AND I were walking in an airport lounge, I don't know where it was. Just as she was about to put her foot down on a moving escalator loads of paparazzi appeared from nowhere. She looked up at me and held out her hand, her expression appealing to me to save her as she fell. I ran to reach out to her, but couldn't get to her in time. The paparazzi then literally swooped upon her, enveloping her.

✦

I had a miscarriage 25 years ago and Yvette is the name I gave to that child. I woke up with a very strong feeling that it had really happened — it seemed so real, and like Diana was a really good friend. I lay in bed for at least another half an hour — I just didn't want to come back down to earth. I felt comforted, and realised that I had also been able to comfort her.

Ann Bensley, 50
Post Office Clerk
Kings Lynn, Norfolk

﹡

A WEEK BEFORE Diana died, my husband passed away and so I was grieving when I heard about her death. I dreamt that I was having a meal in a restaurant with Diana, Harry, William, my three sons and a little girl I didn't know. We were talking about marriage and Diana was telling me about hers — like a woman to woman chat. She turned to me and said, 'You're alright, your husband's wonderful', and I said, 'I know he is' and then suddenly realised that as he had died, she could only know him in death. I said to her, 'Who is this girl?', and she said 'It's Yvette'.

﹡

After Diana did the *Panorama* interview I stopped liking her, but over the past year, I'd started to respect her, particularly because of the work she was doing for charity and for landmines. She was just starting to get herself together. I realised that she had been in the news for my entire life and I'd kind of grown up with her. I remember stories of her trips abroad, particularly when she went to the Taj Mahal and she was alone. I have very strong images of her, but I was pretty unconscious of my feelings about her at the time. Now all of a sudden she's gone. I've been ill with ME for 8 years and used to have nightmares every week. There wasn't one particular thing that would set me off, but it was often images I saw on the television. I was very affected by her death but since dreaming about her, I haven't had a single one. I feel I have let go.

Joanna Hudson, 17
Student
Woodthorpe, Nottingham

✦

I WAS TRAVELLING ON a train and there was an announcement over the Tannoy that Diana had died. Everyone on the train started crying and I thought, Oh my god, I can't believe this is happening. Suddenly all the other people on the train disappeared. A spirit wearing white appeared in the carriage and it was Diana. We were alone. She put her arms around me and cupped my face in her hands. Then she hugged me and rocked me like you would if you were comforting a child. She said, 'Don't be silly, I don't want you to be sad. I'm in a better place. We'll meet again.' It was so intense and very calming, in fact when I woke up, I felt an immense sense of relief. It was like I had really been with her, and she was okay.

✦

When I woke up I felt very disappointed that my dream wasn't real. I thought that Diana was great, despite her problems, her heart was in the right place. She pervaded every part of our lives, and now she's gone, it's left a huge vacuum.

James Cox, 24
Unemployed
Clifton, Bristol

✦

I WAS AT ONE end of the underpass. The crash had just happened and I could see the wreckage in front of me. Diana got out of the car, completely uninjured, and walked to the other end of the tunnel, and then disappeared out of sight. I sensed that the other passengers were dead, but I just stood there watching in stunned silence. It felt so real. The tunnel was quite desolate and I could still smell the smoke in the air.

✦

I usually have very vivid dreams and discuss them with my boyfriend. That morning I told him that I'd dreamt about Princess Diana and then went back to sleep, later waking up to the news of the crash at eleven o'clock. I was obviously a little freaked out by my experience, but didn't attach too much significance to it. The dream was actually a nice one; I felt as though she was just a mate that I was going shopping with, in fact, she was the one with the shopping basket, not me. Although I have never had any dreams about Diana before, I have had several about the Queen. In one I dreamt that I went to Buckingham Palace and had to hide in a food trolley!

Caroline Coyne, 24
Student
Camden, London

I WAS AT THE Glastonbury Music Festival, and Diana had organised some portacabins for the occasion. I was walking down a road and came across a large supermarket. I went inside, only to see Diana there dressed in a very simple, tailored black suit. She said, 'Oh Denise, I want you to know that I've organised the portacabins for everyone to sleep in.' She spoke as if this was one of her charitable works, and her gift to Glastonbury. We walked around, shopping and talking, buying things like baked beans. She looked happy and we were joking about the prices of things on the shelves. Although we were having a great time, all I could think about was the fact that she had got my name wrong. I wondered whether I should tell her about her mistake, but thought, this is Princess Diana, I can't say 'I'm sorry, my name's not Denise.' I thought that she would be offended, so I didn't bother to correct her.

I woke up feeling anxious and sad. Anxious because I didn't want to miss the funeral and sad from the loss of Diana and probably the losses that have occurred in my own life. I don't know why her death hit me so hard, probably because here was someone who 'had it all', riches, beauty, children, world recognition, and in a minute it's all gone. I'm not sure what I identified with because I consider myself a feminist and am a lesbian. I have other female role models rather than Diana. Maybe her vulnerability struck me. I have a sister, Diane, who has lupus and tires very easily, although she is still a very active working person, and mother of two boys. I'm sure part of my dream about Diana is tied to my sister and her vulnerability in life.

Jean Taczak, 50
Systems Engineer,
Telecommunications Company
Reston, Virginia, USA

＊

IN MY DREAM I was sleeping, but kept waking up. I wanted to be up at 6am to watch the funeral of Princess Diana. It was too early so I went back to sleep. I woke up at 5am and said I'd get up and stay up. I had on a voile dress or nightgown. One could see through it. It was pastel, flowered and had slits up the side. Then I went to the kitchen for coffee. I heard a boys choir practising because they were going to sing at the funeral. They were in the living room and didn't see me. I went to my closet to get my purple chenille bathrobe to put on.

＊

I had mixed feelings about her, but I can't say that there are many dreams I have remembered with such clarity. I do feel I have something more to contribute towards Diana, but perhaps this is all it was.

Lesley Russell, 40
Retired Police Officer
Frimley, Surrey

The night of the dream, I woke up to the hotel clock radio, and I hear 'and here is the news: Diana, Princess of Wales has been killed in a car crash'. I have often woken from deep sleep at the precise moment someone is born or dies and would say that my dream coincided with the exact time of Diana's death. In October, by a strange quirk of fate, I visited Paris, and go to the top of the Samaritaine store at sunset. The view is that of my dream.

I was on holiday in Guernsey with a friend and our children at the time. We had rented a car, but road conditions were bad, so we had to drive frustratingly slowly. I served eight years with the Surrey Police Force, five years specialising as one of the first woman Traffic Police Officers. I am an Advanced Trained driver, I adore driving fast. I miss that kind of almost reckless adrenaline fuelled driving. I was retired from the Police in 1983 with injuries I received on duty. Life continually frustrates me, and I would like to make faster progress at work, home and love, yet am fearful of time running out.

shape, but at that moment I see it as like the titanium rocket statue in Moscow which catches the autumn sun. At the top of this shape is a figure, robed in pearlescent clothing. It is a woman and her arms are outstretched, palms towards me, like a Catholic Virgin Mary statue in pose, like the one over the South American city which name I forget. To the left of my vision is a man's face, but I'm not paying real attention to it. Like a magnification of a camera lens, the figure comes into close up. It is Diana, and her face shows extreme distress. Mentally I say, 'Get out of my dream Diana' because I want to get back to the car dream, and perhaps, my man. At that, her mouth goes into the shape of Munch's 'The Scream'. Diana screams in fear and rage, but there is no sound. The blackness of the mouth obliterates the whole scene and I wake up.

✦

I AM THE PASSENGER in a red Ferrari sports car, I am not sure who the driver is, but I think he's an ex-boyfriend I still love, who in fact had a red MX5 in real life. We're driving around tight country lanes and corners, and I feel at the time it's Guernsey, but in retrospect it's Dorset, where we once stayed. The roads are not allowing us to realise any potential to the car, and I'm map reading like a rally driver and getting immensely frustrated that we can't go any faster. I want to put my foot down. Then we reach a blind right-hand bend, and I know that around the corner is some clear road. Like a person flicking TV channels, the whole scene suddenly changes. I am high up and observing an utterly different and incongruous picture. The scene is of an autumn sun-setting sky over a city, it's misty, but you can still see the city lights coming on, as if it were the view from a plane. Rising out of the mist is a solid shining

I had this dream the night I watched Harry on television meeting the Spice Girls and wearing a suit.

Gaynor Williams, 37
Mature Student and
Young Persons Counsellor
Portsmouth

AT THE BEGINNING of November, I had another dream. William and Harry were out on a limb, hanging out, just like ordinary inner city boys. I asked them if they were bored, and they said they were. They were dressed just as Di would have dressed them, immaculate with designer trainers, like catalogue kids. They both seemed shy, particularly Harry. They seemed to be waiting for someone, it wasn't me though — I was the surprise link! I work counselling young people so I wasn't surprised that they responded to me. I asked them if they wanted to come out on the rampage, but had to coax them into coming, as if they weren't sure if they were allowed to have fun. In the dream I nicked a friend's car knowing that I would be in trouble for taking it, but that I would be forgiven. I asked where they wanted to go and they shrugged their shoulders, so I said I would take them to my home town, Coventry. I took them on a strange kind of inner city tour; we were in and out of fields, exploring derelict buildings, walking the streets and, at one point, up a tree house. We were all laughing, particularly Harry.

When I woke up I felt that I had actually experienced flying although I've never flown before. Diana died on my wedding anniversary and I remember saying to my second husband as I watched William and Harry follow the cortège, that I wished my sons would call me — I've been estranged from them for many years. Directly after the funeral, my youngest boy phoned. He had seen the two boys walking behind the coffin and imagined that he could have been one of them. Despite the fact that he has lived much of his life without me, he no longer wanted to do that. My other son called me two days later. In death, she lost her boys and somehow I gained mine.

✦

IN MY FIRST DREAM I was travelling alone by plane and sat down next to a pregnant woman that I recognised. She was some way into her pregnancy and was showing. I was also pregnant but in the early stages. She asked me, 'How do you feel about flying?' I can't remember what I answered but once I heard her voice, I realised it was Diana. I said, 'I'm pregnant, I see that you are too.' She told me to be quiet, that it was a secret, yet anyone could see that she was pregnant. It seemed clear she didn't want to draw further attention to herself, and wanted to remain discreet.

✦

I thought Diana was marvellous and always looked forward to seeing her on the TV. I think she had a very sad life and felt it was right that she spoke about her problems. It made her accessible, more like us, and that was part of her charm. I don't think we'll ever see grief like that again.

My father died of cancer three weeks before I got married and I felt I had to be strong for everyone. I've always felt that I had to carry the load, but I have different responsibilities now – I have my own family and I need to think of them.

Nicolla Mackay, 27
After-Sales Service Rep
Spiarsbridge, Scotland

I WAS PUSHING a cart with Diana in an open coffin through the middle in Sauchiehall Street in Glasgow. People were moving out of the way in front of me. I was crying and the people on the street were also crying and throwing flowers. I was taking her to Kensington Palace but when I got there, it turned out to be two semi-detached council houses merged into one. As I arrived, guards came out, took her from me and closed the door. I felt that it was a job I was given to do, and that I had completed.

That was five years ago. I would usually interpret any female figure in a dream as an aspect of myself. But when Andrew Morton's first book came out a matter of months later, and it was revealed that Diana was passing the information through an intermediary, I thought, 'wow, that dream' — it was strikingly similar to real events.

I admired her as a kind of favourite celebrity, but also I had a lot of respect for Charles. I thought Diana was quite an amazing woman; she handled the media so well and always came out looking best.

It was tragic her being so hunted, as though she was sacrificed — built up and then destroyed. When she died, I cried every day for a week. I can't think of anyone else who filled the gap of an archetypal, female icon. She had that X factor — and it wasn't just because she was blonde and pretty.

Kristina Fletcher, 33
Stand-up comedy actress
Balham, London

I WAS AT A formal event, dressed up and waiting in a line-up to meet Diana. I knew I was there especially to meet her and I was excited. We were introduced, and she said, 'I have to speak to you' and led me to a tiny, cramped library. She was desperate and spoke very quickly. She begged me to take some letters and give them to three people I didn't know: James, Robert and a woman whose name I don't remember. She said that one of them was having a party on Saturday and I could hand them over then. I just thought, these are *your* friends, why me? I don't even know these people. What am I supposed to do, just crash this party? I couldn't understand why she was confiding in me, a total stranger — it was as though she was a prisoner, yet she had an incredible presence; she was lit up.

Actually I think she was a silly girl and had a comfortable life. She rebelled, but was silly to do so. She could have had affairs on the quiet and done it discreetly, and I don't believe the Press would have found out. Then she might have been alive today.

Peter Smith, 60
Retired Financial Director
Richmond, London

✦

I NEVER REALLY HAD a lot of time for Diana, but I had a slightly unusual dream. It was very simple really, I was going out with her on a regular basis and one day she turned round and said it had to stop, it's ended, finished. I said okay, if that's the way it is. There were no phone calls afterwards to discuss it. I was disappointed and upset, but not heartbroken. I had felt that we had something solid and wasn't expecting it.

✦

I have been having a few strange dreams recently. I'm pregnant, so my mum says that it's my hormones. She's been really worried about me as it's been a difficult pregnancy.

Diana's death remained in the front of my mind until I had the dream which was about six weeks later. I'm not so upset now because I think that hopefully she is alright. I felt that she had particular relevance to me because I also have two young boys and I imagined us in the same situation.

Crystal Cooper, 22
Credit Controller
Northampton

✦

I WAS IN Westminster Abbey and all the seats were filled with people quietly chatting to each other. Many of them were friends of mine that I hadn't seen for ages and Prince Charles was also there. Diana stood up in front of everyone and addressed the assembled crowd. 'I'm fine, I'm alright,' she said, 'don't worry', and then everyone started to walk out.

✦

With that I unfortunately rolled over in bed and woke myself up. That Sunday morning I came down to the devastating news. I'd had no reason to dream of Diana that night, as for once I had not bought a tabloid paper, discussed her in any way during the day or seen anything about her on TV. I was shocked days later, after telling people at work about this nondescript man with Diana, to see a picture of Henri Paul as he looked exactly like the man who gave her the keys. I admit I'm rather embarrassed by my dream.

I looked up to her as a role model and was fascinated by her. She was stupid about some things but her good works were genuine. She's been a part of all our lives and I feel we've lost something. But life goes on. I would always look at her in *Hello!* magazine and even though she's dead now, she's still in there.

Xandra Barry, 34
Assistant in film and video industry
Salisbury, Wiltshire

DIANA AND I were in the South of France on a 'gin palace'-type boat – not a particularly smart one, slightly rusty round the edges. We were there on our own. I felt I was with my 'new best friend' and hoped that everyone could see I was with her, Diana, Princess of Wales. I felt so proud and excited to be there. We were larking around and laughing next to a boat on the quay. A man then approached her whom she obviously knew, a small, slightly balding fellow with glasses, who said, 'It's alright, they've gone now'. She asked what he meant and he replied, 'The Press, they've gone now,' and with that he handed her some keys. She turned and smiled sweetly at me.

✴

The Dreams

✴

Diana, Princess of Wales meant many things to many people: fairytale princess, role model, neurotic, goddess, publicity seeker, victim, mother, daughter and friend – and we needed her to be all those things. As with many famous personalities, people felt they knew her. But in our technological age, media has *become* communication, and our connection to Diana was built on an 'image'. Yet paradoxically, as our dreams reveal, she seemed to transcend her iconic status. I personally believe that it wasn't until Diana's death, when we realised she was made of skin and bone and that she could break, that our illusions were shattered.

Yes, this book is about Diana, but it is really about us.

Rita Frances
London

Foreword

IT ALL STARTED, as one might expect, with my own dream about Diana shortly after her funeral. Like millions of others, I remember turning on the television that Sunday morning and watching the news in utter disbelief. Certainly the feelings that I experienced that week – shock, grief and denial – would have been quite appropriate had Diana been someone I knew, or had even met. But she was neither, and it soon became clear that I was not alone in my reaction.

It is relatively common to dream about the Royal Family, particularly the Queen, however, our feelings towards Diana far eclipse that of any other public figure. Exploring the way in which Diana reached ordinary people who never met her, many who were ambivalent towards her, some who loved her and others who disliked her – dreamers find parallels in their own lives with that of a woman who led a life most of us cannot imagine.

Here, they speak for themselves by putting their own dreams into context, and this is undoubtedly where the dreams come alive. There are no psychologists to interpret the dreams, no media pundits, political analysts or royal watchers imparting their wisdom. Collectively, these dreams paint a fascinating picture, leaving the reader to draw their own conclusions.

presenters, journalists and producers at BBC regional radio stations, local newspapers, and the *Big Issue* in Scotland and in Wales, for interviewing me in my quest for contributors, and in some cases, even relating their own dreams. Safi, Jim, Andrea and Pepe and all the staff at the Webshack Internet Cafe in Dean Street, London, for designing the website and for allowing me to begin researching this book from a mobile phone in the ladies' loo.

My friends, who listened to every dream in detail and still had me over to dinner: Hilary Bryans, Diane Daly, Rupert Dickens, Brigitte Downey, Andrew Ferguson, Kathy Forsyth, Jo, Jessica and Christine Feldman, Walter Llewellyn-McKone, Louise Mizen, Jane and Steven Morley, Maritsa Nicola, Mrs Domna Price, Garry Savvin, Maria Trewin, Sue Trewin, Myra, Rita and Sandra Rabee, Bryony Shepherd, Mark and Paula Spangenthal, Steve Shaw, and Maighread Wynn. And to the many friends, friends of friends, mothers of friends, and colleagues of friends who asked everyone they met if they'd had a dream!

My wonderful family: Mum, Dad, Abie, Wendy, Sarah and Edy, and the many friends and relatives who have supported me over the years – you know who you are.

My immense gratitude goes of course to all the dreamers who talked so candidly about their dreams. This is your book. Thank you.

And finally, in memory of Diana, Princess of Wales, with love.

Acknowledgements

My thanks go to...

My publisher, Jeremy Robson of Robson Books, who took my initial call and commissioned *Dreaming of Diana* without hesitation. Always calm, he listened patiently during the many crises encountered in compiling this book, and trusted my instincts when I had yet another 'idea'. Kate Mills, my editor, for her thoughtful advice and steadfast refusal to lose her head, even when I'd left mine at home. I am very grateful that with their support, I have been free to produce the book I wanted to. Charlotte Bush and all the staff at Robson Books for their help and expertise in publishing *Dreaming of Diana*.

Kirsten Parker, my wonderful researcher, who learned to read my mind within an hour of meeting me, and interviewed dreamers with intelligence and sensitivity – you'll go far. And Dominic Streatfeild-James for his assistance in the early stages of the project.

There are many people who have given their invaluable advice and assistance in compiling this book. David May and Helen Swift: friends and former colleagues who were always at the end of a mobile phone, backing me up with their experience. Ion and Simon Trewin who gave of their time and expertise. Jacqui Burdon of the Press Association, Sasha Gibson at Avalon Publicity, John Hind, South West News,

This book is dedicated

to my family

First published in Great Britain in 1998 by Robson Books Ltd,
Bolsover House, 5-6 Clipstone Street, London W1P 8LE

British Library Cataloguing in Publication Data
A catalogue record for this title is available from the British Library

ISBN 1 86105 154 9

Typeset in Gill Sans by FSH Ltd., London
Printed by Butler & Tanner Ltd., Frome and London

Dreaming
of
Diana

THE DREAMS
DIANA, PRINCESS OF WALES,
INSPIRED

Compiled by Rita Frances

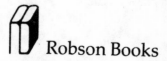

Robson Books

Dreaming
of
Diana